THE STORY OF
ALICE PAUL
and
THE NATIONAL WOMAN'S PARTY

Inez Hayes Irwin

DENLINGER'S PUBLISHERS, LTD.
P.O. Box 76
Fairfax, Virginia 22030

This book contains 512 pages

International Standard Book Number: 0-87714-058-8
Library of Congress Catalog Card Number 63-23006

FOREWORD

The National Woman's Party planned to republish the story of Alice Paul because we wanted the world to know about this wonderful, courageous and dedicated woman who spent her lifetime fighting for a cause—legal equality for women. She died on July 9, 1977, before this printing became a reality, but her spirit remains to inspire us to continue her fight for the Equal Rights Amendment.

Born in Moorestown, New Jersey on January 11, 1885, the daughter of Quaker parents, Alice Paul changed the lives of everyone who came in contact with her. A slender, petite woman with a burning force within her that reached out to others, her greatest gift was inspiring others to follow her cause of justice for women. We have the Equal Rights Amendment pending today because Alice Paul was an inspired leader with a singleness of purpose.

The story of Alice Paul and the National Woman's Party is that of a group of women who dared to defy the system in order to liberate women. They picketed the White House, were arrested, went to prison and braved starvation in hunger strikes. The great victory won by the tactics of these courageous women is not known to many as history books do not tell this story.

A graduate of Swarthmore College in 1905, Alice Paul received her Master's Degree in 1907 and a Ph.D in social work in 1912 from the University of Pennsylvania. After passage of the Woman's Suffrage Amendment in 1920, she felt the need for law degrees and fortified herself with three: an LL.B from Washington College of Law (1922) and an LL.M (1927) and a DC.L (1928) from the American University in Washington.

The Nineteenth Amendment, the right to vote, was won on August 26, 1920. The National Woman's Party, knowing that the struggle for equality was not over, held a commemorative convention in 1923 at Seneca Falls, where the first equal rights convention was held in 1848. Alice Paul presented a proposal to further obtain the rights demanded by Elizabeth Cady Stanton and Lucretia Mott at that Convention. Alice Paul wrote the Equal Rights Amendment and under her leadership, the National Woman's Party had it introduced in Congress in 1923 and for 49 years thereafter.

The original version, called the Lucretia Mott Amendment, read: *"Men and women shall have equal rights throughout the United States and in every place subject to its jurisdiction."*

In the beginning, there was much opposition to the Equal Rights Amendment from women's organizations that felt satisfied with the victory won in gaining the right to vote. They were concerned that the amendment would render invalid all protective legislation for women, especially those laws regarding labor. Alice Paul, ahead of her time in perceiving that most *protective* legislation only furthered discrimination against women, worked relentlessly for the passage of the Equal Rights Amendment.

In 1943, convinced that the amendment would not pass with the original wording, Alice Paul consented to a rewording: *"Equality of rights under the law shall not be denied or abridged by the United States or any State on account of sex."*

Over the years, it was the National Woman's Party, led by Alice Paul, that diligently kept the fires burning for the Equal Rights Amendment, educating other organizations, publishing bulletins, and maintaining an instant information bureau where anyone interested in the Equal Rights Amendment could obtain the exact status of its progress and sponsors day and night.

To date, thirty-five states have ratified the Equal Rights Amendment and only three more are required to make it the twenty-seventh amendment to the United States Constitution.

With the death of Alice Paul, an era has passed. Alice Paul is with God now, but she has left us a heritage to fulfill and a tradition to follow. The full impact of her lifelong efforts to secure equal rights for women in the United States and throughout the world has yet to be felt. We must do our utmost to continue her fight and obtain passage of the Equal Rights Amendment. Alice Paul's spirit remains our inspiration.

Elizabeth L. Chittick, President
National Woman's Party
August 1, 1977

A Brief Summary of National Woman's Party Activities From 1920 to 1977

To write a complete history of the National Woman's Party from 1920 to 1977 would require the writing of another book. This history will be written someday, but for the purpose of this book I will highlight only the more important accomplishments of the Party.

The National Woman's Party, founded in 1913, was incorporated September 20, 1918. After Suffrage was passed, Alice Paul reactivated the Party in 1921 and decided to take up feminist issues only.

In 1922, the following Declaration of Principles was passed:

"That women shall no longer be the governed half of society, but shall participate equally with men in the direction of life . . .

"That women shall no longer be barred from the priesthood or ministry, or any other position of authority in the church, but equally with men shall participate in ecclesiastical offices and social dignities.

"That a double moral standard shall no longer exist, but one code shall obtain for both men and women.

"That exploitation of the sex of women shall no longer exist, but women shall have the same right to the control of their persons as men.

"That women shall no longer be discriminated against in the treatment of sex diseases and in the punishment of sex offenses, but men and women shall be treated in the same way for sex diseases and sex offenses. . . .

"That a woman shall no longer be required by law or custom to assume the name of her husband upon marriage, but shall have the same right as a man to retain her own name after marriage.

"That the wife shall no longer be considered as supported by the husband, but their mutual contribution to the family maintenance shall be recognized.

"That the headship of the family shall no longer be in the husband alone, but shall be equally in the husband and wife. . . .

In short—*that women shall no longer be in any form of subjection to man in law or in custom, but shall be in every way be on an equal plane in rights, as she has been and will continue to be in obligations."*

The party met in 1923 at Senaca Falls. From this meeting the idea of an Equal Rights Amendment was conceived and written by Alice Paul. Over the years, it is true that the one main objective of the National Woman's Party was the Equal Rights Amendment, but under Alice Paul's leadership, they also became interested in world-wide equality for women.

The National Woman's Party wanted the women of the Americas to be recognized as a body of women of the Organization of American States. They attended conferences but were refused recognition or seating. Finally, in 1928 at a Conference in Cuba and with the support of many women from the countries of America, they were able to introduce a resolution which established the Inter-American Commission of Women, now an important adjunct to the Organization of American States.

Alice Paul, with the help of prominent women from all over the world, founded the World Woman's Party on November 19, 1938. This Party was to become the international arm of the National Woman's Party.

On December 12, 1943, with appropriate ceremonies, the National Woman's Party opened the Florence Bayard Hilles Library, the first feminist library. It became known to women all over the world who came for serious research on women's issues. The library has been closed since 1972 for restoration and will reopen as a museum and library. The museum part will contain exhibits of Suffrage costumes, flags, posters and memorabilia of Suffrage days. The library will contain microfilms of the history of the National Woman's Party.

In 1945, when the United Nations was formed in San Francisco, under Alice Paul's leadership, the World Woman's Party and the National Woman's Party were instrumental in having included in the Charter a statement declaring recognition of equality for men and women.

In 1948, the World Woman's Party was successful in persuading the World Court to include a statement supporting the principle of human rights for all.

In 1964, it was the pressure and the lobbying of lawyers of the National Woman's Party that were mainly responsible for the word "sex" being inserted in Title VII-the Civil Rights Act. Alice Paul and her lobbying techniques were without parallel.

Over the years, the National Woman's Party took no stand on issues such as divorce, birth control information or abortion. They did file lawsuits in state court against specific examples of sex discrimination, but other issues mentioned in the 1922 Declaration of Principles were ignored or paid very little attention. They concentrated on discrimination against women, double standards in sex behavior and sex exploitation. They called for full equality under the law. They advocated a complete revision of existing statutes rather than issue-by-issue elimination of laws discriminating against women.

Since the 1960's, the National Woman's Party has concentrated all its efforts solely on passage of the Equal Rights Amendment in Congress and its ratification by the states.

CONTENTS

PART ONE

1913-1914

PAGE

I. INTRODUCTION 3
II. ALICE PAUL 6
III. ALICE PAUL AND LUCY BURNS 14
IV. F STREET AND THE EARLY DAYS 19
V. MAKING THE FEDERAL AMENDMENT AN ISSUE . . 32
VI. PRESSURE ON CONGRESS 50
VII. PRESSURE ON THE PRESIDENT 58
VIII. THE STRUGGLE WITH THE RULES COMMITTEE . . . 67
IX. THE FIRST APPEAL TO THE WOMEN VOTERS . . . 74
X. CONGRESS TAKES UP THE SUFFRAGE AMENDMENT . . 89

PART TWO

1915-1916

I. THE WOMAN VOTERS APPEAL TO THE PRESIDENT
AND TO CONGRESS 101
II. THE NEW HEADQUARTERS AND THE MIDDLE YEARS . . 125
III. THE CONFLICT WITH THE JUDICIARY COMMITTEE . . 132
IV. MORE PRESSURE ON THE PRESIDENT 146
V. FORMING THE WOMAN'S PARTY 152
VI. STILL MORE PRESSURE ON THE PRESIDENT . . . 167
VII. THE SECOND APPEAL TO THE WOMEN VOTERS . . 175
VIII. HAIL AND FAREWELL 187

PART THREE

1917

I. THE PERPETUAL DELEGATION 198
    1. THE PEACEFUL PICKETING 198
    2. THE PEACEFUL RECEPTION 219
    3. THE WAR ON THE PICKETS 227
    4. THE COURT AND THE PICKETS 267
    5. THE STRANGE LADIES 269
II. TELLING THE COUNTRY 300
III. MORE PRESSURE ON CONGRESS 307

CONTENTS

PART FOUR
VICTORY

I.	The New Headquarters and the Later Years	319
II.	Lobbying	325
III.	Organizing	335
IV.	The President Capitulates and the House Surrenders	344
V.	Fighting for Votes in the Senate	348
VI.	Burning the President's Words	363
VII.	The President Appeals to the Senate to Pass the Suffrage Amendment	376
VIII.	Picketing the Senate	382
IX.	The Third Appeal to the Women Voters	390
X.	The President Includes Suffrage in His Campaign for Congress	394
XI.	Burning the President's Words Again	396
XII.	The Watch Fires of Freedom	401
XIII.	The Appeal to the President on His Return	420
XIV.	The Appeal to the President on His Departure	424
XV.	The President Obtains the Last Vote and Congress Surrenders	427
XVI.	Ratification	430
XVII.	The Last Days	478
Index		492

LIST OF ILLUSTRATIONS

Alice Paul . . . . *Frontispiece*

FACING
PAGE

Lucy Burns at the Head of the "Prison Specialists" . . . 16
Why is the Girl from the West Getting all the Attention?
Cartoon by Nina Allender 77
The Suffragist's Dream. *Cartoon by Nina Allender* . . . 148
Inez Milholland in the Washington Parade, March 3, 1913 . . 188
Joy Young at the Inez Milholland Memorial Service . . . 192
Wage Earners Picketing the White House, February, 1917 . . 206
The Thousand Pickets try vainly to Deliver Their Resolutions
to the President, March 4, 1917 210
A Thousand Pickets Marching Around the White House,
March 4, 1917 210
Obeying Orders, Washington Police Arresting White House
Pickets Before the Treasury Building 263
The Patrol Wagon Waiting the Arrival of the Suffrage Pickets . . 263
Burning the President's Words at the Lafayette
Monument, Washington 364
A Summer Picket Line 364
Lucy Branham Burning the President's Words at the
Lafayette Monument 373
The Russian Envoy Banner, August, 1917 373
One of the Watchfires of Freedom 406
A Policeman Scatters the Watchfire 406
Suffragist Rebuilding the Fire Scattered by the Police . . . 409
The Last Suffragist Arrested. The Fire Burns On . . . 409
The Oldest and the Youngest Pickets 460
The Flag Complete 475
Every Good Suffragist the Morning after Ratification.
Cartoon by Nina Allender 484

"But with such women consecrating their lives failure is impossible."

Last words spoken in public by SUSAN B. ANTHONY— *her birthday, 1906.*

"Most of those who worked with me in the early years have gone. I am here for a little time only and my place will be filled as theirs was filled. The fight must not cease; you must see that it does not stop."

SUSAN B. ANTHONY.

PART ONE
1913 and 1914

ALICE PAUL.
Taken the Day Before She Went to Prison.

I

INTRODUCTION

In 1912 the situation in the United States in regard to the enfranchisement of women was as follows:

Agitation for an amendment to the National Constitution had virtually ceased. Before the death of Susan B. Anthony in 1906, Suffragists had turned their attention to the States. Suffrage agitation there was persistent, vigorous, and untiring; in Washington, it was merely perfunctory. The National American Woman Suffrage Association maintained a Congressional Committee in Washington, but no Headquarters. This Committee arranged for one formal hearing before the Senate and the House Committee of each Congress. The speeches were used as propaganda mailed on a Congressman's frank. The Suffrage Amendment had never in the history of the country been brought to a vote in the National House of Representatives, and had only once, in 1887, been voted upon in the Senate. It had not received a favorable report from the Committee in either House since 1892 and had not received a report of any kind since 1896. Suffrage had not been debated on the floor of either House since 1887. In addition, the incoming President, Woodrow Wilson, if not actually opposed to the enfranchisement of women, gave no appearance of favoring it; the great political Parties were against it. Political leaders generally were unwilling to be connected with it. Congress lacked—it is scarcely exaggeration to say—several hundreds of the votes necessary to pass the Amendment. Last of all the majority of Suffragists did not think the Federal Amendment a practical possibility. They were entirely engrossed in State campaigns.

On the other hand, the Suffrage movement, itself, was

3

4

virile and vital. The fourth generation of women to espouse
this cause were throwing themselves into the work with all
the power and force of their able, aroused, and emancipate
generation. The franchise had been granted in six States:
Wyoming, Colorado, Utah, Idaho, Washington, California.
With the winning of Oregon, Kansas, and Arizona in 1912,
the movement assumed a new importance in the national
field. These victories meant that there were approximately
two million women-voters in the United States, that one-
fifth of the Senate, one-seventh of the House and one-sixth
of the electoral vote came from Suffrage States.

It was in December, 1912, as Chairman of the Congressional Committee of the National American Woman Suffrage
Association, that Alice Paul came to Washington.

In the next eight years, this young woman was to bring
into existence a new political Party of fifty thousand members. She was to raise over three-quarters of a million
dollars. She was to establish a Headquarters in Washington
that became the focus of the liberal forces of the country.
She was to gather into her organization hundreds of devoted workers; some without pay and others with less pay
than they could command at other work or with other
organizations. She was to introduce into Suffrage agitation in the United States a policy which, though not new
in the political arena, was new to Suffrage—the policy of
holding the Party in power responsible. She was to institute a Suffrage campaign so swift, so intensive, so compelling—and at the same time so varied, interesting, and
picturesque—that again and again it pushed the war-news
out of the preferred position on the front pages of the
newspapers of the United States. She was to see her Party
blaze a purple, white, and gold trail from the east to the
west of the United States; and from the north to the
south. She was to see the Susan B. Anthony Amendment
pass first the House and then the Senate. She was to see
thirty-seven States ratify the Amendment in less than a

year and a half thereafter. She was to see the President of the United States move from a position of what seemed definite opposition to the Suffrage cause to an open espousal of it; move slowly at first but with a progress which gradually accelerated until he, himself, obtained the last Senatorial vote necessary to pass the Amendment.

What was the training which had developed in Alice Paul this power and what were the qualities back of that training, which made it possible for her to invent so masterly a plan, to pursue it so resistlessly?

II

ALICE PAUL

I watched a river of women,
Rippling purple, white and golden,
Stream toward the National Capitol.

Along its border,
Like a purple flower floating,
Moved a young woman, worn, wraithlike,
With eyes alight, keenly observing the marchers.
Out there on the curb, she looked so little, so lonely;
Few appeared even to see her;
No one saluted her.

Yet commander was she of the column, its leader;
She was the spring whence arose that irresistible
    river of women
Streaming steadily towards the National Capitol.
                    KATHERINE ROLSTON FISHER,
                    The Suffragist, January 19, 1918.

IT is an interesting coincidence that the woman who bore
the greatest single part in the Suffrage fight at the beginning—Susan Anthony—and the woman who bore the
greatest single part at the end—Alice Paul—were both
Quakers.

It is very difficult to get Alice Paul to talk about herself.
She is not much interested in herself and she is interested,
with every atom of her, in the work she is doing. She will
tell you, if you ask her, that she was born in Moorestown,
New Jersey, and then her interest seems to die. She apparently does not remember herself very clearly either as a
child or a young girl. That is not strange. So intently has
she worked in the last eight years and so intensely has she
lived in that work that each year seems to have erased its
predecessor. She is absolutely concentrated on *now*. I

6

asked Alice Paul once what converted her to Woman Suffrage. She said that she could not remember when she did not believe in it. She added, " You know the Quakers have always believed in Woman Suffrage."

Anne Herendeen, in a vivacious article on Alice Paul in *Everybody's Magazine* for October, 1919, says, describing a visit to Moorestown:

" What do you think of all these goings-on? " I asked her mother. She sighed.

" Well, Mr. Paul always used to say, when there was anything hard and disagreeable to be done, ' I bank on Alice.' "

The degree of education in Alice Paul's life and the amount of social service which she had performed are a little staggering in view of her youth. Just the list of the degrees she achieved and the positions she held before she started the National Woman's Party covers a typewritten page. They have even an unexpected international quality. One notes first—and without undue astonishment—that she acquired a B.A. at Swarthmore in 1905; an M.A. at the University of Pennsylvania in 1907; a Ph.D. at the same university in 1912. This would seem enough to fill the educational leisure of most young women, but it does not by any means complete Alice Paul's student career. She was a graduate of the New York School of Philanthropy in 1906. She was a student at the Woodbrooke Settlement for Social Work at Woodbrooke, Birmingham, and in the University of Birmingham, England, in 1907-08; a graduate student in sociology and economics in the School of Economics of the University of London in 1908-09.

She was, in addition, a Resident Worker of the New York College Settlement in 1905-06; a Visitor for the New York Charity Organization Society in the summer of 1906; a Worker in the Summer Lane Settlement, and a Visitor in the Charity Organization Society of Birmingham, England, during the winter of 1907-08; Assistant-secretary to the Dalston Branch of the Charity Organization Society in

London for a half year in 1908; a Visitor for the Peel
Institute for Social Work at Clerkenwell, London, for a half
year in 1908-09; a Resident Worker for the Christian Social
Union Settlement of Hoxton, London, in the summer of
1908. She was also in charge of the Women's Department
of the branch of adult schools at Hoxton in the summer
of 1908.

I asked Mabel Vernon, who went to Swarthmore with
her, about Alice Paul. Her impressions were a little vague
—mainly of a normal, average young girl who had not yet
begun to " show." She remembered that, although biology
was her specialty, Miss Paul was catholic in her choice of
courses; how—as though it were something she expected to
need—she took a great deal of Latin; and that—as though
at the urge of the same intuition—she devoted herself to
athletics. She had apparently no athletic gifts; yet before
she left Swarthmore she was on the girls' varsity basketball
team, was on her own class hockey team, and had taken
third place in the women's tennis tournament. She was a
rosy, rounded, vigorous-looking girl then. When Mabel
Vernon saw her next, she had been hunger-striking in England and was thin to the point of emaciation.

I asked Alice Paul herself about her work with the poor
in England. She said, looking back on it—and it is apparently always a great effort for her to remove her mental
vision from the present demand—that her main impression
was of the hopelessness of it all, that there seemed nothing
to do but sweep all that poverty away. The thing that she
remembers especially now is that they were always burying
children.

The first great, outstanding fact of Alice Paul's training
is that in the English interregnum which divided her American education, she joined the Pankhurst forces. In the
beginning all her work was of the passive kind. She attended
meetings and ushered. She was about to go home; indeed
she had bought her passage when the Pankhursts asked her
to join a deputation to Parliament. This deputation, which

consisted of more than a hundred women, and was led by Mrs. Pankhurst herself, was arrested at the entrance to Parliament. They were detained in the policemen's billiard room of the Cannon Row Police Station, the only place at that station large enough to hold so many women.

The second great outstanding fact of Alice Paul's career in England is that she met Lucy Burns.

Lucy Burns was born in Brooklyn. The facts of her education, although superficially not so multitudinous as those of Alice Paul, are even more impressive in point of international quality. She was graduated from Packer Institute in 1899 and from Vassar College in 1902. She studied at Yale University in 1902-03, at the University of Berlin in 1906-08, at the University of Bonn in 1908-09. She joined the Woman's Social and Political Union of London in 1909 and she worked as an organizer in Edinburgh and the east of Scotland in 1909-12.

Lucy Burns thinks she first met Alice Paul at a Suffrage demonstration. Alice Paul thinks she first met Lucy Burns in that same policemen's billiard room of the Cannon Row Police Station, London. Both these young women remember their English experiences in flashes and pictures. They worked too hard and too militantly to keep any written record; and successive hardships wiped away all traces of their predecessors. At any rate, Alice Paul says that she spoke to Miss Burns because she noticed that she wore a little American flag. Sitting on the billiard table, they talked of home. Alice Paul also says that Lucy Burns, a student at that time of the University of Bonn in Germany, had come to England for a holiday. She entered the militant movement a few weeks after she landed and this was her first demonstration.

The women were held for trial, giving bail for their appearance. Alice Paul had engaged passage home, but she had to cancel it as the trial did not occur until after the date of her sailing. The case was appealed in the courts and was finally dropped by the government.

From this time on, the paths of the two girls kept cross-
ing. Frequently, indeed, they worked together. The next
time Alice Paul was arrested, however, Lucy Burns was not
with her. This was at Norwich. Winston Churchill, a member of the cabinet, was holding a meeting. Outside, Alice
Paul spoke at a meeting too—a protest against the government's stand on Woman Suffrage. On this occasion, she
was released without being tried. At the next Suffrage
demonstration—at Limehouse in London—both girls assisted.
On this occasion, Lloyd-George was holding a meeting.
Miss Paul and Miss Burns were arrested for trying to speak
at a protest-meeting outside, and were sentenced to two
weeks in Holloway Jail. They went on a hunger strike; but
were released after five days and a half.

After they recovered from this experience, Miss Paul and
Miss Burns motored to Scotland with Mrs. Pankhurst and
other English Suffragists, in order to assist with the Scottish campaign. At Glasgow, the party organized a demonstration outside of a meeting held by Lord Crewe, a member
of the cabinet. Arrested, they were released without trial.
Proceeding northward, Miss Paul assisted in organizing the
Suffrage campaign in East Fife, the district of Prime Minister Herbert Asquith. At Dundee, Miss Paul and Miss
Burns took part in a demonstration outside a meeting
held by Winston Churchill. The two American girls and
an English Suffragist were sentenced to ten days in Dundee
Prison. After four days of hunger strike, all were released. Each night during their imprisonment, great crowds
of citizens marched round the prison singing Scotch songs
as a means of showing their sympathy with the campaign.
Upon their release, the Suffragists were welcomed at a
mass-meeting over which the Lord Mayor presided. Thence
they went to Edinburgh where they assisted in organizing
a procession and pageant in Princess Street—one of the
most beautiful and famous thoroughfares of the world. The
pageant of the Scotch heroines who had made sacrifices
for liberty is still remembered in Scotland for its beauty.

The next job was less agreeable. The two American girls were sent to Berwick-on-Tweed to interrupt with a protest a meeting of Sir Edward Grey, then Minister of Foreign Affairs. Miss Paul made the interruption, was arrested, but was released on the following day without going to trial. Miss Burns was not arrested that time.

Next in Bermondsey, one of the slum districts of London, they waged a plain, old-fashioned electoral campaign to defeat a candidate. When this was over, Miss Paul, in company with a Miss Brown, was sent to make a Suffrage protest at the Lord Mayor's Banquet in the Guildhall. They were arrested, of course, and were sentenced to thirty days in Holloway Jail. They hunger struck, and were forcibly fed. This experience left its mark on Miss Paul's health for some time; it was several weeks after her release before she was strong enough to travel. But in January, 1910, she sailed for America—and arrived the pale, emaciated creature who so shocked Mabel Vernon.

Lucy Burns tells an amusing story of Alice Paul's experiences in England. Lord Crewe was to speak at a meeting at Glasgow, and Alice Paul was delegated to represent the Suffragists at that meeting and to heckle the speaker. That meant that she must conceal herself in the building, where the meeting was to take place, the night before. The building was a big, high one—St. Andrew's Hall, the girls remember the name—and it was surrounded by a high, formidable iron fence. The night before Lucy Burns walked with Alice Paul to the Hall and helped her to climb to the top of this fence. Then Alice Paul jumped down into the grounds and Lucy Burns left her there. There was some building going on at this hall and with great difficulty Alice Paul climbed the scaffolding to the high second story and settled herself on a roof to spend the night. It rained all night; and of course she had no protection against the wet. And after all this discomfort, when daylight broke, laborers coming to work on a neighboring building observed the strange phenomenon of a woman lying on a second-story roof. They reported her and she was ignominously led down and out.

In the summer of 1912, Lucy Burns returned to America. Alice Paul visited her in Long Island. For some time now, Alice Paul had been considering the Suffrage situation of the United States in its national aspect. Here, she broached to Lucy Burns her idea of working for a Constitutional Amendment in Washington—her belief that with six States enfranchised—with six States that could be used as a lever on Congress—the time had come when further work in State campaigns was sheer waste. More even than English conditions, American conditions favored the policy of holding the Party in power responsible in regard to Suffrage. In England, there was no body of women completely enfranchised. In America there were approximately two million women voters who, completely enfranchised, could command a hearing from the politicians. She felt that such a campaign in America would be more productive of result for still another reason. In pursuing that policy in England, the Suffragists were often placed in the embarrassing position of defeating Suffragists and putting in anti-Suffragists. But in America, no matter what Party was in power, only Suffrage senators and representatives could be elected from the Suffrage States. In other words, if, in defeating the Party in power they defeated Suffragists—as was inevitable in the Suffrage States—other Suffragists as inevitably took their places. Moreover, there was no immediate motive urging senators and representatives from the Suffrage States—although often they were individually helpful—to convert senators and representatives of their own Party from non-Suffrage States. Were their Party in jeopardy at home, however, that motive was instantly supplied. Also, Alice Paul thought that it was more dignified of women to ask the vote of other women than to beg it of men.

Alice Paul was the first to apply this policy to the Suffrage situation in the United States. As late as 1917, other

Suffrage leaders, as well as members of Congress, were re-iterating that there was no such thing as a Party in power in the United States, that that idea was brought from England by Alice Paul and was not adapted to our American institutions.

The two girls concocted a scheme for starting federal work in Washington. They went with it to the National American Woman Suffrage Association, to Anna Howard Shaw, to Harriot Stanton Blatch, to Mary Ware Dennett. Lucy Burns pictures Alice Paul at that last interview— " a little Quakerish figure, crumpled up in her chair and for the first time I noticed how beautiful her eyes were." Finally Alice Paul went to the Convention of the National American Association at Philadelphia. She talked with Jane Addams. Alice Paul suggested that she be allowed to come to Washington at her own expense to begin work on Congress for the passing of a Constitutional Amendment. She agreed to raise the necessary money. Jane Addams brought this suggestion before the Board of the National American Woman Suffrage Association, urged its acceptance. It was approved. The Board appointed a Committee consisting of Alice Paul, Chairman; Lucy Burns, Vice-chairman; Crystal Eastman. Later in Washington, Mrs. Lawrence Lewis and Mary Beard joined that Committee. Alice Paul went first to Philadelphia and collected money for a few days. Mrs. Lawrence Lewis, who, Miss Paul says, was one of the first to say, " I have always believed that the way to get Suffrage is by a federal amendment," gave her name; gave money; collected money.

And so—all alone—Alice Paul came to Washington.

III

ALICE PAUL AND LUCY BURNS

ALICE PAUL is a slender, frail-looking young woman, delicately colored and delicately made. The head, the neck, the long slim arms, and the little hands look as though they were cut out of alabaster. The dense shadowy hair, scooping with deeper accessions of shadow into great waves, dipping low on her forehead and massing into a great dusky bunch in her neck, might be carved from bronze. It looks too heavy for her head. Her face has a kind of powerful irregularity. Its prevailing expression is of a brooding stillness; yet when she smiles, dimples appear. Her eyes are big and quiet; dark—like moss-agates. When she is silent they are almost opaque. When she talks they light up—rather they glow—in a notable degree of luminosity. Her voice is low; musical; it pulsates with a kind of interrogative plaintiveness. When you ask her a question, there ensues, on her part, a moment of a stillness so profound, you can almost hear it. I think I have never seen anybody who can keep so still as Alice Paul. But when she answers you, the lucidity of exposition, the directness of expression! Always she looks you straight in the eye, and when she has finished speaking she holds you with that luminous glow. Her tiny hands make gestures, almost humorous in their gentleness and futility, compared with the force of her remarks.

In the endless discussions at Headquarters—discussions that consider every subject on earth and change constantly in personnel and point of view—she is always the most silent. But when at last she speaks, often there ensues a pause; she has summed it all up. Superficially she seems cold, austere, a little remote. But that is only because the

14

fire of her spirit burns at such a heat that it is still and white. She has the quiet of the spinning top.

As for her mentality . . . her capacity for leadership . . . her vision. . . . There is no difference of opinion in regard to Alice Paul in the Woman's Party. With one accord, they say, " She is the Party." They regard her with an admiration which verges on awe. Mentally she walks apart; not because she has any conscious sense of superiority, but because of the swiftness, amplitude, and completeness with which her mind marches—her marvelous powers of concentration and her blazing devotion to the work.

I think no better description can be given of her than to quote the exact phrases which her associates use in talking of her. Winifred Mallon speaks of her " burning sincerity." Helena Hill Weed imputes a " prescience " to her. Anne Martin says, " She is the heart, brain, and soul of the Woman's Party," and " Her mind moves with the precision of a beautiful machine." Nina Allender sums her up as " a Napoleon without self-indulgence." She said that when at the hearing in 1915, Congressmen tried to tangle Alice Paul they found it an impossibility; everything in Alice Paul's mentality was so clear; there was nothing to tangle. She added, " There are no two minds to Alice Paul." " My mother describes her," she concluded, " as a flame undyingly burning."

This is Maud Younger's tribute:

She has in the first place a devotion to the cause which is absolutely self-sacrificing. She has an indomitable will. She recognizes no obstacles. She has a clear, penetrating, analytic mind which cleaves straight to the heart of things. In examining a situation, she always bares the main fact; she sees all the forces which make for change in that situation. She is a genius for organization, both in the mass and in detail. She understands perfectly, in achieving the big object, the cumulative effect of multitudes of small actions and small services. She makes use of all material, whether human or otherwise, that comes along. Her work has perpetual growth; it never stagnates; it is always branching out. She is never hampered or cluttered. She is free of the past. Her inventiveness and resourcefulness are endless. She believes absolutely in open diplomacy. She believes that everything should be told; our main argument with her was in regard to the necessity for secrecy in special cases. She is almost without suspicion; and sometimes with a too-great tendency towards kind judgment in the case of the individual. It seems incredible that with all these purely intellectual gifts, she should possess an acute appreciation of beauty; a gift for pageantry; an amazing sense of humor.

Lucy Burns says:

When Alice Paul spoke to me about the federal work, I knew that she had an extraordinary mind, extraordinary courage and remarkable executive ability. But I felt she had two disabilities—ill-health and a lack of knowledge of human nature. I was wrong in both. I was staggered by her speed and industry and the way she could raise money. Her great assets, I should say, are her power, with a single leap of the imagination, to make plans on a national scale; and a supplementary power to see that done down to the last postage stamp. But because she can do all this, people let her do it—often she has to carry her own plans out down to the very last postage stamp. She used all kinds of people; she tested them through results. She is exceedingly charitable in her judgments of people and patient. She assigned one inept person to five different kinds of work before she gave her up. Her abruptness lost some workers, but not the finer spirits. The very absence of anything like personal appeal seemed to help her.

Lucy Burns is as different a type from Alice Paul as one could imagine. She is tall—or at least she seems tall; rounded and muscular; a splendidly vigorous physical specimen. If Alice Paul looks as though she were a Tanagra carved from alabaster, Lucy Burns seems like a figure, heroically sculptured, from marble. She is blue-eyed and fresh-complexioned; dimpled; and her head is burdened, even as Alice Paul's, by an enormous weight of hair. Lucy Burn's hair is a brilliant red; and even as she flashes, it flashes. It is full of sparkle. She is a woman of twofold ability. She speaks and writes with equal eloquence and

Photo Copr. Harris and Ewing, Washington, D. C.

LUCY BURNS AT THE HEAD OF THE "PRISON SPECIALISTS."
These Women, All of Whom Served Terms in Jail, Are Wearing
a Reproduction of Their Prison Garb.

elegance. Her speeches before Suffrage bodies, her editorials in the *Suffragist* are models of clearness; conciseness; of accumulative force of expression. Mentally and emotionally, she is quick and warm. Her convictions are all vigorous and I do not think Lucy Burns would hesitate for a moment to suffer torture, to die, for them. She has intellectuality of a high order; but she overruns with a winning Irishness which supplements that intellectuality with grace and charm; a social mobility of extreme sensitiveness and swiftness. In those early days in Washington, with all her uncompromising militantism, Lucy Burns was the diplomat of the pair; the tactful, placating force.

I asked a member of the Woman's Party who had watched the work from the beginning what was the difference between the two women. She answered, " They are both political-minded. They seemed in those early days to have one spirit and one brain. Both saw the situation exactly as it was, but they went at the problem with different methods. Alice Paul had a more acute sense of justice, Lucy Burns, a more bitter sense of injustice. Lucy Burns would become angry because the President or the people did not do this or that. Alice Paul never expected anything of them."

Both these women had the highest kind of courage. Lucy Burns—although she admits that at Occoquan Workhouse, she suffered from nameless terrors—has a mental poise that is almost unsusceptible to fear. Alice Paul—although she can with perfect composure endure arrest, imprisonment, hunger-striking—acknowledges timidities. She does not like to listen to horrors of any description, especially ghost-stories. They say though that, in the movies, she always particularly enjoyed pirates.

IV

F STREET AND THE EARLY DAYS

WHEN Alice Paul arrived in Washington in December, 1912, she found a discouraging state of things. She had been given the address of Headquarters, but Headquarters had vanished. She had been given a list of people to whom she could turn for help, but most of them had died or moved away. At that time, Mrs. William Kent, who was subsequently to become one of her constant and able assistants, was Chairman of the Congressional Committee of the National American Woman Suffrage Association. Two years before, when her husband was elected to Congress, Mrs. Kent came to Washington. When she was asked to become Chairman of this Committee she was told that it would entail no work. She must merely see that the bill was introduced and arrange hearings before the two committees. There was no thought of putting the Amendment through, and no lobbying for it. The National Association allowed Mrs. Kent ten dollars. At the end of the year she returned change. There were a few Suffrage clubs in Washington, but their activity was merely social. Alice Paul saw that the work had to be started from the very beginning. First of all they had to have Headquarters. She hired a little basement room at 1420 F Street. At a formal opening on January 2, 1913, Mrs. William Kent, presiding, introduced Alice Paul as her successor; and a plan for federal work was laid before the Suffragists of the District of Columbia. Of course no one at the meeting guessed that she was present at a historic occasion.

Alice Paul began work at once. Nina Allender says that one Sunday a stranger called. She was wearing " a slim dress and a little purple hat and she was no bigger," Mrs. Allender held up her forefinger, " than *that*." The call was brief and it was unaccompanied by any of the small talk or the persiflage which distinguishes most social occasions. But when the door closed, a few moments later, mother and daughter looked at each other in amazement. Mrs. Evans had promised to contribute to Suffrage a sum of money monthly. Mrs. Allender had promised to contribute to Suffrage a sum of money monthly. Mrs. Evans had agreed to do a certain amount of work monthly. Mrs. Allender had agreed to do a certain amount of work monthly. Their amazement arose partly from the fact that they had not been begged, urged, or argued with—they had simply been asked; and partly from the fact that, before the arrival of this slim little stranger, they had no more idea of contributing so much money or work than of flying. But they agreed to it the instant she requested it of them.

This is a perfect example of the way Alice Paul works. There may be times when she urges, even begs; but they appear to be rare. She often forgets to thank you when you say yes; for she has apparently assumed that you will say yes. She does not argue with you when you say no— but you rarely say no. She has only to ask apparently. Perhaps it is part the terseness with which she puts her request. Perhaps it is part her simple acceptance of the fact that you are not going to refuse. Perhaps it is her expectation that you will understand that she is not asking for herself but for Suffrage. Perhaps it is the Quaker integrity which shines through every statement. Perhaps it is the intensity of devotion which blazes back of the gentleness of her personality and the inflexibility of purpose which gives that gentleness power. At any rate, it is very difficult to refuse Alice Paul.

A member of the Woman's Party, meeting her for the first time in New York and riding for a short distance in a taxicab with her, says that Alice Paul turned to her as soon as they were alone:

"Will you give a thousand dollars to the Woman's Party?"

"No, I haven't that amount to give."

"Will you give one hundred dollars?"

"No."

"Will you give twenty-five dollars?"

"No."

"Will you——"

"I'll give five dollars."

Mrs. Gilson Gardner says that one day, in the midst of the final preparations for the procession of March 3, she came to Headquarters. Alice Paul, it was apparent, was in a state of considerable perturbation. At the sight of Mrs. Gardner she said, "There's Mrs. Gardner! She'll attend to it." She went on to explain. "The trappings for the horses have been ruined. Will you order some more? They must be delivered tomorrow night." Mrs. Gardner says that she had no more idea how to order a trapping than a suspension bridge, but—magic-ed as always by Alice Paul's personality—she emitted a terrified "Yes," and started out. She walked round and round the block a dozen times, reviewing her problem, and casting about her looks of an appalled desperation. Suddenly she espied a little tailor shop, and in it, at work, a little tailor. She approached and confided her problem to him. Mrs. Gardner kept shop while he went to Headquarters and got the measurements. He delivered the trappings on time.

Later in the history of the Woman's Party, Margery Ross came to Washington to spend the winter with a cousin.

She was young and pretty. She established herself there and began to enjoy herself. She was a Suffragist. One day, out of a clear sky, Alice Paul said: "Miss Ross, will you go to Wyoming on Saturday, and organize a State Convention there within three weeks?" "Why, Miss Paul," the girl faltered, "I *can't*. My plans are all made for the winter. I've only just got here." Nevertheless, in a few days, Miss Ross started for Wyoming. There were only eight members of the Congressional Union in that State, and yet three

weeks later she had achieved a State Convention with one
hundred and twenty delegates.

Perhaps, however, the story which best illustrates Miss
Paul's power to make people work is one of Nina Allender's.
One must remember that Mrs. Allender is an artist. One day
Alice Paul telephoned her to ask her if she would go the
next day to Ohio to campaign for the Woman's Party. Mrs.
Allender, who had no more expectation of going to Ohio
than to the moon, replied: " I'm sorry. It's impossible.
You see, we have just moved. The place is being papered
and painted, and I've got to select the wallpaper." " Oh,
that's all right," Alice Paul suggested. " I'll send a girl
right up there. *She'll pick your paper for you and see that
it's put on.*" In the end, of course, Mrs. Allender chose
her own paper. But although she did not go to Ohio the
next day, she went within a week.

When Alice Paul asked Maud Younger to deliver the
memorial address on Inez Milholland, Miss Younger was at
first staggered by the idea. " I can't," she said. " I don't
know how to do it."

" Oh," directed Alice Paul in a *dégagé* way, " *just write
something like Lincoln's Gettysburg address.*"

The first Headquarters consisted of one long basement
room, partitioned at the back into three small rooms of
which two were storerooms, and one Miss Paul's office. This
opened into a court. Later when the *Suffragist* was published, they had rooms upstairs; sometimes one, sometimes
more, according to their funds. By the first anniversary,
they had expanded to ten rooms. Later still, they had two
whole floors.

Almost all the work was done by volunteers. All kinds of
people worked for them. Comparatively idle women of the
moneyed class gave up matinées, teas, and other social occasions; stenographers, who worked all day long, labored
until midnight. Anybody who dropped into Headquarters
for any purpose was put to work. Once a distinguished
lawyer from a western city called on business with Alice
Paul.

"Would you mind addressing a few envelopes?" asked Alice Paul when the business was concluded. The distinguished lawyer, whose own office was of course manned by a small army of stenographers, smiled; but he took off his coat and went to work.

Alice Paul's swift, decisive leadership was accepted, unquestioningly. Her word was immutable. One day an elderly woman was observed at a typewriter, painfully picking at it with a stiff forefinger. It was obvious that with a great expenditure of time and energy, she was accomplishing nothing.

"Why are you doing that?" somebody asked curiously.

"Because Alice Paul told me to," was the plaintive answer.

Most of the work was done in the big front room. The confusion of going and coming of the volunteer workers; the noise of conflicting activity; conversation; telephones; made concentrated thinking almost impossible. The policeman on the beat said that a light burned in Headquarters all night long. That was true. Alice Paul and Lucy Burns used to work far into the morning because then, alone, were they assured of quiet. There were times though when Alice Paul worked all day, all night and sitting up in bed, into the next morning. She never lost time. Later when she picketed the White House, she used to take a stenographer with her and dictate while on picket duty.

Volunteer work is of course not always to be depended upon. It is eccentric and follows its own laws. There would be periods when Headquarters would be flooded with help. There came intervals when it was almost empty. Sara Grogan, herself a devoted adherent, tells how in this case, she used to go out on the streets and ask strangers to help. Volunteer workers—if they were housekeepers or the mothers of families—learned, on their busy days, to give F Street a wide berth. As they had no time to give and as it was impossible to say no to Alice Paul, the streets about Headquarters were as closed to them as the streets of his creditors to Dick Swiveller. It was perhaps this experience which taught Alice Paul what later became one of her chief assets —her power to put to use every bit of human material that came her way; which developed in her that charitable willingness, when this human material failed in one direction, to try it in another; and another; and another. Rarely did she reject any offer of help, no matter how untrained or seemingly untrainable it was. I asked Mabel Vernon how she got so much work—and such splendid work of all kinds —out of amateurs. She answered, " She believed we could do it and so she made us believe it."

In those days, Alice Paul herself was like one driven by a fury of speed. She was a human dynamo. She made everybody else work as hard as possible, but she drove— although she did drive—nobody so hard as herself. Winifred Mallon said, " I worked with Alice Paul for three months before I saw her with her hat off. I was perfectly astonished, I remember, at that mass of hair. I had never suspected its existence." For a long time, Alice Paul deliberately lived in a cold room, so that she could not be tempted to sit up late to read. It was more than a year before she visited the book-shop opened by a friend because, she said, " I should be tempted to buy so many books there." Anne Martin says that she believes Alice Paul made a vow not to think or to read anything that was not connected with Suffrage until the Amendment was passed. There was certainly no evidence of her reading anything else. They make the humorous observation at Headquarters now that the instant the Amendment had passed both Houses, Alice Paul began to permit herself the luxury of one mental relaxation—the reading of detective stories. But in those early days she worked all the time and she worked at everything. Somebody said to Lucy Burns, " She asks nothing of us that she doesn't do herself," and Lucy Burns answered dryly, " Yes, she's annoyingly versatile."

Not only did Alice Paul ask you to work but after you had agreed to it, she kept after you. " She 'nagged' us "

—they say humorously at Headquarters. Once, just before leaving for Chicago, Alice Paul appointed a certain young person chairman of a certain committee, with power to select chairmen of ten other committees to arrange for a demonstration when the Suffrage Special returned. This was four weeks off and yet in three days from Chicago came a telegram: " Wire me immediately the names of your chairmen! "

But just as Alice Paul never thanked herself for what she was doing, it never occurred to her to thank anybody else. And perhaps she had an innate conviction that it was egregious personally to thank people for devotion to a cause. However that did not always work out in practice, naturally.

Once a woman, a volunteer, who had worked all the morning reported to Alice Paul at noon. She retailed what she had done. Alice Paul made no comment whatever, but asked her immediately if she would go downtown for her. The woman refused; went away and did not come back. Alice Paul asked a friend for an explanation of her absence. " She is offended," her friend explained. " You did not thank her for what she did." " But," exclaimed Alice Paul, " she did not do it for me. She did it for Suffrage. I thought she would be delighted to do it for Suffrage." After that, however, Alice Paul tried very hard to remember to thank everybody. Once a party member said to her, as she was leaving Headquarters, " I have a taxi here, Miss Paul— can't I take you anywhere? " " No," Alice Paul answered abruptly. She was halfway down the stairs when she seemed to remember something. Instantly she turned back and said, " Thank you! " Another time, somebody else announced that she was offended because Alice Paul had not thanked her, and was going to leave. A friend went to Alice Paul.

" Mrs. Blank is leaving us. I am afraid you have offended her."

" Where is she? " Alice Paul demanded, " I will apologize at once."

" For what? " the friend inquired.

" I don't know," Alice Paul answered, " *anything!* "

Like Roosevelt, Alice Paul had a remarkable news sense. She was the joy of newspaper men. Ninety per cent of the Woman's Party bulletins got publicity as against about twenty per cent of others. A New Orleans editor said they were the best publicity organization in the country. Gilson Gardner compares her to a Belasco, staging the scene admirably but, herself, always in the background.

Later, when the first stress was over, her companions spoke of the joy of work with her. They marveled at that creative quality which made her put over her demonstrations on so enormous a scale and the beauty with which she inundated them.

Maud Younger tells of going with her one night to the Capitol steps, when she painted imaginatively, on the scene which lay outstretched before her, the great demonstration which she was planning: wide areas of static color here, long lines of pulsating color there, laid on in great splashes and welts, like a painter of the modern school. Above all, her companions took a fearful joy in the serene way in which she brushed aside red tape, ignored rules. She would decide on some unexpected, daring bit of pioneer demonstration. Her companions would report to her retarding restrictions. "What an absurd rule," she would remark, and then proceed calmly to ignore it. "Oh, Miss Paul, we *can't* do that!" was the commonest exclamation with which the fellow workers greeted her plans. But always they did do it because she convinced them that it could be done. After the death of Inez Milholland, Alice Paul decided to hold a memorial service in Statuary Hall at the Capitol.

"Oh, Miss Paul, we can't do that! Memorial services are held there only for those whose statues are in the Hall." But in the end she did it. When her Committee spoke about it to the officials who have Statuary Hall in charge they said, "One thing we cannot permit. You cannot go up into the gallery because the doors open from that gallery into rooms containing old and valued books and those books might be stolen." The police said, "No, you must not hang curtains over those openings in case a Senator wants to pass through." Later the police themselves were helping Alice Paul to place the purple, white, and gold pennants about the gallery; they themselves were piling around their standards, in order to hold them straight, those same old and valued books; they themselves were standing on step-ladders to help her hang curtains before those unsealable openings.

When the Suffrage Special returned, Alice Paul decided to hold a welcoming banquet in the dining-room of the beautiful new Washington railroad station. She sent somebody to ask this privilege of the authorities. At first, of course, they said, no, but in the end, of course, they said, yes. The Woman's Party hired a band to help in the welcome. Alice Paul observed that the man who played the horn was so tall that he obscured an important detail in the decoration. She asked him to stand in another part of the band group. Of course he answered that that was impossible, that the horn always stood where he was standing, but in the end, of course, he stood where Alice Paul told him to stand.

Late in the history of the Woman's Party, somebody discovered that Alice Paul had never seen an anti-Suffragist. At a legislative hearing during ratification they pointed out one to her—a beautiful one. "She looks like a Botticelli," Alice Paul said—and gazed admiringly at her for the rest of the hearing.

Her companions marveled, I reiterate, at Alice Paul's creative power. That did not manifest itself in demonstrations alone. Her policy had creative quality. It had a wide sweep. It moved on wings and with accumulating force and speed. Her work in Washington started slowly, though with sureness of attack, but all the time it heightened and deepened. From 1913 to 1919 it never faltered. Sometimes changes in outside affairs made changes in her self-evolved plan, but they never stopped it, never even slowed it. From the beginning she saw her objective clearly; and always she made for it. Activities that may often have seemed to the callow-minded but the futile militancy of a group of fanatics were part of a perfectly co-ordinated plan. Moreover, she had always reserve ideas and always a buried ace. Sapient members of the Party—those who were close to her—believe that she used only a part of an enormous scheme; that she was prepared far into the future and for any possible contingency. They wonder sometimes how far that creative impulse reached . . . what form it would later . . . and later . . . and later have taken. Yet she proceeded slowly, giving every new form of agitation its chance; prudent always of her reserves. The instant one kind of demonstration exhausted its usefulness, she moved to the next. She wasted no time on side issues, on petty hostilities, on rivalries with other organizations.

But the quality that, above all, informed her other qualities, the quality that she first of all brought to the Suffrage situation, the quality that made her associates regard her with a kind of awe, was her political-mindedness, and political-mindedness was not at all uncommon in the Woman's Party. It was, perhaps, its main asset, although initiative and efficiency, speed, and courage of the most daring order marked it. But Alice Paul's political mindedness had quality as well as quantity. When Hughes was made the Republican nominee for the 1916 election, Alice Paul asked him to declare for National Suffrage. He was exceedingly dubious. It is obvious that, in asking favors of a politician, it is necessary to prove to him that action on his part will not hurt him in the matter of votes and may help him. On this point, Alice Paul said in effect:

"Your Party consists of two factions, the old, standpat Republicans and the Progressives. Now, if you put a Suffrage plank in your platform, you will not alienate the Progressives, because the Progressives have a Suffrage plank, and the old standpat Republicans will not vote for a Democrat no matter what you put in your platform."

When in the same election campaign Hughes went West, and the West turned to Wilson, it became evident, however much the Woman's' Party diminished the prestige of Wilson, it could not defeat him. Numerous advisers suggested to Alice Paul to withdraw her speakers from the campaign.

Alice Paul answered, " *No; if we withdraw our speakers from the campaign, we withdraw the issue from the campaign.* The main thing is to make the Suffrage Amendment a national issue that the Democrats will not want to meet in another campaign."

After the election, somebody said to her, " The people of the United States generally think you made a great mistake in fighting Wilson. They think your campaign a failure." Alice Paul answered, " In this case, it is not important what the people think *but what the Democratic leaders know.*"

The most magical thing about Alice Paul's political-mindedness was, however, a quality which is almost indescribable. Perhaps it should be symbolized by some term of the fourth dimension—although Helena Hill Weed's happy word " prescience " comes near to describing it. Maud Younger gives an extraordinary example of this. She says again and again, lobbyists would come back from the Capitol with the news of some unexpected manœuver which perplexed or even blocked them. Congressmen, themselves, would be puzzled over the situation. Again and again, she has seen Alice Paul walk to the window, stand there, head bent, thinking. Then, suddenly she would come back. She had seen behind the veil of conflicting and seemingly untranslatable testimony. She had, in Maud Younger's own words, cloven " straight to the heart of things." Often her lobbyists had the experience of explaining to baffled members of Committees in Congress the concealed tactics of their own Committee.

It was small wonder that they were so busy at Headquarters during those first months. They were preparing for a monster demonstration in the shape of a procession which was to occur on March 3, 1913, on the eve of President Wilson's first inauguration. That procession, which was really a thing of great beauty, brought Suffrage into prominence in a way the Suffragists had not for an instant anticipated. About eight thousand women took part. The procession started from the Capitol, marched up Pennsylvania Avenue past the White House and ended in a mass-meeting at the Hall of the Daughters of the American Revolution. Although a permit had been issued for the procession, and though this carried with it the right to the street, the police failed to protect the marchers as had been rumored they would. The end of the Avenue was almost impassable to the parade. A huge crowd, drawn from all over the country, had appeared in Washington for the Inauguration festivities. They chose to act in the most rowdy manner possible and many of the police chose to seem oblivious of what they were doing. Disgraceful episodes occurred. Secretary of War Stimson had finally to send for troops from Fort Meyer. There was an investigation of the action of the police by a Committee of the Senate. The official report is a thick book containing testimony that will shock any fine-minded American citizen. Ultimately, the Chief of Police for the District of Columbia was removed.

The investigation, however, kept the Suffrage procession in the minds of the public for many weeks. It almost overshadowed the Inauguration itself.

On this occasion, the banner—in a slightly modified form to be afterwards always known as the Great Demand banner—was carried for the first time. This banner marched peremptorily through the history of the Woman's Party until the Suffrage Amendment was passed. It said:

WE DEMAND AN AMENDMENT TO THE CONSTITUTION OF THE UNITED STATES ENFRANCHISING THE WOMEN OF THE COUNTRY.

On March 3 there arrived in Washington a man who was that day a simple citizen of the United States. The next day he was to become the President of the United States. As Woodrow Wilson drove from the station through the empty streets to his hotel, he asked, " Where are the people? "

The answer was, " Over on the Avenue watching the Suffrage Parade."

V

MAKING THE FEDERAL AMENDMENT AN ISSUE

THE first great demonstration of the Congressional Committee—the procession of March 3—had been designed to attract the eye of the country to the Suffragists. It succeeded beyond their wildest hopes. Thereafter it became a part of the policy of the Congressional Committee—later, the Congressional Union, and later still, the National Woman's Party—to keep the people watching the Suffragists. The main work of the Congressional Committee, however, focussed directly on Congress, as of course Congress alone could pass a Constitutional Amendment. They appealed to Congress constantly, by different methods, and through different avenues. They appealed to Congress through the President of the United States, through political leaders, through constituents. It is one way of describing their system to say that they worked on Congress by a series of electric shocks delivered to it downwards from the President, and by a constant succession of waves delivered upwards through the people. This pressure never ceased for a moment. It accumulated in power as the six years of this work went on.

When President Wilson arrived in Washington for his inauguration, the first thing brought to his notice was Suffrage agitation. The Congressional Committee thereafter kept Suffrage constantly before him. If not actually opposed to Suffrage in 1913, Woodrow Wilson had every appearance of opposition; certainly he was utterly indifferent to it. But Alice Paul believed that he was amenable to education on the subject, and she proceeded to educate him. Her theory proved to be true, but the process took

32

longer than she had anticipated. Her methods of course aroused storms of criticism; but in the end they triumphed. The President's action during the six years' siege was the attitude of all politicians. That is to say, for a long time he made general statements of a vaguely encouraging nature to the Suffragists, but for a long time he actually did nothing. Every accepted method of convincing him of the justice of the cause was tried. Deputation after deputation waited on him and stated their case. Then he began to move. He came out for Woman Suffrage as a principle; he voted for it in New Jersey but he still believed that the enfranchisement of woman must come by States. In 1917, his position, except for these minor admissions, was exactly that of 1913. As far as the Suffrage Amendment was concerned, he had not budged an inch. The Woman's Party then tried desperate remedies and afterward more and more desperate remedies. These always produced results—towards the end, *immediate* results. But at the beginning of this period, the Suffragists found that the instant they relaxed, the President relaxed; his attention departed from Suffrage. This always happened. Then the Congressional Committee began to exert a little more pressure, and the President's attention came back to Suffrage. In the long attacking process to which Alice Paul subjected him, she put him in untenable position after untenable position. He moved from each one of them by some new concession. In the end, he himself procured the last vote necessary to pass the Amendment in the Senate.

Alice Paul admires Woodrow Wilson profoundly. She admires his powers of leadership; his ideals; his persistence; his steadfastness; his resolution. " He is a man," she says, " who considers one thing at a time. Suffrage was not in his thought at all until we, ourselves, injected it there. And it was not in the center of his thought until the picketing was well along." She believed always that, when the President was made to think that he must act in regard to Suffrage, he would put it through.

Immediately after his inauguration, President Wilson announced that a special session of Congress would be called on April 7. At once the Congressional Committee decided to bring to his attention the fact that there was no subject which more urgently demanded treatment in this session than Woman Suffrage. Three deputations were therefore organized to ask him to recommend the Federal Amendment in the message by which he should convene this special session. These deputations—and all subsequent ones—were organized by Alice Paul.

The first deputation waited on President Wilson on March 17. This deputation consisting of four women was led by Alice Paul herself. Although individual Suffragists had interviewed previous presidents, this was the first deputation which had ever appeared with a request for action before a President of the United States. President Wilson's reply to their remarks was that the subject would receive his most careful attention.

The episode was one of the most amusing of the early history of the Congressional Committee. The President received the deputation in the White House offices. When they entered, they found four chairs arranged in a row with one in front of them, like a class about to be addressed by a teacher. The atmosphere was so tense that all the women felt it and were frightened. Alice Paul spoke first and said that women wanted Suffrage considered by Congress at once, as the most important issue before the country. All spoke in turn. One woman was so terrified that she petrified when her turn came. " Don't be nervous," the President reassured her and she finally proceeded. To this first group the President made the statement that so astounded Suffragists all over the country—that Suffrage had never been brought to his attention, that the matter was entirely new. He added that he did not know his position and would like all information possible on the subject.

The Congressional Committee gave him time to give the subject this careful attention, and then a second deputation waited on the President on March 28 to furnish him with the information he lacked. This deputation was led by Elsie Hill, and it represented the College Equal Suffrage League. The President replied to their remarks that this session of Congress would be so occupied with the tariff and the currency that the Suffrage measure could not be considered.

A third deputation waited on the President on March 31. It was led by Dr. Cora Smith King, and it was composed of influential members of the National Council of Women Voters. This delegation told the President that the women voters, who numbered approximately two million, were much interested in the proposed Suffrage Amendment. They also asked him to recommend it in his message. His reply to them was the same as to the college women: that this special session would be so occupied with the tariff and currency that the Suffrage measure could not be considered.

In the meantime, the Congressional Committee had notified Suffragists all over the United States that a Suffrage Amendment would be introduced in this special session of Congress; asking them to urge the President to indorse Suffrage in his forthcoming message; and to request their Representative in Congress to support Suffrage when it was introduced. Letters poured into Washington from the remotest corners of the country.

This was the beginning of that intimacy which the Congressional Committee—afterwards the Congressional Union, afterwards the National Woman's Party—established with its sympathizers and members all over the country. In the nature of things—the political situation being changeable, and demanding always subtle, delicate, and often swift and decisive handling—the actual work at Washington had to be planned and executed by a limited number. But those few must be able, forceful, and swiftly executive spirits. Their adherents all over the country were however kept as closely and constantly as possible in touch with that changing situation.

In addition, the Congressional Committee did all possible preliminary work with the incoming members of this Congress. The result on the Progressive members was encouraging. Although there was a Woman Suffrage Committee in the Senate, there was none in the House. Thitherto, the Suffrage question had been sent to the Judiciary Committee, the graveyard of the House. As a result of the work of the Congressional Committee, the Progressive Caucus, which met before the new Congress assembled, gave its unqualified indorsement to the proposal to create a Woman Suffrage Committee in the House. The Congressional Committee canvassed the Democratic members of the House and urged them to take similar action. The Democratic Caucus, however, entirely ignored the question.

Having brought Suffrage to the attention of the new President by the monster procession of March 3, the Congressional Committee proceeded to bring it to the attention of the new Congress by a second great demonstration. This was in support of the Federal Amendment, and it took place on the opening day of the special session of the Sixty-third Congress, April 7, 1913. Delegates from each of the 435 Congressional districts in the United States assembled at Washington, bringing petitions from the men and women of their districts, asking for the passing of the Amendment. After the mass-meeting, the delegates marched, each behind her State banner, to the doors of Congress. The procession was greeted at the steps of the Capitol by a group of Congressmen. One of them welcomed the petitioners in a speech pledging his support to their cause. They then led the delegation into the Rotunda, where a long receiving line of members of Congress repeated his welcome. The Suffragists took places which had been set aside for them in the galleries of the Senate and the House and watched the presentation of the petitions.

Immediately after the petitions were presented, Representative Mondell (Republican) of Wyoming, and Senator Chamberlain (Democrat) of Oregon introduced the Suffrage

Amendment. In the Senate this resolution was referred to
the Woman's Suffrage Committee, and in the House to the
Judiciary Committee. Named, as is customary, after those
who introduced it, the measure was known first as the
Chamberlain-Mondell Amendment, and later as the Bristow-
Mondell Amendment. It was in reality the famous Susan
B. Anthony Amendment—first introduced into Congress in
1878 by Senator Sargent of California—exactly as she drew
it up. The Anthony Amendment runs as follows:

Section 1. The right of citizens of the United States to
vote shall not be denied or abridged by any State on account
of sex.
Section 2. Congress shall have power by appropriate legislation to enforce the provisions of this article.

On that same day—April 7, 1913—resolutions were introduced in the House to create a Woman Suffrage Committee
similar to that in the Senate. This was only a tiny gain;
for that Committee was not actually created until September, 1917. But a little later occurred what was a decided
gain—the Senate created a Majority Committee on Woman
Suffrage. The Woman Suffrage Committee in the Senate
had been a Minority Committee thitherto. That meant
that, as its Chairman belonged to the Minority Party, its
existence was purely nominal.

All these four months, the five women who constituted
the Congressional Committee had been working at a tremendous speed. They had been made into a Committee
on the understanding that the Committee would itself raise
the money necessary for its work. Four months' experience
had convinced them that the work of securing a Federal
Amendment required a much greater effort than five women,
working alone, could possibly give to it. The various
State associations composing the National American
Woman Suffrage Association were engrossed in their State
campaigns. Little could be expected from them in the way

of personal service or financial aid. When the Congressional Committee appealed to individuals, they found that these individuals were giving their time and service to the particular State in which they lived. The Congressional Committee realized that they must have an organization back of them to assist with work and money, whose sole object was national work. The Congressional Union for Woman Suffrage was therefore formed by the Congressional Committee, with the approval of the President of the National American Woman Suffrage Association.

The Congressional Union described itself as " a group of women in all parts of the country who have joined together in the effort to secure the passage of an Amendment to the United States Constitution enfranchising women." It offered its members the privilege of making the offices at Washington their headquarters while in the city. It adopted colors—at the happy suggestion of Mrs. John Jay White— of purple, white, and gold. The Union grew rapidly, and was later admitted as an auxiliary to the National American Woman Suffrage Association. The Congressional Committee acted as the Executive Committee of this Congressional Union. Throughout the year the Union was of great assistance to the Committee. It reinforced its work in every possible way.

The Suffrage resolution was now before the Committees in both Houses. The Congressional Union concentrated on securing a hearing before the Senate Committee. Every effort was made to focus the attention of Suffragists and of the country at large on the situation. A hearing was arranged before the Committee, at which Dr. Anna Howard Shaw, President of the National American Woman Suffrage Association, presided. In addition to this public hearing, the members of the Senate Committee were interviewed. And pursuing its course of keeping Suffragists in touch with what was happening at Washington, the Congressional Committee circularized Suffragists all over the country with letters which informed them that the resolution was before the Senate Committee, and asked them to write to this Committee urging a favorable report.

After six months of work occurred the first political triumph of the Congressional Union. On May 13, the Senate Committee voted to make a favorable report upon the Suffrage resolution. There, however, matters rested—with a favorable vote, but still in the Committee. The Suffragists, however, besieged the Committee with requests to make the report and finally, on June 13, the report was made to the Senate—the first favorable one in twenty-one years. This put the measure on the Senate Calendar.

Immediately the Congressional Union turned its attention to proving to the Senate how widespread was the support of this measure in the United States.

A petition was circulated in every State in the Union. It asked for the passage of the Amendment, and was addressed to the Senate. Thousands of signatures were obtained. During June and July, these petitions were collected and brought to Washington. Their arrival at the Capitol on July 31 was the occasion of the third great demonstration. The petitioners came from every State, and they came in every possible way. They came by train, by motor, by caravan. They held meetings and collected signatures to the great petition in the districts through which they passed. All the delegations converged in the little town of Hyattsville, outside Washington. There—at the village grandstand, they were met by members of the Congressional Union and of the Woman Suffrage Committee of the Senate. The reading clerk of the House of Representatives announced the members of the delegations as they arrived in their several motors. Members of the Senate Committee addressed them on behalf of the Congressional Committee of the Congressional Union. The Mayor of Hyattsville delivered to them the key of the town. Mary Ware Dennett replied for the delegates, and accepted the key of the town from the Mayor. The automobiles then formed into a procession,

of which the first motor carried the members of the Senate
Committee. The long line of cars, fluttering flags, and
pennants, and each bearing the banner of its State delegation, proceeded from Hyattsville along the old Bunker Hill
Road to the Capitol. There, the petitions were handed to
the various Senators. Three Senators spoke against Suffrage, but twenty-two in presenting the petitions spoke in
favor of it.

This was the second triumph of the Congressional Union.
Suffrage was debated in Congress—the first time since 1887.

The Congressional Committee now turned its attention to
the work of convincing Congress of the interest in the
Amendment of the women voters of the West. A Convention
of the National Council of Women Voters was held in Washington on August 13, 14, and 15. Emma Smith Devoe,
National President of the Council, and Jane Addams, National Vice-President, presided. Upon a motion by Jane
Addams, the Council passed the following Resolution,
strongly indorsing the Amendment:

Whereas at the present time one-fifth of the Senate, one-
seventh of the House, and one-sixth of the electoral vote comes
from equal Suffrage States; and

Whereas, as a result of this political strength in Congress,
due to the fact that four million women of the United States
are now enfranchised, there is great hope of the passage in the
near future of the Federal Suffrage Amendment; therefore be it

Resolved, That the National Council of Women Voters concentrate its efforts upon the support of this Federal Amendment.

The Rules Committee of the House of Representatives on
August 14 then gave the Council a hearing on the question
of creating a Suffrage Committee in the House.

The Convention ended in a mass-meeting at the Belasco
Theatre, which, in spite of the midsummer heat of Washington, was crowded to the doors. The platform was filled
with Congressmen from Suffrage States. The women
speakers iterated and reiterated the demand of the women

voters of the West for immediate action by Congress, and the Congressmen supported them.

In addition to these—processions, pilgrimages, petitions, deputations, and hearings, hundreds of public meetings organized by the Washington Headquarters—were held everywhere. A constant series of deputations from their own constituencies besieged the members of the Senate. All this was making its inevitable impression on Congress. Those days of the Sixty-third Congressional Session were crowded ones. The President had told the Suffragists that so much time must be given to the tariff and the currency that there would be none left for Women Suffrage. Yet more time was devoted to the Woman Suffrage question than ever before. On September 18, Senator Wesley L. Jones of Washington delivered a speech in the Senate, in which he urged that the Suffrage Resolution should be passed. In the House, a number of Representatives formerly opposed to the resolution now declared that they would support it when it came before them.

In the meantime, the tariff and currency had finally been disposed of. A new Congress was to convene on December 1. Ever since his inauguration, Suffrage agitation of a strong, dignified, and convincing character had been brought to the President's attention. Suffragists hoped, therefore, that the President would feel that he could recommend the Suffrage Amendment to this new Congress. They decided, however, to present the matter to him in a forcible way. A fourth deputation of seventy-three women from his own State of New Jersey came to Washington in the middle of November.

This delegation arrived on Saturday afternoon, November 15. Until Monday morning, they tried in every possible way to arrange for an appointment with the President at the White House. Representative McCoy of New Jersey endeavored to assist them in this matter. Their efforts and his efforts were fruitless.

Monday morning, at 10 o'clock, Alice Paul telephoned

42

the Executive Office that, as it was impossible to find out
what hour would suit the convenience of the President, the
delegation was on its way to the White House. She explained
that they would wait there until the President was ready to
receive them, or would definitely refuse to do so. The clerk
at the Executive Office declared over the telephone that it
would be impossible to see the President without an appointment. He assured Alice Paul that such a thing had never
been done. Representative McCoy called up Headquarters,
and reported his failure to secure an appointment. On
being told that the delegation was going to call on the
President anyway, he protested vehemently against its proceeding to the White House without the usual official preliminaries. Alice Paul's answer was a single statement,—
" The delegation has already started."

In double file the seventy-three New Jersey women
marched through Fifteenth Street, through Pennsylvania
Avenue, past the Treasury Department, and up to the
White House grounds. And, lo, as though their coming
spread paralyzing magic, everything gave way before them.
Two guards in uniform stood at the gate. They saluted
and moved aside. The seventy-three women marched un-
challenged through the grounds to the door of the Executive
Office. An attendant there requested them courteously to
wait until after their two leaders should be presented to
the President by his Secretary.

The request that these seventy-three New Jersey women
made to President Wilson was that he should support the
Constitutional Amendment enfranchising women. President
Wilson replied: " I am pleased, indeed, to greet you and
your adherents here, and I will say to you that I was talking
only yesterday with several Members of Congress in regard
to the Suffrage Committee in the House. The subject is one
in which I am deeply interested, and you may rest assured
that I will give it my earnest attention."

It is to be seen that the President's education had progressed—a little. To previous delegations, he had stated

merely that the tariff and currency would take so much of
the attention of Congress that there would be no time for
the Suffrage question. In advocating a Suffrage Committee
in the House, he had made an advance—tiny, to be sure,
but an advance.

In the last month of 1913 occurred in Washington the
Forty-fifth Annual Convention of the National American
Woman Suffrage Association. The Convention opened
with a mass-meeting at the Columbia Theatre. Dr. Anna
Howard Shaw presided. Jane Addams and Senator Helen
Ring Robinson were the principal speakers. At the opening
meeting of the Convention, Lucy Burns repeated the warn-
ing of the Congressional Union to the Democratic Party:

The National American Women Suffrage Association is assembled in Washington to ask the Democratic Party to enfranchise
the women of America.
Rarely in the history of the country has a party been more
powerful than the Democratic Party is today. It controls the
Executive Office, the Senate, and more than two-thirds of the
members of the House of Representatives. It is in a position to
give us effective and immediate help.
We ask the Democrats to take action now. Those who hold
power are responsible to the country for the use of it. They
are responsible, not only for what they do, but for what they
do not do. Inaction establishes just as clear a record as does
a policy of open hostility.
We have in our hands today not only the weapon of a just case;
we have the support of ten enfranchised States—States com-
prising one-fifth of the United States, one-seventh of the House
of Representatives and one-sixth of the electoral vote. More
than three million, six hundred thousand women have a vote in
Presidential elections. It is unthinkable that a national government which represents women, and which appeals periodically
to the Suffrages of women, should ignore the issue of their right
to political freedom.
We cannot wait until after the passage of the scheduled administration reforms. These reforms, which affect women, should
not be enacted without the consent of women. Congress is free
to take action on our question in the present Session. We ask

the administration to support the Woman Suffrage Amendment in Congress with its full strength.

On December 4, a second meeting was held before the Rules Committee of the House on the creation of a Woman Suffrage Committee in the House of Representatives. Ida Husted Harper reminded the Rules Committee at this hearing that nine States and one Territory had enfranchised their women, and that nearly four million women could vote at a Presidential election. Mary Beard showed by an analysis of the vote which sent President Wilson to the White House that the Democratic strength was already threatened, and how it could strengthen itself by espousing the Suffrage Cause.

Notwithstanding the appeal of the seventy-three New Jersey women, the President's message to Congress on December 2 failed to make any mention whatever of the Suffrage Amendment.

In consequence, a Committee representing each State in the Union was appointed by the Convention of the National American Woman Suffrage Association to wait upon the President and protest. President Wilson was prevented by illness from seeing any visitors during the week the Convention met. The Convention, therefore, authorized the appointment of a Committee of fifty-five delegates, who should remain in Washington until the President was able to see them. The interview took place the following Monday at 12:30. This was the fifth deputation to President Wilson. The President said, according to the *Washington Post* of December 9:

I want you ladies, if possible—if I can make it clear to you—to realize just what my present position is. Whenever I walk abroad, I realize that I am not a free man; I am under arrest. I am so carefully and admirably guarded that I have not even the privilege of walking the street. That is, as it were, typical of my present transference from being an individual with his mind on any and every subject, to being an official of a great Government and, incidentally, or so it falls out under our sys-

tem of Government, the spokesman of a Party. I set myself
this strict rule when I was Governor of New Jersey and have
followed it as President, and shall follow it as President, that
I am not at liberty to urge upon Congress policies which have
not had the organic consideration of those for whom I am
spokesman.

In other words, I have not yet presented to any legislature
my private views on any subject, and I never shall; because I
conceive that to be a part of the whole process of government,
that I shall be spokesman for somebody, not for myself.

When I speak for myself, I am an individual; when I speak
for an organic body, I am a representative. For that reason
you see, I am by my own principles shut out, in the language
of the street, from starting anything. I have to confine myself
to those things which have been embodied as promises to the
people at an election. That is the strict rule I set for myself.

I want to say that with regard to all other matters I am not
only glad to be consulted by my colleagues in the two Houses,
but I hope that they will often pay me the compliment of con-
sulting me when they want to know my opinions on any subject.
One member of the Rules Committee did come to ask me what
I thought about this suggestion of yours of appointing a special
committee for consideration of the question of Woman Suffrage,
and I told him that I thought it was a proper thing to do. So
that as far as my personal advice has been asked by a single
member of the Committee, it has been given to that effect. I
wanted to tell you that to show you that I am strictly living up
to my principles. When my private opinion is asked by those
who are co-operating with me, I am most glad to give it; but I
am not at liberty until I speak for somebody besides myself to
urge legislation upon the Congress.

Dr. Shaw stepped forward to address the President within
the circle of deeply attentive hearers, spoke very quietly and
firmly in her clear and beautiful voice.

"Of the two—the President and Dr. Shaw," said one of
the spectators afterward, "Dr. Shaw spoke with greater
authority, as if with the consciousness of a perfectly just
cause. The President was less assured, more hesitat-
ing." . . .

"As women are members of no political Party, to whom
are they to look for a spokesman?" Dr. Shaw asked.

" You speak very well for yourself," said the President, laughing.

" But not with authority," said Dr. Shaw earnestly.

The deputation then left the President's Office.

Editorially in the *Suffragist* of December 13 appears:

The rule that President Wilson has so strictly set for himself, is a rule not laid down in the Constitution nor in the practice of preceding Presidents, nor in the President's own acts, nor in his own words.

Nevertheless, the statement of President Wilson to the President of the National American Woman Suffrage Association is of great value to the Suffrage movement. The President therein declares that he is only the spokesman of his Party and that he will initiate only legislation which has been indorsed by his Party. He puts the whole question of Federal legislation for Woman Suffrage directly up to the Democratic Party in Congress, and instructs Suffragists throughout the country to hold that Party responsible for the fate of the Constitutional Amendment enfranchising women. He has outlined for us, therefore, the policy of bringing effective pressure to bear on the national Democratic Party from all parts of the country, in an effort to make them realize soon what they must recognize finally, that it is more expedient for them as a Party to advocate Suffrage than to ignore and resist it.

Nevertheless, the President's education had progressed another step. For the first time, he felt the necessity of explaining—and by implication—of excusing himself.

This visit to the President completed the principal work of the year 1913 on the part of the Congressional Committee and the Congressional Union.

Many things had been done in this year, in addition to what has already been indicated. A district of Columbia Branch of the Men's League for Woman Suffrage was organized; this was composed largely of Congressmen. Lectures, receptions, tableaux, benefits, teas had been given, and a Suffrage School opened in Washington. Seven large mass-meetings, exclusive of Convention meetings, were held at Washington. An uninterrupted series of indoor and outdoor meetings, numbering frequently from five to ten a day, constantly reminded Congress of the Suffrage question. A summer campaign, carried on by Mabel Vernon and Edith Marsden, covered the resort regions of New Jersey, Long Island, and Rhode Island, and extended into the South.

Twenty-seven thousand dollars had been raised at the Washington Headquarters, and spent. And there were results. The chief one was that it focussed the attention— not only of Suffragists themselves—but of politicians and the country at large on the Federal Amendment.

June, 1913, brought Presidential Suffrage to the women of Illinois. Only Presidential Suffrage; but that was very important. Astute women everywhere were watching the situation; drawing their own and independent conclusions.

Toward the end of the year, the Congressional Union established an official weekly organ, the *Suffragist*, edited by the well-known publicist, Rheta Childe Dorr. The first issue appeared on November 15, and it has been published ever since.

Lucy Burns, whose editorials were marvels of ironic logic, of forceful condensed expression, succeeded Mrs. Dorr. Then came Vivian Pierce, a trained newspaper woman; Sue White, well-known to Suffragists for her splendid work in Tennessee; Florence Boeckel, able, efficient, untiring. Pauline Clark, Clara Wold, Elizabeth Kalb contributed supplementing editorial work.

The *Suffragist* has reported the activities first of the Congressional Union, and next of the Woman's Party. It is an extremely entertaining periodical, always interesting, often brilliant, essentially readable. It contains editorials, reports, sketches, verse, cartoons. Many famous people have contributed articles. The reports of the workers in the Woman's Party make much the most interesting reading however. Many famous artists have given it drawings. The most pertinent, though, are those contributed by a member of the Congressional Union—Nina Allender.

Mrs. Allender's fertile and original pencil has traced during the entire eight years of its history a running commentary on the progress of the Woman's Party. She has a keen political sense. She has translated this aspect of the feminist movement in terms that women alone can best appreciate. Her work is full of the intimate everyday details of the woman's life from her little girlhood to her old age. And she translates that existence with a woman's vivacity and a woman's sense of humor; a humor which plays keenly and gracefully about masculine insensibility; a humor as realistic, but as archly un-bitter as that of Jane Austen. It would be impossible for any man to have done Mrs. Allender's work. A woman speaking to women, about women, in the language of women.

There is no better place than here to emphasize the work of the Press Department. It will be apparent to the reader, as the story of the Woman's Party unrolls itself, that the work of this department was very difficult and very delicate. The problem was twofold—to keep the action of the party always in the public eye and to bring out the underlying policy. This was not easy when the demonstrations of the Woman's Party were of the kind whose initial effect was to antagonize. Nevertheless, the Press Department minimized that antagonism and minimized by a propaganda which was as restrained in expression as it was vivid in description. Newspaper men generally felt that they could depend on the Woman's Party for news. Florence Brewer Boeckel, who has been press chairman since 1915, is responsible for this magnificent press campaign. But she has not lacked help. Eleanor Taylor Marsh, Alice Gram, Beulah Amidon, and Margaret Grahan Jones, have given her steady assistance.

Early in the year 1914, the Congressional Union resigned from the National American Woman Suffrage Association. The constitution of the National Association permitted a Suffrage body to join it in one of two ways. By one, a new clause imposed a five per cent tax in dues upon its budget. By another, it paid annually one hundred dollars dues. The Congressional Union felt that a five per cent tax upon its budget would seriously cripple its work. The Union offered to become an associated body. The National Association refused this offer, and the Congressional Union, therefore, became an independent organization.

VI

PRESSURE ON CONGRESS

THE *Suffragist* of January 24, 1914, carried the following editorial. In it is repeated the policy which the Congressional Union had in the beginning adopted—that of holding the party in power responsible.

The policy of the Congressional Union is to ask for a Woman Suffrage Amendment from the Party in power in Congress, and to hold them responsible for their answer to its request.

This policy is entirely non-partisan, in that it handles all Parties with perfect impartiality. If the Republicans were in power, we would regard them in their capacity as head of the Government as responsible for the enfranchisement of women. If the Progressives or Socialists should become the majority Party, and control the machinery of Congress, we would claim from them the right to govern ourselves, and would hold them responsible for a refusal of this just demand.

Today the Democrats are in power. They control the executive office, the Senate, and the House. They can, if they will, enfranchise women in the present session; their refusal to do so establishes a record which must necessarily be taken into consideration by women when the Party seeks the re-indorsement of the people at the polls.

This policy simply recognizes the effect of our American system of Government. Ours is a government by Parties. The majority by secret caucus, by the control of committees, by the power of patronage, by their appeal to Party responsibility, by the interest of Party solidarity, control the legislation of the House. The present government recognizes this method of administration with especial, and indeed admirable, frankness. It owes much of its popularity today to its willingness to assume full responsibility for all the legislation enacted in Congress; for whatever is done, and what is not done. The two great measures of the last session, tariff and currency, passed rapidly and successfully through both Houses by the frank use of Party discipline.

Let us by all means deal directly with the people who can give us what we want. The Democrats have it in their power to enfranchise women. . . . This is not only our most logical method of work, but it is also the most economical and expeditious. Assuming that the Democrats yield nothing in the present session, we can, when Congress closes, concentrate our forces on those points where the Party is weakest, and thus become a force worth bargaining with. At the present moment, the Senate is the weakest point in the Democratic armor. To defeat even a few Democratic Senators in November, 1914, would make a serious breach in the Party organization. . . . If, on the other hand, we set out to attack every anti-Suffragist in Congress, we should have hundreds to defeat, and every man would be safe in whose constituency we did not organize. Imagine that, if at the end of arduous labor, we had contrived to defeat a number of Democratic anti-Suffragists, and an equal number of Republican anti-Suffragists, we should by immense sacrifice have completely nullified our own efforts, and left the strength of the Parties just where it was before. . . .

What should we do in our enfranchised States, if we confined ourselves to the plan of supporting individual Suffragists and attacking individual anti-Suffragists, irrespective of their Party affiliations? All the candidates for office in the enfranchised States are Suffragists. Is it suggested that we be inactive in the only places where we possess real political power? Our problem at the present moment is to use the strength of women's votes in national elections so as to force attention to the justice of our claim from the present administration. . . .

But the Congressional Union cannot make it too clear that we are not opposed to any Party today. We are asking the Democrats to help us; we are awaiting their answer. We will frame no policy for or against them or any other Party until this session closes, and the great opportunity of the present Administration has come to an end. We entertain steady and undiminished hopes that the Administration will recognize the justice and expediency of women's claims to self-government. The movement is making immense strides in every part of the country; our present voting strength is great, and will undoubtedly be increased in the present year. It takes no great imaginative reach for the ordinary Congressman to foresee the day when Woman Suffrage will be an established fact throughout these United States.

There is already a strong sentiment in the Upper House for Woman Suffrage, and a rapidly-growing interest in it in the Lower House. We have no reason to expect wilful obstinacy from our American Congressmen. We Americans are adaptable and imaginative, and can shape ourselves with peculiar ease to coming events. The Democratic Party, if it is wise, will pass our Amendment through Congress in the present session.

The first year Congressional Committee, consisting of Alice Paul, Lucy Burns, Mary Beard, Crystal Eastman, and Mrs. Lawrence Lewis, continued their work in 1914 with the Congressional Union under the name of the Executive Committee of the Congressional Union; but it was increased by the addition of Mrs. William Kent, Elsie Hill, Mrs. Gilson Gardner, Mrs. Donald R. Hooker, and Mrs. O. H. P. Belmont.

The year opened with a meeting at the home of Mrs. William Kent in Washington. Plans for the coming year were submitted at that meeting. Among them was one for a nation-wide demonstration on May 2, in which resolutions supporting the Federal Amendment were to be passed. This was to be followed by a great demonstration in Washington on May 9, at which those resolutions should be presented to Congress. Among them also was another plan for the appeal to the women voters of the West for political action in support of a Federal Amendment, if that Amendment had not been passed before the next election. Nine thousand dollars were pledged on the spot for these undertakings. The work on the great demonstration of May 2 began at once, and was pushed rapidly during the opening months of the year.

In the meantime the work on Congress was continued. It will be remembered that a proposal for the formation of a Suffrage Committee in the House had been before the Rules Committee since April 7, 1913, that it had been the subject of two hearings arranged by the Congressional Union. The first action in regard to this was simple and decisive. The Democratic Members of the Rules Committee, who constituted a Majority Committee, met first, apart from their Republican and Progressive colleagues, and, by a vote of four to three, decided against the formation of a Suffrage

Committee. They then went through the form of a meeting with the Republican and Progressive Members on January 24. The resolution, creating the Suffrage Committee, was lost by a vote of four to four.

The Congressional Union, however, realized that the final power with regard to Congressional action was with the Democratic Caucus. They determined therefore—in order that the responsibility for inaction or opposition might be placed on the Democrats as a Party—immediately to appeal to that Caucus to overturn the decision of the Rules Committee. The necessary signatures were secured to a petition calling for the Democratic Caucus of the House to take up the question of the formation of this much-desired Suffrage Committee. The Caucus met on February 3, 1914, to consider this subject. The Democratic Party had a choice of two courses. It could order the Rules Committee, which it of course controlled, to give a favorable report to the House on the resolution creating a Suffrage Committee. Or it could give no order at all of this kind; in which case it revealed itself as responsible for the adverse action of the Rules Committee.

What it did was to adopt a substitute resolution for the resolution providing for the creation of a Committee of Woman Suffrage.

That substitute resolution was: " Resolved, that the question of Woman Suffrage is a State and not a Federal question."

This was the first time in the history of the country that either of the two great Parties had ever caucused on Woman Suffrage.

Editorially the *Suffragist* put the situation pithily to the women of America:

This is the definite lining up of the Democratic Party against Woman Suffrage as a national measure. . . . Unless the Democratic Party reconsiders its present position, Suffragists must necessarily regard that Party as an obstruction in the path of their campaign. . . . They (the Democratic Party) have three votes to lose in the Senate and they lose control of this government. There are nine States in which women vote for United States Senators. The result in the Senatorial elections in these States will undoubtedly depend largely upon the action on Suffrage taken by the Democratic Party.

Although the Congressional Union welcomed any simplification of the Congressional machinery as by the creation of a Suffrage Committee, its object was to secure action on the Suffrage Amendment. Since April 7, 1913, the Amendment had been before the Judiciary Committee in which it had been introduced by Representative Mondell. The Congressional Union asked for a hearing on the Amendment before this Committee. March 3, 1914, was set for that event.

Thitherto, these hearings had been dreary occasions, sparsely attended. There was the half-circle of Committee members, a trifle perfunctory in its attitude, the scattered, tiny audience, very little interested or stirred; the few Suffragists pleading—eloquently, it is true—but pleading; using the inevitable Suffrage arguments, unanswerable, but threadbare. The hearing of March 3 was very different. The Committee was electrically alert. . . . They listened intently. . . . For the first time at a Congressional hearing, propagandistic argument did not appear. The Suffragists appealed to the Committee to report the Suffrage Resolution to the House—not as a matter of justice to women—but as *practical politics.* They pointed out to the Committee that the women voters of the West would hold the Democratic Party responsible for the refusal of this Committee to make that report.

In the meantime, highly important things had been going on in the Senate. It will be remembered that the Suffrage Resolution had been placed upon the Senate Calendar in June, 1913. Ever since that date, it had been awaiting a vote. It could be voted on any time up to the close of the Sixty-third Congress (March 3, 1915).

At the beginning of the year 1914, more votes were pledged in its favor than had carried the Income Tax in the Senate, and sentiment in its favor was steadily increasing among the Senators. Moreover, the prospect that the Referendum elections of the coming autumn would add to the number of Suffrage States promised an increase of Suffrage strength in the Senate. There remained—as it transpired—a whole year before that Congress adjourned, in which the work of obtaining the vote could have gone on. These features of the situation made the Congressional Union most desirous that the Resolution should not be voted upon until every possible vote was won. However, Senator Ashurst, who had reported the Bill to the Senate, had it made " unfinished business " on March 2, 1914. It is the spirit of " unfinished business " that it must be brought up and voted on. In spite of the vigorous protests of the Congressional Union, and of many Suffragists in all parts of the country, it was brought to the vote on March 17. A two-thirds vote was necessary to carry it. It received thirty-five; a majority, it is true, of one vote; but failing of the necessary two-thirds majority by eleven. The Congressional Union blamed the Democratic leaders entirely for this premature vote, as they were fully informed that a vote at that time would mean defeat.

However, this was a memorable moment. It was the first time since 1887 that Suffrage had been voted upon in the Senate. And from the moment on March 2 when it was made " unfinished business " until March 17, when the vote was taken, the Senate debated it almost continuously.

On that same day—March 2—Senator Shafroth of Colorado introduced a resolution providing for a new Suffrage Amendment to the Federal Constitution. This was to become famous as the Shafroth-Palmer Resolution. It offered a path to the enfranchisement of women incredibly cluttered and cumbered. It reads:

Section 1. Whenever any number of legal voters of any State to a number exceeding eight per cent of the number of legal voters voting at the last preceding General Election held in such State shall petition for the submission to the legal voters of said State of the question whether women shall have equal rights with men in respect to voting at all elections to be held in such State, such question shall be so submitted; and if, upon such submission, a majority of the legal voters of the State voting on the question shall vote in favor of granting to women such equal rights, the same shall thereupon be deemed established, anything in the constitution or laws of such State to the contrary notwithstanding.

Compare this with the simplicity and directness of the original Susan B. Anthony Amendment:

Section 1. The right of citizens of the United States to vote shall not be denied or abridged by the United States or by any State on account of sex.
Section 2. Congress shall have power by appropriate legislation to enforce the provisions of this article.

The National American Woman Suffrage Association immediately rallied to the support of the Shafroth-Palmer Amendment; they continued to give to it their undivided work for two years.

But the Congressional Union—I quote the vigorous words of the Report of the Congressional Union for the year 1914:

The Congressional Union immediately announced its determination to support only the original Amendment, known popularly as the Susan B. Anthony Amendment, and in Congress as the Bristow-Mondell Amendment. It maintained that to work at the same time for two Suffrage amendments to the National Constitution would enable the enemies of the bill to play one against the other. Believing that one amendment only must be supported, it felt that it was wise to support the amendment which would give Suffrage itself rather than an amendment which, after the same expenditure of effort would give *only another method of obtaining Suffrage*—that is, would merely establish the initiative on the Suffrage question. The Union, moreover, feeling that the bane of the Suffrage cause at present was too many and not too few referendums, held that to pass a Federal Amendment—which would inaugurate thirty-nine referendum campaigns would involve the movement in a dissipation of resources such as its enemies would most deeply desire. Finally, it held that the passage of one Suffrage amendment to the National Constitution would make it extremely difficult to pass another; so that if the Shafroth Bill became a law, it would probably indefinitely postpone the passage of the Anthony Amendment, and doom the movement to years of referendum campaigns.

Not at all daunted by the action of the Senate in defeating the Susan B. Anthony Amendment, nor by the introduction there of the Shafroth-Palmer Amendment, the Congressional Union at once secured the re-introduction in the Senate of the defeated Amendment. The measure was out of the Senate only twenty-two hours. The following day, Senator Bristow introduced a resolution identical with the one which had been lost. On April 7, it was again reported from the Woman Suffrage Committee, and took its place on the Calendar of the Senate. This was just a year from the date of its original introduction to this Senate. It was the second favorable report of the Senate Committee in one Congress.

Here we leave the work with Congress for a while, and take up the matter of the education of the President. We must go back a few months.

VII

PRESSURE ON THE PRESIDENT

ALTHOUGH five different deputations—Congressional Union members; college women; women voters; New Jersey women; women from all the States—had called on the President, it was apparent that he had undergone no change in his attitude toward the Suffrage question. On February 2, 1914, therefore, another deputation, the sixth—and an exceedingly interesting one—marched to the White House. This deputation included women from the industrial world and they represented more than fifty trades in which women are engaged. They carried banners which bore quotations from the President's *New Freedom:* "We Have Got to Humanize Industry," and "I Absolutely Protest Against Being Put into the Hands of Trustees."

At the mass-meeting, preliminary to waiting upon the President, Melinda Scott, an organizer of the Women's Trade Union League, said:

No one could be serious when they maintained that the ballot will not help the working woman. It has helped the working man to better his conditions and his wages. Men of every class regard the ballot as their greatest protection against the injustice of other men. Women even more than men need the ballot to protect their especial interests and their right to earn a living. . . . We want a law that will prohibit home-work. . . . We hear about the sacredness of the home. What sacredness is there about a home when it is turned into a factory, where we find a mother, very often with a child at her breast, running a sewing machine? Running up thirty-seven seams for a cent. Ironing and pressing shirts seventy cents a dozen, and children making artificial flowers for one cent a gross. Think of it— one hundred and forty flowers for one cent. Taking stitches out of coats, helping their mothers where they have finished them for six cents a coat. These women have had no chance to make laws that would protect themselves or their children. . . .

The organized working woman has learnt through her trade union the power of industrial organization, and she realizes what her power would be if she had the ballot. . . . Men legislating as a class for women and children as a class have done exactly what every other ruling class has done since the history of the world. They discriminate against the class that has no voice. Some of the men say, " You women do not need a ballot; we will take care of you." We have no faith in man's protection. . . . Give us the ballot, and we will protect ourselves.

This army of four hundred arrived safely, with perfect police escort, at the doors of the White House. They were amazed to learn that the President would see only twenty-five of the women. He had said he would " receive the delegation." The selected number then went in, the remaining three hundred and seventy-five waited in line outside.

Margaret Hinchey, a laundry worker of New York, said:

Mr. President: It is shaking and trembling, I, as a laundry worker, come here to speak in behalf of the working women of the United States. I have read about you, and think you are fair, square, on the level, and so much a real democrat, that I believe when it is made clear to you how much we working women, who organize in the factories, the mills, the laundries, and the stores, can help every true democrat, you will use your power to wipe out this great injustice to women by giving us a vote.

Rose Winslow said:

Mr. President: I am one of the thousands of women who work in the sweated trades, and have been since a child, who give their lives to build up these tremendous industries in this country, and at the end of the years of work, our reward is the tuberculosis sanatorium or the street. I do not think to plead with you, Mr. President, nor make a regular speech. I do not speak to Presidents every day; it hasn't been my job, so I don't do it very gracefully.

Here the President interrupted Miss Winslow by stating that he did not see why she should be so nervous, as Presidents are perfectly human. Miss Winslow then continued:

Yes, I know, and that is why I can speak to you, because you are human and have a heart and mind and can realize our great need. I do not need to remind you how we women need the ballot, etc.

The President said:

I need not tell you that a group of women like this appeals to me very deeply indeed. I do not have to tell you what my feelings are, but I have already explained—because I feel obliged to explain—the limitations that are laid upon me as the leader of a Party. Until the Party, as such, has considered the matter of this very supreme importance and taken its position, I am not at liberty to speak of it; and yet, I am not at liberty to speak as an individual, for I am not an individual. As you see, I either speak to it in a message, as you suggest, or I do not speak at all. That is the limitation I am under, and all I can say to you ladies, is that the strength of your agitation in this matter undoubtedly will make a profound impression.

In view of later opinions of the President in regard to his leadership—and in view of the fact that later even Democratic Congressmen referred to his " dictatorship "— his attitude to the women this day was most interesting.

Mrs. Glendower Evans, who was in charge of the deputation, said:

We understand your position and its difficulties quite well, Mr. President, but nevertheless we ask, where can we look for political action? We recognize that the verdict must come not from you alone, but from the whole Party. I do not ask you to break with your Party. What I ask is, will you use your influence within your Party? I do not ask the impossible, though I might from you, for you have done the impossible.

It is apparent that the President's education was progressing. He was beginning to be struck with the strength of the Woman Suffrage agitation; although he still believed himself powerless to help in the work with Congress.

Early in June, 1914, the National Federation of Women's Clubs meeting in Chicago, had given its indorsement, as an organization, to Woman Suffrage. Following this action by the Federation, another delegation—the seventh—of five hundred club women under the leadership of Mrs. Harvey W. Wiley, waited upon the President on June 30. I quote from the *Suffragist:*

The deputation had assembled for a preliminary mass-meeting at the Public Library. . . . Leaving the Library, the deputation, which extended over several blocks, marched in single files to the White House. . . . It passed through the Arcade and into the East Room. . . . Women were massed about the State Apartment, filling it from end to end, and leaving a hollow square in which Mrs. Ellis Logan and Mrs. Wiley and Rheta Childe Dorr awaited the President's arrival. Preceded by his aide, the President entered. . . .

"Mr. President," said Mrs. Dorr, "we are well aware that you are the busiest of men. I shall therefore go directly to the point and tell you that our reason for calling on you today is to ask you if you will not use your powerful influence with Congress to have the Bristow-Mondell Amendment passed in this session."

The President replied:

Mrs. Wiley and Ladies: No one can fail to be impressed by this great company of useful women, and I want to assure you that it is to me most impressive. I have stated once before the position which, as leader of a Party, I feel obliged to take, and I am sure you will not wish me to state it again. Perhaps it would be more serviceable if I ventured upon the confident conjecture that the Baltimore Convention did not embody this very important question in the platform which it adopted because of its conviction that the principles of the Constitution which allotted these questions to the State were well-considered principles from which they did not wish to depart.

You have asked me to state my personal position in regard to the pending measure. It is my conviction that this is a matter for settlement by the States, and not by the Federal Government, and, therefore, that being my personal conviction, and it being obvious that there is no ground on your part for discouragement in the progress you are making, and my passion being local self-government and the determination by the great communities into which this nation is organized of their own policy and life, I can only say that since you turned away from me as a leader of a Party and asked me my position as a man, I am obliged to state it very frankly, and I believe that in stating it I am probably in agreement with those who framed the platform to which allusion has been made.

I think that very few persons, perhaps, realize the difficulty and the dual duty that must be exercised, whether he will or not, by a President of the United States. He is President of the United States as an executive charged with the administration of the law, but he is the choice of a Party as a leader in policy. The policy is determined by the Party, or else upon unusual and new circumstances by the determination of those who lead the Party. This is my situation as an individual. I have told you that I believed that the best way of settling this thing and the best considered principles of the Constitution with regard to it, is that it should be settled by the States. I am very much obliged to you.

The President paused. He looked relieved. There was a moment's silence, and then Mrs. Dorr said:

" May I ask you this question? Is it not a fact that we have very good precedents existing for altering the electorate by Constitutional Amendment? "

The President's face changed. " I do not think," he said, " that that has anything to do with my conviction as to the best way that it could be done."

" It has not," agreed Mrs. Dorr, " but it leaves room for the women of the country to say what they want through the Constitution of the United States."

" Certainly it does," the President said hastily, " there is good room. But I have stated my conviction. I have no right to criticize the opinions of those who have different convictions and I certainly would not wish to do so."

Mrs. Wiley stepped forward. " Granted that it is a State matter," she said, " would it not give this great movement an impetus if the Resolution now pending before Congress were passed? "

" But the Resolution is for an Amendment to the Constitution," the President objected.

" The States would have to pass upon it before it became an Amendment," said Mrs. Wiley. " Would it not be a State matter then? "

" Yes," the President interrupted, " but by a very different process, for by that process it would be forced upon the minority; they would have to accept it."

" They could reject it if they wished to," said Mrs. Dorr. " Three-fourths of the States would have to pass it."

"Yes," the President said, with distinct annoyance, "but the other fourth could not reject it."

"Mr. President," said Mrs. Dorr, "don't you think that when the Constitution was framed it was agreed that when three-fourths of the States wanted a reform, the other fourth should accept it also?"

The President was plainly disconcerted. He stepped back.

"I cannot say," he replied frigidly, "what was agreed upon. I can only say that I have tried to answer your question, and I do not think it is quite proper that I submit myself to cross-examination."

"Very well," Mrs. Dorr said quietly. "We will not cross-examine you further."

"Thank you, Mr. President," said Mrs. Wiley, "for your courtesy in receiving us."

The President bowed. "I am very much obliged to you," he said. "It has been a very pleasant occasion."

In the *Suffragist* Lucy Burns said editorially:

The President has told a deputation of club women that they must win political freedom from State Legislatures; but not from him, not from Congress.

This position is obvious pretense. The national government has the power, granted it by the constitution, to enfranchise women. It has, therefore, the duty of doing so, if women's claim to enfranchisement is just.

The President knows as well as we do the enormous difficulty of winning the vote by amending the Constitution of thirty-nine different States. It is amazing that a man can be found who will calmly direct women to take up this great burden when men are responsible for their need. Men alone, in all but ten States, have the power to change our laws. The good or evil of these laws is their praise or blame. It is a public injustice today that men deny to women in the ballot a means of self-protection which they are glad to possess themselves. Men are ethically on the defensive—particularly the men, or group of men, who from time to time monopolize political power. For the President of the United States, who incorporates in himself the power of the whole nation, and who is, therefore, more responsible than any other person today for the subjugation of women, to declare that he washes his hands of their whole case, is to presume upon greater ignorance among women than he will find they possess.

Nevertheless, we are specifically informed by the President

that it is "not proper" for us to "cross-examine" him on the grounds of his refusal to help us.

Only fitfully do women realize the astounding arrogance of their rulers.

And later:

Some few curious commentaries cropped up editorially. Under the caption, "Heckling the President," the *New York Times* says: "It certainly was not proper. The President of the United States is not to be heckled or hectored or made a defendant. . . . To catechise him when he had finished his speech to them is a thing never done by similar delegations of men."

The *Times* has not grasped the fact that no similar delegation of men is possible. Men approach their own representative. If he disagrees with them, they have a legitimate remedy in their own hands, and can choose another representative at a duly appointed time. Women approach the President as members of a disfranchised class. The President does not represent them. He bears no constitutional relation to them whatever. If the President rejects their appeal, they have no legal means of redress. If they may not question the President on the justice of his refusal to help them, cannot question him gently and reasonably as they did—their position is indeed a subservient one.

And who told the *Times* that men never question the President "after he had finished his speech to them?" While the Tariff Bill was before Congress, representatives of men's interests argued with him for hours. But they were men, and voters.

On January 6, 1915, another deputation—the eighth—of one hundred and fifty Democratic women appeared before the President. Mrs. George A. Armes, President of the Association of the National Democratic Women of America, introduced the speakers, Alberta Hill and Dr. Frances G. Van Gasken. He greeted Miss Hill with marked cordiality and listened attentively as she briefly and with great earnestness pointed out that, while the Federal Government protected men in the exercise of citizenship throughout the United States, a woman lost her right to vote when she crossed the line from a Suffrage to a non-Suffrage State. Miss Hill read the following extracts from the speech delivered by Mr. Wilson on the occasion of the formation of the Wilson and Marshall League at Spring Lake, New Jersey, two months after his nomination.

When the last word is said about politics, it is merely the life of all of us from the point of view of what can be accomplished by legislation and the administration of public offices. I think it is artificial to divide life up into sections: it is all of one piece though you can't attend to all pieces of it at once.

And so when the women, who are in so many respects at the heart of life, begin to take an interest in politics, then you know that all the lines of sympathy and intelligence and comprehension are going to be interlaced in a way which they have never been interlaced before; so that our politics will be of the same pattern with our life. This, it seems to me, is devoutly to be wished.

And so when the women come into politics, they come in to show us all those little contacts between life and politics, on account of which I, for myself, rejoice that they have come to our assistance; they will be as indispensable as they are delightful.

The President listened with close attention, a smile quivering at the corners of his mouth. As she concluded, a ripple of amusement ran around the circle of auditors, and the President laughed outright.

"I cannot argue as well as you can," he told Miss Hill with evident enjoyment. He said further:

I am most unaffectedly complimented by this visit that you have paid me. I have been called on several times to say what my position is in the very important matter that you are so deeply interested in. I want to say that nobody can look on the fight you are making without great admiration, and I certainly am one of those who admire the tenacity and the skill and the address with which you try to promote the matter that you are interested in.

But I, ladies, am tied to a conviction which I have had all my life that changes of this sort ought to be brought about State by State. If it were not a matter of female Suffrage, if it were a matter of any other thing connected with Suffrage, I would hold the same opinion. It is a long standing and deeply matured conviction on my part and therefore I would be without excuse to my own constitutional principles if I lend my support to this very important movement for an amendment to the Constitution of the United States.

Frankly I do not think that this is the wise or the permanent way to build. I know that perhaps you unanimously disagree with me but you will not think the less of me for being perfectly frank in the avowal of my own convictions on that subject; and certainly that avowal writes no attitude of antagonism, but merely an attitude of principle.

I want to say again how much complimented I am by your call and also by the confidence that you have so generously expressed in me, Mrs. Armes. I hope that in some respect I may live to justify that confidence.

VIII

THE STRUGGLE WITH THE RULES COMMITTEE

WE now return to the work in Congress. Again it is necessary to go back into history a few months.

All these months, the work of organizing the nation-wide demonstration of May 2—which had been decided upon at the opening meeting of the Congressional Union for 1914 —had been going on.

The Congressional Union sent organizers into all the States of the Union to make plans for the demonstration. Minnie E. Brooke went through every State in the South. Mabel Vernon, one of the organizers for the Congressional Union, traveled through the southwestern part of the country and up through California, ending her trip in Nevada. Crystal Eastman of the Executive Committee took care of the Northwestern States, Emma Smith DeVoe covered the Far Western States; Jessie Hardy Stubbs, the Middle Western States; Mrs. Lawrence Lewis and Alice Paul, assisted by Olive Hasbrouck, New England and the Middle Atlantic States.

On February 12, the National American Woman Suffrage Association promised its co-operation also, and from that date aided in making the demonstration a success.

The demonstration—taking the form of parades in most cases, meetings in a few—occurred in at least one great city in every State. The following resolution was adopted at the various gatherings.

Resolved, that this meeting calls upon Congress to take immediate and favorable action upon the Bristow-Mondell Resolution enfranchising women.

The culminating demonstration occurred May 9 in Washington. There was a mass-meeting at the Belasco Theatre,

and following this a procession starting promptly at three
o'clock, marched to the Capitol. At the foot of the Capitol
steps, the enormous gathering sang the *Woman's March.*
Then five hundred and thirty-one delegates representing
every Congressional and Senatorial district in the country,
bearing resolutions passed at the country-wide demonstrations, marched up the long steps into the great Rotunda
of the Capitol. A Committee of Senators and Representatives awaited the delegates, received the resolutions and
introduced them on the floor of each House of Congress.

Here, as always, Alice Paul visualized her work in
pageantry. On this occasion, that pageantry was particularly beautiful. Zona Gale writes in the *Suffragist:*

" I shall watch it, but it will not mean anything to me," said
a visitor to me on Saturday, but that night she said: " I leaned
out of my window, and held my screen up with one hand, and
let the sun beat in my face for the forty minutes that you were
passing, and I wept. To think of your being part of it—and
caring like that—and the men there on the sidewalk holding
back, *by what right,* what you ask! "

The effect of this lengthened—and therefore accumulative
—nation-wide demonstration was immediately felt at the
national Capitol. Between the dates of the demonstration
throughout the States May 2, and the demonstration in
Washington, May 9, the Judiciary Committee reported the
Mondell Resolution without recommendation, but with an
overwhelming vote, to the House. This marked an epoch
in the Suffrage work in the United States; for Suffrage had
never been debated on the floor of the House, and not since
1890 had it progressed beyond the Committee stage in the
House. The Resolution rested on May 5 at the foot of the
highly congested House calendar. On May 13, Representative Mondell introduced a Resolution asking time for an
early consideration of the Suffrage Amendment. The adoption of this Resolution meant that the Amendment would
be taken up, debated, and voted on.

The Rules Committee, to which the Resolution was referred, failed to act upon it. Suffragists began to besiege the Rules Committee. The Rules Committee, however, proved unamenable to argument, discussion, or entreaty.

Later in the year, in a speech at the Newport Conference, Lucy Burns said of the Rules Committee that it " adopted devious means for avoiding action on the Suffrage Resolution. It was difficult for them to vote against it, and it seemed difficult for them to vote for it. They apparently decided that the best policy for them to pursue was to take no action at all, so they hit upon the happy expedient of holding no meetings whatever."

A detailed account of the action of the Rules Committee proves the adamancy of Party control. It gives some idea of the obstacles which ingenious politicians can put in the way of citizens, even though those citizens are making a perfectly legitimate request.

Mr. Henry, the Chairman of the Rules Committee, had declared in the spring that he thought it was out of the power of his Committee to take action (i.e. on the matter of the Suffrage Resolution *which was only to allot time in the House for the discussion of the Suffrage Amendment*) since the Suffrage Amendment had not been favorably acted upon at the last Democratic Caucus: " You may tell this to the Press. You may tell it to the newspapers," Mr. Henry said; " my hands are tied."

However, early in June, the *Suffragist* says, " Mr. Henry's view of his political helplessness weakened slightly." He promised to report out the Suffrage Resolution. But he could not be prevailed upon to state when he would do so. The Congressional Union, therefore, organized a series of deputations which visited the Rules Committee during all the long, hot summer and the long, hot fall. Deputations from nearly every State in the Union and from nearly every occupation and profession of women waited upon the members of the Rules Committee. The reader must remember always that they were asking—not that the Amendment be passed—only that a few hours be set aside for the discussion of the Suffrage question in the House of Representatives. Repeated deputations called upon individual members of the Committee. On June 10, the Committee met, but decided to postpone action on the Suffrage question till July 1. Mr. Henry left immediately for Texas. A large deputation came to Washington to be present at the July 1 meeting. Many of the most prominent members of the Club-women's Deputation of five hundred, who had called the afternoon of June 30 on the President, remained in Washington overnight, so that they might be present at the meeting.

When, however, they arrived at the Committee room, they were told that the Committee would not meet, although no notice had been given of any change of date of the meeting. Mr. Henry had not returned to Washington. There was a quorum of the Committee in town; but the Democratic members said that they were bound by a "gentlemen's agreement" among themselves not to meet. August 1 was set for the next meeting.

On July 13, a deputation of more than a hundred members of the Congressional Union, led by Alice Paul, Lucy Burns, and Mrs. Gilson Gardner, called upon the individual members of the Rules Committee. They asked each member to sign a petition requesting the Acting Chairman, Mr. Pou, to call the Committee together for the purpose of reporting out the Resolution on the Suffrage Amendment. This petition was signed by the two Republican members of the Committee in Washington, and the one Progressive member. The two Democratic members then in Washington refused to sign. The petition was presented to Mr. Pou in his office by Representative Mondell.

Mr. Pou rose from his chair, viewing with amazement the numbers of the deputation as they filed into the room till all available space was occupied, leaving the majority of their number in the corridor. Mr. Pou definitely declined to call the meeting, although a quorum of the Committee was in the city, and although all of the Republican members on the Committee and the Progressive member had requested a meeting. Mr. Pou stated that he was bound by a " gentleman's agreement " entered into by the Democratic members to hold no meetings of the Committee before August 1. He said, " The Democratic members agreed not to hold any meetings until August 1. In view of that understanding, I would not feel at liberty to call the Committee together. . . . When the Republicans were in charge, they decided what they were going to do; now that we are in charge, we decide what we are going to do."

On August 1, a deputation consisting of Lucy Burns and Mrs. Gilson Gardner from the Congressional Union accompanied by Maude F. Clark, called upon Mr. Pou. The forthright Lucy Burns began. " Mr. Pou, today is the first day of August. You told us when a Committee of our organization called upon you in July that the Democratic members of the Committee had a ' gentlemen's agreement ' not to hold a meeting until August 1. Now that the day has come we should be glad to know when a meeting of your Committee will be held to consider House Resolution 514, allotting time for the consideration of the Suffrage Amendment in the House."

Mr. Pou informed the delegation that Mr. Henry, Chairman of the Rules Committee, would return to Washington on Monday, August 3, and that a meeting of the Committee would be called for that day. Among other things, Mr. Pou made the significant statement, " The Rules Committee has in its keeping the policy of the Democratic Party in Congress."

On August 3, a second delegation from the Congressional Union, consisting of Alice Paul, Lucy Burns, Mrs. Gilson Gardner, Dr. Clara E. Ludlow, went to attend the promised meeting at the office of the Chairman, Mr. Henry. The elusive Mr. Henry was at last visible in the flesh. He informed these women that no meeting of the Committee had been called for that day. He did not know when it would be called, nor what measures it would consider. He suggested that they call again in a few days.

On August 28, the Rules Committee finally met. A deputation from the Congressional Union presented themselves at the door. The deputation consisted of Mrs. Gilson Gardner, Minnie E. Brooke, Mrs. S. B. McDuffie, Virginia Arnold.

At the door of the Committee room, Mr. Henry's secretary declared that it would be impossible for him to take a message or a card to Mr. Henry.

"I should be glad, then," said the gently diplomatic Mrs. Gardner, "to send a card to other members of the Committee."

"The Chairman has given orders," said the secretary, "that no messages may be sent in to the Committee room."

"I quite understand," said Mrs. Gardner, "that Mr. Henry can speak for the majority members of the Committee, but surely not for the Republican and Progressive members, and I should like your permission to send word in to one of them."

The secretary maintained that this was against Mr. Henry's specific orders.

Mrs. Gardner then went on very gently: "It is not the desire of the deputation to disturb the Committee; but, on the other hand, it is the sense of the deputation that it is necessary to send the Committee a message. What would you suggest that we do?"

The secretary considered and decreed, "A message might be sent in by telephone." Mrs. Gardner accepted the use of Mr. Henry's desk telephone, called up Representative Kelly who was attending the meeting in the adjoining Committee room, and asked if he would bring the Suffrage Resolution to the attention of the Committee. Mr. Kelly promptly promised to call up the Suffrage Resolution if it were possible to do so. This colloquy effectively brought the matter before the Committee.

The Suffrage Resolution was brought up, but a substitute

motion that the Committee adjourn was immediately made and carried. It was a tie vote, but Mr. Henry, as chairman, cast the deciding vote. The Committee accordingly adjourned without having taken action on the Suffrage Resolution.

The Congressional Union, undaunted, maintained its siege of the Rules Committee until Congress adjourned in October. Throughout the remaining months of that Congressional Session, however, the Rules Committee continued its policy of evasion. No action was taken before adjournment.

Of course, all this blocking of their efforts on the part of the Democrats made inevitable the election policy which the Congressional Union was about to adopt—that of holding them " responsible."

IX

THE FIRST APPEAL TO THE WOMEN VOTERS

In the meantime, the Congressional Union had been forming an Advisory Council which continued to support the Congressional Union—and later the Woman's Party—with advice and work during the rest of its history. The personnel of the Advisory Council has changed from time to time; but always it has been a large body and an able one.

The list of membership has included many famous names; women political leaders; women trades-unionists; women of wealth and position; women active in their communities. It included professional women of every sort; doctors, lawyers, clergymen. It included artists of every description; actors, singers, painters, sculptors. It included publicists of every kind; fictionists, poets, dramatists, essayists. It included social workers of every class. And these women have represented all parts of the Union.

On August 29 and 30, this newly-formed Advisory Council met at Newport. Mrs. O. H. P. Belmont did everything to make the occasion a success. She threw open Marble House which, hung with the great purple, white, and gold banners of the Congressional Union and flooded with golden light, made an extraordinary background for the deliberations of the Conference. In every way possible for her she used the beauty and social prestige of Newport to give the occasion dignity, prominence, and publicity. Her daughter, the Duchess of Marlborough, had joined the Congressional Union just previous to this Conference. Little she thought and little the Congressional Union thought that as an English woman, she would be a voter, would be elected to the London City Council before her mother, an American woman, was enfranchised.

74

Here, for the first time, the plan of holding the Democratic Party—the Party in power—responsible for the slowness with which the Suffrage work was progressing, and, in consequence, of working against it, was adopted as a program actually to be carried out.

Lucy Burns made a magnificent speech on that occasion. She pointed out that the Democratic Party was in complete possession of the National Government, controlling the Presidential chair, the Senate, possessing an overwhelming majority in the House. She analyzed the working of Congress: she showed that our government is a government by Party: that no measures of importance had passed through the Sixty-third Congress without the backing of the Party in power: and that no measure could pass that Congress if opposed by that Party.

She amplified this thesis. She showed that the President, the leader of the Party, had seven times refused his powerful aid to the movement. She showed that in the Senate the Democratic leaders blocked the Suffrage measure by bringing it to a vote at a time when they acknowledged it would be defeated. She showed that in the House, the Rules Committee had consistently blocked the Amendment, both by preventing the creation of a Suffrage Committee and by preventing consideration of the Amendment in the House. And she proved by the words of the acting chairman of the Rules Committee that that Committee had in its keeping "the policy of the Democratic Party." She showed that the Democratic Caucus had taken definite action against the Suffrage Amendment. It had declared that Suffrage was not a question for national consideration and so it had refused to sanction the creation of a Suffrage Committee.

Alice Paul, first asking the press to withdraw, outlined the proposed election program. She asked the members of the Conference not to reveal it until the middle of September when the Congressional Union would be ready to put it into practical operation. This is her speech on that occasion:

From the very beginning of our work in Washington, we have followed one consistent policy from which we have not departed a single moment. We began our work with the coming in of the present Congress and immediately went to the Party which was in control of the situation and asked it to act. We determined to get the Amendment through the Sixty-third Congress, or to make it very clear who had kept it from going through. Now, as has been shown, the Democrats have been in control of all branches of the Government and they are therefore responsible for the non-passage of our measure.

The point is first, who is our enemy and then, how shall that enemy be attacked?

We are all, I think, agreed that it is the Democratic Party which is responsible for the blocking of the Suffrage Amendment. Again and again that Party has gone on record through the action of its leaders, its caucus, and its committees so that an impregnable case has been built up against it. We now lay before you a plan to meet the present situation.

We propose going into the nine Suffrage States and appealing to the women to use their votes to secure the franchise for the women of the rest of the country. All of these years we have worked primarily in the States. Now the time has come, we believe, when we can really go into national politics and use the nearly four million votes that we have to win the vote for the rest of us. Now that we have four million voters, we need no longer continue to make our appeal simply to the men. The struggle in England has gotten down to a physical fight. Here our fight is simply a political one. The question is whether we are good enough politicians to take four million votes and organize them and use them so as to win the vote for the women who are still disfranchised.

We want to attempt to organize the women's vote. Our plan is to go out to these nine States and there appeal to all the women voters to withdraw their support from the Democrats nationally until the Democratic Party nationally ceases to block Suffrage. We would issue an appeal signed by influential women of the East addressed to the women voters as a whole asking them to use their vote this one time in the national election against the Democratic Party throughout the whole nine States. Every one of these States, with one exception, is a doubtful State. Going back over a period of fourteen years, each State, except Utah, has supported first one Party and then another. Here are nine States which politicians are thinking about and in these nine States we have this great power. If we ask those women in the nine Suffrage States as a group to withhold their support from this Party as a group which is opposing us, it will mean that votes will be turned. Suppose the Party saw votes falling away all over the country because of their action on the Trust question—they would change their attitude on Trust legislation. If they see them falling away because of their attitude on Suffrage they will change their attitude on Suffrage. When we have once affected the result in a national election, no Party will trifle with Suffrage any longer.

We, of course, are a little body to undertake this—but we have to begin. We have not very much money; there are not many of us to go out against the great Democratic Party. Perhaps this time we won't be able to do so very much, though I know we can do a great deal, but if the Party leaders see that some votes have been turned they will know that we have at least realized this power that we possess and they will know that by 1916 we will have it organized. The mere announcement of the fact that Suffragists of the East have gone out to the West with this appeal will be enough to make every man in Congress sit up and take notice.

This last week one Congressman from a Suffrage State came to us and asked us if we would write just one letter to say what he had done in Congress to help us. He said that one letter might determine the election in his district. This week the man who is running for the Senatorial election in another Suffrage State came to us and asked us to go out and help him in his State—asked us simply to announce that he had been our friend. Now if our help is valued to this extent, our opposition will be feared in like degree.

Our plan is this: To send at least two women to each of those nine States. We would put one woman at the center who would attend to the organizing, the publicity and the distribution of literature. We would have literature printed showing what the Democratic Party has done with regard to Suffrage in the Sixty-third Congress. We would have leaflets printed from the Eastern women appealing to the Western women for help, and we would have leaflets issued showing how much the enfranchised woman herself needs the Federal Amendment because most important matters are becoming national in their organization and can only be dealt with by national legislation. We could reach every home in every one of those nine States with our literature, without very great expense. One good woman at the center could make this message, this appeal from Eastern women, known to the whole State. The other worker would

WHY IS THE GIRL FROM THE WEST GETTING ALL THE ATTENTION?
Nina Allender in *The Suffragist*.

attend to the speaking and in six weeks could easily cover all
the large towns of the State.

This is the plan that we are considering, and that we are
hoping to put through. We would be very much interested to
hear what you think about it and want, of course, to have your
co-operation in carrying it through.

The Conference voted to unite behind the Bristow-Mondell
Amendment in Congress and to support an active election
campaign against candidates of the Democratic Party. It
raised over seven thousand dollars to meet the expense of
this campaign.

The details of the election campaign project were immediately worked out; organizers were selected and after a
farewell garden party on September 14, they started for
the nine enfranchised States. Headquarters were opened in
San Francisco under Lucy Burns and Rose Winslow; in
Denver, Colorado, under Doris Stevens and Ruth Noyes; in
Phœnix, Arizona, under Jane Pincus and Josephine Casey;
in Kansas City, Kansas, under Lola C. Trax and Edna S.
Latimer; at Portland, Oregon, under Jessie Hardy Stubbs
and Virginia Arnold; in Seattle, Washington, under Margaret Whittemore and Anne McCue; at Cheyenne, Wyoming,
under Gertrude Hunter; at Salt Lake City, Utah, under
Elsie Lancaster; at Boise City, Idaho, under Helena Hill
Weed.

In these centers, open-air, drawing-room, and theatre
meetings followed each other in rapid succession. In many
districts, the campaigners canvassed from door to door.
Window-cards, handbills, cartoons, moving-picture films, and
voiceless speeches, calling upon the women voters to refuse
their support to the Party which had blocked the National
Suffrage Amendment, appeared everywhere from Seattle to
Phœnix. A pithily worded *Appeal to the Women Voters*
was placed in the hands of the women voters. Press bulletins
describing the campaign against the Democratic candidates
for Congress and reiterating the record made by the Demo-

cratic Party on the Suffrage question, were issued daily. Literature dealing with the record of the Democratic Party and with the value to the woman voter of a national Suffrage Amendment, were sent to innumerable homes in every Suffrage State.

The *Suffragist*, which teemed with reports of what these vigorous campaigners were doing, presents pictures which could have occurred nowhere in the world but the United States, and nowhere in the United States but the West. The speakers were interesting, amusing, full of information and enthusiasm. With a sympathy and understanding typically western, men and women responded immediately, responded equally to this original campaign.

All the time, of course, these speakers were educating the people of the United States in regard to the work of Congress. This was a new note in Suffrage campaigns; but it was the policy of the Congressional Union at all times whether campaigns were being waged or not.

From the *Suffragist* of September 19, I quote from a report of the enterprising Jessie Hardy Stubbs, who actually began her work on board the North Coast, Limited:

Here we are—all bound for the field of battle. Miss McCue, Miss Whittemore and I are together. Miss Whittemore joined us at Chicago full of earnestness and zeal. We have put up signs in each car that there will be a meeting tonight in the observation car, and that we will speak on the record of the Democratic Party in Congress and Women Suffrage. There is much interest. We have sold ten *Suffragists* today on board the train, secured new subscribers to the *Suffragist*, and contributions for the campaign.

Doris Stevens writes in the *Suffragist* of October 3:

Friday afternoon, Mrs. Lucius M. Cuthbert, a daughter of ex-Senator Hill, gave us a drawing-room meeting in her beautiful Denver home. She invited representative women from all Parties to come and hear of the work of the Union, to which invitation about one hundred women responded. One Democratic lady came up to me after the meeting and said, " I had no idea

you women had been so rebuffed by my Party. I am convinced
that my duty is to the women first, and my Party second."
Another: " You have almost convinced me that we women must
stand together on this national issue." And so it went. And,
as our charming hostess pointed out, the applause was often led
by a prominent Democratic woman. Offers of help, loans of
furniture, and general expressions of eagerness to aid were
made on every side. The meeting was a splendid success, judg-
ing from the large number of women who joined the Union
and the generous collection which was given.

In the *Suffragist* of October 10, Lola Trax writes:

The meeting at Lebanon was especially well advertised. The
moving picture shows had run an advertising slide; the Wednesday prayer meeting had announced my coming, and the Public
Schools had also made announcements to their pupils. The
Ladies' Aid Society invited me to speak in the afternoon, while
they were quilting; and thus another anti-Suffrage argument was
shattered; for quilting and politics went hand in hand.

At Phillipsburg the meeting was on the Court House green.
It is fifty-seven miles from Phillipsburg to Osborne and the trip
has to be made by freight. I was on the road from six-thirty
o'clock in the morning until three P.M. About a dozen passen-
gers were in the caboose on the freight, and we held a meeting
and discussion which lasted about forty-five minutes. Upon
reaching Osborne at three o'clock I found about one hundred
people assembled for an auction sale in the middle of the street.
Cots, tables, and chairs were to be offered at sacrifice prices.
The temptation to hold a meeting overcame fatigue. I jumped
into an automobile nearby and had a most interested crowd until
the auctioneer came. I had been unable to secure the Town
Hall because a troupe of players were making a one night stand
in the town. The meeting at night was also in the open air.

In the *Suffragist* of October 10, Jessie Hardy Stubbs
continues:

On Tuesday evening, September 23, I spoke in the Public
Library, explaining our mission in Oregon. Mr. Arthur L.
Moulton, Progressive Candidate for Congress from the Third
District presided, and made a very clever introductory speech.
Many questions were asked by Democratic women which brought
out a spirited defense on the part of several of those present.

One Democratic woman maintained that it would be a most ungrateful position on the part of the Oregon women to vote against Chamberlain, who had always been a friend of Suffrage, whereupon a distinguished-looking woman arose and said: " Oh, no. It would merely be a case of not loving Chamberlain less, but of loving Suffrage more."

I spoke before the Sheet Metal Workers' Union last night, and expect to address every union before the campaign is over. There are only two women's unions here; the garment workers and the waitresses. We intend to make a canvass of the stores and meet the clerks personally and to get into all the factories, as far as possible, where women are employed, and urge these western women voters to stand by the working women of the East. Tonight we have our first open-air meeting.

In the *Suffragist* of October 31, Gertrude Hunter writes of the campaign in Wyoming:

The meeting last Saturday night was most encouraging. It was a stormy night, and we went in an auto twenty miles from here, through snow banks, and every other difficulty to a rally at a branch home. This was at Grand Canon, and a strongly Democratic precinct. Every one was wildly enthusiastic over the meeting, even the Democratic women telling me how much they appreciated our position. We had a dance immediately after, and I danced with the voters (male) until one-thirty in the morning, when we were all taken to the railroad station in a lumber wagon and four-horse team, a distance of a mile and a half, and came in on a train at two-thirty A.M. I sold twenty *Suffragists* and could have disposed of more if I had had them with me.

Thursday, Friday, and Saturday nights we have big meetings scheduled.

We are now at Egbert on our regular schedule, and in such a snowstorm as I never saw before. However, we have had a good morning in spite of it.

This town is like the others, consisting of a station, a store, and post-office. Not a residence in the place. The people all drove from miles around in a high wind and most unfavorable weather to attend the meeting.

We had the thirty-five mile drive to make to a neighboring town for another meeting and we did it every mile through a high wind and torrents of rain, that flooded the trail with water, as we went over prairie and plowed fields. We did it, however, with only one blow-out, and two very narrow escapes from being completely turned over, getting in at two this morning.

Tomorrow night I shall go to Campstool, where there is a big supper and dance.

I had another very interesting meeting this week at a town fifty miles from here. The " town " consists of a station, the post-office, general store, and a little restaurant; no houses, and only one or two families living there. The meeting was in the school-house and the voters came from miles and miles to attend, at least one hundred and fifty of them, on horseback, in wagons, buggies, and autos. Every one was much interested. The minister, at whose house I was entertained for the afternoon, lived two and one-half miles out in the country, said afterward that the meeting was a thrill to most of them, who had never heard a Suffrage speech in their lives.

These are the solid voters of the community. Many are from the eastern States who are homesteading here. I distributed the literature to every one.

I will probably reach the same number of voters every day this week, or perhaps a few more, as the next town we are going into, Burns, is a trifle larger than Hillsdale.

Miss Brandeis is going from house to house in Cheyenne, distributing our literature and soliciting memberships.

The campaign over, four of these victorious campaigners were welcomed home on the afternoon of November 15, by an enormous audience at the Columbia Theatre in Washington:

Mrs. Latimer said:

The very first thing they said to us in Kansas was, " Well, you are a long way from home ! " and we thought so too.

Kansas, as you know, is a very large State and is an agricultural State, and the consequence was that we had to get in touch with all the farmers and so it was necessary for us to do a great deal of traveling.

After we had established our Headquarters we interviewed the *Kansas City Star,* one of the largest papers in the State. After we had talked with the associate editor and told him what our plan was, that we intended to send a daily bulletin to the eight hundred and eight papers in the State of Kansas, that we were going to every one of the large towns in the State of Kansas, and have just as many meetings as possible, and that we would distribute fifty thousand pieces of literature, he looked at us and said, "Do you realize that this will take eight men and eighteen stenographers?" I said, "Possibly, but two women are going to do it." And two women did do it. The result of that interview was a two and a half column editorial on the editorial page of the *Star*. It was the first time that an interview with a woman had ever appeared on the editorial page, and they told us that even Mr. Bryan had not received two and a half columns on that page. All of our bulletins were very well published after the *Kansas City Star* had taken up our cause. The women of Kansas co-operated with us, and the Progressives and Republicans invited us to speak at their big rallies. Strange as it may seem no one seemed to think we were on the wrong track but the Democrats.

After we had been there for a while we found that the main contest was the Senatorial fight, and so we figured out just how we could keep Mr. Neely out of the Senate. Every one said that as Mr. Murdock was running as a Progressive, and Mr. Curtis as a Republican, it would divide the vote and give the victory to the Democratic Party. We knew that Mr. Neely had received a very large vote from his own district when he ran for Congress—over four thousand majority. So we made up our minds that the thing to do was to reduce the vote in his own district. We thought that this would help to defeat Mr. Neely, and it did. He received from his own district a majority of only eight hundred; that is, the Democratic majority went down to eight hundred from four thousand. In many of the other districts, his majority was still lower. Mr. Taggart, who had a three thousand majority two years ago, went down to three hundred, and Miss Trax was largely responsible for that. We have letters from many of the leading politicians of Kansas saying that our work has been most effective. We have felt all through Kansas that our work was very encouraging.

We had many interesting things happen. The second day we were in the Seventh District we held seven meetings. Six meetings had been planned, but after we reached Dodge City we found there was a political meeting in progress out on the prairie and they telephoned in and asked one of us to come out there and speak to them. If any of you have ever been to Kansas, you know they have schools everywhere, though for miles and miles you never see a house and you wonder where the children come from to go to the schools. At eleven o'clock at night we arrived at the schoolhouse where the meeting was held, and found three hundred people waiting to hear a Suffrage speech. After the meeting the women came up and said, " That is just what we need. We are glad to help the Eastern women, but we do not know anything about it. We are so glad you have come to tell us these things because we did not know them.

The men in the West feel the same way. When I was waiting for a freight train about five o'clock in the morning, a man came up and said, " My wife was at your meeting yesterday afternoon, and I thought I would tell you that I have voted the Democratic ticket for forty years, but I have voted it the last time." That is the spirit of the men. Because they respect their women out there, they do not like to feel that the men in the East and the Democratic Party do not consider the woman movement. People would come in and say, " Well, you are on the right track now," and that seems to be the spirit everywhere in Kansas.

Miss Pincus said:

I am sorry I cannot come to you with the air of a conquering hero, but I am sure that any person who understands the situation in Arizona will acknowledge that the purpose of our campaign was accomplished. Despite the fact that the Democrats were in control—had all the money in the State and owned nearly all the newspapers—a Democratic leader came to my office one day and told me that the Democrats were absolutely sure that the women of Arizona would defeat Smith. He said the Democratic Party was scared to death. It was most amusing. Every candidate who was running, even for State and County offices, felt it necessary to declare that he had always believed in Woman Suffrage, that his mother had believed in Woman Suffrage and that his grandmother believed in it. I suppose you know what action our friends Senator Smith and Congressman Hayden took. Both of them telegraphed from Washington to the Democratic State Convention in session at Phœnix and pledged themselves absolutely to support national Woman Suffrage. Mr. Hayden stood up on the floor of the House and filled three pages of the *Congressional Record* on his attitude on Woman Suffrage and Arizona was simply flooded with this copy.

The women, we found, were very open to reason, and one thing I had not expected to find was how chivalrous all the men were. I have never been so overwhelmed with courtesy and chivalry as I was out in Arizona. Every candidate from every county came into our Headquarters to shake hands and say what a nice day it was and how he had always been in favor of Woman

Suffrage. Each political Party in Arizona claims absolute credit for Woman Suffrage out there. To me, coming from a plain campaign State, New York, it was most encouraging to find all the men such good Suffragists, and I would like to turn all anti-Suffragists into a Suffrage State to let them see how women are treated at election time.

Mrs. Helena Hill Weed said:

I am very glad to be able to report that no Democrat will come to the United States Senate or House of Representatives from Idaho—and the Congressional Union had a hand in it.

We do not claim entire responsibility for the large Republican victory, but we do claim the credit for turning many hundreds of votes from the Democratic Party. When I reached Idaho I found the question simmered down to the Senatorial race. The two candidates were Senator Brady, Republican, and ex-Governor Hawley, who was running on the Democratic ticket.

I began by sending out copies of all of our literature and the current number of the *Suffragist* to every editor, club woman, minister, or other person of influence. I began with a meeting which was organized by the working women in the hotel where I was stopping. I told them of our work and what it meant. Many of the women had worked in the East and they knew what conditions were among the laboring women there, and they said they never before realized that they could do anything to help the women in the East. About three days after the meeting a woman came into my office and said, " I want to tell you, Mrs. Weed, that that meeting is going to bring out at least two hundred Republican votes in my ward which are never cast, and is going to turn many more." I positively could not fill the requests that were made to speak and explain the Congressional Union policy. Men and women of the labor unions were much enthused over our work and we won hundreds and hundreds of votes simply because our policy was non-partisan.

We put it straight up to Mr. Hawley that an indorsement of President Wilson's administration meant the indorsement of the administration's refusal to allow a discussion and a vote on Suffrage. We put it up to him that it made no difference how good a Suffragist he personally might be, if he ran on a platform which contained, as did his, a blanket indorsement of *all* of President Wilson's policies, including his refusal to allow a discussion and a vote on Suffrage. We pointed out to him that his personal belief in Suffrage was of little avail to us if he could not or would not bring the Party which he was supporting to cease its hostility to our Amendment. We reminded him of the Democratic Congressmen from Suffrage States who had sat in the Sixty-third Congress and who had professed a deep interest in Suffrage but who had accomplished nothing as far as actually bringing Suffrage to pass was concerned, because of the continued hostility of the Democratic Party which was in control of all branches of the Government. We told him that we felt duty bound to make known to the women voters the hostile record of his national Party on Woman Suffrage, and to ask them to refuse their support to that Party until it ceased blocking our Amendment.

They understood the point very quickly and saw that as far as the individual was concerned there was nothing to choose from between Mr. Hawley and Senator Brady—both were equally good Suffragists, as far as their personal stand was concerned. It was only when it came to considering their Party affiliations that one could discriminate between them. We always emphasized the fact that we were not indorsing the Republican, the Progressive, the Socialist, or the Prohibition Party, but were merely asking the women to refuse support to the Party which had the power to give Suffrage and which up to the present had used its power only to block that measure. We explained that we would have opposed any of the other Parties, had they possessed the power which the Democratic Party possessed, and had they used that power in the same obstructive way.

I am absolutely sure that the Congressional Union has the right policy for us to follow and that through this policy we are going to win the passage of the Federal Amendment.

Incidentally the referendum in 1914 in Nevada and Montana gave Suffrage to women.

Although the Congressional Union never deviated from its policy of devoting itself to the Federal Amendment, yet it was deeply interested in the success of these referendum campaigns and gave aid when it seemed needed. The Congressional Union sent Mabel Vernon, a national organizer, to help in the Nevada campaign. At the close of the campaign an enthusiastic audience welcomed Mabel Vernon home.

Miss Vernon said:

In the West they do not have the feeling that Suffrage is an old, old story. They were very willing to go to a Suffrage meeting, particularly in the mining camps, where to advertise that a woman is going to speak is almost enough to cause them to close down the mines in order that they might hear her. This summer Miss Martin, the State president, and I went all over the State in a motor, traveling about three thousand miles. We would travel sometimes one hundred and twenty miles in order to reach a little settlement of about one hundred people, sixty voters perhaps. We had the conviction that if Suffrage was going to win in Nevada, it was going to win through the votes of those people who lived in the remote places. We knew Reno. We knew it well. We knew it was not to be counted upon as giving any majority in favor of Suffrage. That was the object of the motor trip this summer.

We traveled for miles and miles without seeing one sign of life. There was only the sand, the sage-bush, and the sky. Even though we did not arrive until ten o'clock at night at the place where we were to speak, we always found our crowd waiting for us. There was one mining camp, one of the richest camps there now, where the men said, " We will give you ninety per cent, ladies, there is not a bit of doubt about it." When the returns came in from that camp, there were eleven votes against it and one hundred and one for it. The politicians laughed at us because we were so confident. " Don't you appreciate that many men who promised to vote for you just want to make you feel good and haven't any intention of doing it? " they would say. When the returns came in I took a great deal of satisfaction in showing them that the men had kept their promises.

The position that Nevada has geographically had a great deal to do with it: We made a house-to-house canvass to find out if the majority were in favor of Suffrage and we found that women out there would say, " Of course I believe in Suffrage; I used to vote myself in Idaho." One woman told me, " I feel very much out of place here in Nevada because I haven't the right to vote. I voted for years in Colorado." It would have been an easy thing to prove that at least seventy-five per cent of the women in Nevada were in favor of Woman Suffrage. When the men said, " We are willing that Nevada women shall have the vote when the majority of them want it," we could say that the majority of the women in the State of Nevada do want it.

X

CONGRESS TAKES UP THE SUFFRAGE AMENDMENT

THE effect of this campaign—the first of the kind in the history of the United States—was as though acid had been poured into the milk of the Democratic calm and security. Within a few days of the appearance of the Congressional Union speakers, the Democratic papers were full of attacks on the Congressional Union. The following from the *Wyoming Leader* of October 6 is typical of the way the Democratic papers handled the Congressional Union workers:

Monday afternoon, they desecrated a charitable gathering of the Ladies' Hospital Aid. . . . If it was nothing more than the harmless effort of a couple of women to earn some Congressional coin, it might be overlooked, and these two women with fatherly tenderness, told to go back home. But it involves an insult to the intelligent citizenship of this State. It attempts to compromise and bring into disrepute the practical workings of Woman Suffrage in this, the original Suffrage State. It proposes to prostitute religion, charity, fraternity, and society itself, to the ambition of a place-and-plunder-hunting politician. These women go into gatherings to insult and outrage harmony and good-will among women who themselves avoid politics in their meetings.

They could not have selected a meeting at which it was so plainly out of place as a meeting of hospital workers. These women had gathered together to promote the good work of mercy and charity in our community. They were Republicans, Progressives, and Democrats in their preferences. . . .

The editor of the *Leader* has met and talked with these two women and believes they do not realize the insult they are offering to the women of Wyoming.

The Republican papers of course instantly came to the rescue of the Congressional Union organizers. The *Cheyenne Tribune* said editorially on October 16:

Democratic newspapers like the *Wyoming Leader* are finding fault with the Woman Suffrage Congressional Union for sending representatives into this State to work against the Democratic candidate for Congress.

This is a free country, and Wyoming a Woman Suffrage State, and if worthy, respectable women come into Wyoming, the first State to grant the franchise to women, and conduct a decent campaign for the principles of Woman Suffrage, they should be treated courteously and given a respectful hearing.

They rightly hold the Democratic Party responsible for its self-evident opposition to the cause of Woman Suffrage, and rightly are seeking to defeat Democratic candidates for Congress by endeavoring to get woman voters to vote against them.

As to the actual effects, I quote from the report of the Congressional Union for Woman Suffrage for the year 1914:

One of the strongest proofs of the results accomplished in Washington was given when Judge W. W. Black, Democratic candidate for the United States Senate, called at the head-quarters of the Congressional Union in Seattle, and urged the organizers in charge, in the words of the *Seattle Sunday Times,* "to go home and wage a campaign for female Suffrage, and let the Democratic Congressional candidates in this State alone. Judge Black disclaimed personal interest," continued the *Seattle Times,* "and insisted that his is merely a fatherly concern for the two young Suffrage leaders. To demonstrate that he was not concerned personally, Judge Black told the two workers that he was going to be elected, anyway."

Shortly before election day, Democratic leaders in Colorado formed a Democratic woman's organization for the purpose of actively combating the Congressional Union's work among the women voters.

Further striking evidence of the importance which the Democratic leaders of Colorado attached to the Union's activities was furnished by a leaflet sent far and wide through the State, issued from the Colorado Democratic State Headquarters, under the names of Wellington H. Gates, Leo U. Guggenheim, and John

T. Barnett, National Democratic Committeemen. The leaflet began: "Permit us to call your attention to the apparent aims and purposes of the organization calling itself *The Congressional Union.*"

It then devoted four pages to letters and statements opposing the policy of the Union, and ended with an appeal to the women voters to elect the Democratic candidates for Congress "with larger majorities than ever before, to show the world that the Democratic women of Colorado are not only loyal, but consistent, voters."

This was the last leaflet sent to the voters by the State Democratic Committee. From the first word to the last, it dealt only with the Congressional Union. Could better evidence be desired of the important part which the Democrats themselves felt that Suffrage was playing in the election?

Nowhere did the Congressional Union election work arouse greater opposition than in Utah. "Intimidation, coercion, and what were equivalent to threats of political banishment from the State of Utah," said the *Republican Herald* of Salt Lake City (October 15), "were exercised toward Miss Elsie Agnes Lancaster, the New York Suffragist, by W. R. Wallace, the Democratic generalissimo, and his gang of political mannikins."

"They invited' Miss Lancaster," the *Herald* continued, "to come to Democratic State Headquarters, and there kept her on the grill for two and a half hours. This term of cross-examination, during which she was under fire of cross-questioning and denunciation from practically all of the Democratic politicians present, was a vain endeavor to have her bring to an immediate close her campaign against the Democratic nominees for the United States Senate and Congress. For two hours and a half, the hundred pounds of femininity withstood the concentrated cross-fire of the ton of beef and brawn represented by the dozen or more distinguished Democrats who acted as attorney, judge, and jury all in one. After they had finished, she went her way, telling Mr. Wallace that neither he nor his hirelings could swerve her from her duty in Utah as a representative of the Congressional Union for Woman Suffrage.

"The greatest outburst of Generalissimo Wallace," concludes the *Herald*, "was when, in a moment of rage, he brought his fist down on the table and threatened to advertise Miss Lancaster the country over by means of the Associated Press as being in league with 'sinister influences' in Utah."

One of the candidates for Congress from Kansas (Representative Doolittle) called at the Washington Headquarters of the

Union shortly after the inauguration of work in Kansas, and urged the Union to withdraw its campaigners from his district, at least, if not over all the Western States. Finding the Union determined to continue its opposition through the women voters, as long as his Party continued its opposition to the National Amendment, Mr. Doolittle delivered a speech in the House of Representatives (occupying more than a page of the *Congressional Record*), denouncing the Union, and assuring the members of Congress that its appeal to the women voters was not authorized by the Suffragists of the country.

Representative Hayden of Arizona also endeavored, in a speech in the House, to answer the appeal of the Congressional Union to the Western women to cast their votes against him, together with the other national Democratic candidates. Nearly three pages of the *Record* was consumed by Mr. Hayden's speech, which he reprinted, and sent far and wide through the State of Arizona in an attempt to counteract the havoc which it was apparently believed was being wrought by the Congressional Union workers.

A prominent Democratic candidate for the Arizona Legislature testified to the fear which the Union campaign had aroused among the Democratic element in that State by an appeal to Dr. Cora Smith King, a member of the Advisory Council of the Congressional Union, urgently imploring her to use her influence with the Union to terminate its election activities in Arizona. Dr. King replied: " The more the local Democrats complain, the more they advertise the slogan of the Congressional Union, that the Democrats put Suffrage second to Party. Do, for Heaven's sake, raise the Democratic roof in Washington for involving you in this dilemma."

Among the concrete results showing the effectiveness of the Congressional Union election activities was the inclusion of a Federal Suffrage Amendment plank in the platforms of each of the State parties in Colorado, the first time that this occurred in that State, and the inclusion of a similar plank in the Arizona Democratic platform.

Another result was the conversion of Senator Smith of Arizona to a belief in the Federal Amendment. On September 28, Senator Smith and Representative Hayden, the two Democratic candidates who were running for Congress from Arizona, sent the following telegram to Mrs. Frances Munds, candidate for State Senatorship on the Democratic ticket: " Our record in Congress shows that we are for National Woman Suffrage. If you think best, offer as plank in State platform the following: ' We pledge our candidates for United States Senator and Representative in Congress to vote at all times for National Woman Suffrage.' "

The Democratic Committee adopted and strengthened this platform.

All candidates, indeed, seemed to develop a marked increase in the fervor of their allegiance to the Suffrage Amendment. Senator Chamberlain of Oregon, in his last edition of street-car cards before election day, headed his poster with a declaration of his support of National Woman Suffrage as the leading argument for his re-election.

Not only the Congressional candidates, but minor Democratic workers, suddenly developed unsuspected interest in the cause of Woman Suffrage. Said the *Examiner* of Yuma, Arizona (October 24, 1914), in commenting on the situation: " We view with amazement the efforts of the Democratic bosses to be in favor of Equal Suffrage."

And so in each of the States.

No more conclusive proof of the support given by the women voters to the Union's campaign could be afforded than the readiness with which they became members and active workers.

In undertaking the election campaign, the Union had expected that in the beginning only the humble members of the rank and file would respond to its appeal. It had fully realized that the rank and file are more easily reached by new work than are the leaders. It was with amazement, therefore, as well as gratification that it greeted the co-operation of the leading women voters of the West. Their willingness to subordinate Party interest to the National Suffrage cause furnished the strongest assurance of the speedy organization of the women's vote to such a power as to make it a determining factor in the outcome of things at Washington.

The rank and file, however, equalled the leaders in the enthusiasm with which they supported the campaign. Women who had never before been active in Suffrage work were aroused to an effective support of the Congressional Union's policy. Said the *Tribune* of Pendleton, Oregon (October 16), for instance, in commenting on this situation:

" Large numbers of women who had not even registered until the campaign of the Congressional Union began, have made it their duty to do so in order that they may cast their ballot on this one issue alone. They had not been especially interested in the general political campaign, but seeing the opportunity to

94

assist in the enfranchisement of other women, they have come bravely to the front with offers of assistance."

One of the illuminating features of the campaign was the aid given to the Union in its election work by prominent Democratic women. This support came from the Democratic women of the East as well as of the West. For example, Mrs. George A. Armes, President of the District of Columbia Branch of the National Wilson and Marshall League, wrote to the Chairman of the Union during the election days: " I have come to the conclusion that the greatest service I can render to the National Democratic Party is to help to bring it to realize that true democracy involves Suffrage for women as well as for men. I know that it will come to a realization of the truth if it sees that it can no longer count upon the women's vote in the West if it opposes the Suffrage Amendment. I am, therefore, heartily with the election campaign of the Congressional Union in its appeal to the women voters to cast their votes against all Democratic candidates for Congress."

Women voted in the election for forty-five members of Congress. The Democratic Party ran candidates for forty-three members in these States. The Congressional Union opposed all these candidates. Out of the forty-three Democratic candidates, only twenty were elected. In some of these districts undoubtedly the women affected these results.

I quote the same report:

Basing our estimate on the charges made by friends of the candidates whom we were forced, by reason of the action of their Party, to oppose, the Congressional Union campaign defeated Representative Neely of Kansas, Mr. Flegel of Oregon, and Representative Seldomridge of Colorado; and contributed in large measure to the defeat of Mr. Hawley of Idaho, Mr. James H. Moyle of Utah, and Mr. Roscoe Drumheller of Washington, and greatly lessened the majorities of Senator Smith of Arizona, Senator Thomas, and Mr. Keating of Colorado.

The campaign of the Congressional Union accomplished exactly what its members hoped and expected that it would accomplish. If their purpose had been merely to unseat Democrats, they would, of course, have taken the districts in the United States where the Democrats had won by very slight majorities. When they went into such strongly Democratic States as Arizona and Colorado, they did not expect to unseat any of the Democratic candidates in those States. Their purpose was to make Woman Suffrage an ever-present political issue in the States where women have political power until all the women of the United States shall be enfranchised, and to lay in those States the foundations for permanent and constantly-growing support of the franchise work at Washington. They succeeded in making the record of the Democratic Party on Woman Suffrage (an issue which would not otherwise have been heard of) widely known and hotly discussed in the Suffrage States.

In the meantime, Suffrage had come up again and again in Congress. On October 10, 1914, during discussion of the Philippine Bill, conferring a greater measure of self-government on Filipino men, Representative Mann of Illinois proposed on that date that the franchise measure in the Bill be so amended as to give the vote to women on the Islands. This Amendment was lost by a vote of fifty-eight to eighty-four. On October 12, Representative J. W. Bryan of Washington, Progressive, proposed three other Amendments: One, making women eligible to vote in school elections, which was lost by a vote of eleven to twenty-seven; one giving the vote to women property-owners, which was lost by a vote of nine to twenty-seven, and one giving the Philippine legislature power to extend the right of Suffrage to women at any future time, which was lost by a vote of eleven to twenty-seven. The Amendments were defeated by strictly Party votes, the Democrats voting almost solidly against them, while the Progressives and Republicans supported them.

This Session of Congress adjourned on October 4, 1914. At its close, the Suffrage Amendment was upon the calendar of the Senate and the House, ready for a vote. In the House, however, the Rules Committee must apportion time for the vote. Mr. Mondell's Resolution providing for this —and for which successive deputations had besieged the Rules Committee—was still before the Rules Committee.

The short Session—the last Session of the Sixty-third Congress—opened on December 7. President Wilson's message, read to Congress on December 8, made no mention of the Woman Suffrage question, though it expressly recommended the Bill granting further independence to the men of the Philippines.

In December, therefore, Anne Martin, who had brought to brilliant victory the campaign in Nevada, came to the Congressional Union's Headquarters in Washington. She called on the President to ask his assistance in furthering the passage of the Bristow-Mondell Amendment.

In referring to the victory in Nevada, the President said: "That is the way I believe it should come, by States."

Miss Martin then pointed out to the President the immense difficulties involved in State campaigns. She said: "The referendum campaigns are killing work, and the women of America are working for the passage of this Federal Amendment in order to end the long struggle."

Miss Martin referred to the President's attitude toward the Filipinos. She said she had read with interest that part of his message to Congress in which he advocated a larger measure of self-government for them. She pointed out that Suffragists were asking for an extension of the same right to American women, and urged him to give equal support to the Amendment enfranchising his country-women.

The Congressional Union began to send deputations to the refractory Rules Committee, immediately upon the return of the Committee members to Washington. On December 9, Mrs. William Kent and Mrs. Gardner called upon Chairman Henry as soon as he reached the city. To their great astonishment, they were promptly assured by Mr. Henry that the Rules Committee would report favorably House Resolution No. 514—providing time for the consideration of the Suffrage Amendment in the House—which had been before it since May 13.

"Mr. Henry said," says the *Suffragist* of December 12, "that he had always desired to make a favorable report of the Suffrage

rule; certain 'sinister influences,' however, working upon some
of the members of this Committee had made it impossible
for the Committee to take action upon it during the last
Session. Mr. Henry did not state what the 'sinister influences'
were, nor why they had been removed immediately after the
election."

He also assured representatives of the Union that the
Rules Committee would shortly bring the Amendment to a
vote in the House.

"There is every reason to believe," said Mrs. Gilson Gardner commenting on Mr. Henry's glib change of front, "that
the Party leaders have met and studied the Democratic returns from the campaign States."

On January 12, the Resolution on the Susan B. Anthony
Amendment was debated for over six hours in the House
and voted upon the same day. One hundred and seventy-
four votes were cast for the Amendment, two hundred and
four against it. Forty-six members were recorded as not
voting. Of the forty-six, twelve were paired in favor, and
six paired against it. The Amendment thus failed by
seventy-eight votes of the necessary two-thirds.

It is a favorite trick with politicians to bring up the
Amendment in the short session of a dying Congress. They
can vote no and still have a chance, in the new Congress,
to redeem themselves before election.

The *Suffragist* of January 23 quotes some of the reasons
for opposing the Amendment:

That Woman Suffrage cannot be supported because of a man's
respect, admiration, and reverence for womanhood.
That five little colored girls marched in a Suffrage parade in
Columbus, Ohio.
That women must be protected against themselves. They
think they want to vote. As a matter of fact, they do not want
to vote, and man, being aware of this fact, is obliged to prevent
them from getting the ballot that they do not want
That the ballot would degrade women.
That no man would care to marry a Suffragist.
That women do not read newspapers on street cars.

That women do not buy newspapers of Ikey Oppenstein, who keeps the stand on the corner.

That no man would care to marry a female butcher.

That no man would care to marry a female policeman.

That Woman Suffrage is a matter for the States to determine.

That Mrs. Harriot Stanton Blatch once marched in a procession in which she carried a banner inscribed, " One million Socialists vote and work for Suffrage."

That Inez Milholland married a Belgian and once referred to a cabinet-officer as a joke.

That women fail to take part in the " duty of organized murder " and might therefore vote against war.

PART TWO

1915-1916

THE WOMAN VOTERS APPEAL TO THE
PRESIDENT AND TO CONGRESS

THE new—the Sixty-fourth—Congress did not meet until December in 1915. This is the first and only summer in President Wilson's administration in which Congress was not in session. Normally, Congress meets every other summer, but President Wilson has called three special sessions in the alternate years. In consequence, that year in Washington is less full than others with work with Congress or the President. In the meantime, however, the Congressional Union did not permit the people of the United States to forget the Suffrage fight.

Alice Paul now felt that it was necessary to swing in the support of the country back of the Suffrage demand for the Federal Amendment. She felt that this could only be accomplished by a nation-wide organization which, dissipating no energy in State work, would focus on Congress.

At a meeting of the Advisory Council in New York City on Wednesday, March 31, she outlined plans for the coming year. She said in part:

We want to organize in every State in the Union. We will begin this by holding in each State a Convention on the same lines as this Conference, at which we will explain our purposes, our plans, and our ideals. At each of these Conferences, the members will select a State Chairman, who will appoint a Chairman of each of the Congressional constituencies in her State. Each Convention will also adopt a plan of State organization, suited to the needs of their locality. Each Convention too will send Representatives to a culminating Convention of women voters, to be held at San Francisco during the course of the Panama-Pacific Exposition, on September 14th, 15th, and 16th. At this first Convention of women voters to be held on their own

101

territory in behalf of the National Suffrage Amendment, delegates will be appointed to go to Washington, D. C., the week Congress opens, to lay before their Representatives and the leaders of the majority Party in Congress, the demand of women voters for the national enfranchisement of women. During the opening week in Congress, too, the pageant on the life of Susan B. Anthony, along the lines which Hazel Mackaye has just outlined to you, will be given. We want to make Woman Suffrage the dominant political issue from the moment Congress reconvenes. We want to have Congress open in the midst of a veritable Suffrage cyclone.

During the Sixty-third Congress, we have been able, with very little organized support, to force action on the Federal Suffrage Amendment. When we have an active body of members in every State in the Union uniting in this demand, I believe that we will be able to get our Amendment passed.

The organization of the various State Conventions progressed rapidly from week to week. An incredible amount of work was done—and done with the swift, broad, slashing strokes which always characterized the Congressional Union work. This, of course, brought the Congressional Union into prominence everywhere; but the eye of the country was held by a new type of demonstration which, following her genius for picturesque publicity, Alice Paul immediately began to produce. The stage was the entire United States of America, and the leading woman in the —one would almost call it a pageant—was Sara Bard Field of California. The prologue opened at the Panama-Pacific Exposition of 1915.

Through Mrs. Kent an exhibit booth for the Congressional Union for Woman Suffrage was secured in the Educational Building at the Panama-Pacific Exposition. The Record of the Sixty-third Congress was exhibited there, and the people in charge invited detailed inspection from visitors. All American visitors were asked to look up the record of their Congressman, to discover how he voted on the Suffrage Amendment: they were asked to sign the monster petition to Congress. This booth, always decorated with purple, white, and gold, was to become during the year the scene of meeting after meeting; all characterized by the picturesqueness which would inevitably emerge from a combination of the Congressional Union with California.

Sara Bard Field, in the *Suffragist* of September 11, thus describes it:

A world passes by. It looks reverently at the firmly-sweet face of Susan B. Anthony, whose portrait hangs upon the wall. It scans the record of the vote of the Sixty-third Congress. . . . It peers with curious smiles at the brief array of lady dolls which mutely proclaim the voting and non-voting States for women, and the forces which prevent Suffrage. . . .

The first California Conference of the Congressional Union was held in San Francisco June 1 and 2. Every part of the State and every political Party was represented at the gathering. Florence Kelley, National Secretary of the Consumers' League, appealed to the women of the West for aid in the battle of Eastern women for Suffrage in the following eloquent words:

I come from a State in which women have been trying to get Suffrage for twenty-seven years. We are forced to come to you women of California and ask you to stand behind us; and we are thankful that California has re-enlisted for Suffrage. Women in California have talked to me about the ease with which they won Suffrage, and praise their men-folk. I would like to say there was nothing the matter with my father. He was a Suffragist. There is nothing the matter with our men in the State of New York. Our trouble is with the steerage. They inundate our shores year after year. We slowly assimilate and convert; but each year there is the same work to do over —the same battle with ignorance and foreign ideas of freedom and the " place of woman."

Mrs. Kelley gave instance after instance of the humiliation to which women working on the New York Suffrage petition had been put by naturalized foreign residents. She pointed out the curious, paradoxical inconsistency of granting foreigners the vote, and yet denying it to American women.

She described with a real dramatic effect the incident of the President's trip to Philadelphia, when he welcomed a great army of naturalized immigrants, and denied a hearing to American women.

"There are some of our men," she commented, "the mechanics of whose minds we do not understand. George Washington, you may remember, in Woodrow Wilson's *History of the United States*, had no mother."

Mrs. Kelley told of the battle women, themselves sworn to enforce the law, have to fight if they are without the ballot. She went into her experiences as a voteless citizen of Illinois, when she was a factory inspector there.

Eastern women have been degraded by sixty-eight years of beggary. They have begged of the steerage; they have begged of politicians; now they find it possible to come West and ask the co-operation of their own sisters. But I come to you with a nobler argument when I ask you to support the work of the Congressional Union for Woman Suffrage. Do not do it for us, even though we have borne the rigor and heat of the day in the long fight for enfranchisement. Do it for the children of the future: let them come into a noble heritage through us.

The climax of this Conference came the final day when, at the Inside Inn ball-room of the Exposition, the representatives of the eleven enfranchised States, the Territory of Alaska and in addition the enfranchised nations, meeting on the same platform, told what freedom for women had accomplished in their nations and States. The great ball-room was decorated with purple, white, and gold banners of the Union, and massed with golden acacia. Many of the women representatives wore the costumes of their native land. Mayi Maki, a Finnish girl typically blonde, in the striking peasant costume of Finland, spoke. Mrs. Chem Chi, a Chinese woman, in the no less striking costume of China, spoke. Representatives of New Zealand, the Isle of Man, Norway, Iceland, and Denmark spoke.

The Congressional Union celebrated Bunker Hill Day,

June 17, by another charming occasion. It dedicated to
the Massachusetts exhibit a miniature reproduction of
Bunker Hill monument, thrown into relief by a black-velvet
background, which bore the history of the notable women
of the State.

It was a brilliant day, sunny and clear. The Massachusetts Building, a facsimile of the noble State House of
Boston, situated between the gorgeous bay of San Francisco and the iridescent Marin shore on the one hand, and
the long line of orientally colored Exposition Buildings on
the other, was decorated for the occasion with the red, white,
and blue of the national flag, and the white of the great
State flag.

A procession of Suffragists, headed by Gail Laughlin,
wearing the purple, white, and gold regalia, and escorted
by a special military band, marched behind a large purple,
white, and gold flag, and between an avenue of purple,
white, and gold flags up to the Massachusetts Building,
where they were confronted by a great banner, bearing the
words of the Susan B. Anthony Amendment.

Gail Laughlin, who was educated in Massachusetts, said
in part:

There were Pilgrim mothers in those days, as well as Pilgrim
Fathers, though they were singularly absent from history. You
will find nothing of them in the schoolbooks; you have to go
to the sources from which histories are made. Then Mary
Warren, advisor of Knox and Adams and Jefferson; and Hannah
Winthrop and Abigail Adams begin to stand out beside the men
who are said to have made the history of that time. Was it not
Abigail Adams who wrote to her husband at the Continental
Congress when the very document we women are now striving
to change was drawn up: " If you do not free the women of the
nation, there will be another revolution." I consider Abigail
Adams the first member of the Congressional Union for Woman
Suffrage.

There was Julia Ward Howe, the author of *The Battle Hymn
of the Republic,* and Harriet Beecher Stowe, who so largely
helped in the freeing of the slaves; and Lucy Stone, that staunch
Abolitionist and Suffragist—all closely linked with Massa-

chusetts' great history. It was Lucy Stone who, when protest was made that she injected "too much suffrage" into her Abolitionist speeches, declared, "I was a woman before I was an Abolitionist."

Later, at a mass-meeting of the Congressional Union, Maud Younger, who, in Washington, was to become so steadfast a worker for the Congressional Union, spoke. Maud Younger is one of the most picturesque of the many picturesque figures among the native daughters of California: a student of economic conditions; a feminist; much traveled; an ex-president of the Waitresses' Union; her life is as inextricably mixed with the Labor and Suffrage history of California as later it was bound with the Woman's Party. On this occasion, she said:

The burden of the women of the unenfranchised States, their struggles, is ours more than it ever was; our freedom is not our own while they are unenfranchised. I realized in the East that we women can spend a lifetime for Suffrage, if we continue to work State by State only. Do you realize that, since we won our vote in California, Ohio has been twice defeated, and Michigan twice defeated? . . . I heard Frank P. Walsh, Chairman of the Industrial Railways Commission, say in Washington: "The ballot for women will only come through the persistent and unremitting effort of the women in the free States."

Maud Younger was followed by Andrew Gallagher, equally important, and equally as picturesque a figure among the Native Sons of California. Mr. Gallagher is an ex-champion amateur heavyweight of the Pacific Coast; a labor leader; a power in California politics. He said in part:

In those days when Suffrage hopes were dark in California, Labor stood by women; as we stood for State Suffrage, so now we stand for National Suffrage. If Labor can help to bring about the passage of the National Woman Suffrage Amendment, then Labor will put its shoulder to the wheel, and do all in its power to force its adoption.

The Political Convention of Woman Voters held in San Francisco in September at the Panama-Pacific Exposition, carried out all these traditions of picturesqueness. Mrs. O. H. P. Belmont opened the Convention. Mrs. Fremont Older, the novelist, spoke. Dr. Yami Kin, the first woman physician in China—bringing to the event a picturesque touch of internationalism by wearing a pale blue brocaded mandarin coat—spoke in excellent English. Mme. Ali Kuli Khan, the wife of the Persian Minister, and Mme. Maria Montessori, the famous Italian physician and educator, also spoke.

Mrs. Belmont said:

We women of the North, of the South and of the East, branded on account of sex, disfranchised as criminals and imbeciles, come to the glorious West, where the broad vision of its men has seen justice.

Mrs. Older said:

I thought that Woman Suffrage was like Utopia; when women were good enough to vote, the men would give it to them; but I have learned that Utopias are not given away; they must be fought for.

Dr. Yami Kin said:

All countries look to North and West for inspiration and help in their march toward freedom.

Mme. Montessori said:

We have watched individual States in your country give justice to women, one by one. Now we are waiting for the United States to declare its women free.

The Convention passed Resolutions calling upon the Sixty-fourth Congress to vote for the Susan B. Anthony Amendment. Sara Bard Field and Frances Joliffe were selected as envoys to carry the Resolution across the country to Congress. A plan was made for the envoys to travel slowly eastward, holding meetings and collecting signatures to the petition; arriving in Washington the day Congress assembled. Mabel Vernon acted as advance guard for this expedition and was more responsible than anybody else for its success.

The final ceremony of the Convention took place in the Court of Abundance on the night of the day which had been designated by the directors of the Exposition as the Congressional Union for Woman Suffrage Day. On that evening, Mr. M. H. DeYoung, on behalf of the directors of the Exposition, presented Mrs. Belmont for the Congressional Union with a bronze medal in recognition of the work of the Congressional Union. Ten thousand people gathered there to witness it. They listened rapt to the speeches, and then —lighting their way by thousands of golden lanterns—accompanied the envoys to the gates.

The national Suffrage Edition of the *San Francisco Bulletin*, edited by Mrs. O. H. P. Belmont, assisted by Doris Stevens as city editor, Mrs. John Jay White as art editor and Alice Paul as telegraph editor, charmingly described the scene:

The great place was softly and naturally lit except for the giant tower gate flaming aloft in the white light, which focussed on it as on some brilliant altar. Far below, like a brilliant flower bed, filling the terraced side from end to end, glowed the huge chorus of women, which was one of the features of the evening. Those at the top—hardly women—were the girls of the Oriental School, from midget size up, in quaintly colorful native costumes. In the foreground were the Finnish, Swedish, and Norwegian girls in their peasant costumes, and, stretching the length of the stage, like a great living flag of the Congressional Union, were massed Union members in surplices of the organization colors. The effect was one of exotic brilliancy.

Back of the stage, curtaining the great arch, fluttered the red, white, and blue emblem of the nation that women have sacrificed as much to upbuild as the men; but significantly waving with the Stars and Stripes hung the great Suffrage banner, that ringingly declared: WE DEMAND AN AMENDMENT TO THE

CONSTITUTION OF THE UNITED STATES ENFRAN-
CHISING WOMEN. And the great crowd in the Court
joined in the swelling song that another band of women across
the sea, fighting for liberty, had originated. Every one was
catching the words:

> " Shout, shout, up with your song!
> Cry with the wind, for the dawn is breaking.
> March, march, swing you along,
> Wide blow our banners, and hope is waking."

And then came the envoys, delegated by women voters to
carry the torch of liberty through the dark lands and keep it
burning. And the dark mass below the lighted altar-tower
caught the choristers' spirit, and burst into cheers.

The chorus also sang the *Song of the Free Women,* written
by Sara Bard Field to the music of the *Marseillaise.*

The envoys spoke. Their words were greeted with cheers.
One of the nation's greatest actresses, Margaret Anglin, said
a few fitting farewell words to them in the name of the women
of the world.

Then, all at once, the great, brightly-colored picture and its
dark background began to disintegrate and fade. The Court
darkened, but bright masses of women were forming in procession to escort the envoys to the gates of the Exposition. Orange
lanterns swayed in the breeze; purple, white, and gold draperies
fluttered, the blare of the band burst forth, and the great surging
crowd followed to the gates.

There, Ingeborg Kindstedt and Maria Kindberg, of Providence, Rhode Island, who had purchased the car that is to take
the crusaders on their long journey, met the procession. The
Overland car was covered with Suffrage streamers. Miss
Kindberg was at the wheel. To the wild cheering of the crowd,
Miss Joliffe and Mrs. Field, the two envoys for Washington,
were seated. The crowd surged close with final messages.
Cheers burst forth as the gates opened, and the big car swung
through, ending the most dramatic and significant Suffrage Convention that has probably ever been held in the history of the
world.

And so Alice Paul's stupendous pageant—whose stage
was the entire United States—opened.

The petition which the envoys were to carry across the
country to Washington was, even when it left California,

the largest ever signed in one place. It was **18,333** feet long, and contained **500,000** names.

Very soon after the envoys started, President Wilson made his first declaration for Suffrage. He also went to New Jersey and voted for it.

Frances Joliffe was called back to California by illness in her family at the beginning of the journey. Sara Bard Field, therefore, continued alone across the continent with her two Swedish convoys. It was a remarkable trip, filled with unexpected adventure. A long procession of Mayors and Governors welcomed Mrs. Field in her nationwide journey. Everywhere she advertised the Democratic record in Congress. One of the early mishaps was to get lost in the desert of Utah. They wandered about for a whole day, and regained the highway in time to arrive in Salt Lake City at five o'clock in the afternoon. Later in Kansas came a more serious mishap. But let Mrs. Field speak for herself. No better picture can be given of her picturesque journey than her own reports, published from time to time in the *Suffragist*.

From Fallon, Nevada, Mrs. Field wrote:

Here we are in the heart of Nevada's desert, having traveled already over three hundred and eighty miles of every kind of country—meadow land, green, luxurious ranches, rolling hill country, steep mountain grades, the grass lands of the Sierras, and now through the bare but beautiful desert.

We reached Reno at midnight on Sunday after a vision of the sublime chaos of the Sierras at night.

At night, from a car flying the Congressional Union colors and the Amendment banner, Miss Martin and I spoke in the streets of Reno. The crowd listened with close attention, and pressed closely about the car to sign the petition.

At noon today, we left Reno for the most trying and perilous part of our journey. We are traveling across some six hundred miles of barren land known as the "Great American Desert." Our next destination is Salt Lake City.

From Salt Lake City, Mrs. Field wrote:

The State Capitol, where each meeting was held, stands on a hill. The world is at its feet. The mountains wall the entire city. . . . While the earth was glowing in the light of a flaming sunset, and the mountains about stood like everlasting witnesses, Representative Howell of Utah pledged his full and unqualified support to the Susan B. Anthony Amendment in the coming session of Congress.

At Colorado Springs, their reception was almost a pageant. Marching to music, a procession of women clad in purple, white, and gold surplices and carrying banners, accompanied the Suffrage car to the City Hall where they sang *The March of the Women* and *The Song of the Free Women*. The Mayor of Colorado Springs greeted them with a welcoming speech.

In the bogs of southern Kansas, the Suffrage car had an adventure. The *Suffragist* says:

Pulling into Hutchinson on Monday evening over muddy roads, the car plunged suddenly into a deep hole filled with water. The body of the *Flier* was almost submerged. The petitioners, fearing to step out of the car, sat and called " Help! " into the darkness of the night until their voices were hoarse. No response came from the apparently deserted country. But they knew there was a farmhouse about a mile back. So Sara Bard Field, little but brave, slipped away from her place on the back seat; before her companions knew it, was almost up to her waist in slimy mud. Hardly able to pull one foot out of the mud to plant it ahead of the other, she finally, after a two hours' struggle, reached the ranch, where the farmer and his son were roused from their sleep (for it was now midnight) and told of the women's plight. In a little while, horses were harnessed and a rescue party was on its way; but not until three o'clock did the women start toward Hutchinson tired and wet, and covered with mud.

In Kansas City, Missouri, the Suffragists, accompanied by a procession of automobiles, impressively long, called first on Mayor Jost and then on Senator Reed. The difference between Suffrage and non-Suffrage States became immediately evident from Mayor Jost's attitude; for, while he bade the envoys welcome, he declined to state his own convictions on the purposes of their journey. There was no doubt about Senator Reed's conviction. He had voted against the Suffrage measure in the last Session. The women made speeches. In answer, Senator Reed spoke several sentences in such a low and indistinct manner that no one in the crowd that overflowed his office could understand him, and a man in the delegation called out, " You need say only one word, Senator." There were more speeches from the women, and, when Senator Reed saw that something must be said, he finally declared he " would take the matter into consideration."

Mrs. Field writing of Missouri, said:

" In the enemy's country,"—that is what the newspapers said of our arrival in Missouri, the first non-Suffrage State we reached. Such kind, genial, hospitable "enemies." I wish all enemies were of their disposition. For a whole day and night, Kansas City, Missouri, was alive with Suffrage enthusiasm; great crowds attended our advent everywhere. We never spoke that whole day, from our noon meeting on the City Hall steps until the last late street meeting at night, but we had more people to talk to than our voices could reach. As our auto procession passed down the street, crowds gathered to see it; and the windows of every business house and office building were lined with kindly faces. Often, there was applause and cheers; when these were lacking, there was a peculiar sort of earnest curiosity. And, oh the Suffragists! I wish that every western voting woman who is making a sacrificial effort at all for National Suffrage could have seen those grateful women. " The greatest day for Suffrage Kansas has ever seen," said some of the older Suffrage workers: " How good of the western women to come to our aid! " At the City Club meeting, which was packed, Mr. Frank P. Walsh predicted National Suffrage in 1916. There was good fellowship over a Suffrage dinner, and earnest street meetings afterwards; gravely interested crowds attended, and the newspapers gave large space. The whole city talked National Suffrage for at least two days.

At Topeka occurred another adventure. A great crowd awaited the Suffrage automobile for two hours. But sixty miles away, afflicted with tire trouble and engine difficulties,

the car stood stationary for those two hours. And all the
time, the valiant Mabel Vernon talked, hoping against hope
that the arrival of the car would interrupt her speech. She
says that in those two hours she talked everything she ever
knew, guessed, hoped, or wished for Suffrage.

The Chicago reception was unusually picturesque. Enthusiasm was heightened by the fact that the women voters
were holding a Convention there, and they added their welcome to that of the city.

At eleven o'clock in the morning, fifty automobiles, flying
the Suffrage colors, and filled with Suffrage workers from
all organizations, met Mrs. Field at her hotel. Then the
long line of cars escorted by mounted officers, passed
through the crowded streets to the Art Museum on the wide
Michigan Boulevard. Here was a stage equal in impressive-
ness, although of quite a different kind, to that of the Court
of Abundance, which saw the envoys depart down their
nation-wide trail. Back of them was the great silver-
gray Lake; in front of them, the long line of monolithic
Chicago skyscrapers, grim and weather-blackened; and on
both sides the wide expanses of the Boulevard. The Suffrage women, a mass of brilliant color, covered the steps of
the Museum. At the top a chorus of a hundred women
grouped about the band. From the bronze standard in
the center of the steps hung the Amendment banner. And
in their midst, like, as somebody has said—" a brown
autumn leaf blown from the West "—Sara Bard Field in
her simple traveling suit punctuated all that vividness.

Mayor Thompson said:

Speaking for the City of Chicago, which I have the honor to
represent, I can say that we wish you God-speed and much
success in your mission.

He further told Mrs. Field:

We have watched the growth of the Suffrage movement with
great interest, and as you know, we have partial Suffrage in

Illinois. I hope it will not be long before women have full Suffrage here and throughout the nation.

Mrs. Field replied:

I like Mayor Thompson's way of putting it. At Kansas City the other day, the Mayor quite flustered me with his speech. He said so many things about women—for instance, that woman was a Muse that soared; that she was the poetry of our existence; and something about the sun, moon, and stars. Then he added that he did not think women should be allowed to vote. I think Mayor Thompson's method is much better.

"My recollections yesterday," Mrs. Field wrote to the *Suffragist*, "are a confused mass of impressions—music and cheers—throngs of men, women, and children—colors flying in the sunshine, and great crowds surging and pressing about."

In Indianapolis, there gathered to meet the envoys the largest street meeting ever held in Indiana in behalf of Suffrage. The *Indianapolis News* of November 8 says:

Mrs. Sara Bard Field, brown-eyed and slender, saw men gather at the curbing in the shadows of the Morton Monument, on the State House steps, shortly after noon today—watched them smile as she began her talk for Woman Suffrage, then saw their faces grow serious as they stepped nearer. Then she smiled herself, and her argument poured forth while "old hands" in the State House coterie and machine politicians stood with open mouths and drank in her pleadings.

There is only space for glimpses of this picturesque single pilgrimage from now on to its reception at Washington. At Detroit, they were welcomed by a glowing evening reception. A long procession of automobiles, decorated with yellow flags, yellow pennants, yellow balloons, and illuminated yellow lanterns, met them on the outskirts of the city, and escorted them to the steps of the County Building. Here four stone urns foamed with red fire. "The scene was," one of the papers said, "like pictures of Rome in the time of the Cæsars. . . ." In Cleveland, they held an open-air meeting in the public square in the midst of a whirling snowstorm. A drum, a trombone, and a cornet escorted them—with an effect markedly comic—through the echoing corridors of the City Hall to the Mayor's office; escorted them, after the official call, onto the street again. In New York came their first real accident. On the way to Geneva, the axle broke. The Rochester motor companies declared it was impossible to do anything for a day at least; but Mrs. Field telephoned to the head office at Toledo, and a new axle appeared in Rochester at seven o'clock in the evening. However, the envoys had to drive through cold and a light fall of snow until half-past one in the morning, in order to make the meeting at Syracuse the next day. . . . In Albany, preceded by a musical car which played *The Battle Hymn of the Republic*, they proceeded to the enormous Capitol Building, where Governor Whitman, surrounded by his staff, met them. The Governor was amazed that a woman had driven the car all the way from San Francisco, and even more amazed at the size of the envoy. " I thought you would be six feet tall," he said. . . . At Providence, after a rousing welcome in Boston—where Governor Walsh met the envoys, and the enormous crowd which accompanied them, in the beautiful rotunda of the State House—the little car, which now registered nearly five thousand miles of hard travel, was put on the boat, and its occupants brought to New York City. The weather-beaten automobile, bearing the slogan on the front, ON TO CONGRESS !, and on the back, the great Demand banner, WE DEMAND AN AMENDMENT TO THE CONSTI-TUTION OF THE UNITED STATES ENFRANCHIS-ING WOMEN, followed one hundred other cars, beautifully decorated with purple ribbons, with gold and white chrysan-themums and with floating golden balloons, blazed—among the jet-black motors and the glossy green busses of Fifth Avenue—a path of purple and gold. A huge meeting was held in the ball-room at Sherry's at which Mrs. O. H. P. Belmont, Frances Joliffe, and Florence Kelley spoke for the Suffragists. Sara Bard Field closed the meeting. The

Tribune said: " A tired little woman in a travel-worn brown suit, she stood in the glitter of Sherry's ball-room, and held out a tired little brown hand."

" We want to help you, the voting women of the West," she pleaded; " will you let us? " " The audience," the *Suffragist* says, " was moved to tears and action: six thousand dollars was contributed to the Congressional Union."

The late Mayor Mitchell telephoned to the meeting his regret that he was unable to be present because of illness; but he received the envoys at his home, and added his name to the petition.

At Washington, the envoys were met by an escort, planned and directed for the Congressional Union by Mary Austin, the celebrated novelist. It comprised a group of mounted women, representing the eleven States and Alaska, in all of which women are enfranchised; another group, representing the thirty-seven unenfranchised States; great numbers of flag and banner bearers, wearing long, purple capes with deep yellow collars and white stoles; hundreds of women carrying purple, white, and gold pennants.

The party started at once for the Capitol to the music first of the *Marseillaise* and then of *Dixie*.

There were two picturesque features of the parade. The famous petition itself, bearing five hundred thousand signatures, unrolled to the length of one hundred feet, and carried by twenty bearers, was the focus for all eyes. A replica of the Liberty Bell, lavishly decorated in purple, white, and gold, and mounted on the same truck which had carried it through the Pennsylvania State campaign, of course attracted almost an equal degree of attention.

At the top of the high broad Capitol steps Senator Sutherland of Utah and Representative Mondell, surrounded by a group of Senators and Representatives, formed a reception committee. To music, Sara Bard Field and Frances Joliffe marched up the steps followed by the petition bearers and attendants. The envoys made speeches and Senator Sutherland and Representative Mondell replied to them.

From the Capitol, the party proceeded to the White House.

President Wilson received the envoys in the East Room. Anne Martin introduced Sara Bard Field and Frances Joliffe.

In closing, Miss Joliffe said: " Help us, Mr. President, to a new freedom and a larger liberty."

Sara Bard Field emphasized that same note:

. . . and, Mr. President, as I am not to have the woman's privilege of the last word, may I say that I know what your plan has been in the past, that you have said it was a matter for the States. But we have seen that, like all great men, you have changed your mind on other questions. We have watched the change and development of your mind on preparedness, and we honestly believe that circumstances have so altered that you may change your mind in this regard.

Mrs. Field then requested the President to look at the petition. He advanced, unrolled a portion of it, and examined it with interest.

The President said:

I did not come here anticipating the necessity of making an address of any kind. As you have just heard (and here the President smiled), I hope it is true that I am not a man set stiffly beyond the possibility of learning. I hope that I shall continue to be a learner as long as I live.

I can only say to you this afternoon that nothing could be more impressive than the presentation of such a request in such numbers and backed by such influence as undoubtedly stands behind you. Unhappily it is too late for me to consider what is to go into my message, because that went out to the newspapers at least a week ago; and I have a habit—perhaps the habit of the teacher—of confining my utterances to one subject at a time, for fear that two subjects might compete with one another for prominence. I have felt obliged in the present posture of affairs to devote my message to one subject, and am, therefore, sorry to say that it is too late to take under consideration your request that I embody this in my message. All I can say with regard to what you are urging at present is this: I hope I shall always have an open mind, and I shall certainly take the greatest pleasure in conferring in the most serious way with my colleagues at the other end of the city with regard to what is the right thing to do at this time concerning this great matter. I am always restrained, as some of you will remember, by the consciousness that I must speak for others as well as for myself as long as I occupy my present office, and, therefore, I do not like to speak for others until I consult others and see what I am justified in saying.

This visit of yours will remain in my mind, not only as a very delightful compliment, but also as a very impressive thing which undoubtedly will make it necessary for all of us to consider very carefully what is right for us to do.

It will be noted that in this speech, the President referred to the " influence " behind the women. He speaks of the " impressive " quality of this demonstration.

From now on the strength of the woman voters became a dominant note in the work with both the President and Congress.

On December 12, a great mass-meeting of welcome to the envoys was held in the Belasco Theatre. Forty-five thousand dollars was pledged there for the work with Congress.

The Sixty-fourth Congress convened December 6.

The Susan B. Anthony Amendment, at the request of the Congressional Union, was introduced in the Senate on December 7 by Senator Sutherland of Utah and in the House on December 6 by Representative Mondell of Wyoming. Other members introduced the identical measure the same day. In the Senate, it was referred to the Committee on Woman Suffrage and in the House to the Judiciary Committee.

On December 16 occurred a Suffrage hearing before the Judiciary Committee. It will be remembered that this was the first hearing since the Congressional Union had campaigned against the Democratic Party. It was one of the most stormy in the history of the Congressional Union. Later a Republican Congressman referred to it, not as the "hearing," but as the "interruption." The storm did not break until after two hours in which the speakers of the other Suffrage Association had been heard, and the following members of the Congressional Union: Mrs. Andreas Ueland, Jennie C. Law Hardy, Florence Bayard Hilles, Mabel Vernon, all introduced by Alice Paul.

At this point, there occurred among the Democratic members of the Committee a sudden meeting of heads, a disturbed whispering. To informed lookers-on, it became evident that it had just dawned on them that the pale, delicate, slender slip of a girl in a gown of violet silk and a long Quakerish white fichu was the power behind all this agitation, that redoubtable Alice Paul who had waged the campaign of 1914 against them.

As Alice Paul rose to introduce one of the speakers, Mr. Taggart of Kansas interrogated her. It will be remembered that this was the Mr. Taggart whose majority had been diminished, by the Woman's Party campaign, from three thousand to three hundred.

Mr. Taggart to Miss Paul: Are you here to report progress in your effort to defeat Democratic candidates?

Miss Paul: We are here to talk about this present Congress —this present situation. We are here to ask the Judiciary Committee to report this bill to the House.

Mr. Taggart: I take this occasion to say as a member of this committee that if there was any partisan organization made up of men who had attempted to defeat members of this committee, I do not think we would have given them a hearing. And if they had been men, they wouldn't have asked it.

Miss Paul: But you hear members of the Republican Party and of the Prohibition Party.

Mr. Webb: They aren't partisan. (Laughter).

Mr. Taggart, coming back to the attack: You didn't defeat a single Democratic Member of Congress in a Suffrage State.

Miss Paul, quickly: Why, then, are you so stirred up over our campaign? (Audible murmur from Republican left wing).

Mr. Webb: I move a recess of this committee for one hour.

After the recess Miss Paul rose to introduce Helen Todd of California.

Mr. Williams put the following question to her:

Miss Paul, would you state to me the names of the candidates for Congress which your organization opposed in the State of Illinois?

Miss Paul: We conducted our campaign only in the nine States in which women were able to vote for members of Congress. In no way did we participate in the campaign in Illinois.

Miss Paul then introduced Helen Todd. After Miss Todd had spoken, Frances Joliffe and Sara Bard Field spoke.

Later Alice Paul said:

In closing the argument before this committee, may I summarize our position? We have come here to ask one simple thing: that the Judiciary Committee refer this Suffrage Amendment, known as the Susan B. Anthony Amendment, to the House of Representatives. We are simply asking you to do what you can do—that you let the House of Representatives decide this question. We have tried to bring people to this hearing from all over the United States to show the desire of women that this should be done.

I want to emphasize just one point, in addition, that we are absolutely non-partisan. We are made up of women who are strong Democrats, women who are strong Republicans, women who are Socialists, Progressives—every type of women. We are all united on this one thing—that we put Suffrage before everything else. In every election, if we ever go into any future elections, we simply pledge ourselves to this—that we will consider the furtherance of Suffrage and not our party affiliations in deciding what action we shall take.

Mr. Williams, of Illinois: Is it your policy to fight this question out only as a national issue? Do you make any attempt to secure relief through the States?

Miss Paul: The Congressional Union is organized to work for an Amendment to the National Constitution. We feel that the time has come, because of the winning of so many Suffrage States in the West, to use the votes of women to get Suffrage nationally. In the earlier days in this country, all the Suffrage work was done in the States, but the winning of the Western States has given us a power which we did not have before, so we have now turned from State work to national work. We are concentrating on the national government.

Mr. Gard: Miss Paul, is it true that you prefer to approach

this through the State legislatures than to approach it directly through the people?

Miss Paul: We prefer the quickest way, which we believe is by Congressional action.

Mr. Taggart: Why did you oppose the Democrats in the last election?

Miss Paul: We came into existence when the administration of President Wilson first came in. We appealed to all members of Congress to have this Amendment put through at once. We did get that measure out upon the floor of the House and Senate, but when it came to getting a vote in the House we found we were absolutely blocked. We went again and again, week after week, and month after month to the Democratic members of the Rules Committee, who controlled the apportioning of the time of the House, and asked them to give us five or ten minutes for the discussion of Suffrage. Every time they refused. They told us that they were powerless to act because the Democrats had met in caucus and decided that Suffrage was a matter to be decided in the States and should not be brought up in Congress. (Here Miss Paul, moving the papers in front of her, deftly extracted a letter.) I have here a letter from Mr. Henry, Chairman of the Rules Committee, in which he says: " It would give me great pleasure to report the Resolution to the House, except for the fact that the Democratic caucus, by its direct action, has tied my hands and placed me in a position where I will not be authorized to do so unless the caucus is reconvened and changes its decision. I am sure your good judgment will cause you to thoroughly understand my attitude."

(This interesting revelation was greeted by appreciative grins from the Republican members.)

After we had been met for months with the statement that the Democratic Party had decided in caucus not to let Suffrage come up in Congress, we said, " We will go out to the women voters in the West and tell them how we are blocked in Washington, and ask them if they will use their vote for the very highest purpose for which they can use it—to help get votes for other women."

We campaigned against every one of the forty-three men who were running for Congress on the Democratic ticket in any of the Suffrage States; and only nineteen of those we campaigned against came back to Washington. In December, at the close of the election, we went back to the Rules Committee. They told us then that they had no greater desire in the world than to bring the Suffrage Amendment out. They told us that we had

misunderstood them in thinking that they were opposed to having
Suffrage come up in Congress. They voted at once to bring
Suffrage upon the floor for the first time in history. The whole
opposition of the Democratic Party melted away and the decision
of the party caucus was reversed.

The part we played in the last election was simply to tell the
women voters of the West of the way the Democratic Party had
blocked us at Washington and of the way the individual members of the Party, from the West, had supported their Party in
blocking us. As soon as we told this record they ceased blocking us and we trust they will never block us again.

Question: But what about next time?

Miss Paul: We hope we will never have to go into another
election. We are appealing to all Parties and to all men to put
this Amendment through this Congress and send it on to the
State Legislatures. What we are doing is giving the Democrats
their opportunity. We did pursue a certain policy which we
have outlined to you as you requested. As to what we may do
we cannot say. It depends upon the future situation.

Question: But we want to know what you will do in the 1916
election?

Miss Paul: Can you possibly tell us what will be in the platform of the Democratic Party in 1916?

Mr. Webb: I can tell one plank that will not be there, and
that is a plank in favor of Woman Suffrage.

Question: If conditions are the same, do you not propose to
fight Democrats just the same as you did a year ago?

Miss Paul: We have come to ask your help in this Congress.
But in asking it we have ventured to remind you that in the next
election one-fifth of the vote for President comes from Suffrage
States. What we shall do in that election depends upon what
you do.

Mr. Webb: We would know better what to do if we knew
what you were going to do.

Mr. Gard: We should not approach this hearing in any
partisan sense. What I would like is to be informed about
some facts. I asked Mrs. Field what reason your organization
had for asking Congress to submit this question to States that
have already acted upon it. Why should there be a resubmission
to the voters by national action in States which have either voted
for or against it, when the machinery exists in these same States
to vote for it again?

Miss Paul: They have never voted on the question of a National Amendment.

Mr. Gard: The States can only ratify it. You would prefer that course to having it taken directly to the people?

'Miss Paul: Simply because we have the power of women's votes to beck up this method.

Mr. Gard: You are using this method because you think you have power to enforce it?

Miss Paul: Because we know we have power.

Mr. Taggart: The women who have the vote in the West are not worrying about what women are doing in the East. You will have to get more States before you try this nationally.

Miss Paul: We think that this repeated advise to go back to the States proves beyond all cavil that we are on the right track.

Mr. Taggart: Suppose you get fewer votes this time? Do you think it is fair to those members of Congress who voted for Woman Suffrage and have stood for Woman Suffrage, to oppose them merely because a majority of their Party were not in favor of Woman Suffrage?

Miss Paul: Every man that we opposed stood by his Party caucus in its opposition to Suffrage.

Mr. Volstead: This inquiry is absolutely unfair and improper. It is cheap politics, and I have gotten awfully tired listening to it.

Mr. Taggart: Have your services been bespoken by the Republican committee of Kansas for the next campaign?

Miss Paul: We are greatly gratified by this tribute to our value.

Mr. Moss: State just whether or not it is a fact that the question is, What is right? and not, What will be the reward or punishment of the members of this committee? Is not that the only question that is pending before this committee?

Miss Paul: Yes, as we have said over and over today. We have come simply to ask that this committee report this measure to the House, that the House may consider the question.

Mr. Moss: Can you explain to the committee what the question of what you are going to do to a member of this committee or a Congressman in regard to his vote has to do with the question of what we should do as our duty?

Miss Paul: As I have said, we don't see any reason for discussing that.

Mr. Webb: You have no blacklist, have you, Miss Paul?

Miss Paul: No.

Mr. Taggart: You are organized, are you not, for the chastisement of political Parties that do not do your bidding at once?

Miss Paul: We are organized to win votes for women and our method of doing this is to organize the women who have the vote to help other women to get it.

The meeting then adjourned.

Before going on with the work for 1916, it is perhaps expedient to mention here one of two interesting events. The *New York Tribune* announced on November 5 that, " accepting the advise of Mrs. Medill McCormick of Chicago, the National American Woman Suffrage Association announced yesterday that it had instructed the Congressional Committee not to introduce the Shafroth-Palmer Resolution in the Sixty-fourth Congress." This meant, of course, that there would in the future be no division of the energies of the Suffrage forces of the country; that all would work for the Susan B. Anthony Amendment.

II

THE NEW HEADQUARTERS AND THE
MIDDLE YEARS

THE second event of 1915 of less importance nationally, but of great practical importance to the Congressional Union, was the removal of Headquarters from the dark, congested rooms in F Street to Cameron House, sometimes known as the Little White House. Cameron House has held, ever since its construction, a vivid place in Washington history. It has been occupied by Senator Donald Cameron; Vice-President Garret A. Hobart; Senator Mark Hanna. The famous breakfasts given by Senator Hanna, to which President McKinley often came, occurred here. Presidents, such as John Quincy Adams, Harrison, Taylor, and Fillmore; statesmen, such as Webster, Clay, Cass, and Calhoun; historians, such as Prescott, Bancroft, and Washington Irving, have frequented it. The Little White House is situated at 21 Madison Place, just across Lafayette Square from the big White House. From the windows of the big White House could be seen great banners of purple, white, and gold, waving at the windows of the Little White House.

Cameron House was charming inside and out. Outside, a great wistaria vine made in the spring a marvel of its façade, and inside a combination of fine proportions and a charming architectural arrangement of the rooms gave it that *gemütlich* atmosphere necessary to a rallying spot. When you entered, you came into a great hall, from which a noble staircase made an effective exit, and in which a huge fireplace formed a focussing center. All winter long, a fire was going in that fireplace; there were easy chairs in front of it, and straying off from it. The Little White House

125

became a place where people dropped in easily. This big reception hall always held a gay, interesting, and interested group, composed of Party members resident there; sympathizers and workers who lived in Washington; people from all over the United States who had come to Washington on a holiday. The organizers were always returning from the four corners of the country with a harvest of news and ideas and plans before starting off for new fields.

Perhaps there is no better place than here to speak of the work of those remarkable young women—the organizers. It will be remembered that from the time of the formation of the Congressional Committee to the time when the Senate passed the Anthony Amendment was about six years and a half. Yet in 1919, Maud Younger said to me, " There have been three generations of organizers in this movement." That was true. Not that they served their average of two years and left. Most of them who came to work for the Party stayed with it. It was only that, as the work grew, developed, expanded, more organizers and even more became necessary. And perhaps it is one of the chief glories of the Woman's Party that these organizers came to them younger and younger, until at the end they were fresh, beautiful girls in their teens and early twenties.

The first group consisted of:

Mabel Vernon; Elsie Hill; Margaret Whittemore; Doris Stevens; Mrs. Sinclair Thompson; Virginia Arnold.

The second group consisted of:

Iris Calderhead; Vivian Pierce; Beulah Amidon; Lucy Branham; Hazel Hunkins; Clara Louise Rowe; Joy Young; Margery Ross; Mary Gertrude Fendall; Pauline Clarke; Alice Henkel; Rebecca Hourwich.

The third group consisted of:

Julia Emory; Betty Gram; Anita Pollitzer; Mary Dubrow; Catherine Flanagan.

The difficulties which lay in the path of the organizers cannot possibly be exaggerated: the work they accomplished cannot possibly be estimated. Their story is one of those scaled chapters in the history of feminism, the whole of which will never be known. With her usual astuteness Alice Paul always chose young, fresh, convinced, inspiring, and inspired spirits. Always she preferred enthusiasm to experience. Before an organizer left Headquarters for parts unknown, Alice Paul talked with her for several hours, going over her route, indicating the problems which would arise and—in her characteristic and indescribable Alice Paul way —suggesting how they were to be met; holding always above these details the shining object of the journey; managing somehow to fill her with the feeling that in spite of many obstacles, she would conquer all these new worlds. "No matter," she always concluded, "what other Suffragists may say about us, pay no attention to it; go on with your work. Our fight is not against women."

Sometimes these girls would come into towns where there not only existed no Suffrage organization but there had never been a Suffrage meeting. Sometimes they would have a list of names of people to whom to go for help; sometimes not that. At any rate they went to the best hotel and established themselves there. Then they found Headquarters, preferably in the hotel lobby; but if not there, in a shop window. Next they saw the newspapers. Inevitably it seemed—Alice Paul's sure instinct never failed her here —they were incipient newspaper women. From the moment they arrived, blazing their purple, white, and gold, the papers rang with them, and that ringing continued until they left. They called on the women whose names had been given them, asked them to serve on a committee in order to arrange a meeting. At that meeting, to which National Headquarters would send a well-known speaker, the work would be explained, the aims of the Woman's Party set forth, its history reviewed. When the organizer left that town, she left an organization of some sort behind her. Alice Paul always preferred, rather than a large, inactive membership, a few active women who, when needed, could bring pressure to bear from their State on Washington.

In the course of its history, the Woman's Party has organized at some time in every State of the Union.

Whenever the organizers came back to Washington, Miss Paul always sent them to the Capitol to lobby for a while. This put them in touch with the Congressional situation. Moreover, Congressmen were always glad to talk with women who brought them concrete information in regard to the country at large, and particularly in regard to the Suffrage sentiment and the political situation in their own States, which they had often not seen for months. On the other hand, when the organizers embarked on their next journey, editors of small towns were always very grateful for the chance of talking with these informed young persons, who could bring their news straight from the national news-mint.

But one of the great secrets of Alice Paul's success was that she freshened her old forces all the time, by giving them new work, brought new forces to bear all the time on the old work. If organizers showed the first symptoms of growing stale on one beat, she transferred them to another. Most of them performed at some time during their connection with the Woman's Party every phase of its work. Perpetual change . . . perpetual movement . . . the onward rush of an exhilarating flood . . . that was the feeling the Woman's Party gave the onlooker.

I reiterate that it would be impossible to do justice, short of a book devoted entirely to their efforts, to these organizers. They turn up everywhere. They do everything! They know not fatigue! There is no end to their ingenuity and enthusiasm.

In spite of all this intensive thinking, and its result in action, the Congressional Union had its lighter moments, and many of them.

On Valentine's Day, 1916, a thousand Suffrage valentines were despatched to Senators and Representatives by members of the Congressional Union living in their districts; the President and Vice-President were not forgotten. They were of all kinds and descriptions. Recalcitrant politicians were especially favored. The Rules Committee, for instance, were showered. One of Mr. Henry's valentines took the form of an acrostic:

> H is for Hurry—
> Which Henry should do.
>
> E is for Every—
> Which includes women too.
>
> N is for Now—
> The moment to act.
>
> R is for Rules—
> Which must bend to the fact.
>
> Y is for You—
> With statesmanlike tact.

Mr. Pou's valentine showed an exquisitely ruffled little maiden, with heel-less, cross-gartered slippers and a flower-trimmed hat, curtseying to a stocked and ruffled gentleman who is presenting her with a bouquet. Underneath it says:

> The rose is red,
> The violet's blue,
> But VOTES are better
> Mr. Pou.

One to Representative Williams of the Judiciary Committee ran:

> Oh, will you will us well, Will,
> As we will will by you,
> If you'll only will to help us
> Put the Amendment through!

Representative Webb's valentine bore the words, " From a fond heart to a Democratic (?) Congressman," with the following verse:

> Federal aid he votes for rural highways,
> And Federal aid for pork each to his need;
> And Federal aid for rivers, trees, and harbors,
> But Federal aid for women?—No, indeed!

Representative Fitzgerald received:

> Your Party's health is very shaky,
> The Western women say,
> They scorn a laggard lover
> And will not tell him " Yea,"
> But pass the Suffrage measure,
> Then watch Election Day!

Congressman Mondell's valentine was a red heart, on which was written:

> Oh, a young Lochinvar has come out of the West,
> Of all the great measures his bill was the best!
> So fearless in caucus, so brave on the floor
> There ne'er was a leader like young Lochinvar!

On May Day, the Woman's Party hung a May basket for the President. It was over-brimming with purple, white, and gold flowers, and, concealed in their midst, was a plea for the Susan B. Anthony Amendment.

Later, in May, on Representative Williams's birthday, he was invited by Representative Kent to go with him into the visitors' lobby. There he met Gertrude and Ruth Crocker of the Congressional Union, who were carrying on a tray, made of the Congressional Union banner and the American flag, a huge birthday cake. It was frosted and set with fifty-nine candles, each emerging from a small, yellow rose and bore an inscription in purple letters:

May the coming year bring you joy and the Susan B. Anthony Amendment.

A few days later, when Representative Steele reached his office, he found on his desk a purple basket filled with forget-me-nots. The card bore this inscription:

"Forget me not" is the message
I bring in my gladsome blue;
Forget not the fifty-six years that have gone
And the work there is still to do;
Forget not the Suffrage Amendment
That waits in committee for you.

The first National Convention of the Congressional Union was held at Cameron House from December 6 to December 13, 1915. The following ten members were elected for the Executive Committee: Alice Paul; Lucy Burns; Mrs. O. H. P. Belmont; Mrs. John Winters Brannan; Mrs. Gilson Gardner; Mrs. William Kent; Mrs. Lawrence Lewis; Elsie Hill; Anne Martin; Mrs. Donald R. Hooker.

III

THE CONFLICT WITH THE JUDICIARY COMMITTEE

BOTHERATION

("Why do you come here and bother us?"—Chairman Webb,
at the Suffrage hearing in Washington.)

Girls, girls, the worst has happened;
　　Our cause is at its ebb.
How could you go and do it!
　　You've bothered Mr. Webb!
You came and asked for freedom,
　　(As law does not forbid)
Not thinking it might bother him,
　　And yet, it seems, it did.

Oh, can it be, my sisters,
　　My sisters can it be,
You did not think of Mr. Webb
　　When asking to be free?
You did not put his comfort
　　Before your cause?　How strange!
But now you know the way he feels
　　I hope we'll have a change.

Send word to far Australia
　　And let New Zealand know,
And Oregon and Sweden,
　　Finland and Idaho;
Make all the nations grasp it,
　　From Sitka to El Teb,
We never mention Suffrage now;
　　It bothers Mr. Webb!

ALICE DUER MILLER.

132

OUR IDEA OF NOTHING AT ALL

("I am opposed to Woman Suffrage, but I am not opposed to woman."—Anti-Suffrage speech of Mr. Webb of North Carolina.)

Oh, women, have you heard the news
Of charity and grace?
Look, look, how joy and gratitude
Are beaming in my face!
For Mr. Webb is not opposed
To woman in her place!

Oh, Mr. Webb, how kind you are
To let us live at all,
To let us light the kitchen range
And tidy up the hall;
To tolerate the female sex
In spite of Adam's fall.

Oh, girls, suppose that Mr. Webb
Should alter his decree!
Suppose he were opposed to us—
Opposed to you and me.
What would be left for us to do—
Except to cease to be?

ALICE DUER MILLER.

DURING 1916, the central department of the Congressional Union—the legislative—was in the hands of Anne Martin who after her notable success in making Nevada a free State and with the added advantage of being a voter herself, was particularly fitted for this work. Anne Martin showed extraordinary ability in building back-fires in Congressional Districts, in keeping State and district chairmen informed of the actions of the representatives, in getting pressure from home upon them and in organizing the lobbying. Maud Younger, as chairman of the Lobby Committee, composed of women voters, assisted her. Lucy Burns edited the *Suffragist*.

The friends of the Susan B. Anthony Amendment were

surprised—and of course delighted—when through the tireless efforts of Anne Martin—the Suffrage Bill came out of committee and onto the calendar of the Senate on January 8. In the House at first, the situation seemed equally encouraging. But unexpected obstacles manifested themselves; continued to multiply and grow. Presently there developed between the Judiciary Committee and the Suffragists a contest similar to that of 1914 between the Rules Committee and the Suffragists, but more intense.

The Judiciary Committee as usual referred the Amendment to a sub-committee. Anne Martin lobbied the members of the sub-committee and in consequence of this pressure, the sub-committee on February 9, voted the report out— although without recommendation, to the full committee which would meet on February 15.

At this meeting, by a vote of nine to seven, the Judiciary Committee referred the Suffrage Resolution back to the subcommittee with instructions to hold it until December 14— nearly a year off. This was an unusual thing to do. After a sub-committee has reported a measure to the committee, it is customary to allow at least a week to elapse before it is acted upon, so that the members who are absent may be present when the committee, as a whole, votes upon it. There is a gentleman's agreement to this effect.

In her *Revelations of a Woman Lobbyist*, in *McCall's Magazine*, Maud Younger thus describes the meeting of February 15:

The day ended as discouragingly as it had begun and I reported the situation to Mr. John Nelson, of Wisconsin, the only man on the committee who showed genuine enthusiasm.

"Your Amendment can't come up tomorrow," he assured me. "There's a gentleman's agreement that no action shall be taken on a bill for a week after the sub-committee reports it out. The matter lies over so that the members may be notified to be present. Your Amendment will come up next week.",

Relying on this reprieve, I felt no apprehension when Anne and I went to the Capitol next morning. Standing in the anteroom of the Judiciary Committee's chamber, we watched the members passing through. The committee went into executive session and the door closed.

"There's the gentleman's agreement," I said to Anne. "Nothing can happen."

"No," she answered meditatively.

We waited. An hour passed and Mr. Carlin came out. He walked close to Anne and said with a laugh as he passed her, "Well, we've killed Cock Robin."

"Cock Robin?" said Anne, puzzled, looking after him.

Mr. Nelson came out, much perturbed, and explained. Upon motion of Mr. Carlin the Judiciary Committee had voted to send the Amendment back to the sub-committee to remain until the following December.

This was in direct violation of the gentleman's agreement but our opponents had the votes, nine to seven, and they used them. Our Amendment was killed. Every one on the committee said so. Every one in Congress with whom we talked said so. The newspaper men said so. Soon every one believed it but Alice Paul, and she never believed it at all.

"That's absurd!" she said impatiently. "We have only to make them reconsider."

At once she went over the list of our opponents to decide who should make the move. "Why, William Elza Williams, of Illinois, of course. He will do it." She sent me to see him.

Mr. Williams was necessary not only for purposes of reconsideration, but because, when he had changed his vote, we would have a majority in committee. But he did not see the matter at all in the same light in which Miss Paul saw it. He had not the least intention of changing his vote. I pointed out that the women of Illinois, being half voters, had some claims to representation, but he remained obdurate.

When this was reported to Miss Paul she merely said, "Mr. Williams will have to change his vote. Elsie Hill can attend to it."

So Elsie, buoyant with good spirits, good health, and tireless enthusiasm, pinned her smart hat on her reddish-brown hair and set out through Illinois for Mr. Williams's vote.

Presently the ripples of Elsie's passing across the Illinois prairies began to break upon the peaceful desk of Mr. Williams in Washington. I found him running a worried hand through his hair, gazing at newspaper clippings about Mr. Williams and his vote on the Judiciary Committee. Resolutions arrived from Labor Unions asking him to reconsider; letters from constituents, telegrams, reports of meetings, editorials.

On March 8, a deputation of twenty members of the Congressional Union, led by Maud Younger, called on Representative Williams. I quote the *Suffragist*:

Mr. Williams received the women with cordiality and Miss Younger at once laid before him the object of the visit.

"On the fifteenth of February," said Miss Younger, "the subcommittee reported out the Suffrage Amendment. We are told that there is a gentleman's agreement to the effect that when a sub-committee reports, no action shall be taken that day but the matter shall lie over for a week. Four of our supporters were absent on the day of the report and the opposition sent the Amendment back to sub-committee. There were nine votes cast in favor of sending it back, and seven against. We feel that it was you who cast the deciding vote, for if you had voted with supporters of Suffrage, the vote would have been a tie, and the Amendment would not now be in sub-committee.

You told me that you were in favor of having this matter remain in committee until December, because you felt it would be embarrassing to some men who would run for office next fall. As a trades-unionist, as well as a woman voter, I feel that the eight million working women of this country are entitled to as much consideration as are a few politicians."

Miss Younger then introduced Mrs. Lowell Mellett, of Seattle, Washington; Mrs. William Kent, of California; Mrs. Gilson Gardner, Mrs. Charles Edward Russell, of Illinois; Anne Martin, of Nevada; each of whom made an appeal to Mr. Williams to give his support to a report from the Judiciary Committee during the present session.

Miss Martin said:

You are in what seems to us a very undesirable position. You are a Representative from a Suffrage State, from a State where women have the right to vote for President. You are a professed Suffragist, yet you are the only member of that committee who is a Suffragist and who is in the position of having voted with the professed anti-Suffragists against a hearing. . . . We urge you to do everything in your power to reconsider the smothering of this resolution, and bring up the question in committee again as soon as possible, to report it to the House and then to leave to the Rules Committee the question of what time it shall have for discussion in this session. We urge this most earnestly.

Mr. Williams replied:

I am pleased to hear from you ladies and to know fully your side of this case.

If I remember correctly the conversation you refer to in which I spoke of some embarrassment—not to myself, but to some of my colleagues—I think I stated the condition of the calendar and the business of this session. I have not double-crossed anybody. I have not taken any sudden change of front. I have told every representative of the Suffrage organization who has visited me that I do not favor a report at this first session of the Sixty-fourth Congress. I gave, as my primary reason, the crowded condition of the business of this Congress. I incidentally—sometimes in a good-natured way, as I remember—stated that it did not embarrass me to vote on the question because I was already on record, but it might embarrass some of my colleagues. My real views have been that Congress has duties in this, a campaign year, when all members hope to leave at a reasonable time within which to make their campaign; that this session is not a good time to take upon ourselves the consideration of any unimportant question that can be disposed of just as well at the next session.

With a campaign approaching and two national conventions in June, I do not believe it wise for your cause to crowd this matter on now. I do not believe that it would get that consideration that you will get after the election and after these necessary matters—matters of importance and urgent necessity—are disposed of.

I am opposed to smothering anything in committee. I do not propose to smother this in committee. I intend, when I think it is the proper time, to vote the Susan B. Anthony Amendment out and vote for it in the House. Now that is my intention. I have not said that I would not do so at this session. I think the strongest that I have put it is that I would not do so unless the work of the session is cleared away so that we can get to it.

Now I have said more than that. At any time that you get a full attendance of the committee, or those absent represented by pairs so that both sides are represented, and no advantage can be taken and no criticism made of what takes place, whenever there is what is equivalent to a full committee present, I am willing that the committee shall again vote on the question and determine whether they want it out now.

Miss Younger: Before the conventions will meet in June, Congress will have been in session six months, and we ask you for only one day out of the six months. Some of those other questions, such as preparedness, are not ready to come before Congress.

Mr. Williams: You would not be satisfied with one day.

Miss Martin: That is all we had last time and we were satisfied.

Mrs. Russell: Whatever action Congress takes or does not take on preparedness, we women will have to stand for it. Any program that Congress puts through we shall be involved in. Isn't that just one more reason why we ought to have a vote promptly?

Mr. Williams: Yes, but you cannot get it in time for the emergency that is now before us. I believe this: If women had full political rights everywhere there would not be any war. But that cannot be brought about in time for this emergency.

" We cannot conceive," said one member of the delegation at this juncture, " of any situation which will not permit of three-quarters of an hour being taken on the floor of the House for a vote."

Mr. Williams: We have no right to refuse to submit it. I would not smother it in committee at all, but I believe the committee has a right to exercise their discretion as to when it shall be submitted. . . . How do you take my suggestion? I am willing that a vote may be had at any time if there is the equivalent of a full attendance of the committee. Can that be secured?

Miss Martin: I have been working with this committee for nearly three months, and I do not know of any session at which they have all been present. You impose upon us now a condition that you did not exact when this Amendment was smothered.

I think that we must regard a motion to postpone until after election as an action unfriendly to Suffrage.

Mr. Williams: It may be. I do not see how it can be.

" Last year," a member of the delegation then reminded Mr. Williams, " the Amendment was postponed and voted on immediately after the elections were safely over. The plan now is to postpone it until after the elections to the Sixty-fifth Congress are over and no one's election will be jeopardized. We do not like to have the vote taken in each Congress immediately after election."

Miss Martin: We are not saying anything with reference to a vote on the floor of the House at this time. We are simply asking that the Judiciary Committee perform its function and judge the bill on its merits and make its report to the House. Does not that appeal to you?

Mr. Williams: Yes, it does. I am told I am the only member of the committee who voted to postpone the Amendment, who is a Representative from a Suffrage State. Somehow or other you have put the burden on me.

Miss Martin: You are. The burden is on you.

Miss Younger: If we could prove to you that with your vote we would have a majority of the committee, would you be willing to vote to report it out to the House.

Mr. Williams: There would be ten besides myself favorable to reporting it out? Yes, if you have the ten.

Miss Martin: I have them right here. You are the eleventh. We have those ten votes.

Mr. Williams: Well, I hope you have. May I ask you just to read them?

Miss Martin: These are the ten who are for reporting the Amendment: Representatives Thomas, of Kentucky; Taggart, of Kansas; Dale of New York; Neely, of West Virginia; Volstead, of Minnesota; Nelson, of Wisconsin; Morgan, of Oklahoma; Chandler, of New York; Dyer, of Missouri, and Moss, of West Virginia. That makes ten.

Mr. Williams: And Mr. Williams will make eleven. When will it be possible to get them all together?

Miss Martin: We were hoping to do that by tomorrow. Mr. Dale was here but he has been called back to New York. Mr. Moss has been seriously ill but has promised to attend the meeting tomorrow. I will read the names of the men who are against a report. They are all anti-Suffragists and you are classified with them: Representatives Webb, of North Carolina; Carlin, of Virginia; Walker, of Georgia; Gard, of Ohio; Whaley, of South Carolina; Caraway, of Arkansas; Igoe, of Missouri; Steele, of Pennsylvania, and, until now, yourself.

Mr. Williams: If a majority of the committee want to reconsider it I will vote in favor of it.

Miss Martin: What would you do if we could only get ten Suffrage members present tomorrow and they were a majority of those present?

Mr. Williams: Let us not make any further agreement. I have agreed to your former proposition and I will stand by my word.

Miss Martin: We are sure you will.

After the deputation had left his office Mr. Williams promised Miss Younger and Miss Martin that, whenever the requisite number of friends of Suffrage were present at a meeting of the Judiciary Committee, he himself would move a reconsideration of the question.

Again I quote Miss Younger's, *Revelations of a Woman Lobbyist:*

We now had a majority of one on the committee. We had only to get the majority together. It seemed a simple thing to do, but it wasn't.

The number of things that could take a Congressman out of town on Tuesday and Thursday mornings, the number of minor ailments that could develop on those days was appalling. It seemed that every time a Congressman faced something he did not want to do, he had a headache.

Monday after Monday, Wednesday after Wednesday, we went from office to office, inquiring solicitously about each man's health. Was he quite well? Did he have a headache or any symptoms of internal disorders? Was his wife in good health? His children? Could any business affairs arise to take him out of town next day? . . .

The weeks went by and we were not able to get our majority together.

"You think you're going to bring that question up again," said Mr. Webb, the chairman. "No power on earth will do it. It's locked up in sub-committee till next December, and it's going to stay there."

This was repeated to Miss Paul. "Nonsense!" she said. "Of course it will be brought up."

But why should all this petty bickering, this endless struggling with absurdities be necessary in order to get before Congress a measure dealing with a question of public good? No man would run his private business that way. Yet that is the way public business is done.

Finally after weeks of working and watchful waiting I reported to Anne on Wednesday that a majority of our members were in town and well. We were jubilant. Early next morning we were before the doors of the Judiciary Committee to see them file in. They arrived one by one, solemn, nervously hurrying by, or smiling in an amused or friendly way. Mr. Hunter Moss, our staunch friend, appeared. Mr. Moss was dying of cancer. Though often too ill to leave his bed, he asked his secretary to notify him whenever Suffrage was to come up so that he might fight for it. Mr. Moss was our tenth man. We recounted them anxiously. Ten supporters, ten opponents—where was Mr. Dale of New York? I flew downstairs to his office—I don't

know who went with me but I have a faint memory of red hair
—and there he was in his shirt sleeves calmly looking over his
mail.

"Hurry!" we cried. "The committee is ready to meet.
Every one's there except you!"

He reached for his coat but we exclaimed, "Put it on in the
hall!" and hurrying him out between us we raced down the
corridor, helping him with the coat as we ran, then into the
elevator and up to the third floor and to the committee room.
We deposited him in one vacant seat. Our majority was complete!

As we stood off and looked at our eleven men sitting there
together, gathered with so much effort and trial, no artist was
ever prouder of a masterpiece than we. We stood entranced sur-
veying them until Mr. Webb sternly announced that the committee would go into executive session which meant that we
must go.

In the anteroom other Suffragists gathered, also the newspaper men. Every one said that in a few moments the Amendment would be reported out. But the minutes ran into hours.
Our suspense grew. Each time those closed doors opened and
a member came out we asked for news. There was none.
"Carlin's got the floor."

The morning dragged past. Twelve o'clock came. Twelve-
thirty. One o'clock. The doors opened. We clustered around
our supporters and eagerly asked the news.

Well, Carlin got the floor and kept it. He took up the time.
It got late and the members were hungry and wanted to go to
luncheon, and there would have been a lot of wrangling over
the Amendment. So they adopted Carlin's motion to make Suffrage the special order of business two weeks from today.

"It's all right," our friends consoled us. "Only two weeks'
delay!"

But why two weeks? And why had Mr. Carlin, our avowed
and bitter enemy, himself made the motion to reconsider, tacking
to it the two weeks' delay, unless something disastrous was
planned?

Now began a care and watchfulness over our eleven, in comparison to which all our previous watchfulness and care was as
nothing. Not only did we know each man's mind minutely from
day to day, but we had their constituents on guard at home.

Washington's mail increased. One man said, "I wish you'd
ask those Pennsylvania ladies to stop writing me!" Mr. Morgan
said, "My secretary has been busy all day long answering letters

from Suffragists. Why do you do it? You know I'm for it."
Mr. Neely, at a desk covered with mail, broke forth in wrath,
eyes blazing, "Why do you have all those letters written to me
as though you doubted my stand? I'm as unchangeable as the
Medes and Persians!"

On the 27th of March, the day before the vote, telegrams
poured in. We stumbled over messenger boys at every turn in
the House office building. Late that afternoon as Anne and I
went into Mr. Taggart's office we passed a postman with a great
bundle of special-delivery letters.

Mr. Taggart was last on the list. Every one else was pledged
to be at the meeting next day.

"Yes, I'll be there," said Mr. Taggart slowly and ominously.
"But I'll be a little late."

"Late!" We jumped from our seats. "Why, it's the special
order for ten-thirty!"

Well, I may not be very late. I've got an appointment with
the Persian Ambassador—Haroun al Raschid," said he, and
looked at each of us defiantly.

We pleaded, but in vain. Without Mr. Taggart we had not
a majority. What could we do? We discussed it while we
walked home in the crisp afternoon air. There was no Persian
ambassador in America, but a chargé d'affaire, and his name was
not Haroun al Raschid, but Ali Kuli Kahn. We smiled at Mr.
Taggart's transparency, but we were alarmed. Our Amendment
hung on Mr. Taggart's presence.

Suppose after all he did intend to consult Persia on some
matter of moment to Kansas? To leave no loop-hole unguarded,
Mary Gertrude Fendall next morning at nine o'clock took a taxi
to the Persian legation and left it on the corner. At ten o'clock
she was to ring the bell, ask for Mr. Taggart, drive him in
haste to the Capitol and deposit him in the midst of our majority. As she walked up and down, however, the problem
became acute, for how could she get him out of the legation
when he did not go in? At last, ringing the bell, seeing one
attaché and then another, she became convinced that nothing was
known of the Kansas Congressman in the Persian legation, so
she telephoned us at the Capitol.

This confirmed our fears. Every one else was present; Mr.
Taggart was not in his office; no one knew where he was. Ten-
thirty came; ten forty-five. There was nothing of the vanquished
in the faces of our opponents. Mr. Carlin grinned affably at
all of us, and the grin chilled us. We looked anxiously from
one to another as the meeting began. Ten supporters—ten op-

ponents. Mr. Taggart, wherever he was, had our majority. The minutes dragged. Our friends prolonged the preliminaries. A stranger near me pulled out his watch. I leaned over and asked the time. " Five minutes to eleven." And just at that moment, looking up, I saw Mr. Taggart in the doorway—Mr. Taggart, very much of a self-satisfied, naughty little boy, smiling triumphantly. That did not matter. Our majority was complete.

The committee went into executive session, and we moved to the anteroom. " A few minutes and you'll have your Amendment reported out," said the newspaper men. " It's all over but the shouting." The situation was ours. Suffrage was the special order; nothing could be considered before it, and we had a majority. As the moments passed we repeated this, trying to keep up our courage. For time lengthened out. We eyed the door anxiously, starting up when it opened. We caught glimpses of the room. The members were not sitting at their places, they were on their feet, shaking their fists.

" They're like wild animals," said one member who came out.

" But what's happening? " There was no answer. The door closed again.

Slowly we learned the incredible fact. When the door had shut upon us, Mr. Carlin immediately moved that *all constitutional amendments be indefinitely postponed.*

Now there were many constitutional amendments before that committee, covering many subjects; marriage, divorce, election of judges, a national anthem, prohibition. Mr. Carlin, to defeat us, had thrown them all into one heap. A man could not vote to postpone one without voting to postpone them all. He could not vote against one without voting against them all. Were these men actually adult human beings, legislating for a great nation, for the welfare of a hundred million people?

The motion threw the committee into an uproar. Our friends protested that it could not be considered; Suffrage was the special order of the day. Mr. Moss moved that the Suffrage Amendment be reported out. The chairman ruled this out of order. Now there was a majority in that committee for Suffrage and a majority for prohibition, but they were not the same majority. One of the strongest Suffragists represented St. Louis with its large breweries. If he voted against postponing the Prohibition Amendment he could never again be re-elected from St. Louis. Yet he could not vote to postpone it without postponing Suffrage also.

Through the closed door came the sound of loud, furious voices. We caught glimpses of wildly gesticulating arms, fists in air, contorted faces. One o'clock approached. Mr. Moss came out and crossed quickly to the elevator. We hurried after him.

" Indefinitely postponed," he said indignantly, not wanting to talk about it.

" But our majority? "

" We lost one."

" Who? "

" I cannot tell." He stepped into the elevator. The other men came trooping out. Our defeat was irrevocable, they all said. Nothing could be done until the following December.

" You see," said Mr. Taggart, looking very jubilant for a just-defeated Suffragist, " You women can all go home now. You needn't have come at all this session. But of course you women don't know anything about politics. We told you not to bring up Suffrage before election. Next December, after election, we may do something for you."

Our opponents, secure in victory, grew more friendly; but as they warmed, our supporters became colder. Mr. Chandler flatly refused to stay with us.

" I've voted for your Amendment twice," he said, " and I won't vote for it again this session. That's final."

I also heard rumors of Mr. Neely's refusing to vote for it, so I caught him in a corridor and hurried beside him, talking as I walked.

" That true," he said. " I won't vote for it again this session. It's no use talking. I am as unchangeable as the Medes and Persians."

" But that's just what you said when you were receiving so many letters that you thought we doubted you! You said nothing could——"

" I've got some bills of my own to get out of this committee," said he, waving aside the Medes and Persians. " I won't get them out if you keep bringing up this Suffrage. Good day."

In commenting upon the action of the Judiciary Committee, Miss Alice Paul said:

The action of the Democratic leaders at Washington in again blocking the Suffrage Amendment by postponing indefinitely its consideration in the Judiciary Committee is an additional spur to Suffragists to press forward with their plan of going out through the Suffrage States to tell the women voters—particularly those who are supporting the Democratic Party—of the opposition which the Party is giving to the Federal Amendment at Washington.

We have now labored nearly a third of a year to persuade the Democratic leaders in Congress to allow the Amendment to be brought before the members of the House for their consideration. The rebuff in the committee today shows the necessity of not delaying longer in acquainting the four million voting women with what is going on in Congress.

Many months still remain, in all probability, before Congress adjourns. We will do our utmost in these months to create such a powerful party of voting women in the West as to make it impossible for the Democratic leaders at Washington longer to continue their course of refusing to let this measure come before the House for even the few minutes necessary for discussion and a vote.

Miss Younger says further:

The following Tuesday found me as usual in the Judiciary Committee room. When I appeared in the doorway there was a surprised but smiling greeting.

" You haven't given up yet? "

" Not until you report our Amendment."

For the first time Mr. Webb smiled. There was surprise in his voice. " You women are in earnest about this."

IV

MORE PRESSURE ON THE PRESIDENT

IN the meantime the work with the President was going on.
Mr. Wilson was about to make a speaking trip which included Kansas. This would be the first time since his
inauguration that he would visit a Suffrage State.

On January 26, 1916, Mrs. William Kent and Maud
Younger waited on the President to ask him to receive a
delegation of women in a forthcoming visit to New York.
In presenting this request, Mrs. Kent sounded a note which
was beginning to become the dominant strain in the Suffrage
demands of the western women.

" Women are anxious to express to you, Mr. President,"
she said, " the depth of earnestness of the demand for
Woman Suffrage. We as western women and as citizens
are accustomed to having a request for political consideration received with seriousness; and we feel keenly the injustice of the popular rumor that such delegations are planned
to annoy a public official. We hope that you will appreciate
the dignity and propriety of such a representative appeal as
the women of New York are now making."

President Wilson said that such an assumption was entirely absent from his mind. He added that he had decided
to make it a rule during his trip to New York and throughout the Middle West not to receive any delegations whatever,
since he would " get in wrong," as he said, if he received one
and not another; it was very possible, however, that he
might be approached by deputations which he would be able
to receive.

As Mrs. Kent and Miss Younger came out from this call
on the President, the evening papers were on the stands.

146

They announced that the next day in New York the President would receive fifteen hundred ministers.

On the morning of January 27, 1916, over a hundred women, organized by Doris Stevens and led by Mrs. E. Tiffany Dyer, assembled in the East Room of the Waldorf Astoria Hotel. Fifteen minutes later they sent up a note asking for a ten-minute audience with the President, that New York women might lay their case for federal action upon Suffrage before him. Secretary Tumulty sent back the following note:

For the President, I beg to acknowledge the receipt of your note requesting a Conference with him to discuss the Suffrage Amendment. I very much regret that the President's engagements make it impossible to arrange this matter as you have so generously suggested. When a representative from your committee called at the White House the President informed her of the crowded condition of his calendar today.

JOSEPH TUMULTY.

As this note merely said that no time had been set aside for a deputation of women, and did not say that it would be impossible to see him at all, a second note was sent, asking for just five minutes and offering to wait as long as necessary. In the meantime, an interview between Mr. Tumulty and Mrs. Amos Pinchot took place. Mrs. Pinchot reported to the deputation that the President and his Secretary were " conferring." For two hours the women waited, holding a meeting. Some of the women thought it was undignified to wait since the President had stated in his note that an appointment had not been secured.

" But," said Mrs. Carol Beckwith, " why quibble about our undignified position here in the Waldorf? Our political position is undignified, and that is what we should remedy."

At a quarter past eleven, the President appeared.

In answer to the speeches of Mrs. Dyer, Mrs. Henry Bruere, Mary Ritter Beard, President Wilson said:

I ought to say, in the first place, that the apologies, I think, ought to come from me, because I had not understood that an appointment had been made. On the contrary, I supposed none had been made, and, therefore, had filled my morning with work, from which it did not seem possible to escape.

I can easily understand the embarrassment of any one of your representatives in trying to make a speech in this situation. I feel that embarrassment very strongly myself, and I wish very much that I had the eloquence of some of your speakers, so that I could set my views forth as adequately as they set forth theirs.

It may be, ladies, that my mind works slowly. I have always felt that those things were most solidly built that were built piece by piece, and I felt that the genius of our political development in this country lay in the number of our States, and in the very clear definition of the difference of sphere between the State and Federal Government. It may be that I am a little old-fashioned in that.

When I last had the pleasure of receiving some ladies urging the Amendment that you are urging this morning, I told them that my mind was unchanged, but I hoped open, and that I would take pleasure in conferring with the leaders of my Party and the leaders of Congress with regard to this matter. I have not fulfilled that promise, and I hope you will understand why I have not fulfilled it, because there seemed to be questions of legislation so pressing in their necessity that they ought to take precedence of everything else; that we could postpone fundamental changes to immediate action along lines in the national interest. That has been my reason, and I think it is a sufficient reason. The business of government is a business from day to day, ladies, and there are things that cannot wait. However great the principle involved in this instance, action must of necessity in great fundamental constitutional changes be deliberate, and I do not feel that I have put the less pressing in advance of the more pressing in the course I have taken.

I have not forgotten the promise that I made, and I certainly shall not forget the fulfillment of it, but I want to be absolutely frank. My own mind is still convinced that we ought to work this thing out State by State. I did what I could to work it out in my own State in New Jersey, and I am willing to act there whenever it comes up; but that is so far my conviction as to the best and solidest way to build changes of this kind, and I for my own part see no reason for discouragement on the part of the women of the country in the progress that this movement has been making. It may move like a glacier, but when it does move, its effects are permanent.

THE SUFFRAGIST'S DREAM.

PRESIDENT WILSON: My dear young lady, you have saved my life. How can I thank you?

Nina Allender in *The Suffragist*.

I had not expected to have this pleasure this morning, and therefore am simply speaking offhand, and without consideration of my phrases, but I hope in entire frankness. I thank you sincerely for this opportunity.

Smiling the President turned to leave the room, when Mrs. Beard reminded him that the Clayton Bill, with its far-reaching effects on the working-man, had not been gained State by State.

" I do not care to enter into a discussion of that," he said sharply.

In February, President Wilson visited Kansas in his " Preparedness Tour." As soon as it became known that he was coming to Topeka, the heads of various Civic and Suffrage organizations in Kansas telegraphed him, asking for an interview.

Secretary Tumulty answered by telegram that the crowded condition of the Topeka program would not permit of this arrangement.

The Kansas women telephoned that they were sure the President could spare them five minutes, and they would await him at the State House, immediately after the party arranged in his honor.

When Secretary Tumulty alighted from the President's car in Topeka, the inspired, swift, and executive Mabel Vernon met him with a note from the Kansas women asking the President to see them. To do this, she had had to run the gauntlet of a large force of police, Secret Service men and the National Guard.

Mr. Tumulty said that he could give no answer at that time, but that later the delegation could telephone him at Governor Capper's house, where President and Mrs. Wilson were entertained. Governor Capper was a strong Suffragist. The women did call later, but Secretary Tumulty explained then that it would be impossible for the President to see them. After much talk, an arrangement was made that the delegation should come to the Governor's house at twenty minutes before one. The thermometer was at zero, and snow was falling, but the women waited before Governor Capper's house for an hour. Finally the President came out. The delegation, following the purple, white, and gold, marched up the steps in double file. Lila Day Monroe made a little speech, and handed the President the petition. The President murmured:

I appreciate this call very much. . . . I appreciate it very much. . . . I am much obliged, much obliged. . . . Pleased to meet you . . ." he repeated at intervals, but he gave no expression of opinion.

After the deputation of women had filed by, the President handed the petition to one of the Secret Service men, who buttoned it up in his inside pocket.

V

FORMING THE WOMAN'S PARTY

The Congressional Union was now to undertake another gigantic task—the formation of a new political Party.

For this purpose, a conference of national officers, state officers, members of the Advisory Council of the Congressional Union from the unenfranchised States met at the Little White House April 8 and 9, 1916. Brilliant speeches were made by Anne Martin and Lucy Burns. Alice Paul summed the whole matter up in her usual convincingly incisive and logical way:

This is the third time we have called together the members of our Advisory Council and our state and national officers to lay before them a new project. The first time was at Newport when we proposed a campaign against all Democratic candidates for Congress in the Suffrage States. The second time was a year ago in New York when we proposed to convert the Congressional Union into a national organization with branches in the different States. Today we want to lay another plan before you for your consideration—that is the organization of a political Party of women voters who can go into this next election, if it is necessary to go into it, as an independent Party.

I think we are all agreed on certain essential points. First—from what source our opposition comes. We are agreed that it comes from the Administration. We do not have to prove that. Second—we are agreed as to where our power lies—that is in the Suffrage States. Third—we are agreed as to the political situation. We know that the two Parties are about equal, that both want to win. We know that the Suffrage States are doubtful States and that every one of those States is wanted by the political Parties. We know that many of the elections will be close. The State of Nevada was won by only forty votes in the last Senatorial election. In Utah it was a week before the campaign was decided. In Colorado, the same. Going back over a period of twenty years it would have been necessary to have

152

changed only nine per cent of the total vote cast in the presidential elections in order to have thrown the election to the other Party. This gives us a position of wonderful power, a position that we have never held before and that we cannot hope to hold again for at least four years, and which we may not hold then.

We have been working for two years to effect an organization in the Suffrage States and have finally completed such an organization. Our last branch was formed about ten days ago in the State of Washington. We now have to demonstrate to the Administration, to the majority Party in Congress, that the organization in the Suffrage States does exist and that it is a power to be feared. There are many months still remaining, probably, before Congress will adjourn. If in these months we can build up so strong an organization there that it really will be dangerous to oppose it, and if we can show Congress that we have such an organization, then we will have the matter in our hands.

We have sent a request to our branches in the East to select one or more representative women who will go out to the West and make a personal appeal to the women voters to stand by us even more loyally than they have before—to form a stronger organization than has ever before existed.

Today we must consider what concrete plan we shall ask these envoys who go out to the West to propose to the voting women. I do not think it will do very much good to go through the voting States and simply strengthen our Suffrage organizations. That will not be enough to terrify the men in Congress. Suffrage organizations, unfortunately, have come to stand for feebleness of action and supineness of spirit. What I want to propose is that when we go to these women voters we ask them to begin to organize an independent political Party that will be ready for the elections in November. They may not have to go into these elections. If they prepare diligently enough for the elections they won't have to go into them. The threat will be enough. We want to propose to you that we ask the women voters to come together in Chicago at the time that the Progressives and Republicans meet there in June, to decide how they will use these four million votes that women have, in the next election.

Now, if women who are Republicans simply help the Republican Party, and if women who are Democrats help the Democratic Party, women's votes will not count for much. But if the political Parties see before them a group of independent women voters who are standing together to use their vote to promote Suffrage, it will make Suffrage an issue—the women voters at once become a group which counts; whose votes are wanted. The Parties will inevitably have to go to the women voters if the latter stand aloof and do not go to the existing political Parties. The political Parties will have to offer them the thing which will win their votes. To count in an election you do not have to be the biggest Party; you have to be simply an independent Party that will stand for one object and that cannot be diverted from that object.

Four years ago there was launched a new Party, the Progressive Party. It really did, I suppose, decide the last Presidential election. We can be the same determining factor in this coming election. And if we can make Congress realize that we can be the determining factor, we won't have to go into the election at all.

What I would like to propose, in short, is that we go to the women voters and ask them to hold a convention in Chicago the first week in June, and that we spend these next two months in preparation. We could not have a better opportunity for preparation than this trip of the envoys through every one of the Suffrage States, calling the women together to meet in Chicago, the place where the eyes of the whole country will be turned in June.

We want very much to know what you think about this plan and whether you will help us in carrying it through. It is not an easy thing to launch a new Party and have it stand competition with the Republican and Democratic Parties. If we undertake it, we must make it a success. We must make it worthy to stand beside these great Parties. That is the biggest task that we have ever dreamed of since we started the Congressional Union.

It was unanimously decided by the Conference to send an appeal to all members in the Suffrage States to meet in Chicago on June 5, 6, and 7, to form a Woman's Party. Envoys to carry this appeal to the West were elected.

Mrs. W. D. Ascough, Harriot Stanton Blatch, Abby Scott Baker, Lucy Burns, Agnes Campbell, Mrs. A. R. Colvin, Anna Constable, Edith Goode, Jane Goode, Florence Bayard Hilles, Julia Hurlburt, Caroline Katzenstein, Winifred Mallon, Mrs. Cyrus Mead, Agnes Morey, Katherine Morey, Gertrude B. Newell, Mrs. Percy Read, Ella Riegel, Mrs. John Rogers, Mrs. Townsend Scott, Helen Todd, Mrs. Nelson Whittemore.

All of these women were chosen by State groups of the National Woman's Party; they therefore went to the West as the spokesmen of the unenfranchised women of their own States. Ahead of them went the organizers.

This Suffrage Special must not be confused with Hughes' "Golden Special," which in October—six months later—toured the West and with which the National Woman's Party had no connection.

Five thousand people gathered in the Union Station at Washington to see the envoys off—what the *Washington Times* describes as a "banner-carrying, flag-waving, flower-laden cheering crowd." Automobiles flying the tri-color brought the envoys to the station. Two buglers sounded the assembly for the farewell. The Naval Gun Factory Band greeted them with the *Marseillaise*, and in the half-hour before the train's departure, it continued to play martial music. When it struck up *Onward Christian Soldiers* and *America*, the crowd sang with them.

The envoys made a tremendous impression in the West. Whenever their train arrived—purple, white, and gold decorations floating from all the windows—that arrival became an event and created excitement.

"I wish you might see some of these meetings," Abby Baker wrote to the *Suffragist* of April 29, "and see the looks of amusement of the men as our train pulls in, gay with our Congressional Union colors. They invariably call out, 'Here come the Suffragettes,' but very soon they are saying, 'She's all right,' and 'That's straight lady,' or some such approving phrase, and as the train pulls out of the station, we hear, 'Bully for you!' 'Good luck!' and so forth."

"At Williams, Arizona," said another letter in the same number of the *Suffragist*, "there was nothing in sight but a water tank, a restaurant, a picture postal card shop, and yet we had a tremendous meeting."

At El Tova, in the same State, they carried the message of the unenfranchised women of the East to the very rim of the canyon, a mile below sea level!

Leaving very early in the morning, at Maricopa they found a group of women waiting, who said plaintively, " Oh, if you could only stop longer, so that we might drum up all the women out of the sage brush! "

It was not the people alone or the civic authorities who made this trip of the envoys so attractive. When the Suffragists came to breakfast on the road from Maricopa to Tucson, they found that the management of the railway had decorated the breakfast tables in the dining car with purple, white, and gold—sweet peas and yellow laburnums. At Tucson, Eugene Debs came with the crowd to meet them.

At a meeting in Cheyenne, Mrs. Blatch was presented with a framed copy of a facsimile of the Governor's signature attached to the act enfranchising the women of Wyoming when the State came into the Union.

In San Francisco, where there was a large meeting in the Civic Auditorium, presided over by Gail Laughlin, Sara Bard Field spoke. At the close of the meeting, she asked if the people present who put Suffrage before Party affiliations would say, " I will." The audience arose as one man, and answered roundly, " I will."

At Sacramento, California, where they were given a reception and luncheon by the Chamber of Commerce, the annual fruit show was in progress and the envoys were presented with an immense box of raisins and two boxes of Sacramento Valley cherries.

At Seattle, the station was decorated with Congressional Union banners; the national colors; hanging baskets of flowers. A bugler called together the big crowd—including the Acting Mayor—which had gathered to welcome the envoys.

" Ladies," Mrs. Blatch ended her speech, " we are here after your votes." A man's voice in the audience cried:

" You'll get them," and when Mrs. Blatch said, " Men, we
need yours too," the whole crowd burst into applause.

Immediately after the address, the envoys were taken on
a tour of the city in a procession of a hundred and fifty
automobiles, all, of course, flying the purple, white, and
gold. They attended court, where Seattle's only woman
judge, a member of the Congressional Union, presided—
Reah Whitehead.

It was in Washington State that the doctrine of Suffrage
first reached what the *Suffragist* described as " the height of
its career." Lucy Burns, as the guest of Flight Lieutenant
Maroney of the Naval Militia at Washington, flew to a
height of fourteen hundred feet over Seattle, scattering
leaflets as she went. When she started, Miss Burns carried
a Congressional Union banner, but the eighty-mile-an-hour
gale soon tore it from her hand. When last seen, it reposed
gracefully on the roof of a large Seattle mill. At Belling-
ham occurred one of the biggest out-of-door meetings the
envoys had had. For a solid block, the street was packed
with people from one side to the other.

At Spokane, they participated in an interesting and
rather poignant event, the planting of a tree in memory of
May Arkwright Hutton, pioneer Suffragist of Washington.

At Helena, Montana, a huge mass-meeting was held in the
Auditorium. A sand storm, which had greeted their arrival,
grew worse towards night, the wind howling louder and
louder. In the midst of Mrs. Rogers's speech the lights suddenly went out. She did not even hesitate, and in the
absolute darkness continued to urge women to stand by
women. There was not a sound from the audience; they
listened in perfect quiet till the end.

In one State, the Governor declared the coming of the
Suffrage Special a legal holiday. Everything on wheels
turned out to meet the envoys at the train, including the
fire engine.

A Convention at Salt Lake City on May 11 closed the
swing of the Suffrage Special round the circle of the twelve

free States, and brought the Western tour to its highest
stage of success. The envoys passed from the station under
a great purple, white, and gold flag, through a lane of
women, their arms full of spring blossoms, to a long line of
waiting automobiles flying banners of purple, white, and
gold.

The Convention passed resolutions demanding from Congress favorable action on the Suffrage Amendment in the
present session and elected three women voters to carry these
resolutions to Congress.

These women accompanied the envoys to Washington.
There they were welcomed by a luncheon in the Union Station. Then, in automobiles, brilliantly decorated, they drove
through streets lined with huge posters which said COME TO
THE CAPITOL. As they approached the Capitol, two buglers,
from the broad platforms at the top of the high, wide stairway, alternately sounded a note of triumphant welcome. A
huge chorus of women in white sang *America*. Through
the aisle formed on the Capitol steps by ribbons held in the
hands of other women in white, the envoys passed up the
steps into the Rotunda. In the Rotunda, they grouped
themselves into a semi-circle facing another semi-circle—
nearly a hundred Senators and Representatives. The
Senate had taken a recess especially to meet these
women.

The envoys, elected at the Salt Lake City Convention, then
presented to the assembled Congressmen the resolutions
passed at that Convention and speeches followed.

While the envoys were rousing the West, the Congressional
Union was sending deputations to great political leaders in
the hope of getting declarations of support which would
influence the coming National Political Conventions. To a
deputation consisting of Mary Beard, Elizabeth Gerberding,
Alice Carpenter, and Mrs. Evan Evans, Theodore Roosevelt,
who had long been converted to the principle of Suffrage,
announced himself in favor of the Federal Amendment and
promised his active support in the campaign. This was of

course an encouraging episode in the story of the National Amendment.

Three weeks later came the next important event in the history of the Congressional Union—the launching of a Woman's Party on July 5 at the Blackstone Theatre in Chicago. At this time Chicago was the center of publicity; the strategic point as far as the press was concerned. The Woman's Party Convention met before the Conventions of the Republicans and Democrats. The reporters, gathered there and waiting in idleness for these later occasions, looked upon the Woman's Party Convention as a gift of the gods.

Helena Hill Weed presented a report of the Credentials Committee, of which she was Chairman. She said:

This is not a delegated body.

It is a mass convention of all members of the Congressional Union to form a Woman's Party, made up of enfranchised women of the eleven full Suffrage States, and of Illinois, where women may vote for President of the United States.

There are two classes of delegates in this convention—members of the Union in these twelve Suffrage States, who have the right to speak and vote in the convention; and members of the Union in the thirty-six unfree States, who may speak from the floor, but may not vote.

As registration is still going on, it is impossible to give a final vote of the number of delegates attending. Over fifteen hundred delegates have already registered.

Maud Younger was temporary Chairman of the Convention and keynote speaker. She said in part:

A new force marches on to the political field. For the first time in a Presidential election women are a factor to be reckoned with. Four years ago, women voted in six States—today in twelve, including Illinois. These States with their four million women constitute nearly one-fourth of the electoral college and more than one-third of the votes necessary to elect a President. With enough women organized in each State to hold the balance of power, the women's votes may determine the Presidency of the United States.

160

The Woman's Party has no candidates and but one plank, the enfranchisement of the women of America through a Federal Amendment.

Anne Martin was chosen permanent Chairman of the Party; Phœbe A. Hearst, Judge Mary A. Bartelme, Vice-Chairmen; Mabel Vernon, Secretary.

The Party platform, adopted unanimously amid cheers, reads:

The National Woman's Party stands for the passage of the Amendment to the United States Constitution known as the Susan B. Anthony Amendment, proposing an Amendment to the Constitution of the United States extending the right of Suffrage to women:

Resolved by the Senate and House of Representatives of the United States of America in Congress assembled (two-thirds of each House concurring therein) that the following article be proposed in the legislatures of the several States as an Amendment to the Constitution of the United States, which, when ratified by three-fourths of the said legislatures, shall be valid as part of such Constitution, namely:

Article 1, Section 1. The right of citizens of the United States to vote shall not be denied or abridged by the United States or by any State on account of sex.

Section 2. Congress shall have power, by appropriate legislation, to enforce the provisions of this article.

The National Woman's Party, convinced that the enfranchisement of women is the paramount issue, pledges itself to use its united vote to secure the passage of the Susan B. Anthony Amendment, irrespective of the interests of any national political Party, and pledges its unceasing opposition to all who oppose this Amendment.

Sara Bard Field closed that first meeting with an eloquent invocation to the spirit of freedom, quoting from Alfred Wallace the words he used just before his death:

All my long life and investigations have shown me that there is one supreme force needed in the universe for growth, either material or spiritual, physical or mental—and that force is freedom.

An evening session of the Woman's Party Convention, held also at the Blackstone Theatre, was made interesting and picturesque by the presence of representatives of all the political Parties.

The Convention appointed women representing the Woman's Party, to speak at the Republican, Democratic, and Progressive Conventions.

Incidental to the Convention a big "Suffrage First" luncheon was given in the Auditorium Hotel. So many hundreds of applicants for tickets had to be refused that finally tickets of admission for standing room were sold. Every inch of steps was occupied when the luncheon began. Remarkable speeches were made by Rheta Childe Dorr, the famous publicist, and one of the early editors of the *Suffragist*; by Crystal Eastman, one of the founders of the Congressional Union, brilliant speaker, writer, and editor; Inez Milholland Boissevain, who, before the year was out, was to end, with such tragic abruptness, a vivid and devoted life; Helen Keller, whose unexampled achievement is known to the whole world.

The publicity which the Woman's Party received was extraordinary. The Convention lasted three days and the meetings were packed. Arthur Brisbane pointed out the difference between the clock-like organization of the women and the hap-hazard organization of the men.

Ida M. Tarbell, describing the Woman's Party in the *New York World* of June 7 and 8, 1916, says:

The new Woman's Party had permitted representation of five different political Parties to appear before them and briefly present their various claims to the Suffrage of women. "We do not ask you here to tell us what we can do for your Parties, but what your Parties can do for us," Miss Martin told the speakers in a tone of exultant sweetness which sent a cheer from shore to shore of the human sea that filled the house. . . .

"Votes don't matter," Benson shouted at them, "nothing but education matters. Women, like men, don't know how to vote. Nevertheless, if you have nothing but ignorance you have a right to contribute that. As for the Socialists, we shall continue to vote for Suffrage, as we always have done, if no women vote for us."

Much as they gasped at Benson's defiance of their " power," they took it like sports, and sent him to his seat with rounds of cheers and long waving of their lovely banners. (They have a wonderful eye for color, these new politicians.)

But when Mr. Hammond—confident and bland—assured them the Republican Party offered them protection from invaders, they jeered at him. He did not understand that they are their own protectors and war scares are not going to stampede them.

Another thing that the gentlemen must have noticed—used as they are to the same game—and that was, that no amount of eloquence made the faintest scratch on the rock-ribbed determination of the women. The one and only thing they wanted to know, so the women told the men after they had gone through their ordeals, was whether or no they proposed to support the Susan B. Anthony Amendment. That was the only possible interest they had in what the gentlemen could say. Was it, yes or no?

The Republican and Progressive Conventions began in Chicago the day the Woman's Party Convention ended. The delegates elected by the women spoke before the Resolution Committee of both these Conventions.

The hearing before the Republicans was held in the vast Coliseum. Representatives of the National American Woman Suffrage Association addressed the Committee. Anti-Suffragists followed. In closing, their last speaker said:

" We will now leave you to the tender mercies of those who demand."

The Woman's Party then took the hearing in charge.

The hearing of the Woman's Party before the Progressive Convention was held at eight o'clock the same evening in the South Parlor of the Auditorium Hotel.

Later, members of the Woman's Party went to St. Louis where the Democrats were holding their Convention. When they arrived they found there was no room in the hotel which could be used for Headquarters. Most of them, a little discouraged, went in to breakfast. While they sat at the table, a newspaper man approached. " Where are your

Headquarters?" he asked. "Here," Alice Paul answered instantly. After breakfast she chose a table in a conspicuous part of the hotel lobby; covered it with Woman's Party literature, hung a purple, white, and gold banner back of it. The hotel, seething with the activity due to the fact that Democratic Headquarters was there, took no notice of what she was doing. Nobody said anything to her. Gradually Alice Paul hung purple, white, and gold banners everywhere in that corner of the lobby. Nobody remonstrated. Perhaps by this time, the hotel authorities decided that her color scheme was decorative. At any rate, the Woman's Party maintained that corner as Headquarters. It was a conspicuous spot; everybody had to pass it to go to the elevator. They could not have hired a place so advantageously situated.

Newspaper cartoonists began to introduce the new Party into their pictures. Alice Paul in the figure of a little deer, big-eyed and wistful, stood timidly among a group which included the elephant, the donkey and the bull moose.

The Woman's Party found every sentiment in favor of Suffrage among the Democratic delegates until Secretary of War Baker arrived from Washington bringing the platform drawn up by Wilson. Then the atmosphere changed. Newspaper men, who told the Woman's Party delegates of the encouraging condition earlier, now said: "There is no chance of getting what you want."

When later the Resolutions Committee met, representatives from the Woman's Party waited all night outside the door in a last effort to influence the members of the Committee going in and out of the Committee Rooms. The entire platform was accepted, with very slight changes, as it had been originally drafted in Washington. It contained a recommendation that the question of Woman Suffrage be confined to the States.

The Progressives endorsed National Suffrage. This was the first time a national political Party had ever endorsed the Federal Amendment; for although the Progressives, the

Socialists, and the Prohibitionists had endorsed the principle of Suffrage in 1912, they had apparently never heard of the principle of Federal Suffrage. The platforms of the other two Parties were unsatisfactory as far as the Federal Amendment was concerned.

The Republican Suffrage plank was:

The Republican Party, reaffirming its faith in a government of the people, by the people, and for the people, as a measure of justice to one-half the adult population of this country, favors the extension of Suffrage to women, but recognizes the right of each State to settle this question for itself.

The Democratic Suffrage plank ran:

We recommend the extension of the franchise to the women of the country by the States upon the same terms as to men.

These two planks also marked a great advance; for it was the first time the major political Parties had ever mentioned Suffrage.

Now every effort of the Woman's Party was directed to getting the Presidential candidates, Wilson and Hughes, to come out for National Suffrage.

Alice Paul's campaign, conducted on Hughes, was particularly vigorous. It was nation-wide in its extent. She sent telegrams all over the country asking people to urge this upon him. She sent numberless women to plead with Hughes. She sent women to Roosevelt and to other prominent Republicans and Progressives to get them to use their influence with Hughes. Every Republican member of Congress was lobbied to write to Hughes or to see him.

Hughes found himself bombarded. Letters inundated him from all over the nation. Newspapers besieged him with editorials. Most important of all, Alice Paul herself went to him. Then it was that she presented an unanswerable argument which has already been quoted.

Your Party consists of two factions, the old stand-pat Republicans and the Progressives. Now if you put a Suffrage plank in your platform, you will not alienate the Progressives, because the Progressives have a Suffrage plank and the old stand-pat Republicans will not vote for a Democrat, no matter what you put in your platform.

At a great mass-meeting in Carnegie Hall, Hughes accepted the nomination. He did not, however, satisfactorily mention Woman Suffrage. That evening an unknown man came up to the box where Alice Paul was sitting and introducing himself as Hughes's representative, asked her what she thought of the program. " Utterly unsatisfactory," said Alice Paul; " it did not mention Federal Suffrage." That night Alice Paul and other Suffragists went early to the public reception given to Hughes at the Hotel Astor. They told every Senator, Congressman, and plain individual whom they knew there: " When you congratulate Mr. Hughes, tell him how disappointed you were that he did not mention Federal Suffrage."

In a telegram sent on August 1 to Senator Sutherland of Utah, Hughes declared himself in favor of the Federal Amendment. It was the first time any Presidential candidate of either of the two big political Parties had publicly declared the Federal Amendment a part of his policy.

On June 19, President Wilson sent to Mrs. Carrie Chapman Catt, president of the National American Woman Suffrage Association, the following letter, which is a reply to a telegram from her asking what the Suffrage plank in the Democratic platform meant:

MY DEAR MRS. CATT:

I was away from the city and did not get your telegram of June sixteenth promptly.

I am very glad to make my position about the Suffrage plank adopted by the convention clear to you, though I had not thought that it was necessary to state again a position I have repeatedly stated with entire frankness. The plank received my entire approval before its adoption and I shall support its principle with sincere pleasure. I wish to join my fellow-Democrats in recommending to the several States that they extend the Suffrage to women upon the same terms as to men.

Cordially and sincerely yours,

WOODROW WILSON.

VI

STILL MORE PRESSURE ON THE PRESIDENT

On June 12, 1916, Sara Bard Field sent a telegram to President Wilson. Mrs. Field was a Democrat, but she was, first of all, a Suffragist. In that telegram, she urged the President to support the Suffrage Amendment. She promised, if the Democratic Party would do this, that she herself would gladly campaign for him in the Western States without remuneration. She promised him also the services of at least five other influential Democratic women. The President answered:

DEAR MRS. FIELD:
Your frank and kindly telegram of June 12 sent from St. Louis was warmly appreciated. I have been in frequent conference with my Party associates about a platform declaration with regard to Woman Suffrage and sincerely hope the outcome has been acceptable to you.
In haste, with sincerest appreciation,
Cordially yours,
WOODROW WILSON.

On June 21, President Wilson received Mrs. D. E. Hooker of Richmond, who came to him as a delegate from the Virginia Federation of Labor. Mrs. Hooker placed in the President's hands resolutions passed by the Federation, demanding favorable action on the Federal Amendment this session.
" This is very strong," said President Wilson.
The *Suffragist* of July 1 says:

Mrs. Hooker then urged upon the President, very movingly, the humiliation, from the standpoint of a Southerner and a woman, of going before the entire population of men now enfranchised, and begging them each personally to approve of

167

woman's right to full citizenship. Tears came into her eyes as she spoke, and the President seemed rather touched. He said consolingly that she must not mind the criticism she encountered in a good work. "Every one in the public eye," the President said, "is deluged with criticism. You simply must do what you believe to be right."

Mrs. Hooker went on to explain the political difficulties of the State by State road to National Woman Suffrage.

President Wilson seemed very little impressed by these facts. "Every good thing," he said, "takes a great deal of hard work."

Mrs. Hooker made a very strong point of the indefensible behavior of the House Judiciary Committee in blocking the Suffrage Amendment and refusing to allow the representatives of the people an opportunity to vote upon it. "Whatever one may think of Woman Suffrage," she said, "tying the Amendment up this way before an election is wrong; and the blame will fall squarely on the Democratic Party."

"You must see the members of the Judiciary Committee about that," said the President, with a considerable tactical skill. "I do not think I should interfere with the action of a Committee of Congress."

"Have you never done it before, Mr. President?" asked Mrs. Hooker. The President explained that he had done it only under pressure of a national emergency.

The interview lasted about half an hour. The President's manner was kindly and friendly, but he made it very plain that he interpreted the Democratic platform plank to mean the limitation of the Suffrage movement to State activities, and that he was still opposed to the Federal Suffrage Amendment.

Later, Mrs. Field replied to the President's letter:

I am sorry to have to tell you that not only is the platform declaration not acceptable to me, and to hundreds of thousands of voting women of the West, but that we also greatly deprecate the interpretation which you gave of this plank to Mrs. D. E. Hooker of Richmond.

It is my sincere hope as a Democratic woman that you will not allow any menace to the Democratic Party in the fall election through your unwillingness to face the desire of the West for speedy action upon the Susan B. Anthony Amendment.

On July 3, a delegation representing the Woman's National Democratic League, composed, according to the

Washington Times, of some of the most distinguished ladies of the Congressional and official sets, went to inform the President that the League had raised a thousand dollars as a contribution towards his re-election. Afterwards, Mrs. F. B. Moran, a grand-niece of Martha Washington, and it may be almost unnecessary to state, a member of the Congressional Union, requested a five minute interview with the President.

Mrs. Moran said:

I am really afraid for my Party. The women in the West are far superior to us. They have power, and they know how to use it. There are four million of them, and they are heartily in favor of the Federal Suffrage Amendment because they do not wish to be disfranchised when they pass beyond the limits of their own State. It is not a question of their threatening us. It is a question of our realizing what they are going to do. You can get the Suffrage Amendment through Congress, and, if you do not do it, these women will regard you as responsible.

President Wilson said, in answer, that he could not interfere with the action of Congress. He believed that Suffrage should be established on the secure foundation of separate State action. " You should work from the bottom up, not from the top down," the President said. " Women should be patient, and continue to work in the admirable way they have worked in the past."

On July 4, President Wilson reviewed a Labor parade in connection with the laying of the corner-stone of the Labor Temple of the American Federation of Labor in Washington, D. C., and at its close he addressed the marchers. He had just declared that he stood for the interests of all classes, when Mabel Vernon, who sat on the platform a few feet away, called in a voice which has a notably clear, ringing quality, " Mr. President, if you sincerely desire to forward the interests of all the people, why do you oppose the national enfranchisement of women? "

The President answered, " That is one of the things which we will have to take counsel over later."

When the President was closing his speech, Mabel Vernon called again; " Answer, Mr. President, why do you oppose the national enfranchisement of women? "

The President did not answer.

The Secret Service men with almost an exquisite courtesy gently hurried Miss Vernon away.

On July 24, another deputation of prominent Democratic women called on the President. The deputation included Mrs. George W. Lamont, Harriot Stanton Blatch, Mina Van Winkle, Helen Todd. I quote the *Suffragist:*

Mrs. Lamont, who introduced the group to President Wilson, said: " I have come to you, Mr. President, as a Democratic woman. I used to be first a Democrat and then a Suffragist; now I am a Suffragist first." She asked the President if he realized how painful a position he created for Democratic women when he opposed the enfranchisement of their sex and forced them to chose between their Party allegiance and their loyalty to women throughout the nation.

Mrs. Blatch told President Wilson of the strength of the sentiment for Woman Suffrage she had found in the West on her recent trip in the Suffrage Special through the equal Suffrage States and of the extraordinary difficulties she had experienced in her own life trying to win Suffrage by amending the constitution of her State.

" I am sixty years old, Mr. President," said Mrs. Blatch, " I have worked all my life for Suffrage; and I am determined that I will never again stand up on the street corners of a great city appealing to every Tom, Dick, and Harry for the right of self-government. When we work for a Federal Amendment, we are dealing at last with men who understand what we are talking about and can speak to us in our tongue. We are not asking for an easy way to win the vote. It is not easy to amend the United States Constitution. We are asking for a dignified way; and we ought to be able to rely on the chivalry of our representatives, particularly of the southern representatives, to accord to women a self-respecting method of working out their enfranchisement."

Miss Helen Todd told the President of her experience in a State campaign in Texas, when Democratic members of the Legislature refused to submit the question to the voters, saying bluntly that they controlled eleven votes in the upper house and that those eleven could keep the Suffrage Amendment " tied up " indefinitely. " Women go to Democrats in Congress and are told they must appeal to State Legislatures. They go to Democratic State Legislatures, who refuse to allow the electors of their own State to vote upon the question at all. " What are women to do, Mr. President? " said Miss Todd, " when they are played with in this cat and mouse fashion? "

The interview was in many respects interesting. President Wilson did not mention the States' rights formula. He said he was unable to help the Suffrage Amendment in Congress because his Party was opposed to it. It was the President's theory, he explained, that a Party leader should not go so far in advance of his adherents as to withdraw himself from them, and make united action impossible upon the other issues before the country.

The impression was strongly conveyed, however, that this opposition from the President's Party was not necessarily permanent. " In four years, or in two years," said Mr. Wilson, impressively but vaguely, " the situation might be different. At present many members of the Democratic Party are opposed to Woman Suffrage on account of the negro question." " But," said one of his visitors, " if women were given the vote throughout the United States the percentage of the white vote to the negro vote would be increased." " You have not explained that to the men in Congress," President Wilson said.

In answer to the statement that the Democratic Party would lose the support of women in the West and therefore of western electoral votes if they persisted in opposing women's national enfranchisement, President Wilson said he did not believe women would vote in a national election on the Suffrage issue. " If they did that," said Mr. Wilson, with superb and quite unconscious insolence, " they would not be as intelligent as I think they are."

The women came away from this meeting convinced that the President would do nothing for the Federal Amendment.

On September 8, however, President Wilson spoke at Atlantic City before a Convention of the National American Woman Suffrage Association. It was the first time he had ever addressed a Suffrage meeting. That was, of course, in itself, significant. I quote the *Suffragist:*

I have found it a real privilege to be here tonight and to listen to the address which you have heard. Though you may not all of you believe it, I would a great deal rather hear some one else speak than speak myself, but I should feel that I was omitting a duty if I did not address you tonight and say some of the things that have been in my thoughts as I realized the approach of this evening and the duty that would fall upon me.

The astonishing thing about this movement which you represent is not that it has grown so slowly, but that it has grown so rapidly. No doubt for those who have been a long time in the struggle, like your honored president, it seems a long and arduous path that has been trodden, but when you think of the cumulating force of this movement in recent decades, you must agree with me that it is one of the most astonishing tides in modern history.

Two generations ago, no doubt, Madam President will agree with me in saying it was a handful of women who were fighting this cause. Now it is a great multitude of women who are fighting it. And there are some interesting historical connections which I would like to attempt to point out to you. One of the most striking facts about the history of the United States is that at the outset it was a lawyer's history.

There was a time when nobody but a lawyer could know enough to run the government of the United States, and a distinguished English publicist once remarked, speaking of the complexity of the American government, that it was no proof of the excellence of the American Constitution that it had been successfully operated, because the American could run any constitution. But there have been a great many technical difficulties in running it.

And then something happened. A great question arose in this country which, though complicated with legal elements, was at the bottom a human question, and nothing but a question of humanity. That was the slavery question, and is it not significant that it was then, and then for the first time, that women became prominent in politics in America? Not many women. Those prominent in that day are so few that you can almost name them over in a brief catalogue, but nevertheless, they then began to play a part in writing not only, but in public speech, which was a very novel part for women to play in America; and after the Civil War had settled some of what seemed the most difficult legal questions of our system, the life of the nation began not only to unfold but to accumulate.

Life in the United States was a comparatively simple matter at the time of the Civil War. There was none of that underground struggle which is now so manifest to those who look only a little way beneath the surface. Stories such as Dr. Davis has told tonight were uncommon in those simpler days.

The pressure of low wages, the agony of obscure and unremunerated toil did not exist in America in anything the same proportions that they exist now. And as our life has unfolded and accumulated, as the contacts of it have become hot, as the populations have assembled in the cities, and the cool spaces of the country have been supplanted by the feverish urban areas, the whole nature of our political questions has been altered. They have ceased to be legal questions. They have more and more become social questions—questions with regard to the relations of human beings to one another—not merely their legal relations, but their moral and spiritual relations to one another.

And this has been most characteristic of American life in the last few decades, and as these questions have assumed greater and greater prominence, the movement which this association represents has gathered cumulative force. So that if anybody asks himself, "What does this gathering force mean?" if he knows anything about the history of the country, he knows that it means something that has not only come to stay, but has come with conquering power.

I get a little impatient sometimes about the discussion of the channels and methods by which it is to prevail. It is going to prevail, and that is a very superficial and ignorant view of it which attributes it to mere social unrest. It is not merely because the women are discontented. It is because the women have seen visions of duty, and that is something which we not only cannot resist, but, if we be true Americans, we do not wish to resist.

So that what we have to realize in dealing with forces of this sort is that we are dealing with the substance of life itself.

I have felt as I sat here tonight the wholesome contagion of the occasion. Almost every other time that I ever visited Atlantic City I came to fight somebody. I hardly know how to conduct myself when I have not come to fight against anybody, but with somebody. I have come to suggest, among other things, that when the forces of nature are steadily working and the tide is rising to meet the moon, you need not be afraid that it will not come to its flood.

We feel the tide: we rejoice in the strength of it and we shall not quarrel in the long run as to the method of it. Because, when you are working with masses of men and organized bodies of opinion, you have got to carry the organized body along.

The whole art and practice of government consists, not in moving individuals, but in moving masses. It is all very well to run ahead and beckon, but, after all, you have got to wait for the mass to follow. I have not come to ask you to be patient, because you have been, but I have come to congratulate you that tnere was a force behind you that will, beyond any peradventure, be triumphant and for which you can afford a little while to wait.

This speech is, of course, often exquisitely phrased. However, it promised nothing. The Woman's Party was not deceived by it.

It is to be seen that President Wilson was moving—slowly, to be sure; one cautious foot carefully planted before the other cautious foot moved—in the right direction. He had progressed a measurable distance from the man who just after his inauguration admitted he had never considered the subject of Suffrage. However, he still held to his idea of the " State-by-State " progress for the enfranchisement of women. But he was to change even in that, as will subsequently be seen.

VII

THE SECOND APPEAL TO WOMEN VOTERS

On August 10, 11, and 12, of 1916, the newly formed National Woman's Party held a conference at the Hotel Antlers in Colorado Springs, to formulate a policy for the coming presidential campaign.

In Washington, Senators and Representatives read avidly the newspaper accounts of this convention.

Politically, it was a tremendously impressive gathering. Prominent women came from all the Western States to decide how they should endeavor to mobilize the women's votes. Greatly alarmed at this drifting away of members, the Democratic Party sent prominent Democratic women to plead with them not to leave the Party and to represent to them that Peace was more important than Suffrage. The Republicans sent important Republican women to plead with them to give their support to Hughes since he had come out for the Federal Suffrage Amendment.

Finally the Democratic leaders appealed to the President to counteract the attacks being made on the Party, on the score of its Suffrage record. The President, thereupon, despatched to the Thomas Jefferson Club of Denver the following letter which was read at a banquet the last day of the Conference.

THE WHITE HOUSE,
WASHINGTON, D. C., August 7, 1916.

MY DEAR FRIENDS:

I wish I could meet you face to face and tell you in person how deeply I appreciate the work your organization has done and proposes to do for the cause of democracy and popular government.

I am told that yours was the first woman's Democratic voters' organization in America, and I am sure that as such it must have

175

been the instrument of impressing your convictions very deeply upon the politics of your State.

One of the strongest forces behind the Equal Suffrage sentiment of the country is the now demonstrated fact that in the Suffrage States women interest themselves in public questions, study them thoroughly, form their opinions and divide as men do concerning them. It must in frankness be admitted that there are two sides to almost every important public question, and even the best informed persons are bound to differ in judgment concerning it. With each difference in judgment, it is not only natural, but right and patriotic, that the success of opposing convictions should be sought through political alignment and the measuring of their strength at the polls through political agencies. Men do this naturally, and so do women; though it has required your practical demonstration of it to convince those who doubted this. In proportion as the political development of women continues along this line, the cause of Equal Suffrage will be promoted.

Those who believe in Equal Suffrage are divided into those who believe that each State should determine for itself when and in what direction the Suffrage should be extended, and those who believe that it should be immediately extended by the action of the national government, by means of an amendment to the Federal Constitution. Both the great political Parties of the nation have in their recent platforms favored the extension of Suffrage to women through State action, and I do not see how their candidates can consistently disregard these official declarations. I shall endeavor to make the declaration of my own Party in this matter effectual by every influence that I can properly and legitimately exercise.

Woman's part in the progress of the race, it goes without saying, is quite as important as man's. The old notion, too, that Suffrage and service go hand in hand, is a sound one, and women may well appeal to it, though it has long been invoked against them. The war in Europe has forever set at rest the notion that nations depend in time of stress wholly upon their men. The women of Europe are bearing their full share of war's awful burden in the daily activities of the struggle, and more than their share as sufferers. Their fathers and husbands and sons are fighting and dying in the trenches; but they have taken up the work on the farms, at the mill, and in the workshop and counting houses. They bury the dead, care for the sick and wounded, console the fatherless, and sustain the constant shock of war's appalling sacrifices.

From these hideous calamities we in this favored land of ours
have thus far been shielded. I shall be profoundly thankful, if,
consistently with the honor and integrity of the nation, we may
maintain to the end our peaceful relations with the world.
Cordially and sincerely yours,
WOODROW WILSON.
To the officers and members of the
Jane Jefferson Club of Colorado.

The Woman's Party did not care for whom the women
cast their protest vote—Republicans, Socialists, Prohibitionists—they cared only that women should not vote for the
Democrats. They knew if this protest vote was large
enough, whoever was elected would realize that opposition
to Suffrage was inexpedient.

At Colorado Springs the National Woman's Party passed
the following resolutions:

Resolved that the National Woman's Party, so long as the
opposition of the Democratic Party continues, pledges itself to
use its best efforts in the twelve States where women vote for
President to defeat the Democratic candidate for President; and
in the eleven States where women vote for members of Congress
to defeat the candidates of the Democratic Party for Congress.

Immediately the campaign began. It was the biggest campaign—the most important ever waged by the Woman's
Party. A stream of organizers started for the Western
States to prepare the way for the speakers. How hard, and
how long, and how intensively these girl organizers worked
will never be known because, in the very nature of things,
there could be no adequate record of their efforts. Then
came a stream of speakers, relay after relay—convinced,
informed, experienced—and inspired. Among them were
Harriot Stanton Blatch, Sara Bard Field, Ida Finney Mackrille, Mrs. William Kent, Mrs. H. O. Havemeyer, Helen
Todd, Maud Younger, Rose Winslow, Gail Laughlin. The
brilliant, beautiful Inez Milholland Boissevain, doomed soon
to die so untimely but so glorious a death, was appointed
special flying envoy to make a twelve mile swing through

the twelve western Equal Suffrage States; to bring to the enfranchised women of the West an appeal for help from the disfranchised women of the East.

The campaign of 1916 was characterized by the swiftness of attack and efficiency of method which characterized the campaign of 1914, but it was carried out on a much larger scale. In Washington, Headquarters boiled . . . bubbled . . . seethed. . . .

From Washington there sifted into the West tons of campaign literature: miles of purple, white, and gold banners; acres of great across-the-street streamers. In the West itself, Woman's Party speakers addressed every kind of meeting known to our civilization: indoor meetings; outdoor meetings; luncheons; banquets; labor unions, business men's organizations; in churches, factories, theatres; at mining camps, county fairs. They took advantage of impromptu meetings in the streets; small ready-made meetings at clubs; large advertised mass-meetings. And Inez Milholland's activities as a flying envoy—and in that, her last fight she did fly—were the climax of it all.

The slogan of the Wilson party was, " He kept us out of war." The slogan of the Woman's Party developed, " He kept us out of Suffrage."

The Democrats, remembering the results of the campaign of 1914, were far from indulgent of this small army, the members of which were all generals.

In Denver, Elsie Hill the Woman's Party organizer was arrested and hurried to the police station in a patrol wagon. The only charge against her was that she had distributed literature telling the Democratic record on Suffrage.

In Colorado Springs, the Federal Amendment banner was " arrested " and locked up for the night in jail.

In Chicago, described by the *Chicago Tribune* as the " pivotal point of the 1916 election," this hostility was much more violent. The day that Wilson spoke there a hundred women, some of them carrying inscribed banners, stationed themselves at the entrance to the auditorium where he was to appear. They were attacked by groups of men, who tore their banners out of their hands, and demolished them. Several women were thrown to the ground, and one, still clinging to the banner, was dragged across the street.

This was followed by an attack upon Minnie E. Brooke, one of the Woman's Party speakers. She was alone, walking quietly down Michigan Boulevard. She had a small purple, white, and gold flag in her hand, and was wearing the regalia of the Woman's Party. Suddenly two men darted up to her, and tried to tear her colors away. In the struggle she was thrown down and would have fallen in front of an automobile had not a hotel employee run to her assistance.

However, in the out-of-way country places in the Western States, the Woman's Party speakers were received with that hearty hospitality, that instant and instinctive chivalry, which marks the West. In this campaign, they made a point of appearing in the State and County Fairs which characterized the late summer and early fall months.

On Frontier Day, at the Douglas County Grange at Castle Rock, Colorado, Elsie Hill spoke—to a grandstand crowded with people—between the end of the relay race (in which the riders changed horses and saddles) and the beginning of the steer-roping contest. On the stand were massed men, women, and children. Just over the fence crowded hundreds of cowboys and farmers.

Street processions also characterized this campaign. At night in Salt Lake City occurred an extraordinary parade— a river of yellow. The squad of mounted policemen who headed the procession wore the purple, white, and gold regalia of the Woman's Party. Marching women carried lighted yellow Japanese lanterns. The people who filled the automobiles carried yellow lanterns. The huge Amendment banner was yellow. Yellow banners were strung across the streets.

Billboards and posters appeared everywhere which adjured voters not to support Wilson or any Democratic candidates for Congress. In Tucson and Prescott, Arizona, these great banners were surreptitiously cut down. In California, the Democrats placed counter placards beside these disturbing posters. In San Francisco, armed patrols guarded the two conflicting posters in one hotel lobby.

The Woman's Party speakers took advantage of all kinds of situations. In one town, Maud Younger found that a circus had arrived just ahead of her. There was no adequate hall for a meeting; and so the circus men offered her their tent; they even megaphoned her meeting for her. In another town, a County Fair was being held. Maud Younger appealed to the clowns to give her a chance to speak, and they let her have their platform and the spot-light while they were changing costumes. In San Francisco, Hazel Hunkins scattered thousands of leaflets from an aeroplane flying over the city. Red Lodge, Montana, sent to the train, which brought Abby Scott Baker to them, a delegation of members of the Grand Army of the Republic, the leader bearing a large American flag. They conducted her in state through the town to the hall where she was to speak.

Perhaps no campaign was more interesting than that of Rose Winslow in Arizona. Vivian Pierce, whose experienced newspaper hand on the *Suffragist* helped to make that paper the success it so swiftly became, thus describes her work:

Rose Winslow represented the workers. She spoke for the exploited women in Eastern industry. In her own person to her audiences she typified her story of those imprisoned in factories and slums, unable to fight their own battles. Her words had the authenticity of an inspired young evangelist. She herself had come up out of that darkness; and the men of the mines and lumber camps, the women of the remote Arizona towns, listened to her with tears pouring down their faces. One does not see Eastern audiences so moved. At Winslow . . . this girl, pleading for working women, the most exploited class in industry, appealed to the men of the great Santa Fé railroad shops that animate the life of that remote region on the edge of the " Painted Desert." Rose Winslow had been warned that if she spoke at this town, she would be " mobbed " by the Wilson Democrats. After her impassioned story, told one noon hour, the men of the shops crowded around this young woman from the East, " one of our own people," as one man said, and asked her what they could do for the women of the East. . . .

In the remote copper camps around Jerome and Bisbee, the story of the industrial workers who have merely asked for a chance to help themselves, made a deep impression on the foreign-born voters of this section. There were Poles, Finns, and Lithuanians in the great audience held in that copper town that is the working-man's annex to Bisbee. That audience both laughed and cried with Rose Winslow, and then crowded around to greet her in her own language.

From the vividly colored fastness of the miners' villages in this wild mountain region, to border towns like Nogales, though but a short step geographically, the temper and character of the cities change. . . . In places like Nogales, the soldiers who could not go home to vote turned the Woman's Party meetings into near-riots, so anxious were these victims of a peace adminis-tration to hear what the ladies had to say about Wilson. The soldiers registered their approval by helping take up collections, though even the provost guard could not remove them to give space to citizens able to register their protests.

An event equally picturesque marked the closing of the campaign on the night of Sunday, November 5, on the plat-form of the Blackstone Theatre, Chicago. There, Harriot Stanton Blatch, acting as the spokesman of the disfran-chised women of the East, called up by long-distance tele-phone a series of mass-meetings, one in each of the twelve Suffrage States and repeated their message — a final appeal to the women voters of the West to cast their ballots on the following Tuesday against President Wilson.

The result of the election is summed up in the *Suffragist* of November 11:

In Illinois, the only State where the vote of women is counted separately, over seventy thousand more women voted against Mr. Wilson than for him. . . .

The reports indicate that the Woman's Party campaign was as successful in holding the woman's vote in line in the other eleven States as in Illinois. While ten of these States went for Wilson, they did not do so, as has been claimed, by the woman's

182

vote. Mr. Wilson received in these States almost the solid Labor vote, the Progressive, and the farmer's vote. The popular majority which Mr. Wilson received in the twelve Suffrage States amounted only to twenty-two thousand one hundred seventy-one out of a popular vote, according to the latest returns, of more than four million, eight hundred and ten thousand in the same States. This does not include the Socialist and Prohibition vote, which was very heavy in some of the Western States. . . .

We were not concerned with the result of the election. Ours was a campaign in which it made no difference who was elected. We did not endorse any candidate. We did not care who won. We were not pro-Republican, pro-Socialist, pro-Prohibition—we were simply pro-woman. We did not endeavor to affect the result in the non-Suffrage States. What we did try to do was to organize a protest vote by women against Mr. Wilson's attitude towards Suffrage. This we did. Every Democrat who campaigned in the West knows this. The Democratic campaign in the West soon consisted almost entirely of an attempt to combat the Woman's Party attack.

Tribute to the strength of the Woman's Party campaign is contained in the remark of a woman who had in charge the campaign of the Democratic women voters. Out of six leaflets which her organization got out, five were on the subject of Suffrage. A reporter remonstrated with her in regard to Suffrage not being an issue in the West. She agreed with him, but, she added, " We have to combat the Woman's Party."

The whole Western campaign of the Republicans was conducted as if they were assured of victory. In many cases the organizers of the Woman's Party told the Republicans in the East that they were going to lose in certain districts. "Nonsense," laughed the Republicans, "we are sure to win there, absolutely sure." Alice Paul in Chicago received reports from campaigners through the West and all predicted Democratic victory. She went to Republican Headquarters with these reports, but she could not convince the Republicans of the truth of them.

Senator Curtis, Secretary of the Republican Senatorial Committee, said he got more information as to the situation in the West from the Woman's Party than he got from any other source.

It became apparent soon that Wilson was going to win. It was then that advisors came to Alice Paul and said, "Withdraw your speakers from the campaign, so that you will not have the humiliation of defeat before the country."

And it was then that Alice Paul answered, "No. *If we withdraw our speakers from the campaign, we withdraw the issue from the campaign. We must make this such an important thing in national elections that the Democrats will not want to meet it again.*"

Commenting on this campaign, Alice Paul said the Democrats made a strong appeal to the women voters but for the Republicans the women did not exist, and in fact the chief recognition that the Republicans made of the women in the West was to send there the Hughes so-called "Golden Special," which, on leaving Chicago, announced that it was *not* a "Suffrage Special."

After the campaign was over, Vance McCormick, Chairman of the Democratic Party, was talking with a member of his committee. He said, in effect: "Before the election of 1918, we must patch up our weak places. Our weakest spot is the Suffrage situation. We must get rid of the Suffrage Amendment before 1918 if we want to control the next Congress."

The Sixty-fourth Congress met for its second and last session on December 4, 1916. President Wilson delivered a message which made no reference to the subject of Woman Suffrage. The Congressional Union, always having advance information, knew this beforehand. And so on that occasion, by a bit of direct action, they brought Suffrage vividly to the attention of President Wilson, Congress, and the whole country. This was the only action of the Woman's Party which Alice Paul did not give out beforehand to the press.

Early that morning, before the outer doors were opened,

five women of the Congressional Union appeared before the Capitol. After a long wait the doors were opened, and— the first of a big crowd—they placed themselves in the front row of the gallery just to the left of the big clock. They faced the Speaker's desk, from which the President would read his message. These five women were: Mrs. John Rogers, Jr.; Mrs. Harry Lowenburg; Dr. Caroline Spencer; Florence Bayard Hilles; Mabel Vernon. In a casual manner, other members of the Union seated themselves behind them and on the gallery steps beside them: Lucy Burns; Elizabeth Papandre; Mildred Gilbert; Mrs. William L. Colt; Mrs. Townsend Scott.

Mabel Vernon sat in the middle of the five women in the front row. Pinned to her skirt, under the enveloping cape which she wore, was a big banner of yellow sateen. After the five women had settled themselves, Mabel Vernon unpinned the banner and dropped it, all ready for unrolling, on the floor. At the top of the banner were five long tapes —too long—Mabel Vernon now regretfully declares. At the psychological moment, which had been picked beforehand, in President Wilson's speech—he was recommending a greater freedom for the Porto Rican men—Mabel Vernon whispered the series of signals which had previously been decided on. Immediately—working like a beautifully co-ordinated machine—the five women stooped, lifted the banner, and, holding it tightly by the tapes, dropped it over the balcony edge. It unrolled with a smart snap and displayed these words:

MR. PRESIDENT, WHAT WILL YOU DO FOR
WOMAN SUFFRAGE?

Then the women sat perfectly still, in the words of the *Washington Post* " five demure and unruffled women . . . with the cords supporting the fluttering thing clenched in their hands."

The effect was instantaneous. The President looked up, hesitated a moment, then went on reading. All the Con-

INEZ MILHOLLAND.
In the Washington Parade, March 3, 1913.

gressmen turned. The Speaker sat motionless. A buzz ran wildly across the floor. Policemen and guards headed upstairs to the gallery where the women were seated; but their progress was inevitably slow as the steps were tightly packed with members of the Congressional Union. In the meantime, one of the pages, leaping upward, caught the banner and tore it away from the cords in the women's hands. " It it hadn't been for those long tapes," Mabel Vernon says, " they never could have got it until the President finished his speech."

The episode took up less than five minutes' time. Until the President finished his message, it seemed to be completely forgotten. But the instant the President with his escort disappeared through the door, every Congressman was on his feet staring up at the gallery.

The Woman's Party publicity accounts of this episode— multigraphed the night before—were in the hands of the men in the Press Gallery the instant after it happened. This is a sample of the perfect organization and execution of the Woman's Party plans.

Of course, this incident was a front page story in every newspaper in the United States that night despoiling the President of his headlines. It is now one of the legends in Washington that in the midst of the dinner given to the President by the Gridiron Club shortly after, the identical banner was unfurled before his eyes.

The following week, at the first meeting of the Judiciary Committee since the Presidential Campaign, the report of the Federal Suffrage Amendment was made without recommendation to the House of Representatives.

VIII

HAIL AND FAREWELL

TO INEZ MILHOLLAND BOISSEVAIN

'For Lycidas is dead, dead ere his prime;
Young Lycidas, and hath not left his peer."
—MILTON.

Inez, vibrant, courageous, symbolic,
How can death claim you?
Many he leads down the long halls of silence
Burdened with years,
Those who have known sorrow
And are weary with forgetting,
The young who have tasted only gladness
And who go with wistful eyes,
Never to see the sharp breaking of illusion.
For these—
We who remain and are lonely
Find consolation, saying
" They have won the white vistas of quietness."

But for you—
The words of my grief will not form
In a pattern of resignation.
The syllables of rebellion
Are quivering upon my lips!
You belonged to life—
To the struggling actuality of earth;
You were our Hortensia and flung
Her challenge to the world—
Our world still strangely Roman—
" Does justice scorn a woman? "

Oh! Between her words and yours the centuries seem
Like little pauses in an ancient song,
For in the hour of war's discordant triumph
You both demanded " Peace "!

187

And I, remembering how the faces of many women
Turned toward you with passionate expectation,
How can I find consolation?

Inez, vibrant, courageous, symbolic,
Can death still claim you?
When in the whitening winter of our grief
Your smile with all the radiance of spring,
When from the long halls of silence
The memory of your voice comes joyously back
To the ears of our desolation—
Your voice that held a challenge and a caress.
You have gone—
Yet you are ours eternally!
Your gallant youth,
Your glorious self-sacrifice—all ours!
Inez, vibrant, courageous, symbolic,
Death cannot claim you!

RUTH FITCH.
The Suffragist, December 30, 1916.

THE most poignant event—and perhaps the most beautiful
in all the history of the Congressional Union—took place
on Christmas Day of this year, the memorial service in
memory of Inez Milholland.

Inez Milholland was one of the human sacrifices offered on
the altar of woman's liberty. She died that other women
might be free.

In the recent campaign, she had spoken in Wyoming,
Idaho, Oregon, Washington, Montana, Utah, Nevada, and
California. In her memorial address, Maud Younger said:

The trip was fraught with hardship. Speaking day and night,
she would take a train at two in the morning, to arrive at eight;
and then a train at midnight, to arrive at five in the morning.
She would come away from audiences and droop as a flower.
The hours between were hours of exhaustion and suffering.
She would ride in the trains gazing from the windows, listless,
almost lifeless, until one spoke; then again the sweet smile, the
sudden interest, the quick sympathy. The courage of her was
marvelous.

At a great mass-meeting at Los Angeles, in October, she was saying—in answer to the President's words, "The tide is rising to meet the moon; you will not have long to wait," —"How long must women wait for liberty?" On the word *liberty*, she fell fainting to the floor. Within a month, she was dead.

That Christmas Day, Statuary Hall in the Capitol of the United States was transformed. The air was full of the smells of the forest. Greens made a background—partially concealing the semi-circle of statues—at the rear; laurel and cedar banked the dais in front; somber velvet curtains fell about its sides. Every one of the chairs which filled the big central space supported a flag of purple, white, and gold. Between the pillars of the balcony hung a continuous frieze; pennants of purple, white, and gold—the tri-color of these feminist crusaders.

The audience assembled in the solemn quiet proper to such an occasion, noiselessly took their seats in the semi-circle below and the gallery above. The organ played *Ave Maria*. Then again, a solemn silence fell.

Suddenly the stillness was invaded by a sound—music, very faint and faraway. It grew louder and louder. It was the sound of singing. It came nearer and nearer. It was the voices of boys. Presently the beginning of a long line of boy choristers, who had wound through the marble hallway, appeared in the doorway. They marched into the hall chanting:

> " Forward, out of error,
> Leave behind the night,
> Forward through the darkness,
> Forward into light."

Behind came Mary Morgan in white, carrying a golden banner with the above words inscribed on it. This was a duplicate of the banner that Inez Milholland bore in the first Suffrage parade in New York. Behind the golden banner came a great procession of young women wearing straight surplices; the first division in purple, the next in white, the last in gold, carrying high standards which bore the tri-color. Before each division came another young girl in white, carrying a golden banner—lettered.

One banner said:

GREATER LOVE HATH NO MAN THAN THIS THAT HE
LAY DOWN HIS LIFE FOR A FRIEND

Another banner said:

WITHOUT EXTINCTION IS LIBERTY, WITHOUT
RETROGRADE IS EQUALITY

The last banner said:

AS HE DIED TO MAKE MEN HOLY LET US DIE
TO MAKE MEN FREE

These white-clad girls stood in groups on both sides of the laurel-covered dais against the shadowy background of the curtains. The standard-bearers in the purple, the white, the gold, formed a semi-circle of brilliant color which lined the hall and merged with the purple, white, and gold frieze above them. They stood during the service, their tri-colored banners at rest.

There followed music. The choristers sang: *Forward Be Our Watchword.* The Mendelssohn Quartet sang: *Love Divine* and *Thou Whose Almighty Word.* Elizabeth Howry sang first *All Through the Night* and, immediately after, Henchel's ringing triumphant *Morning Song.* It is an acoustic effect of Statuary Hall that the music seems to come from above. That effect added immeasurably to the solemnity of this occasion.

Tribute speeches followed, Anne Martin introducing the speakers. Mrs. William Kent read two resolutions: one prepared under the direction of Zona Gale, the other by Florence Brewer Boeckel. Maud Younger delivered a beautiful memorial address.

" And so ever through the West, she went," Miss Younger said in part, " through the West that drew her, the West that loved her, until she came to the end of the West. There where the sun goes down in glory in the vast Pacific, her life went out in glory in the shining cause of freedom. . . . They will tell of her in the West, tell of the vision of loveliness as she flashed through her last burning mission, flashed through to her death, a falling star in the western heavens. . . . With new devotion we go forth, inspired by her sacrifice to the end that this sacrifice be not in vain, but that dying she shall bring to pass that which living she could not achieve, full freedom for women, full democracy for the nation. . . ."

At the end the quartet sang, *Before the Heavens Were Spread Abroad.* Then the procession re-formed, and marched out again as it had come, a slow-moving band of color which gradually disappeared; a river of music which gradually died to a thread, to a sigh . . . to nothing. . . . As before the white-surpliced choristers headed the procession, chanting the recessional, *For All the Saints.* Their banners lowered, the girl standard-bearers—first those in floating gold, then those in drifting white, then those in heavy purple—followed. From the far-away reaches of the winding marble halls sounded the boyish voices. Faintly came:

> O, may Thy Soldiers, faithful, true and bold,
> Fight as the Saints who nobly fought of old,
> And win with them the victor's crown of gold.
> Alleluia!

And fainter still:

> But, lo, there breaks a yet more glorious day,
> The Saints triumphant rise in bright array.

The voices lost themselves in the distance, merged with silence. The audience still sat moveless, spellbound by all this beauty and grief. Suddenly the *Marseillaise* burst from the organ like a call to the new battle. Instantly, it was echoed by the strings.

On January 9, the President received a deputation of three hundred women. This deputation brought to him the resolutions passed at memorials held in commemoration of Inez Milholland from California to New York.

Sara Bard Field said in part:

Since that day (a year ago) when we came to you, Mr. President, one of our most beautiful and beloved comrades, Inez Milholland, has paid the price of her life for a cause. The untimely death of a young woman like this—a woman for whom the world has such bitter need—has focussed the attention of men and women of this nation on the fearful waste of women which this fight for the ballot is entailing. The same maternal instinct for the preservation of life—whether it be the physical life of a child, or the spiritual life of a cause—is sending women into this battle for liberty with an urge that gives them no rest night or day. Every advance of liberty has demanded its quota of human sacrifice, and, if I had time, I could show you that we have paid in a measure that is running over. In the light of Inez Milholland's death, as we look over the long backward trail through which we have sought our political liberty, we are asking, how long, how long, must this struggle go on?

Mr. President, to the nation more than to women themselves is this waste of maternal force significant. In industry, such a waste of money and strength would not be permitted. The modern trend is all towards efficiency. Why is such waste permitted in the making of a nation?

Sometimes I think it must be very hard to be a President, in respect to his contacts with people, as well as in the grave business he must perform. The exclusiveness necessary to a great dignitary holds him away from the democracy of communion necessary to full understanding of what the people are really thinking and desiring. I feel that this deputation today fails in its mission if, because of the dignity of your office and the formality of such an occasion, we fail to bring to you the throb of woman's desire for freedom and her eagerness to ally herself with all those activities to which you yourself have dedicated your life. When once the ballot is in her hand, those tasks which this nation has set itself to do are her tasks as well as man's. We women who are here today are close to this desire of woman. We cannot believe that you are our enemy, or are indifferent to the fundamental righteousness of our demand.

We have come here to you in your powerful office as our helper.

JOY YOUNG AT THE INEZ MILHOLLAND MEMORIAL
SERVICE.

We have come in the name of justice, in the name of democracy, in the name of all women who have fought and died for this cause, and in a peculiar way, with our hearts bowed in sorrow, in the name of this gallant girl who died with the word " Liberty " on her lips. We have come asking you this day to speak some favorable word to us, that we may know that you will use your good and great office to end this wasteful struggle of women.

The President replied:

Ladies, I had not been apprised that you were coming here to make any representation that would issue an appeal to me. I had been told that you were coming to present memorial resolutions with regard to the very remarkable woman whom your cause has lost. I therefore am not prepared to say anything further than I have said on previous occasions of this sort.

I do not need to tell you where my own convictions and my own personal purpose lie, and I need not tell you by what circumscriptions I am bound as leader of a Party. As the leader of a Party, my commands come from that Party, and not from private personal convictions.

My personal action as a citizen, of course, comes from no source, but my own conviction, and there my position has been so frequently defined, and I hope so candidly defined, and it is so impossible for me until the orders of my Party are changed, to do anything other than I am doing as a Party leader that I think nothing more is necessary to be said.

I do want to say this: I do not see how anybody can fail to observe from the utterance of the last campaign that the Democratic Party is more inclined than the opposition Party to assist in this great cause, and it has been a matter of surprise to me, and a matter of very great regret, that so many of those who are heart and soul for this cause seem so greatly to misunderstand and misinterpret the attitudes of Parties. In this country, as in every other self-governing country, it is really through the instrumentality of Parties that things can be accomplished. They are not accomplished by the individual voice, but by concentrated action, and that action must come only so fast as you can concert it. I have done my best, and shall continue to do my best to concert it in the interest of a cause in which I personally believe.

In Maud Younger's delightful *Revelations of a Woman Lobbyist*, in *McCall's Magazine*, she thus describes that scene:

The doors opened, and, surrounded by Secret Service men, President Wilson entered. He came quickly forward, smiling as he shook my hand. Contrary to the general impression, President Wilson has a very human, sympathetic personality. He is not the aloof, academic type one expects of a man who, avoiding people, gets much of his knowledge from books and reports. Though he appears to the general public as in a mist on a mountain top, like the gods of old, he is really a man of decided emotional reactions.

I answered his greeting briefly, giving him the resolutions I held, and presented Mrs. John Winters Brannan, who handed him the New York memorial without speaking at all. We were saving time for his declaration. Then came Sara—small, delicate Sara Bard Field, a woman of rare spirituality and humor—whom we had chosen to speak for us.

She began to talk very nobly and beautifully, while the President listened cordially. But suddenly a cold wave passed over him. Sara had quoted Mr. Hughes. At that name, the President's manner chilled. The look in his eyes became so cold that, as Sara says, the words almost froze on her lips. She finished in an icy stillness, and after a moment the President spoke.

Instead of the assurances we had expected, we heard words to the effect that he could not dictate to his Party. We must first concert public opinion. It was his last gleam, for, looking about him and seeing amazement, disappointment, indignation, he grew still colder. With a last defiant glance at us all he abruptly left the room. Secret Service men, newspaper men, and secretaries followed him. Where the President of the United States had been was now a closed door.

Stunned, talking in low, indignant tones, we moved slowly out of the East Room and returned to our Headquarters. There we discussed the situation. We saw that the President would do nothing for some time, perhaps not until the eve of the Presidential election in 1920. He said we must concert public opinion. But how? For half a century women had been walking the hard way of the lobbyist. We had had speeches, meetings, parades, campaigns, organization. What new method could we devise?

PART THREE
1917

I

THE PERPETUAL DELEGATION

ON THE PICKET LINE

The avenue is misty gray,
And here beside the guarded gate
We hold our golden blowing flags
And wait.

The people pass in friendly wise;
They smile their greetings where we stand
And turn aside to recognize
The just demand.

Often the gates are swung aside:
The man whose power could free us now
Looks from his car to read our plea—
And bow.

Sometimes the little children laugh;
The careless folk toss careless words,
And scoff and turn away, and yet
The people pass the whole long day
Those golden flags against the gray
And can't forget.

BEULAH AMIDON.
The Suffragist, March 3, 1917.

1. *The Peaceful Picketing*

BEFORE we examine the consideration which actuated the
National Woman's Party in waging the picket campaign of
1917, let us see where President Wilson stood at the beginning of the war; let us briefly recapitulate the steps which
brought him there.

It will be remembered that, shortly after the President took his seat in March, 1913, he told a deputation from the Congressional Committee that Suffrage was a question to which he had given no thought and on which he had no opinion. During the year, no longer stating that he knew nothing about Suffrage, he gave as a reason for inaction that the Congressional program was too crowded to consider it. By the end of the year, he had reached the point where he stated that he could take no action on the Suffrage Amendment until commanded by his Party.

In 1914, he continued to state that he was prohibited from acting because of being bound by his Party until June, when he seized on the excuse of States Rights further to explain his inaction. In the autumn of 1915 he first came out personally for Suffrage by voting for it in New Jersey but still refused to support it in Congress. His next step forward came in June, 1916, when he caused the *principle* of Suffrage to be recognized in the Party platform, though as yet neither he nor the Party had endorsed the Federal Amendment. In September of that same year—after the Woman's Party had begun its active campaign in the Suffrage States—the President took another step and addressed a Suffrage Convention of the National American Woman's Suffrage Association. But as yet he was not committed to the Federal Amendment, had not begun to exert pressure on Congress.

The situation of the President and the Woman's Party at this juncture may be summed up in this way. Wilson, himself, was beginning to realize that the Suffrage Amendment must ultimately pass. But he had just been re-elected. He was safe for four years; he could take his time about it. The Woman's Party on the other hand, realized that the President being safe for four years, no political pressure could be exerted upon him. They realized that they must devise other methods to keep Suffrage, as a measure demanding immediate enactment, before him.

In the meantime, a feeling of acute discontent was growing

in the women of the United States. The older women—
and they were the third generation to demand the vote—
were beginning to ask how long this period of entreaty must
be protracted. The younger women—the fourth generation
to demand the vote—were becoming impatient with the out-
worn methods of their predecessors. Moreover, when the
disfranchised women of the East visited the enfranchised
States of the West, their eyes were opened in a practical
way to the extraordinary injustice of their own disfranchisement. Equally, the enfranchised women of the West, moving to Eastern States, resented their loss of this political
weapon. On many women in America the militant movement
of England had produced a profound impression.

A new note had crept into the speeches made by the members of the Woman's Party—the note of this impatience and
resentment. It will be remembered that Mrs. Kent told the
President that the women voters of the West were accustomed to being listened to with attention by politicians, and
that they resented the effort to make it seem that they were
merely trying to bother a very busy official. Mrs. Blatch
had told him that the time had gone by when she would
stand on street corners and ask the vote from every Tom,
Dick, and Harry; that she was determined to appeal instead
to the men who spoke her own language and who had in
charge the affairs of the government.

Doris Stevens, in an interview in the *Omaha Daily News*
for June 29, 1919, voices perfectly what her generation was
feeling.

A successful young Harvard engineer said to me the other
day, " I don't believe you realize how much men objected to
your picketing the White House. Now I know what I'm talking
about. I've talked with men in all walks of life, and I tell you
they didn't approve of what you women did."

This last with warmer emphasis and a scowl of the brow. " I
don't suppose you were in a position to know how violently men
felt about it."

I listened patiently and courteously. Should I disillusion
him? I thought it was the honest thing to do. " Why, of course

WAGE EARNERS PICKETING THE WHITE HOUSE, FEBRUARY, 1917.

men didn't like it. Do you think we imagined they would? We knew they would disapprove. When *did men ever* applaud women fighting for their own liberty? We are approved only when we fight for yours!"

" You don't mean to say you planned to do something knowing men would not approve?"

I simply had to tell him, " Why, certainly! We're just beginning to get confidence in ourselves. At last we've learned to make and stand by our own judgments."

" But going to jail. That was pretty shocking."

" Yes, indeed it was. It not only shocked us that a government would be alarmed enough to do such a thing, but what was more to the point, it shocked the entire country into doing something quickly about Woman Suffrage."

It will be seen by the foregoing pages of this book that Suffragists had exhausted every form of Suffrage agitation known to the United States. In particular, they had sent to the President every kind of deputation that could possibly move him.

They decided to send him a perpetual deputation.

Alice Paul, in explanation of her strategy in this matter, uses one of the vivid figures that are so typical of her: " If a creditor stands before a man's house all day long, demanding payment of his bill, the man must either remove the creditor or pay the bill."

At first, the President tried to remove the creditor. Later he paid the bill.

At ten o'clock on January 10, 1917, the day after the deputation to the President, twelve women emerged from Headquarters and marched across Lafayette Square to the White House. Four of them bore lettered banners, and eight of them carried purple, white, and gold banners of the Woman's Party. They marched slowly—a banner's length apart. Six of them took up their stand at the East gate, and six of them at the West gate. At each gate—standing between pairs of women holding on high purple, white, and gold colors—two women held lettered banners.

One read:

MR. PRESIDENT WHAT WILL YOU DO FOR
WOMAN SUFFRAGE?

The other read:

HOW LONG MUST WOMEN WAIT FOR LIBERTY?

These were the first women to picket the White House.

The first picket line appeared on January 10, 1917; the last, over a year and a half later. Between those dates, except when Congress was not in session, more than a thousand women held lettered banners, accompanied by the purple, white, and gold tri-colors, at the White House gates, or in front of the Capitol. They picketed every day of the week, except Sunday; in all kinds of weather, in rain and in sleet, in hail, and in snow. All varieties of women picketed: all races and religions; all cliques and classes; all professions and parties. Washington became accustomed to the dignified picture—the pickets moving with a solemn silence, always in a line that followed a crack in the pavement; always a banner's length apart; taking their stand with a precision almost military; maintaining it with a movelessness almost statuesque. Washington became accustomed also to the rainbow splash at the White House gates—" like trumpet calls," somebody described the banners. Artists often spoke of the beauty of their massed color. In the daytime, those banners gilded by the sunlight were doubly brilliant, but at twilight the effect was transcendent. Everywhere the big, white lights—set in the parks on such low standards that they seemed strange, luminous blossoms, springing from the masses of emerald green shrubbery—filled the dusk with bluish-white splendor, and, made doubly colorful by this light, the long purple, white, and gold ribbon stood out against a back-ground beautiful and appropriate; a mosaic on the gray of the White House pavement; the pen-and-ink blackness of the White House iron work; the bare, brown crisscross of the White House trees, and the chaste colonial simplicity of the White House itself.

With her abiding instinct for pageantry and for telling picturesqueness of demonstration, Alice Paul soon punctuated the monotony of the picketing by special events. Various States celebrated State days on the picket line. Maryland was the first of these, and the long line of Maryland women bearing great banners, extended along Pennsylvania Avenue the entire distance from the East gate to the West gate. Pennsylvania Day, New York Day, Virginia Day, New Jersey Day, followed. The Monday of every week was set aside finally for District of Columbia Day.

The New York delegation carried on their banners phrases from President Wilson's book, *The New Freedom.*

LIBERTY IS A FUNDAMENTAL DEMAND OF THE HUMAN SPIRIT.

WE ARE INTERESTED IN THE UNITED STATES, POLITICALLY SPEAKING, IN NOTHING BUT HUMAN LIBERTY.

On College Day, thirteen colleges were represented, the biggest group from Goucher College, Baltimore. Then came Teachers' Day; Patriotic Day, and Lincoln Day. On Patriotic Day, one of the banners read:

DENMARK ON THE VERGE OF WAR GAVE WOMEN THE VOTE.

WHY NOT GIVE IT TO AMERICAN WOMEN NOW?

On Lincoln Day, they said:

WHY ARE YOU BEHIND LINCOLN?

AFTER THE CIVIL WAR WOMEN ASKED FOR POLITICAL FREEDOM.

THEY WERE TOLD TO WAIT—THIS WAS THE NEGRO'S HOUR.

IN 1917, AMERICAN WOMEN STILL ASK FOR FREEDOM.

WILL YOU, MR. PRESIDENT, TELL THEM TO WAIT—THAT THIS IS THE PORTO RICAN'S HOUR?

On Sunday, February 18, came Labor Day on the picket line. It was, of course, impossible for wage-earning women to picket the White House on any other day. They represented not only office workers, but factory workers from the great industrial centers. Many of them had come from other cities.

Susan B. Anthony's birthday, February 15, was celebrated impressively, although it rained and snowed heavily. Three new banners appeared that day. The first—big enough and golden enough even to suit that big, golden woman—bore quotations from Susan B. Anthony:

WE PRESS OUR DEMAND FOR THE BALLOT AT THIS TIME IN NO NARROW, CAPTIOUS, OR SELF-SEEKING SPIRIT, BUT FROM PUREST PATRIOTISM FOR THE HIGHEST GOOD OF EVERY CITIZEN, FOR THE SAFETY OF THE REPUBLIC, AND AS A GLORIOUS EXAMPLE TO THE NATIONS OF THE EARTH.

The second Susan B. Anthony banner said:

AT THIS TIME OUR GREATEST NEED IS NOT MEN OR MONEY, VALIANT GENERALS OR BRILLIANT VICTORIES, BUT A CONSISTENT NATIONAL POLICY BASED UPON THE PRINCIPLES THAT ALL GOVERNMENTS DERIVE THEIR JUST POWERS FROM THE CONSENT OF THE GOVERNED.

The third Susan B. Anthony banner said:

THE RIGHT OF SELF-GOVERNMENT FOR ONE-HALF OF ITS PEOPLE IS OF FAR MORE VITAL CONSEQUENCE TO THE NATION THAN ANY OR ALL OTHER QUESTIONS.

On March 2, 1917, the Congressional Union and its Western organization, the Woman's Party, met in joint convention and organized themselves into the National Woman's Party.

On that occasion, Alice Paul said:

We feel that by combining the Congressional Union and the Woman's Party we shall bring about a unity in organization which will make impossible duplication, difference of opinion, and divergence of method. By uniting we make, moreover, for unity of spirit in the whole Suffrage movement, bringing the voters and non-voters together in a movement in which they should both be integral parts.

The original purpose for which the Woman's Party, as an organization confined to women voters alone, was formed, has, we believe, been served. In the first three years of our work we endeavored to call the attention of political leaders and Congress to the fact that women were voting and that these voting women were interested in Suffrage. But words alone did not have much effect. We found we had to visualize the existence of voting women out in the West and their support of the Suffrage Amendment. The Woman's Party was formed as one means of doing this.

The Woman's Party did, I believe, have an effect on the political leaders. It was very clear, I think, at the convention in Chicago and in St. Louis that the idea that women were voting and that those women were interested in the Federal Amendment was at last appreciated. This November's election completed our work in getting that fact into the minds of Congressmen and political leaders. There is no longer any need to draw a line around women voters and set them off by themselves in order to call attention to them. They now enter into the calculations of every political observer.

If we amalgamate and make ourselves one great group of voters and non-voters all working for the Federal Amendment, the question arises: What name shall we be called by, the Congressional Union or the Woman's Party? Our Executive Committee felt that we ought to keep the name of the Woman's Party, because it stands for political power.

The objections brought against this are, I think, two. First, that non-voters should not, according to custom, be part of a political Party; second, that if they are included, that Party will not command as much respect as would a Party composed solely of voters. There are non-voters in the Socialist, the Progressive, and the Prohibition Parties; there is no reason why, if we are interested in precedent and custom, they should not be in our Party also. As to the second point: The Congressional Union has the reputation of being an active, determined, and well-financed organization. When the political world realizes that this young Woman's Party has been strengthened by the influx of twenty-five thousand workers of the Congressional Union ready to give their service and money it will consider that the Woman's Party stands for more power than if formed of the women of the Western States only.

All of us in the Congressional Union feel an affection for it. But that is no reason for continuing the organization. The Congressional Union has served a useful purpose, we believe. But now that we have created the Woman's Party we ought, it seems to me, to develop and make that the dominant Suffrage factor in this country because that, through its name and associations, throws the emphasis more than does the Congressional Union on the political power of women.

The following officers were elected unanimously at the morning session: Chairman of the National Woman's Party, Alice Paul; Vice-Chairman, Anne Martin; Secretary, Mabel Vernon; Treasurer, Gertrude Crocker. The executive board elected were: Lucy Burns, Mrs. O. H. P. Belmont, Mrs. J. W. Brannan, Mrs. Gilson Gardner, Abby Scott Baker, Mrs. William Kent, Maud Younger, Doris Stevens, Florence Bayard Hilles, Mrs. Donald Hooker, Mrs. J. A. H. Hopkins, and Mrs. Lawrence Lewis.

At that Convention, various resolutions were passed; the most notable in regard to the attitude of the National Woman's Party towards the rapidly developing war situation. That resolution runs as follows:

Whereas the problems involved in the present international situation, affecting the lives of millions of women in this country, make imperative the enfranchisement of women,

Be it resolved that the National Woman's Party, organized for the sole purpose of securing political liberty for women, shall continue to work for this purpose until it is accomplished, being unalterably convinced that in so doing the organization serves the highest interests of the country.

And be it further resolved that to this end we urge upon the President and the Congress of the United States the immediate passage of the National Suffrage Amendment.

It was decided to present these resolutions to the President. Shortly after, Dudley Field Malone, Collector of the

Port of New York, on behalf of the Woman's Party, informed the President that a deputation would visit him for that purpose.

This demonstration was not so much a protest at the failure of the first administration to pass the Anthony Amendment, or at the adjournment of Congress without passing it, as a presentation of the demands of the National Woman's Party immediately upon the opening of President Wilson's second term.

During the first three days in March, Washington filled steadily with inauguration crowds. When they got off the train, the Great Demand banner of the National Woman's Party confronted them, and girls handed them slips inviting them to the demonstration of the National Woman's Party at the White House on Inauguration Day and to the mass-meeting of the National Woman's Party to be held that night. Girls also stood in theatre lobbies, handing out more of these slips. Girls made the rounds of the government departments, handing out still more. Everywhere great posters said:

COME TO THE WHITE HOUSE ON MARCH 4.

COME IN THOUSANDS.

Inauguration Day dawned a day of biting wind and slashing rain.

Outside Headquarters was turmoil; inside a boiling activity. Hundreds of women were preparing to picket the White House. To accommodate them, a rubber company, hastily summoned, had commandeered one room and was selling rain-coats; tarpaulin hats; rubbers.

An extraordinary, a magnificent demonstration followed. To the music of several bands, nearly a thousand pickets circled the White House four times—a distance of four miles. Vida Milholland, the younger sister of Inez Milholland, marched at the head, carrying on a golden banner her sister's last words for Suffrage.

The Great Demand banner followed, carried by Mrs. Benton Mackaye:

WE DEMAND AN AMENDMENT TO THE CONSTITUTION OF THE UNITED STATES ENFRANCHISING WOMEN.

Beulah Amidon carried the Suffrage banner which Inez Milholland bore in the first Suffrage procession in New York:

> Forward, Out Of Darkness,
> Leave Behind The Night.
> Forward Out Of Error,
> Forward Into Light.

Behind there came hundreds of women bearing the purple, white, and gold. They were divided according to States; and before each division marched the State flag of the division. The drenching rain fell steadily. The pavements turned to shallow lakes, and the banners—their brilliancy accentuated by the wet—threw long, wavy reflections on the glassy, gray streets. They were of course expecting this demonstration at the White House, and, as though it were dangerous, unusual precautions had been taken against it. Every gate was locked. The Washington force of police officers, augmented by police from Baltimore and by squads of plain-clothes men, guarded the grounds without and within. Gilson Gardner said the President seemed to think the women were going to steal his grass roots.

There was no one at the locked gates to receive the women or the resolutions except the guards; these guards protested that they had not been ordered to receive either. The women visited every gate, but received the same answer. The cards of the leaders were finally handed over to a guard to present at the White House. He tried to deliver them, but was reprimanded for leaving his post, and sent back. Learning that the cards would be delivered at the end of the day, as is the custom with visiting-cards of casual visitors at the White House, the thousand pickets took up their march again.

Gilson Gardner wrote of this demonstration:

The weather gave this affair its character. Had there been fifteen hundred women carrying banners on a fair day, the sight would have been a pretty one. But to see a thousand women— young women, middle-aged and old women—and there were women in the line who had passed their three score and ten— marching in a rain that almost froze as it fell; to see them standing and marching and holding their heavy banners, momentarily growing heavier—holding them against a wind that was half gale—hour after hour, until their gloves were wet, their clothes soaked through; to see them later with hands sticky from the varnish from the banner poles—bare hands, for the gloves had by this time been pulled off, and the hands were blue with cold—to see these women keep their lines and go through their program fully, losing only those who fainted or fell from exhaustion, was a sight to impress even the dulled and jaded senses of one who has seen much.

One young woman from North Dakota I saw clinging to the iron pickets around the White House, her banner temporarily abandoned, fighting against what was to her a new feeling, faintness resulting from the pain in her hands. She was brought to the automobile in which I was riding before she actually fell to the ground; but after a short rest she was back in the line, and finished with the others.

There is no doubt that what Gilson Gardner said was true—the weather gave this affair its character.

People passing by, thrilled by the gallantry of the marchers, joined the procession. And as Gilson Gardner says, it was not because it was a pretty sight, or because these women were all young. Anna Norris Kendall of Wisconsin, seventy-two years old, and the Rev. Olympia Brown, eighty-two years old, one of the pioneer Suffragists of the country, both took part.

That day, a newly elected Congressman drove about Washington, showing the city to his wife. He had always

THE THOUSAND PICKETS TRY VAINLY TO DELIVER THEIR RESO-
LUTIONS TO THE PRESIDENT, MARCH 4, 1917.

A THOUSAND PICKETS MARCHING AROUND THE WHITE HOUSE,
MARCH 4, 1917.

been a Suffragist. She had always been an anti-Suffragist. The sudden sight of the thousand women marching in the rain not only converted her, but it produced such an effect on her she burst into tears.

Later, President Wilson sent a letter to the National Woman's Party, acknowledging the resolutions presented to him by the deputations of March 4, and concluded: " May I not once more express my sincere interest in the cause of Woman Suffrage? "

Congress adjourned on March 3, 1917. The pickets adjourned with it. On April 2, a Special War Session of Congress convened. The *Suffragist* gives an interesting description of that interesting day.

Just half an hour before Congress formally opened, the Suffrage sentinels at the Capitol took their places. . . . There was tensity in the atmosphere. The Capitol grounds were overrun with pacifists from many cities wearing white-lettered badges; and with war advocates, as plainly labeled, with partisan demands. They swarmed over the Capitol grounds unmolested, though extra precautions were taken throughout the day and in the evening when troops of cavalry were called out. The silent sentinels stood unmoved the while for democracy while peace and war agitation eddied around them.

The pickets convened with Congress. They continued to stand at the gates of the White House, but they extended their line to the Capitol. Three pickets, led by Elsie Hill, took up their station by the House entrance and three by the Senate entrance. At night—this evoked from the newspapers sly allusions to the Trojan horse—they used to store their banners in the House Office Building.

On April 7, the United States declared itself to be at war with Germany.

After war was declared, the Woman's Party continued— and continued with an increasing force and eloquence—to demand the enfranchisement of the women of the United States by Constitutional Amendment. This brought down upon their heads a storm of criticism; antagonism; hostility. But Alice Paul was not deflected by it from her purpose. She recalled that, at the outbreak of the Civil War, Suffragists of that day, were entreated to relinquish their Suffrage work in favor of war work. They were promised that, at the end of the war, they would be enfranchised. Susan B. Anthony complied with great reluctance, carried on, against her will, by the majority of those who surrounded her.

At the end of the war, the black man was enfranchised. The white women had been asking for the vote ever since.

Every effort was made to shake this young leader in her fearless stand. All kinds of people came to her and begged her to give up the picketing. One strong friend, a newspaper man, said, " It's as though you opened the windows and said, ' There's a nice big cyclone coming. Come out of your cyclone-cellars, girls, and let's go in it! ' " Denunciations, violence, mobs, murders were predicted.

There was no officer of the National Woman's Party who did not realize what it meant to go on with such a fight at such a time.

They determined, whatever befell, not to lower their banners; to hold them high.

Alice Paul announced in the editorial columns of the *Suffragist*, that members of the Woman's Party would, if they so desired, work for war through various organizations, especially organized for war work, but that the Woman's Party itself would continue to work only for the enfranchisement of women.

The eyes of the world were now turned on the White House. Distinguished men from all over the country visited the President. Foreign missions came one after another.

Picturesque events continued to happen on the picket line. Arthur Balfour, the leader of the British Mission, called at the White House to pay his respects. He was confronted with forty pickets. Their banners were inscribed with the President's own words:

WE SHALL FIGHT FOR THE THINGS WHICH WE HAVE ALWAYS HELD NEAREST OUR HEARTS—FOR DEMOCRACY, FOR THE RIGHT OF THOSE WHO SUBMIT TO AUTHORITY TO HAVE A VOICE IN THEIR OWN GOVERNMENTS.—President Wilson's War Message, April 2, 1917.

This quotation from the President's words became a slogan among the Suffragists.

The pickets recalled that when Arthur Balfour used to emerge into Downing Street, where the English militants were producing a demonstration, he always wore a bunch of violets in his buttonhole, to show his sympathy with them.

The spring brought its usual beautiful metamorphosis to Washington. If the pickets had seemed beautiful in the winter, they were quadruply so when the fresh green came. Everywhere that luxuriance of foliage, exquisitely tender and soft, which marks Washington, made an intensive background for their great golden banners and their tri-color. The pickets found it a delightfully humorous coincidence that, when they came to take up their station at the White House, the White House lawns were ablaze with their tri-color—the white of hyacinths, the purple of azalea, and the gold of forsythea. The Little White House itself was not exempt from this burst of bloom. The huge wistaria vine on its facade turned to a purple cascade; and out of it spirted the purple, white, and gold of their tri-color and the red, white, and blue of the national banner. When the French Commission, including Joffre and Viviani, passed all this massed color, they leaped to their feet, waving their hats and shouting their approval.

On June 20, the Mission headed by Bakmetief, sent by the new Russian Republic which had just enfranchised its women, was officially received by President Wilson. When they reached the White House gates, they were confronted by a big banner—since known as the " Russian " banner—borne by Lucy Burns and Mrs. Lawrence Lewis.

PRESIDENT WILSON AND ENVOY ROOT ARE DECEIVING RUSSIA. THEY SAY " WE ARE A DEMOCRACY. HELP US WIN THE WAR SO THAT DEMOCRACIES MAY SURVIVE."

WE WOMEN OF AMERICA TELL YOU THAT AMERICA IS NOT A DEMOCRACY. TWENTY MILLION WOMEN ARE DENIED THE RIGHT TO VOTE. PRESIDENT WILSON IS THE CHIEF OPPONENT OF THEIR NATIONAL ENFRANCHISMENT.

HELP US MAKE THIS NATION REALLY FREE. TELL OUR GOVERNMENT THAT IT MUST LIBERATE ITS PEOPLE BEFORE IT CAN CLAIM FREE RUSSIA AS AN ALLY.

The appearance of this banner produced strange results. A man standing at the White House gates leaped at it—the instant the Russian Mission had vanished—and tore the sign from its supports.

The crowd closed in around them. The two women continued to, stand facing them. Nina Allender, who saw this from across the street, said that the surging back and forth of straw hats as the crowd closed in upon the women gave her a sense of faintness. " One instant the banners were there, the next there were only bare sticks."

Later, a prominent member of the Mission said to a no less prominent American, " You know, it was very embarrassing for us, because we were in sympathy with those women at the gates."

The next day, June 21, Lucy Burns and Katherine Morey carried a banner which was the duplicate of the one borne the day before to the lower White House gate. Before they could set it up some boys destroyed it. The police did not interfere; they looked placidly on. Immediately other banners were sent off from Headquarters. Hazel Hunkins carried one which said harmlessly:

DEMOCRACY SHOULD BEGIN AT HOME.

The crowds gathered and surged up and down the street but the two pickets stood motionless. Nothing happened for a while. Then a man, who stopped to congratulate Miss Hunkins, was applauded by the crowd. It is an interesting example of mob psychology that after this applause such an incident as happened five minutes later could happen. A woman of the War Department, who had been boasting that morning in her office that she was going to do this, attacked Hazel Hunkins. She tore the banners and spat on them. The avenue was crowded with government clerks and they immediately fell on the banners and destroyed them after a struggle. Katherine Morey, who was lunching at Headquarters, says in almost Bunyanesque language: " And I heard a great roar." She ran towards the White House gates and saw that the mobs had charged the pickets, had torn the banners into shreds. The mob then rushed to the other gate, picketed by Catherine Lowry and Lillian Crans. After a struggle, their banners also were destroyed. Lillian Crans ran to Headquarters for another banner, carrying the news of what had happened.

Immediately, there emerged from the Little White House four women led by Mabel Vernon, carrying purple, white, and gold banners. It was a moment of tension, and the pickets were white-faced with that tension. This silent, persistent courage had, however, its inevitable effect on the crowd. It fell back. Before it could recover from its interval of indecision, the police met the groups of girls, and conducted them to their places. Police reserves ultimately appeared, and cleared the crowd from Pennsylvania Avenue. The pickets kept guard the rest of the day in peace. One of them even did her war-time knitting.

About this time a prominent newspaper man was sent to

Alice Paul by the powers that be, on a mission of intervention. He told her it was feared the President might be assassinated by some one in the crowds that the pickets collected.

"Is the Administration willing to have us make this public?" Alice Paul asked.

"Oh, no!" was the answer.

Alice Paul replied, "The picketing will go on as usual."

So now Major Pullman, Chief of Police for the District of Columbia, called at Headquarters. He told Alice Paul that if the pickets went out again they would be arrested. Alice Paul answered in effect:

"Why has picketing suddenly become illegal? Our lawyers have assured us all along that picketing was legal. Certainly it is as legal in June as in January." She concluded, "The picketing will go on as usual."

Major Pullman then told her again that the pickets would be arrested if they went out.

Alice Paul replied, "The picketing will go on as usual."

The next morning, June 22, Miss Paul telephoned Major Pullman that the pickets were going out with the banners. Rows of policemen stood outside Headquarters. However, that did not daunt the pickets. Suffragists began to come out; return; emerge again. All this made so much coming and going that, when Mabel Vernon appeared, carrying a box under her arm, nobody paid any attention. That box, however, contained a banner. Miss Vernon crossed to the park and sat down. Presently Lucy Burns came out of Headquarters and walked leisurely in one direction; a little later Katherine Morey came out, and strolled in another direction. At a given moment these two women met at the East gate of the White House. Mabel Vernon joined them with the banner. They set it up and stood undisturbed in front of the White House for several minutes. Suddenly one of the policemen caught sight of them: "The little devils!" he exclaimed: "Can you beat that!"

The banner carried the President's own words: " We shall fight for the things, etc."

The day before the police had been in a bad quandary. Now they were in a worse one: it did not seem reasonable to arrest such a banner. One policeman did, however, start to do so. " My God, man, you can't arrest that," another policeman remonstrated. " Them's the President's own words." They did make the arrest, though—after seven minutes of indecision. When the prisoners arrived at the police station Lucy Burns asked what the charge was: " Charge! Charge!" the policeman said, obviously much puzzled: " We don't know what the charge is yet. We'll telephone you that later."

These two, Lucy Burns and Katherine Morey, were the first of the long list of women to be arrested for picketing the White House. They were, however, never brought to trial.

2. *The Peaceful Reception*

THE YOUNG ARE AT THE GATES

If any one says to me: " Why the picketing for Suffrage? " I should say in reply, " Why the fearless spirit of youth? Why does it exist and make itself manifest? "

Is it not really that our whole social world would be likely to harden and toughen into a dreary mass of conventional negations and forbiddances—into hopeless layers of conformity and caste, did not the irrepressible energy and animation of youth, when joined to the clear-eyed sham-hating intelligence of the young, break up the dull masses and set a new pace for laggards to follow?

What is the potent spirit of youth? Is it not the spirit of revolt, of rebellion against senseless and useless and deadening things? Most of all, against injustice, which is of all stupid things the stupidest?

Such thoughts come to one in looking over the field of the Suffrage campaign and watching the pickets at the White House and at the Capitol, where sit the men who complacently enjoy the rights they deny to the women at their gates. Surely, nothing but the creeping paralysis of mental old age can account for the phenomenon of American men, law-makers, officials, administrators, and guardians of the peace, who can see nothing in the intrepid young pickets with their banners, asking for bare justice but common obstructors of traffic, naggers—nuisances that are to be abolished by passing stupid laws forbidding and repressing to add to the old junk-heap of laws which forbid and repress? Can it be possible that any brain cells not totally crystallized could imagine that giving a stone instead of bread would answer conclusively the demand of the women who, because they are young, fearless, eager, and rebellious, are fighting and winning a cause for all women—even for those who are timid, conventional, and inert?

A fatal error—a losing fight. The old stiff minds must give way. The old selfish minds must go. Obstructive reactionaries must move on. The young are at the gates!

Lavinia Dock.

The Suffragist, June 30, 1917.

This hostility in June had worked up suddenly after the five quiet months, during which the Woman's Party had been peacefully picketing the White House. Perhaps their immunity was at first due to the fact that when the picketing in January began, the people in Washington did not expect it to last. " When the rain comes, they will go," Washingtonians said, and then, as the line still continued to appear, " When the snow comes, they will go." But, instead of going with the rain, the pickets waited for Smith, the janitor, to bring them slickers and sou'westers. And instead of leaving with the snow, they only put on heavier coats. The pickets became an institution.

It is true, too, that, though that picket line was a surprise to every one (and to many a shock) to some it was a joke.

There was one Congressman, for instance, who took it humorously. He said to Nina Allender, when the Suffragists began to picket the Special War Session of Congress:

" The other day, a man covered the gravestones in a cemetery with posters which read: ' Rise up! Your country needs you!' Now that was poor publicity. I consider yours equally poor."

" But," replied Mrs. Allender, " we are not picketing a graveyard. We are picketing Congress. We believe there are a few live ones left there."

The Congressman admitted that he had laid himself wide open to this.

But, from the very beginning, there were those who did not consider it a joke. The first day the pickets appeared, a gentleman—old and white-haired—stopped to stare at the band of floating color. He read the words:

MR. PRESIDENT, HOW LONG MUST WOMEN WAIT FOR LIBERTY?

Then he took off his hat, and held it off, bowing his white head to each of the six silent sentinels. Having passed them, he covered his head again. But he repeated this reverential formality as he passed the six women at the other gate.

One Washingtonian took his children out to see the picket

line. He told them he wanted them to witness history in the making.

That first day when the President came out for his daily afternoon drive, he seemed utterly unaware of the pickets; but the next day he laughed with frank good nature as he passed, and thereafter he too bared his head as he drove between them.

It was the intention at first for these sentinels to keep complete silence. But, as the throngs hurrying past began to question them, continued to question them, conversation became inevitable.

The commonest question, of course, was, " Why are you doing this? "

The pickets always answered, " The President asked us to concert public opinion before we could expect anything of him. We are concerting it upon him." The second most popular question was, " Why don't you go to Congress? " The answer, " We have—again and again and again; and they tell us if the President wants it, it will go through."

That hurrying crowd was made up of many types. In the early morning and the late afternoon, government clerks predominated. Almost as many were the sight-seers from every part of the country. Then there were diplomats, newspaper-men, schoolboys, and schoolgirls, and the matinée crowds. In the streets came the endless file of motor-cars, filled mainly with women going to teas. Many people pretended not to see the sentinels. They would walk straight ahead with an impassive expression, casting furtive, side-long glances at the banners. Again and again, the pickets enjoyed the wicked satisfaction of seeing them walk straight into the wire wickets which enclosed the Pennsylvania Avenue trees. At first, Congressmen tried not to see what was going on. After a while, however, they too stopped to chat with the pickets. One Congressman told Mrs. Gilson Gardner that he felt there was " something religious about that bannered picket line; that it had already become to him a part of the modern religion of this country."

Another Congressman, who had been opposed at first to the picketing, called out one day, " That's right. Keep it up! Don't let us forget you for a moment! "

All kinds of pretty incidents occurred. Once, Ex-Senator Henry W. Blair visited the picket line. He had been a friend of Susan B. Anthony, and he made the first speech ever delivered in the Senate in favor of Suffrage. White-haired, keen-eyed, walking with a crutch and a stick, he came along the line of pickets, greeting each one of them in turn— ninety years old.

" And I, too, have been a picket," said General Sherwood to them.

" I salute you as soldiers in a great revolution," said one chance passer-by to the Women Workers' Delegation on Labor Day. And—struck apparently by the high spiritual quality in the beautiful procession—a woman, a stranger to them, remarked to the pickets: " I wonder if you realize what a mediæval spectacle you young women present. You have made us realize that this cause is a crusade."

Workmen digging trenches in the streets discussed the matter among themselves. Picketing is an institution very dear to the heart of Labor. These men showed their sympathy by devising and making supports for the banners. They offered to make benches for the pickets, but agreed with the women when they said that sentinels must stand, not sit, at their posts.

When the Confederate Reunion occurred in Washington, many of the feeble, white-haired men in their worn Confederate grey and their faded Confederate badges, stopped to talk with the pickets. I quote the *Suffragist:*

" We-all came out early to see the sights," said one. " We went three times around this place, and I thought the big house in the center was the White House. But we weren't sure—not until you girls came out with your flags and stood here. ' This is sure enough where the President lives,' I said, ' here are the Suffrage pickets and there are the purple and gold flags we read about down home.' You are brave girls."

One old soldier, hat off, said, " I have picketed in my time.
And now it is your turn, you young folks. You have the courage.
You are going to put it through."

That was the note many of them sounded. " Girls, you are
right," a third encouraged them. " I have been through wars,
and I know. You-all got to have some rights."

Even the anti-Suffragists were moved sometimes. One of them
said: " I have never been impressed by Suffragists before, but
the sincerity you express in being willing to stand here in all
weathers for the thing you believe in makes me think that there is
something in the Suffrage fight after all."

And yet, Suffragists themselves were occasionally antag-
onistic. " You have put the Suffrage cause back fifty
years! " said one. She little suspected that, within a year,
the House of Representatives would have passed the Amendment; within less than two years thereafter the Senate.

People went further than words. Many paused to shake
hands. Many asked to be allowed to hold the banners for
a moment.

Once a bride and groom—very young—stopped. The
groom talked to one picket, the bride to another. The man
said: " I think this is outrageous. I have no sympathy with
you whatever. I wouldn't any more let my wife——" At
that moment the little bride came rushing up, radiant. " Oh,
do you mind," she said to her husband, " if I hold one of
those banners for a while? "

" No, if you want to," the bridegroom answered.

And she took her stand on the picket line.

Children stopped to spell out the inscriptions, and sometimes asked what they meant.

Once, a group of boys from a Massachusetts school inquired what the colors stood for, and asked to have the
slogan translated. As by one impulse, they lifted their hats
and said, " You ought to have it now."

Occasionally, distinguished visitors leaving the White
House would smile their appreciation and approval. On
one occasion Theodore Roosevelt beamed vividly on the

pickets, waving his hat as he passed. As the weather changed and the winter storms began, the gaiety in the attitude of their audience deepened to a real admiration. With the rains, the pickets appeared in slickers and rubber hats. This was not, of course, unendurable. But, when the freezing cold came, often with snow and swirling winds, picketing became a real hardship. There were days when it was almost impossible to stand on the picket line for more than half an hour at a time. At regular intervals, Smith, the janitor, assisted at times by a little colored boy, used to appear from Headquarters, trundling a wheelbarrow. That wheelbarrow was piled high with hot bricks covered with gunny-sacking. He would distribute the bricks among the pickets and they would stand on them. An observer said that, when the relay of pickets, leaving at the end of the day, stepped down from the bricks at the word of command, it was like a line of statues stepping from their pedestals.

But others—and sometimes strangers—sought to mitigate for the pickets the rigors of the freezing weather. One woman, coming regularly every day in her car, brought thermos bottles filled with hot coffee. On one occasion, a young girl—a passing volunteer—came on picket duty in a coat too light and shoes too low. While she stood there, a closed limousine drew up to the curb. A woman alighted and forced the girl to retire to her car and put on her fur coat and her gaiters. The stranger held the banner while the warming-up process was going on. She offered to organize a committee, made up of older women, who would collect warm clothing for the pickets. In point of fact, the Virginia and Philadelphia branches of the Congressional Union presented the pickets with thick gloves, spats, and slickers for rainy days. Thousands of men and women from all over the country sent suggestions for their comfort.

Official kindness, even, was not lacking. One superlatively cold day, an attaché of the President invited the whole company of pickets into the East Room of the White House.

The superintendents of the Treasury Building and the War Department Annex extended to them similar invitations.

The police were, at the beginning, friendly, not only in words but in acts. An officer stopped one day, after telephoning at the near police box, to say: "You are making friends every minute. Stick to it! Do not give up. We are with you and admire your pluck." The majority of them did not like to do what afterwards they had to do.

As for the White House guards—they were the champions of the pickets. At the outbreak of the war, the White House gates were closed for the first time in its history. The pickets without often informed the guards within as to the kind of vehicle that demanded entrance of them. The guards came to treat them as comrades patrolling the same beat. Once, when the pickets were five minutes late, one of these guards said: "We thought you weren't coming, and we'd have to hold down this place alone."

When the pickets re-convened with the Special War Session of the Sixty-fifth Congress on April 2, the White House police were most demonstrative in their welcome. They were glad to see them back: they said they had missed them. And indeed they had come to look on the women as a kind of auxiliary police force. Once, when somebody asked a policeman, "When is the President coming out?" Mary Gertrude Fendall said, "I guess you'd like a dollar for every time people ask you that." The policeman answered, "I'd rather have a dollar for every time they ask when are the Suffragists coming out?" The country at large had accepted the pickets. The directors of the sight-seeing busses pointed them out as one of the city's sights. Tourists said, oftener and oftener, "Well, we weren't quite sure where the White House was until we saw you pickets." And when these tourists used to crowd about the gates, waiting for the President's limousine to come out, and the signal was flashed that the Presidential motor had started, the guards pressed the crowds away. "Back!" they would order. "Back!

Back! All back but the pickets! No one allowed inside the line but the pickets!"

As can be imagined, Headquarters was a busy place during the picketing; and sometimes a hectic one. Later, of course, when the arrests began, and mobs besieged it, it seethed with excitement. It was not easy always to find women with the leisure and the inclination to serve on the picket line before the arrests. But, when arrests began and imprisonments followed, naturally it became increasingly difficult.

Many members of the Woman's Party in Washington looked on their picketing as a part of the day's work. Mrs. William Kent, who said that no public service she had ever done gave her such an exalted feeling, always excused herself early from teas on Monday. "I picket Mondays from two to six," she explained simply.

Watchers said that those high groups of purple, white, and gold banners coming down the streets of Washington were like the sails, magically vivid and luminous, of some strange ship. They were indeed the sails of a ship—the mightiest that women ever launched—but only the women who manned those sails saw that ship.

3. *The War on the Pickets*

"I have no son to give my country to fight for democracy abroad and so I send my daughter to Washington to fight for democracy at home."

Mrs. S. H. B. Gray of Colorado.

It will be remembered that the arrest of Lucy Burns and Katherine Morey—the first of a series extending over more than a year—occurred on June 22.

On June 23, Mrs. Lawrence Lewis and Gladys Greiner were arrested in front of the White House. On the same day, Mabel Vernon and Virginia Arnold were arrested at the Capitol.

On June 25, twenty women bore Suffrage banners to their stations. The slogans on these banners were:

HOW LONG MUST WOMEN WAIT FOR LIBERTY?

MR. PRESIDENT, YOU SAY "LIBERTY IS A FUNDAMENTAL DEMAND OF THE HUMAN SPIRIT."

WE ADDRESS OUR DEMAND FOR THE BALLOT AT THIS TIME IN NO NARROW, CAPTIOUS, OR SELFISH SPIRIT, BUT FROM PUREST PATRIOTISM FOR THE HIGHEST GOOD OF EVERY CITIZEN FOR THE SAFETY OF THE REPUBLIC AND AS A GLORIOUS EXAMPLE TO THE NATIONS OF THE EARTH.

Twelve women were arrested. They were: Mabel Vernon, Lucy Burns, Gladys Greiner, Katherine Morey, Elizabeth Stuyvesant, Lavinia Dock, Berta Crone, Pauline Clarke, Virginia Arnold, Maude Jamison, Annie Arniel, and Mrs. Townsend Scott.

On Tuesday, June 26, nine women were arrested for carrying the same banners. They included some of the women from the day before, and, in addition, Vivian Pierce and Hazel Hunkins.

227

A high-handed detail of this arrest was that the women were overpowered by the police before they had proceeded half a block.

Most of these women were released after each arrest. The last six to be arrested were asked to return to court for trial.

On June 27, six American women were tried in the police court of the District of Columbia.

These women were: Virginia Arnold, Lavinia Dock, Maud Jamison, Katherine Morey, Annie Arniel, Mabel Vernon.

The women defended themselves. Mabel Vernon, who conducted the case, demanded that the banners they had carried be exhibited in court. It made a comic episode in the midst of the court proceedings when the policeman, who had been sent for them, returned, bristling all over his person with banner sticks, and trailing in every direction the purple, white, and gold. The courtroom crowd burst out laughing when they read the legend:

MR. PRESIDENT, YOU SAY " LIBERTY IS THE FUNDAMENTAL DESIRE OF THE HUMAN SPIRIT."

There was a technical discussion as to how much sidewalk space the young women occupied, and how near the White House palings they stood. The Suffrage group had photographs which showed the deserted pavements at the time of the arrests.

The women cross-examined the police who testified that there was no crowd at that time of the morning and that the women stood with their backs to the White House fence.

The Judge said: " If you had kept on moving, you would be all right."

" I find these defendants guilty as charged," was his verdict, " of obstructing the highway in violation of the police regulations and the Act of Congress, and impose a fine of twenty-five dollars in each case, or in default of that, three days' imprisonment."

The six young women refused to pay the fine. They were each sentenced to three days in the District jail.

When the first pickets came out of jail, a hundred women, representing many States, gave them a reception breakfast in the garden of Cameron House.

A subsequent chapter will relate the prison experiences of these women and of the long line of their successors.

The next picket line went out on Independence Day, July 4, 1917. Five women marched from Headquarters bearing purple, white, and gold banners. They were: Helena Hill Weed, Vida Milholland, Gladys Greiner, Margaret Whittemore, Iris Calderhead. Helena Hill Weed carried a banner:

GOVERNMENTS DERIVE THEIR JUST POWER FROM
THE CONSENT OF THE GOVERNED.

Following the advice of the Judge, they kept moving. Across the street, a crowd had gathered in expectation of arrests. Standing about were policemen—a newspaper man said twenty-nine. The police walked along parallel with the women, and the crowd followed them. As the banner-bearers crossed the street to the White House, the police seized them before they could get onto the sidewalks. An augmenting crowd surged about them. Some of the on-lookers protested, but most of them took their cue from the police, and tore the flags away from the women. Apart from the pickets, Kitty Marion, who for some weeks had been selling the *Suffragist* on the streets, was attacked by a by-stander who snatched her papers away from her, tearing one of them up. Miss Marion was arrested. She protested at the behavior of her assailant and he was arrested too. Hazel Hunkins, who was not a part of the procession, came upon a man who had seized one of the banners carried by the pickets and was bearing it away. Miss Hunkins attempted to get it from him, and she also was arrested.

The police commandeered automobiles, and commenced bundling the women into them.

Immediately another group of women came marching up Pennsylvania Avenue on the opposite side of the street. This second group contained Mrs. Frances Green, Mrs. Lawrence Lewis, Lucile Shields, Joy Young, Elizabeth Stuyvesant, Lucy Burns. Joy Young, who is a little creature, led this group. They reached the West gate of the White House, and there the police arrested them. A Washington paper described with great glee how, like a tigress, little Joy Young fought to retain her banner, and how finally three policemen managed to overpower her. The women were booked for " unlawful assembly " all except Kitty Marion, who was charged with " disorderly conduct."

Helena Hill Weed and Lucy Burns cross-examined the witnesses on behalf of the women. Mrs. Weed insisted that the torn, yellow banner should be brought into court. Throughout the trial, it hung suspended from the Judge's bench—GOVERNMENTS DERIVE THEIR JUST POWERS FROM THE CONSENT OF THE GOVERNED. Lucy Burns, examining the police officers, asked why citizens carrying banners on June 21 were protected by the police, and on July 4 arrested for doing the same thing. The officer replied that they were protected on June 21 because he had no orders for that day. The orders which came later were, he said, not to allow picketing, though he admitted there were no directions about seizing banners. The women brought out by skillful cross-questioning that it was the action of the police which had collected a disorderly crowd, and not the marching of the two groups of women; that at the former trial of a group of Suffrage pickets, the Judge himself had declared that marching pickets did not violate the law.

Lucy Burns summed up the case for the Suffragists as follows:

I wish to state first—she said—as the others have stated, that we proceeded quietly down the street opposite the White House with our banners; that we intended to keep marching; that our progress was halted by the police, not the crowd. There was no interference on the part of the crowd until after the police had arrested us and turned their backs on the crowd. Our contention is as others have stated that the presence of the crowd there was caused by the action of the police and the previous announcement of the police that they would arrest the pickets, and not by our action which was entirely legal.

In the second place I wish to call your attention to the fact that there is no law whatever against our carrying banners through the streets of Washington, or in front of the White House. It has been stated that we were directed by the police not to carry banners before the White House, not to picket at the White House. That is absolutely untrue. We have received only one instruction from the chief of police and that was delivered by Major Pullman in person. He said that we must not carry banners outside of Headquarters. We have had no other communication on this subject since that time.

We, of course, realized that that was an extraordinary direction, because I don't think it was ever told an organization that it could not propagate its views, and we proceeded naturally to assume that Major Pullman would not carry out that order in action because he would not be able to sustain it in any just court.

We have only been able since to judge instructions by the action of the police, and the actions of the police have varied from day to day, so that as a point of fact, we don't know what the police have been ordered to do—what is going to be done. On one occasion we stepped out of Headquarters with a banner— the so-called Russian banner—and it was torn to fragments before we had reached the gate of our premises, although Major Pullman had given no notice to us at that time. Another time we proceeded down Madison Place with banners, walking in front of the Belasco Theatre, and were arrested. Another time we were allowed to proceed down Madison Place and the north side of the Avenue and were not molested.

Now the district attorney has stated that on account of the action of this court a few days ago, we knew and deliberately did wrong. But we were advised then by the Judge—and he was familiar with the first offense—that we would have been all right if we had kept on walking. On July 4 we kept on walking and this is the result of that action.

I myself was informed on June 22 by various police, that if I would keep on walking, my action would be entirely legal. We were innocent of any desire to do anything wrong when we left our premises.

It is evident that the proceedings in this court are had for the purpose of suppressing our appeal to the President of the United States, and not for the purpose of accusing us of violating the police regulations regarding traffic in the District of Columbia.

The eleven women were found " Guilty," and sentenced to pay a fine of twenty-five dollars or to serve three days in the District jail. They refused to pay the fine, and were sent to jail. The case against Hazel Hunkins was dismissed. Kitty Marion was found " Not Guilty," of disorderly conduct.

In the meantime, Alice Paul had been seized with what looked like a severe illness. A physician finally warned her that she might not live two weeks. It was decided, on July 14, to send her to a hospital in Philadelphia for treatment. The day before she left, a meeting of the Executive Board was held at her bedside in the Washington hospital. Although later diagnosis proved more favorable, and Miss Paul was to be away from Washington only a month, many of the women present at that meeting believed that they would never see her again. That was a poignant moment, for the devotion of her adherents to their leader can neither be described nor measured. But they felt that there was only one way to serve her if she left them forever and that was to carry out her plans. . . . The next day they went out on the picket line.

That next day was the French national holiday—July 14. The Woman's Party had, as was usual with them when they planned a demonstration, announced this through the press.

On the anniversary of the fall of the Bastille, therefore, three groups of women carrying banners, one inscribed with the French national motto: LIBERTY, EQUALITY, FRATERNITY, and the Woman's Party colors, marched one after another from Headquarters.

In the first group were Mrs. J. A. H. Hopkins, Mrs. Paul Reyneau, Mrs. B. R. Kincaid, Julia Hurburt, Minnie D. Abbot, Anne Martin.

In the second group were, Amelia Himes Walker, Florence Bayard Hilles, Mrs. Gilson Gardner, Janet Fotheringham.

In the third group were, Mrs. John Winters Brannan, Mrs. John Rogers, Jr., Louise P. Mayo Doris Stevens, Mary H. Ingham, Eleanor Calnan.

A big crowd, attracted by the expectation of excitement, had collected outside Headquarters. The police made no effort to disperse them. When the first group appeared, there was some applause and cheering. They crossed the street, and took up their station at the upper gate of the White House. As nothing happened to the first group, the second group, led by Amelia Himes Walker, emerged from Headquarters and took up a position at the lower gate of the White House. However, the instant the two groups had established themselves, the policemen, who had been making a pretense of clearing the sidewalks, immediately arrested them.

The third group of pickets, however, came forward undismayed, their flags high. The crowd applauded them; then fell back and permitted the pickets to take their places. The police in this third case waited for four minutes, watches in hand. Then they arrested the women on the charge of " violating an ordinance."

At the station the sixteen women were booked for " unlawful assembly." On July 17, Judge Mullowney, sentenced the sixteen women to sixty days in Occoquan Workhouse on the charge of " obstructing traffic."

A detailed consideration of the treatment of the pickets in Occoquan and the Jail is reserved for a later chapter. It will, therefore, be stated briefly here that these sixteen women were pardoned by the President after three days in Occoquan. However, they were submitted to indignities there such as white prisoners were nowhere else compelled to endure. When J. A. H. Hopkins and Gilson Gardner were permitted to visit their wives, they did not at first recognize them in the haggard, exhausted-looking group of creatures in prison garb, sitting in the reception room. One of the women, however, seeing her husband, half rose from her chair.

"You sit down!" Superintendent Whittaker yelled, pointing his finger at her.

J. A. H. Hopkins, who had been a member of the Democratic National Campaign Committee of 1916, went immediately to the President and told him the conditions under which these women were being held. Gilson Gardner, a well-known newspaper man who had supported Wilson throughout the previous election campaign, wrote a long communication to the President on the same subject. Dudley Field Malone, Collector of the Port of New York and one of the President's closest friends and warmest advisors, who was later in so gallant a way to show his disapproval of the Suffrage situation, saw the President also. President Wilson professed himself as being "shocked" at his revelations. He said he did not know what was going on at Occoquan.

"After this, Mr. President," Mr. Malone replied, "you *do* know."

After her release, Mrs. J. A. H. Hopkins wanted to find out whether this pardon also meant that the President supported their Amendment. She therefore wrote him the following letter:

MY DEAR MR. PRESIDENT:
The pardon issued to me by you is accompanied by no explanation. It can have but one of two meanings—either you have satisfied yourself, as you personally stated to Mr. Hopkins, that I violated no law of the country, and no ordinance of this city, in exercising my right of peaceful petition, and therefore you, as an act of justice, extended to me your pardon, or you pardoned me to save yourself the embarrassment of an acute and distressing political situation.

In this case, in thus saving yourself, you have deprived me of the right through appeal to prove by legal processes that the police powers of Washington despotically and falsely convicted me on a false charge, in order to save you personal or political embarrassment.

As you have not seen fit to tell the public the true reason, I am compelled to resume my peaceful petition for political liberty. If the police arrest me, I shall carry the case to the Supreme Court if necessary. If the police do not arrest me, I shall believe that you do not believe me guilty. This is the only method by which I can release myself from the intolerable and false position in which your unexplained pardon has placed me.

Mr. Hopkins and I repudiate absolutely the current report that I would accept a pardon which was the act of your good nature.

In this case, which involves my fundamental constitutional rights, Mr. Hopkins and myself do not desire your Presidential benevolence, but American justice.

Furthermore, we do not believe that you would insult us by extending to us your good-nature under these circumstances.

This pardon without any explanation of your reasons for its issuance, in no way mitigates the injustice inflicted upon me by the violation of my constitutional civil right.

Respectfully yours,
ALISON TURNBULL HOPKINS.

After having written this letter, quite alone and at the crowded hour of five o'clock in the afternoon, Mrs. Hopkins carried a banner to the White House gates, and stood there for ten minutes. The banner said: WE ASK NOT PARDON FOR OURSELVES BUT JUSTICE FOR ALL AMERICAN WOMEN. A large and curious crowd gathered, but nobody bothered her. While she stood there, the President passed through the gates and saluted.

On Monday, July 23, exactly a month from the time that the police had first interfered with the picketing and the Suffragists, the daily Suffrage picket was resumed. The crowds streaming home in the afternoon from the offices, laughed when they saw the banners at the White House gates again. Some stopped to congratulate the women.

Time went on and still the President did nothing about putting the Amendment through. As always when it was not strikingly brought to his attention, Suffrage seemed to pass from his mind. It became again necessary to call his attention to the Amendment. Often it seemed as though the President's attention could be gained only by calling the country's attention to his inaction.

Within a week appeared a new banner. Elihu Root, the Special Envoy of the United States to Russia, had just come home from a country which had enfranchised its women. With the other members of the American Mission to Russia, he called at the White House, and at the gates he was confronted by these words:

TO ENVOY ROOT:

YOU SAY THAT AMERICA MUST THROW ITS MANHOOD IN THE SUPPORT OF LIBERTY.

WHOSE LIBERTY?

THIS NATION IS NOT FREE. 20,000,000 WOMEN ARE DENIED BY THE PRESIDENT OF THE UNITED STATES THE RIGHT TO REPRESENTATION IN THEIR OWN GOVERNMENT.

TELL THE PRESIDENT THAT HE CANNOT FIGHT AGAINST LIBERTY AT HOME WHILE HE TELLS US TO FIGHT FOR LIBERTY ABROAD.

TELL HIM TO MAKE AMERICA FREE FOR DEMOCRACY BEFORE HE ASKS THE MOTHERS OF AMERICA TO THROW THEIR SONS TO THE SUPPORT OF DEMOCRACY IN EUROPE.

ASK HIM HOW HE COULD REFUSE LIBERTY TO AMERICAN CITIZENS WHEN HE HAS FORCED MILLIONS OF AMERICAN BOYS OUT OF THEIR COUNTRY TO DIE FOR LIBERTY.

For two hours, Lucy Ewing and Mary Winsor stood holding this banner. It attracted the largest crowd that the pickets had as yet experienced. But the police managed them perfectly—although in the courts there had been plenty of testimony that they could not manage similar crowds—and without a word of protest—although half a block was completely obstructed for two hours.

The following day saw scenes the most violent in the history of the pickets. This was August 14. Catherine Flanagan's story of this period of terror is one of the most thrilling in the annals of the Party:

That day a new banner was carried for the first time by Elizabeth Stuyvesant—the "Kaiser" banner. The banner read:

KAISER WILSON, HAVE YOU FORGOTTEN YOUR SYMPATHY WITH THE POOR GERMANS BECAUSE THEY WERE NOT SELF-GOVERNING?

TWENTY MILLION AMERICAN WOMEN ARE NOT SELF-GOVERNING. TAKE THE BEAM OUT OF YOUR OWN EYE.

I do not remember when Elizabeth took this banner out, but I think she was on the four o'clock shift. For a half an hour people gathered about the banner. The crowd grew and grew. You felt there was something brewing in them, but what, you could not guess. Suddenly it came—a man dashed from the crowd and tore the banner down. Immediately, one after another, the other banners were torn down. As fast as this happened, the banner bearers went back to Headquarters; returned with tri-colors and reinforcements; took up their stations again. Finally the whole line of pickets, bannerless by this time, marched back to Headquarters. The crowd, which was fast changing into a mob, followed us into Madison Place. As the pickets emerged again, the mob jumped them at the very doors of Cameron House, tore their banners away from them and destroyed them. By this time the mob, which had become a solid mass of people, choking the street and filling the park, had evolved a leader, a yeoman in uniform, who incited everybody about him to further work of destruction. Suddenly, as if by magic, a ladder appeared in their midst. A yeoman placed it against Cameron House, and accompanied by a little boy, he started up. He pulled down the tri-color of the Woman's Party which hung over the door. In the meantime, it was impossible for us to take any banners out. We locked the door, but two strange women, unknown to the Woman's Party, came in. They opened a window on the second floor and were about to push the ladder, on which the sailor and the little boy still stood, back into the street when Ella Morton Dean drew them away.

At the other side of the house and at the same moment, another member of the crowd climbed up the balcony and pulled down the American flag which hung beside the tri-color. Immediately Virginia Arnold and Lucy Burns appeared on the balcony carrying, the one the Kaiser banner and the other the tri-color. The crowd began to throw eggs, tomatoes, and apples at them, but the two girls stood, Virginia Arnold white, Lucy Burns flushed, but—everybody who saw them comments on this—with a look of steady consecration, absolutely moveless, holding the tri-color which had never before been taken from its place over the door at Headquarters.

Suddenly a shot rang out from the crowd. A bullet went through a window of the second story, directly over the heads of two women who stood there—Ella Morton Dean and Georgiana Sturgess—and imbedded itself in the ceiling of the hall. The only man seen to have a revolver was a yeoman in uniform, who immediately ran up the street. By this time Elizabeth Stuyvesant had joined Lucy Burns and Virginia Arnold on the balcony; others also came. Three yeomen climbed up onto the balcony and wrested the tri-color banners from the girls. As one of these men climbed over the railing, he struck Georgiana Sturgess. "Why did you do that?" she demanded, dumbfounded. The man paused a moment, apparently as amazed as she. "I don't know," he answered; then he tore the banner out of her hands and descended the ladder. Lucy Burns, whose courage is physical as well as spiritual, held her banner until the last moment. It seemed as though she were going to be dragged over the railing of the balcony, but two of the yeomen managed to tear it from her hands before this occurred. New banners were brought to replace those that had disappeared.

While this was going on, Katherine Morey and I went out the back way of Headquarters, made our way to the White House gates, unfurled a Kaiser banner, and stood there for seventeen minutes unnoticed. There was a policeman standing beside each of us, but when the yeoman who had led the mob and who was apparently about to report for duty, tore at the banner, they did not interfere. We were dragged along the pavements, but the banner was finally destroyed.

By this time the crowd had thinned a little in front of Headquarters. The front door had been unlocked when we went back. Five different times, however, we and others, led always by Lucy Burns, made an effort to bear our banners to the White House gates again. Always, a little distance from Headquarters, we were beset by the mob and our banners destroyed.

About five o'clock, the police reserves appeared and cleared the street. Thereupon, every woman who had been on picket duty that day, bearing aloft the beautiful tri-color, went over to the White House gates, marched up and down the pavements three times. The police protected us until we started home. When, however, our little procession crossed the street to the park, the crowd leaped upon us again, and again destroyed our banners. Madeline Watson was knocked down and kicked. Two men carried her into Headquarters.

While the crowd was milling its thickest before Headquarters, somebody said to a policeman standing there, "Why don't you arrest those men?" "Those are not our orders," the policeman replied.

Twenty-two lettered banners and fourteen tri-color flags were destroyed that day.

During all the early evening, men were trying to climb over the back fence of the garden to get into Cameron House. None of us went to bed that night. We were afraid that something—we knew not what—might happen.

The next day, August 15, was only a degree less violent. The Suffrage pickets went on duty as usual at twelve o'clock, and picketed all that afternoon.

All the afternoon yeomen, small boys, and hoodlums attacked the women without hindrance. Elizabeth Stuyvesant was struck by a soldier who destroyed her flag. Beulah Amidon was thrown down by a sailor, who stole her flag. Alice Paul was knocked down three times. One sailor dragged her thirty feet along the White House sidewalk in his attempts to tear off her Suffrage sash, gashing her neck brutally. They were without protection until five o'clock.

During this time they lost fifty tri-color banners and one Kaiser banner.

The pickets were, of course, constantly going back to Headquarters for new banners, and constantly returning with them.

At five o'clock, in anticipation of the President's appearance, and while still the turmoil was going on, five police officers quickly and efficiently cleared a wide aisle in front of each gate, and as quickly and as efficiently drove the mob across the street. The President, however, left by a rear gate.

On the next day, August 16, the policy toward the pickets changed again. Fifty policemen appeared on the scene, and

240

instead of permitting Suffragists to be attacked by others, they attacked them themselves. Virginia Arnold was set upon by three police officers. Before she could relinquish her banner to them, her arms were twisted and her hands bruised. Elizabeth Stuyvesant, Natalie Gray, and Lucy Burns were all severely handled by the police. Elizabeth Smith and Ruth Crocker, who were carrying furled flags, were knocked down. When men, more chivalrous-minded than the crowd, came to their rescue, they were arrested.

In the late afternoon, the crowd grew denser. The police, therefore, ceased their efforts, and waited while the crowd attacked the women and destroyed their banners An officer threatened to arrest, one young woman who defended her banner against an assailant.

"Here, give that up!" called the second officer to a girl who was struggling with a man for the possession of her flag.

During these days of mob attacks, the pickets had been put to it to get outside Headquarters to some coign of vantage where they could stand for a few seconds before the inevitable rush. For the first time in the history of their picketing the girls could not carry their banners on poles. Either the mobs seized them or the policemen who lined the sidewalks outside Headquarters. The pickets carried them inside their sweaters and hats, in sewing bags, or pinned them, folded in newspapers or magazines, under their skirts. One picket was followed by crowds who caught a gleam of yellow at the hem of her gown. When they got to the White House, the pickets held the banners in their hands. Lucy Burns kept sending out relays with new banners to take the place of those which were torn.

Catherine Flanagan says that on August 16 when the four o'clock shift of the picket line started out, Lucy Burns pointed to rolls of banners done up in various receptacles and said, "Take out as many of these as you can carry and keep them concealed until it is necessary to use them." The eight pickets distributed the banners in different parts of their clothes, and approaching the White House by various

routes, suddenly lined themselves against the White House
fence, each unfurling a Kaiser banner at the word of command. They were faced by forty policemen, policewomen,
and secret service men. Instantly the police were on them.
The pickets held the banners as long as it was physically
possible—it took three policemen to remove each banner.
The policemen heaved sighs of relief, as though their work
for the day was done, turned, and moved to the edge of the
pavement. Instantly, eight more banners appeared and as
instantly they fell on the pickets again. This happened
seven times. As often as the police turned with captured
banners in their hands, reinforcing pickets in the crowd
handed fresh banners to the pickets at the gates. Fifty-six
Kaiser banners were captured this day. When the Kaiser
banners were exhausted, the eight pickets returned to Headquarters and soon emerged bearing the tri-color. The tactics of the police changed then. They did not, themselves,
attack the pickets, but they permitted the crowds to do so.
In all, one hundred and forty-eight flags were destroyed.

On August 17, Major Pullman, police head of Washington, called upon Alice Paul, and warned her that young
women carrying banners would be arrested.

Alice Paul replied, " The picketing will go on as usual."
In a letter to his friend, Major Pullman, quoted in the
uffragist of August 25, Gilson Gardner put the case con-
sely and decisively. . . .

You must see, Pullman, that you cannot be right in what you
ve done in this matter. You have given the pickets adequate
otection; you have arrested them and had them sent to jail
d the workhouse, you have permitted the crowds to mob them,
d then you have had your officers do much the same thing by
cibly taking their banners from them. In some of these ac-
ns, you must have been wrong. If it was right to give them
otection and let them stand at the White House for five months,
h before and after the war, it was not right to do what you
later.
You say it was not right and that you were " lenient," when

you gave them protection. You cannot mean that. The rightness or wrongness must be a matter of law, not of personal discretion, and for you to attempt to substitute your discretion is to set up a little autocracy in place of the settled laws of the land. That would justify a charge of "Kaiserism" right here in our Capitol city.

The truth is, Pullman, you were right when you gave these women protection. That is what the police are for. When there are riots they are supposed to quell them, not by quelling the "proximate cause," but by quelling the rioters.

I know your police officers now quite well and I find that they are most happy when they are permitted to do their duty. They did not like that dirty business of permitting a lot of sailors and street riffraff to rough the girls. . . .

It is not my opinion alone when I say that the women were entitled to police protection, not arrest. President Wilson has stated repeatedly that these women were entirely within their legal and constitutional rights, and that they should not have been molested. Three reputable men, two of them holding office in this Administration, have told me what the President said, and I have no reason to doubt their word. If the President has changed his mind he has not changed the law or the Constitution, and what he said three weeks ago is just as true today.

In excusing what you have done, you say that the women have carried banners with "offensive" inscriptions on them. You refer to the fact that they have addressed the President as "Kaiser Wilson." As a matter of fact, not an arrest you have made—and the arrests now number more than sixty—has been for carrying one of those "offensive" banners. The women were carrying merely the Suffrage colors or quotations from President Wilson's writings.

But suppose the banners were offensive? Who made you censor of banners? The law gives you no such power. Even when you go through the farce of a police court trial, the charge is "obstructing traffic," *which shows conclusively that you are not willing to go into court on the real issue.*

No. As chief of police you have no more right to complain of the sentiments on a banner than you have of the sentiments in an editorial in the *Washington Post,* and you have no more right to arrest the banner-bearers than you have to arrest the owner of the *Washington Post.* So long as the law against obscenity and profanity is observed, you have no business with the words on the banners. Congress refused to pass a press censorship law. There are certain lingering traditions to the effect that a people's

liberties are closely bound up with the right to talk things out
and those who are enlightened know that the only proper answer
to words is words.

During the entire afternoon of that day—August 17—
the day that Major Pullman called on Alice Paul—the sentinels stood at their posts. One of the banners read:

ENGLAND AND RUSSIA ARE ENFRANCHISING WOMEN
IN WAR TIME;

Another:

THE GOVERNMENT ORDERS OUR BANNERS DESTROYED
BECAUSE THEY TELL THE TRUTH.

At intervals of fifteen minutes—for two hours—the
pickets were told by a captain of police that they would be
arrested if they did not move. But they held their station.
At half-past four, the hour at which the thousand of government clerks invade the streets, there was enough of a
crowd to give the appearance that the pickets were "blocking traffic." Lavinia Dock; Edna Dixon; Natalie Gray;
Madeline Watson; Catherine Flanagan; Lucy Ewing, were
arrested soon after four o'clock. Their trial lasted just
forty minutes. One police officer testified that they were
obstructing traffic. They all refused to pay the ten dollar
fine, which, though it would have released them, would also
have been an admission of guilt, and Police Magistrate
Pugh sentenced them to serve thirty days in the Government
Workhouse.

On August 23, six women appeared at the White House,
bearing banners. They were, Pauline Adams; Gertrude
Hunter; Clara Fuller; Kate Boeckh; Margaret Fotheringham; Mrs. Henry L. Lockwood. All of their banners quoted
words from the President's works:

I TELL YOU SOLEMNLY, LADIES AND GENTLEMEN, WE CAN-
NOT POSTPONE JUSTICE ANY LONGER IN THESE UNITED

STATES, AND I DON'T WISH TO SIT DOWN AND LET ANY MAN TAKE CARE OF ME WITHOUT MY HAVING AT LEAST A VOICE IN IT; AND IF HE DOESN'T LISTEN TO MY ADVICE I AM GOING TO MAKE IT AS UNPLEASANT FOR HIM AS I CAN.

In ten minutes they were all arrested. When they appeared before Police Magistrate Pugh, Clara Kinsley Fuller said in part:

I am the editor, owner, and publisher of a daily and weekly newspaper in Minnesota. I pay taxes to this government, yet I have nothing to say in the making of those laws which control me, either as an individual or as a business woman. Taxation without representation is undemocratic. For that reason, I came to Washington to help the Federal Amendment fight. When I learned that President Wilson said that picketing was perfectly legal, I went on the picket line and did my bit towards making democracy safe at home, while our men are abroad making democracy safe for the world.

Margaret Fotheringham, a school-teacher, said:

I have fifteen British cousins who are in the fighting line abroad. Some are back very badly wounded, and others are still in France. I have two brothers who are to be in our fighting line. They were not drafted; they enlisted. I am made of the same stuff that those boys are made of; and, whether it is abroad or at home, we are fighting for the same thing. We are fighting for the thing we hold nearest our hearts—for democracy.

To these pleas, Judge Pugh answered that the President was "not the one to petition for justice"; that the people of the District virtuously refrained from picketing the White House for the vote for themselves "for fear the military would take possession of the streets."
I quote the *Suffragist* of September 2.

Here is a sample of Judge Pugh's logic:
" These ladies have been told repeatedly that this law was ample to prevent picketing in front of the White House, or anywhere else on the sidewalks of the District of Columbia; that it was not the fashion to petition Congress in that way, to stand in front

of the White House, the President's mansion, to petition somebody else, a mile and a half away. The President does not have
to be petitioned. . . . You ladies observe all the laws that give
you benefits, property rights that legislatures composed of men
have passed . . . and those that are aimed at preserving the
peace and good order of the community you do not propose to
observe."

And much more to the same effect, which proved that Judge
Pugh knew nothing of the long vigil of the pickets at the doors
of Congress, and apparently nothing of the President's actual
dictatorship.

Finally he admitted that he did not care to send "ladies of
standing" to jail, and would refrain if they promised to stop
picketing, although they were not charged with picketing. In
the face of the dead silence that followed, he pronounced sentence: A fine of twenty-five dollars or thirty days at Occoquan
Workhouse. Every woman refused to pay the fine.

Attorney Matthew O'Brien represented the women in the District Court, appealing finally from the judgment of the court.

On August 28, the same women, with Cornelia Beach,
Vivian Pierce, Maud Jamison, and Lucy Burns, were again
arrested, and given the same sentence. An appeal was
granted them again, the Judge announcing that this was the
last appeal he would give in the picketing cases until a decision had been given by the Court of Appeals.

On September 4, the day of the parade of the drafted men,
thirteen women were arrested. They were: Abby Scott
Baker, Dorothy Bartlett, Annie Arniel, Pauline Adams,
Mrs. W. W. Chisholm, Lucy Burns, Margaret Fothering-
ham, Lucy Branham, Julia Emory, Eleanor Calnan, Edith
Ainge, Maude Malone, Mary Winsor.

The banner these women bore was inscribed:

MR. PRESIDENT, HOW LONG MUST WOMEN BE DENIED A VOICE
IN THE GOVERNMENT THAT IS CONSCRIPTING THEIR SONS?

They were sent to Occoquan for sixty days.

At this vivid interval in the history of the Woman's Party
occurred a notable incident.

Dudley Field Malone, who had long been a staunch friend of the Woman's Party—and one of the few men who had been willing to make a sacrifice for Suffrage—resigned his position as Collector of the Port of New York as a protest against the intolerable Suffrage situation. This was a *beau geste* on the part of Mr. Malone. There are those who believe that that gallant deed will go rolling down the centuries gathering luster as it rolls. It had an inevitable effect, not only on the members of the Woman's Party, but on the members of other Suffrage organizations as well, and it produced a profound impression on the country at large.

His letter of resignation reads as follows:

New York, N. Y., Sept. 7, 1917.

THE PRESIDENT,
  THE WHITE HOUSE,
    WASHINGTON, D. C.
DEAR MR. PRESIDENT:

Last autumn, as the representative of your Administration, I went into the Woman Suffrage States to urge your re-election. The most difficult argument to meet among the seven million voters was the failure of the Democratic Party, throughout four years of power, to pass the Federal Suffrage Amendment, looking towards the enfranchisement of all the women in the country. Throughout those States, and particularly in California, which ultimately decided the election by the votes of women, the women voters were urged to support you, even though Judge Hughes had already declared for the Federal Suffrage Amendment, because you and your Party, through liberal leadership, were more likely nationally to enfranchise the rest of the women of the country than were your opponents.

And if the women of the West voted to re-elect you, I promised them I would spend all my energy, at any sacrifice to myself, to get the present Democratic Administration to pass the Federal Suffrage Amendment.

But the present policy of the Administration, in permitting splendid American women to be sent to jail in Washington, not for carrying offensive banners, nor for picketing, but on the technical charge of obstructing traffic, is a denial even of their constitutional right to petition for, and demand the passage of, the Federal Suffrage Amendment. It, therefore, now becomes my profound obligation actively to keep my promise to the women of the West.

In more than twenty States it is a practical impossibility to amend the State constitutions; so the women of those States can only be enfranchised by the passage of the Federal Suffrage Amendment. Since England and Russia, in the midst of the great war, have assured the national enfranchisement of their women, should we not be jealous to maintain our democratic leadership in the world by the speedy national enfranchisement of American women?

To me, Mr. President, as I urged upon you in Washington two months ago, this is not only a measure of justice and democracy, it is also an urgent war measure. The women of the nation are, and always will be, loyal to the country, and the passage of the Suffrage Amendment is only the first step toward their national emancipation. But unless the government takes at least this first step toward their enfranchisement, how can the government ask millions of American women, educated in our schools and colleges, and millions of American women in our homes, or toiling for economic independence in every line of industry, to give up by conscription their men and happiness to a war for democracy in Europe while these women citizens are denied the right to vote on the policies of the government which demands of them such sacrifice?

For this reason many of your most ardent friends and supporters feel that the passage of the Federal Suffrage Amendment is a war measure which could appropriately be urged by you at this session of Congress. It is true that this Amendment would have to come from Congress, but the present Congress shows no earnest desire to enact this legislation for the simple reason that you, as the leader of the Party in power, have not yet suggested it.

For the whole country gladly acknowledges, Mr. President, that no vital piece of legislation has come through Congress these five years except by your extraordinary and brilliant leadership. And millions of men and women today hope that you will give the Federal Suffrage Amendment to the women of the country by the valor of your leadership now. It will hearten the mothers of the nation, eliminate a just grievance, and turn the devoted energies of brilliant women to a more hearty support of the government in this crisis.

As you well know, in dozens of speeches in many States I have advocated your policies and the war. I was the first man of your Administration, nearly five years ago, publicly to advocate preparedness, and helped to found the first Plattsburg training camp. And if, with our troops mobilizing in France, you will give American women this measure for their political freedom, they will support with greater enthusiasm your hope and the hope of America for world freedom.

I have not approved all the methods recently adopted by women in the pursuit of their political liberty; yet, Mr. President, the Committee on Suffrage of the United States Senate was formed in 1883, when I was one year old; this same Federal Suffrage Amendment was first introduced in Congress in 1878; brave women like Susan B. Anthony were petitioning Congress for the Suffrage before the Civil War, and at the time of the Civil War men like William Lloyd Garrison, Horace Greeley, and Wendell Phillips assured the Suffrage leaders that if they abandoned their fight for Suffrage, when the war was ended the men of the nation, " out of gratitude," would enfranchise the women of the country!

And if the men of this country had been peacefully demanding for over half a century the political right or privilege to vote, and had been continuously ignored or met with evasion by successive Congresses, as have the women, you, Mr. President, as a lover of liberty, would be the first to comprehend and forgive their inevitable impatience and righteous indignation. Will not this Administration, re-elected to power by the hope and faith of the women of the West, handsomely reward that faith by taking action now for the passage of the Federal Suffrage Amendment?

In the port of New York, during the last four years, billions of dollars in the export and import trade of the country have been handled by the men of the customs service; their treatment of the traveling public has radically changed, their vigilance supplied the evidence for the Lusitania note; the neutrality was rigidly maintained; the great German fleet guarded, captured, and repaired; substantial economies and reforms have been concluded, and my ardent industry has been given to this great office of your appointment. But now I wish to leave these finished tasks, to return to my profession of the law, and to give all my leisure time to fight as hard for the political freedom of women as I have always fought for your liberal leadership.

It seems a long seven years, Mr. President, since I first campaigned with you when you were running for Governor of New Jersey. In every circumstance throughout those years, I have served you with the most respectful affection and unshadowed devotion. It is no small sacrifice now for me, as a member of your Administration, to sever our political relationship. But I think it is high time that men in this generation, at some cost to themselves, stood up to battle for the national enfranchisement of American women. So in order effectively to keep my promise made in the West, and more freely to go into this larger field of democratic effort, I hereby resign my office as Collector of the Port of New York, to take effect at once, or at your earliest convenience.

Yours respectfully,

DUDLEY FIELD MALONE.

On September 13, six pickets left Headquarters at half-past four in the afternoon. They were: Katherine Fisher, Mrs. Frederick Willard Kendall, Mrs. Mark Jackson, Ruth Crocker, Nina Samardin, Eleanor Gwinter. The two lettered banners were borne by Miss Fisher and Mrs. Kendall:

HOW LONG MUST WOMEN WAIT FOR LIBERTY?

MR. PRESIDENT, WHAT WILL YOU DO FOR WOMAN SUFFRAGE?

They marched straight to the lower gate. A crowd had already collected there. Another crowd lined the edge of the sidewalk across the street on Lafayette Square. There were two police officers on the White House sidewalk, and several across the way.

The crowd made way for the group of pickets, and they took their accustomed places at the gate. For a few minutes nothing happened. During all these days of roughness and riot, it had been very difficult to take pictures. It seemed as though the thing the police most feared was the truth. They would not permit the moving-picture men to record these vivid events. They even confiscated cameras. Photographers ran the risk always of having their cameras destroyed. On this day, Gladys Greiner, a Suffragist, was taking pictures of the crowd. As she leveled her kodak at a police captain, he kicked her. She continued to take her pictures nevertheless. A sailor and a marine, both in uniform, instead of moving as the police had ordered, came closer and closer to the pickets. Suddenly, the sailor snatched the banner from the pole. The two men tore the banner into pieces; passed the scraps to their friends. The police looked on without interference. Then they arrested the women. They were taken to Judge Mullowny.

Judge Mullowny had been away for two months from the bench. In the meantime, his ideas on the offense of picketing had undergone another change. His first decision in regard to the Suffragists was that they obstructed traffic, and, in regard to the banners, that they "had nothing to do with the case." Later, he decided that the banners were " treasonable." Now, in regard to their banner, *How Long Must Women Wait for Liberty*, he decided: " Since this banner is unlikely to give offense, I will give you women a light sentence this time."

All evidence except that of the two policemen was ruled out. In regard to the conduct of the police captain in kicking Miss Greiner, the Judge said: " I have nothing to do with those things; they have nothing to do with the case."

He asked, " Would you pay a fine instead of going to prison, if I made the fine fifty cents? "

" Not if you made it five cents," replied Mrs. Kendall, who spoke for the six prisoners.

He therefore sentenced them to thirty days in the government workhouse.

On September 22, four more Suffragists were arrested. They were Peggy Baird Johns, Margaret Wood Kessler, Ernestine Hara, Hilda Blumberg. They carried a new banner this time, quoting words from an early work of the President. It said:

PRESIDENT WILSON, WHAT DID YOU MEAN WHEN YOU SAID, " WE HAVE SEEN A GOOD MANY SINGULAR THINGS HAPPEN RECENTLY. WE HAVE BEEN TOLD THAT IT IS UNPATRIOTIC TO CRITICIZE PUBLIC ACTION. WELL, IF IT IS, THERE IS A DEEP DISGRACE RESTING UPON THE ORIGIN OF THIS NATION. THIS NATION ORIGINATED IN THE SHARPEST SORT OF CRITICISM OF PUBLIC POLICY. WE ORIGINATED, TO PUT IT IN THE VER-

NACULAR, IN A KICK AND IF IT IS UNPATRIOTIC TO KICK, WHY, THEN THE GROWN MAN IS UNLIKE THE CHILD. WE HAVE FOR- GOTTEN THE VERY PRINCIPLE OF OUR ORIGIN IF WE HAVE FORGOTTEN HOW TO OBJECT, HOW TO RESIST, HOW TO AGI- TATE, HOW TO PULL DOWN AND BUILD UP EVEN TO THE EXTENT OF REVOLUTIONARY PRACTICES IF IT BE NECESSARY TO READJUST MATTERS. I HAVE FORGOTTEN MY HISTORY IF THAT BE NOT TRUE HISTORY."

The *Suffragist* of September 29 describes this event:

When the pickets this week took up their stations at the East gate of the White House, and unfurled the " seditious " utter- ance of the President himself, the banner was almost immediately confiscated by the two police officers who had hurried to the spot. They seemed anxious to keep from the little pressing crowd the fact that the President had once been not only a Democrat, but a democrat.

The two officers then stood directly in front of the little group of women carrying tri-colored flags, with their backs to what crowd there was. More than half of the wide White House sidewalks were vacant of pedestrians. The officers had evidently been ordered to let the crowd collect for a certain number of minutes before they arrested the women. They betrayed not the slightest interest in the spectators, but watched their victims with bored attention as they waited for the patrol. . . .

The four young women were, on the following day, after the usual court proceeding, sentenced to thirty days in the govern- ment workhouse for " obstructing traffic."

A brief statement was made by each of the little group. " We are not citizens," said these young women. " We are not repre- sented. We were silently, peacefully attempting to gain the freedom of twenty million women in the United States of America. We have broken no law. We are guilty of no crime. We have been illegally arrested. We demand our freedom, and we shall continue to ask for it until the government acts."

They were given thirty days in the workhouse.

The last picketing of the Emergency War Session of the Sixty-fifth Congress took place on October 6, the day Con- gress adjourned. There were eleven women in this picket line: Dr. Caroline Spencer, Vivian Pierce, Louise Lewis

Kahle, Rose Winslow, Joy Young, Matilda Young, Minnie
Henesy, Kate Heffelfinger, Maud Jamison, Lou C. Daniels.

Alice Paul led them. Congress was adjourning. The
work of the Woman's Party was going on smoothly. For
the first time, Alice Paul felt that she had the leisure to go
to jail.

In the *Suffragist* of October 13, Pauline Jacobson of the
San Francisco Bulletin thus describes their arrest:

I had had much of the Western prejudice against the "militant
movement" that the live Suffrage battle had become in this
country. I had thought from the newspaper reports that have
gone forth concerning the action of these "militant Suffragists,"
that "picketing" was rowdy and unlovely. I found it a silent,
a still thing—a thing sublime. . . .

The sun, which never seems bright to me under these paler
Eastern skies, slanted chill and thin through the falling golden
foliage of autumn trees lining the broad avenue on which the
White House stands. Diagonally across, flying the Suffrage
colors, stands the handsome old Cameron House, the Headquarters of the Woman's Party.

Suddenly that chill avenue vista became vibrant with color,
with fluttering banners, wide-striped of purple, white, and gold,
borne aloft on tall, imposing, war-like spears. Down the
Avenue they fluttered slowly, as if moved by some mysterious
force. Then I saw the force that was sending those banners
forward through the careless crowds.

There were eleven women, each bearing high her colored
banner. The leader, a woman frail, and slight, and very pale,
her eyes and face really lit with exaltation of purpose, carried
a white flag on which was printed: "Mr. President, what will
you do for Woman Suffrage?" Then behind them followed the
others with the vivid purple and gold flags on the spear-headed
staffs. They looked neither to the right nor to the left. They
seemed to me to walk so lightly that the great banners carried
them; and there was the glow in all of their eyes though their
faces were quite unsmiling.

The street in an instant had become alive with people who
gathered about, followed, or lined the curbs, men and women—
the women for the most part curious, the men for the most part
disdainful, insolent, or leering. It was not a Western crowd;
there was no generosity in it.

But silently, perceived by all but perceiving none, the women

marched straight ahead. As they neared the White House a
sailor sprang forward and tore the banner from one picket,
threw it on the ground, and trampled on it. The young girl
who had carried it stooped down and silently rescued her banner.
I thought there was tenderness in the way she smoothed it out
and tried to fasten it again to her tall staff. Four banners were
torn and mutilated like that. Each girl, without a word, like the
first, tried to protect her flag.

And then, like a flash, those eleven women, a few feet apart,
were flanking either side of the wide White House gates like
living statues, only their colored banners fluttering upward.
They stood facing the coming and going crowd silently. There
was the pale little leader with her staff bare; the crowd had torn
away that simple question on the white flag. . . .

Then came shouted orders, the sudden waving of blue-coated
arms, and the elbowing to the front of blue coats with much gold
braid. The police were scattering the curious crowd. Above
their orders came the clang of the patrol. Next the eleven
statues had disappeared from the White House gates. They were
being crowded to the front by the fat officer in the uniform.
They were still silent and still proud. There was something
majestic even in the way each stooped her head to enter the
small door of the patrol wagon. And the last uniformed officer
who had gathered together the brilliant flags sat in front, where
they still fluttered triumphant in the wind as the patrol clanged
off and the crowd shouted.

I followed them to the police station. It seemed to me there
was strange delay in the procedure of accepting bail for people
charged with so simple an offense—for they were charged with
" obstructing traffic." That same day, I had seen dense crowds
watching the World Series returns, with mounted police to clear
a space for the cars. There were no arrests for blocking traffic.
They were finally released on bail for trial the following Monday.

The eleven women were tried on October 8. They refused
to recognize the Court. They would not be sworn. They
would not question witnesses. They would not speak in their
own behalf.

Alice Paul said—I quote the *Suffragist*:

We do not wish to make any plea before this Court. We do
not consider ourselves subject to this Court since, as an unenfranchised class, we have nothing to do with the making of the
laws which have put us in this position.

The Judge did not sentence the eleven women. He suspended sentence and restored the bail furnished by the Suffragists for their appearance. For this surprising change of front, no reason was given. Though apparently inconsistent, it was perfectly consistent with the policy of an Administration quite dazed and uncertain in regard to its treatment of the picketing women.

In point of fact, the Court did not sentence the women because Congress was adjourning. They did not dismiss the charge, however.

Regarding the freeing of the pickets Miss Paul said:

We are glad that the authorities have retreated at last from their untenable position, and grown wary of prosecuting women for peacefully petitioning for political liberty.

The action of the Court this morning makes more glaring than ever the injustice of holding nineteen women on sixty and thirty day sentences in Occoquan Workhouse for the same offense of petitioning for liberty which we committed. We will use our unexpected freedom to press our campaign with ever-increasing vigor.

On October 15, four pickets, under suspended sentence from their picketing of October 6, went out again. They were Rose Winslow, Kate Heffelfinger, Minnie Henesy, Maud Jamison. The police were taken absolutely by surprise. It was ten minutes before the patrol wagons appeared. In the meantime, of course, a crowd gathered to see what was going to happen. When the patrol stopped at the curb, an officer approached the pickets. " Move on! " he ordered, and, before the pickets could move on, or even make a reply—" I will put you under arrest," and immediately, " You are under arrest." Rose Winslow, one of the pickets, lifted her banner high, and marched with the air of a conqueror to the waiting patrol. The crowd burst into spontaneous applause.

In court Rose Winslow said:

We have seen officers of the law permit men to assault women, to destroy their banners, to enter their residences. How, then, can you ask us to have respect for the law? We thought that by dismissing the Suffragists without sentence this Court had finally decided to recognize our legal right to petition the government. We shall continue to picket because it is our right. On the tenth of November there will be a long line of Suffragists who will march to the White House gates to ask for political liberty. You can send us to jail, but you know that we have broken no law. You know that we have not even committed the technical offense on which we were arrested. You know that we are guiltless.

Judge Mullowny gave them the choice between a twenty-five dollar fine and six months in the district workhouse. They, of course, refused to pay the fine.

At half-past four on October 20, Alice Paul led a deputation of three pickets to the West gate of the White House. The others were Dr. Caroline Spencer, Gladys Greiner, Gertrude Crocker. Alice Paul carried a banner with the words of President Wilson which had appeared recently on the posters for the Second Liberty Bond Loan of 1917:

THE TIME HAS COME TO CONQUER OR SUBMIT. FOR US THERE CAN BE BUT ONE CHOICE. WE HAVE MADE IT.

Dr. Caroline Spencer's banner bore the watchword of '76:

RESISTANCE TO TYRANNY IS OBEDIENCE TO GOD.

They were arrested as soon as the police had permitted what seemed a sufficient crowd to gather, placed in the patrol wagon, and taken to the district jail.

The officer testified as follows—the italics are my own:

I made my way through the crowd that was surrounding them, and told the ladies *they were violating the law by standing at the gates,* and would not they please move on.

Assistant District Attorney Hart asked: Did they move on?

Lee answered: *They did not, and they did not answer either.*

Hart: What did you do then?

Lee: Placed them under arrest.

The two women who carried the banners—Alice Paul and Caroline Spencer—were sentenced to seven months in jail; the other two pickets were offered the choice of a five dollar fine or thirty days, and, of course, took the thirty days.

On the same occasion, Rose Winslow and those who were arrested with her, Maud Jamison, Kate Heffelfinger, Minnie Henesy—both on October 4 and October 15—came up for further sentence. Rose Winslow described very vigorously the confusion of the Suffragists who, she admitted, were not more nonplussed than Judge Mullowny admitted the Court was. She said:

> You sentence us to jail for a few days, then you sentence us to the workhouse for thirty days, then sixty, and then you suspend sentence. Sometimes we are accused of carrying seditious banners, then of obstructing traffic. How do you expect us to see any consistency in the law, or in your sentences?

The Court smiled, and pronounced an additional thirty days, saying: " First, you will serve six months, and then you will serve one month more."

Alice Paul had been in jail ever since October 20. When the news first got out, women came from all over the country to join the picket forces. It was decided that on November 10, forty-one women should go out on the picket line as a protest against her imprisonment. But on the night of November 9, these forty-one women—accompanied by sympathizers and friends—went down to the jail where their leader was confined. Headquarters had heard from Alice Paul from time to time, and Alice Paul had heard from Headquarters— by means of a cleaning-woman in the jail. In her *Jailed for Freedom*, Doris Stevens tells how she went down to the jail and talked to Alice Paul from the yard. Catherine Flanagan and Mrs. Sophie Meredith had communicated with her in this same manner. And once Vida Milholland came and sang under her window. But this was the first time that a deputation visited their imprisoned leader.

The house in which Warden Zinkham lived was close to the wing in which Alice Paul was imprisoned. The leader of the delegation, Katherine Morey, accompanied by Catherine Flanagan, went to Zinkham's door and rang the bell; asked to see him. They were told that he was ill and could not be seen. Immediately, the two girls gave a prearranged signal to the silent crowd of pickets back of them. With one accord, they ran and grouped themselves under Alice Paul's window. Before the guards could rush upon them and push them out of the yard, they had managed to call up to her their names; the large sum of money which that day had come into the Treasury; that forty-one of them would protest against her imprisonment on the picket line the next day.

The next morning, the picket line of forty-one women marched from Headquarters in five groups. The first was led by Mrs. John Winters Brannan.

As usual, the pickets bore golden-lettered banners. As usual, they bore purple, white, and gold flags. As usual, they walked slowly—always a banner's length apart. They moved over to Pennsylvania Avenue; took up their silent statuesque position at the East and West gates of the White House.

The thick stream of government clerks, hastening with home-going swiftness, paused to look at them. Involuntarily they applauded the women when they were arrested. This happened almost immediately, the police hurrying the pickets into the line of waiting patrols. Suddenly the crowd raised a shout:

" There come some more!"

The second picket line numbered ten women.

They also bore golden lettered banners. They also bore flags of purple, white, and gold. They were arrested immediately.

The applause continued to grow and grow in volume.

Immediately a third group appeared, and after they had been arrested, a fourth; and, on their arrest, a fifth. For half an hour a continuous line of purple, white, and gold blazed its revolutionary path through the grayness of the November afternoon.

Mary A. Nolan of Florida headed the fifth group of pickets. Little, frail, lame, seventy years old, her gallantry elicited from the two lines of onlookers applause, cheers, calls of encouragement.

"Keep right on!" one voice emerged from the noise. "You'll make them give it to you!"

The women of the first group were: Mrs. John Winters Brannan, Belle Sheinberg, L. H. Hornesby, Paula Jakobi, Cynthia Cohen, M. Tilden Burritt, Dorothy Day, Mrs. Henry Butterworth, Cora Weeks, Peggy Baird Johns, Elizabeth Hamilton, Ella Guilford, Amy Juengling, Hattie Kruger.

The women of the second group were: Agnes H. Morey, Mrs. William Bergen, Camilla Whitcomb, Ella Findeisen, Lou Daniels, Mrs. George Scott, Mrs. Lawrence Lewis, Elizabeth McShane, Kathryn Lincoln.

The women of the third group were: Mrs. William Kent, Alice Gram, Betty Gram, Mrs. R. B. Quay, Mrs. C. T. Robertson, Eva Decker, Genevieve Williams.

The women of the fourth group were: Mrs. Charles W. Barnes, Kate Stafford, Mrs. J. H. Short, Mrs. A. N. Beim, Catherine Martinette.

The women of the fifth group were: Mrs. Harvey Wiley, Alice Cosu, Mary Bartlett Dixon, Julia Emory, Mary A. Nolan, Lucy Burns.

The forty-one women were tried on November 12. They were charged with " obstructing traffic," and pleaded " Not Guilty." The police sergeants and plain-clothes men gave their testimony which was refuted absolutely by witnesses for the defendants—Helena Hill Weed, Olivia Dunbar Torrence, Marie Manning Gasch, Mary Ingham.

Mrs. John Winters Brannan said:

The responsibility for an agitation like ours against injustice rests with those who deny justice, not those who demand it. Whatever may be the verdict of this Court, we shall continue our agitation until the grievance of American women is redressed.

Mrs. Harvey Wiley said:

I want to state that we took this action with great consecration of spirit. We took this action with willingness to sacrifice our personal liberty in order to focus the attention of the nation on the injustice of our disfranchisement, that we might thereby win political liberty for all the women of the country. The Constitution says that Congress shall not in any way abridge the right of citizens peacefully to assembly and petition. That is exactly what we did. We peacefully assembled and then proceeded with our petition to the President for the redress of our grievance of disfranchisement. The Constitution does not specify the form of petition. Ours was in the form of a banner. To say that we " broke traffic regulations " when we exercised our constitutional right of petition is therefore unconstitutional.

Judge Mullowny admitted the embarrassment of the Administration.

" The trouble of the situation is that the Court has not been given power to meet it," he complained. " It is very, very puzzling."

A little after three o'clock, he dismissed the pickets without imposing sentence. He said he would take the case under advisement.

An hour later, twenty-seven of the women who had just been tried—with, in addition, Mrs. William L. Colt, Elizabeth Smith, Matilda Young, Hilda Blumberg—emerged from Headquarters. They walked twice up and down in front of the White House before they took their places at the gates.

The police were dumbfounded by their unexpected onslaught. There were no patrols waiting. But they pulled themselves together, arrested the pickets, and commandeered cars in which to take them to the police headquarters.

The thirty-one women were ordered to appear in court on November 14. There, after waiting all the morning, Judge Mullowny told them to come back Friday.

At Headquarters, it was believed that this was not only a challenge to the quality of their spirit, but to the degree of their patience.

Many women had come from a long distance to make this protest. Not all could spare the time, money, and vitality. Their answer to that challenge was instant and convincing. On the afternoon of November 13, the picket line went out again—thirty-one of them.

The pickets blazed their way through dense, black throngs. The crowd was distinctly friendly.

Suddenly one of the banners disappeared; another and another until six of them were destroyed; the bare poles proceeded on their way however. The same person accomplished all this—the uniformed yeoman who dragged Alice Paul across thirty feet of pavement on August 15. But this time, the crowd—friendly—manifested its disapproval, and the police arrested him. The pickets stood for a long time, their line stretching from gate to gate, until they began to think that the Administration had changed its tactics. Then suddenly the patrol wagon gong sounded in the distance. Presently they were all arrested.

Many of the pickets had been tried the day before. As their bail had not been refunded, they refused to give more. They were kept that night in the house of detention. As this institution had but two rooms with eight beds each, some of the women slept on the floor. They were tried and sentenced the next day. One of them—the aged Mrs Nolan—got six days, three fifteen days, twenty-four thirty days, two—Mrs. Lawrence Lewis and Mrs. John Winters Brannan—sixty days, and one—Lucy Burns—six months.

It was this group of women who went through the Night of Terror, subsequently to be described.

On November 17, three more women—Mrs. Harvey Wiley, Mrs. William Kent, and Elizabeth McShane—were sentenced to fifteen days on the November 10 charges.

All these prisoners except four were sent to the Occoquan Workhouse.

Habeas corpus proceedings became necessary—owing to conditions which will presently be set forth—and a writ was procured; but only after numberless obstacles were surmounted. The case came up in the United States District Court at Alexandria, Virginia, with Judge Edmund Waddill sitting. Judge Waddill ordered the prisoners transferred to the jail on the ground that they should have been confined there instead of at Occoquan Workhouse. Later the Court of Appeals reversed this decision. In the meantime, brought to the jail, the government was faced with the necessity of forcibly feeding the majority of these women, already weakened from hunger-striking.

Here, perhaps, is the place to tell of a curious incident that happened during Alice Paul's jail term. For this to strike the reader with the force it deserves, he must remember that Alice Paul was held almost incommunicado, that she saw but two friends from the outside, and then only for a few minutes, that she could not confer with her counsel, Dudley Field Malone, who had to overcome extraordinary obstacles—had finally to threaten habeas corpus proceedings and to see high officials who were his personal friends—to get to her. Two newspaper men were admitted, but they were friendly to the Administration.

One evening, at nine o'clock—an hour when all the prisoners were supposed to be in bed—the door opened and a stranger entered her room. He proved to be David Lawrence, a newspaper man, very well known as one who was closely associated with the Administration. He did not say that he had come from the Administration, but, of course, it is obvious that if he had not been in favor with the Administration, he would not have been admitted. He stayed two hours, and Miss Paul talked over the situation with him.

I now quote Miss Younger, who has told this episode on many platforms:

He asked Miss Paul how long she and the other pickets would give the Administration before they began picketing again. She said it would depend upon the attitude the Administration and Congress seemed to be taking toward the Federal Amendment. He said he believed the prohibition bill would be brought up and passed, and after that was out of the way the Suffrage bill would be taken up.

He asked if we would be content to have it go through one House this session and wait till the next session for it to pass the other House. Miss Paul said that if the bill did not go through both Houses this session, the Woman's Party would not be satisfied.

Then the man said he believed that the President would not mention Suffrage in his message at the opening of Congress, but would make it known to the leaders of Congress that he wanted it passed and would see that it passed.

He said in effect: Now the great difficulty is for these hunger-strikers to be recognized as political prisoners. Every day you hunger-strike, you advertise the idea of political prisoners throughout the country. It would be the easiest thing in the world for the Administration to treat you as political prisoners; to put you in a fine house in Washington; give you the best of food; take the best of care of you; but if we treat you as political prisoners, we would have to treat other groups which might arise in opposition to the war program as political prisoners too, and that would throw a bomb in our war program. It would never do. It would be easier to give you the Suffrage Amendment than to treat you as political prisoners.

On November 27 and 28, a few days after Miss Paul's strange experience—suddenly, quite arbitrarily, and with no reason assigned—the government released all the Suffrage prisoners.

The speakers of the Woman's Party began telling this story of the visit to Alice Paul's cell, everywhere. It finally appeared in the *Milwaukee Leader* and in the *San Francisco Bulletin* in an article written by John D. Barry. The National Association Opposed to Woman Suffrage immediately questioned the truth of this episode.

Congress reconvened on December 3. The President, true to David Lawrence's prophecy, did not mention Suffrage in his message to Congress. However, on January 9, 1918, on the evening of the victorious vote in the House—as will subsequently and in more detail again be told—the President declared for the Federal Amendment.

Minnie Bronson, the General Secretary of the National Association Opposed to Woman Suffrage, immediately sent Alice Paul a letter of apology for questioning the truth of her statement. In that letter, she repeats Maud Younger's statement in regard to this visit to Alice Paul in prison, and says:

The inference contained in this article that the President of the United States would under cover assist a proposition which he had publicly and unqualifiedly repudiated, seemed to us unworthy of his high office, and we felt justified in defending him from what seemed an unwarranted and unbelievable accusation.

However, the President's subsequent public support of the Federal Suffrage Amendment, his announcement coming on the eve of the vote in the House of Representatives, indicates the truth of your original assertion, and we therefore deem it incumbent upon ourselves to apologize for having questioned Miss Younger's statement.

We are sending a copy of this letter to the President and members of Congress.

Very truly yours,
MINNIE BRONSON.

Perhaps a word should be said of description—and even of explanation—in regard to the crowds who harried the Suffragists. Of course, in all crowds there is a hoodlum element, and if that element is not held down by the police, it rapidly becomes the controlling power; tends to become more and more destructive. The police, as has been indicated from time to time, adopted various policies. At first, they maintained order. Then they began to permit the rowdy element in the crowds to do as it pleased. Later, they even worked with these destructive forces.

Men were heard to say, one to another, " Stick around here. Something's going to happen this afternoon. I saw it this morning." To them, of course, it was merely an entertaining exhibition.

Photo Copr. Harris and Ewing, Washington, D. C.

OBEYING ORDERS.

WASHINGTON POLICE ARRESTING WHITE HOUSE PICKETS BEFORE
THE TREASURY BUILDING.

Photo Copr. Harris and Ewing, Washington, D. C.

THE PATROL WAGON WAITING THE ARRIVAL OF THE
SUFFRAGE PICKETS.

An enlisting sergeant used often to make his way through the crowds saying, " Now you have shown your spirit, boys, come and enlist! "

At all times, however, the people who annoyed, and later ill-treated the girls, were very young men—often in uniform. After a while there appeared men in plain clothes with groups of men in khaki, or yeomen, who were obviously in the crowd for the purpose of making trouble for the Suffragists. These people did not like cameras, and the moving picture people who, appreciating the news value of the situation, tried to get views of the crowd, did so at the risk of having their cameras smashed. Indeed, Helena Hill Weed once dispersed a crowd by pointing a camera at them. This was the worst element the pickets had to deal with— unthinking young men of a semi-brutalized type. Of course, boys took their cue from their elders, and snatched or destroyed banners where they could. After a demonstration, you would come across groups of them, marching with the tattered banners that they had managed to steal.

" When is the shooting going to begin? " one little boy was heard to ask once.

In the very midst of the riots, one would come across older men cutting up banners into small pieces which they gave away as souvenirs.

Of course, there were chivalrous spirits who protested against the treatment of the pickets by the police—protested even after they were threatened with arrest. Some of them were actually arrested, and one of them fined.

Often—very often indeed—the waiting crowds broke into spontaneous applause when group after group marched from Headquarters into the certainty of arrest. Those who were Anglo-Saxons inevitably admired the sporting quality of these women.

Perhaps a negro street sweeper summed it up better than anybody else. He said: " I doan know what them women want, but I know they ain't skeered! '

The reader is probably asking by this time what was the

effect of the picketing on the Woman's Party itself. The first reaction was exactly what he would guess—that members resigned in large numbers. The second, however, was one which he might not expect—that new members joined in large numbers. In other words, the militant action which alienated some women brought others into the organization; women who were aroused by the simple and immediate demands of the Woman's Party and by the courage and the forthrightness with which it pushed those demands; women who had become impatient at the *impasse* to which the older generation of Suffrage workers had brought the Suffrage Amendment. The majority of the people who deserted came back later.

As far as money was concerned, the effect was magical. In some months during the picketing the receipts were double what they had been the corresponding months of the previous year when there had been no picketing. Once those receipts jumped as high as six times the normal amount. This was what happened in England during the militant period.

4. *The Court and the Pickets*

" So long as you send women to prison for asking for justice,
so long will women be ready to go in such a cause.'
    ANNE MARTIN to the judge before whom she was tried.

After Judge Waddill's decision that the commitment of the
pickets to Occoquan was illegal, the pickets filed sixteen suits
for damage. Eight of these were against Whittaker, Superintendent of the Workhouse at Occoquan, and his assistant,
Captain Reams, on account of their brutal treatment of the
women while at Occoquan Workhouse. They were filed in
the United States Court for the Western District of Virginia at Richmond. The other eight were against the Commissioners of the District of Columbia and Superintendent
Zinkham of the District Jail for the unlawful transfer of the
pickets to the institution of Whittaker at Occoquan. These
suits were filed in the Supreme Court of the District of
Columbia at Washington.

The appeals in the cases of two groups of women arrested
August 23 and 28 came up in the District of Columbia
Court of Appeals on January 8, 1918, before Chief Justice
Smyth, and Justices Robb and Van Orsdel. Matthew
O'Brien, of Washington, and Dudley Field Malone, of New
York, appeared for the Suffragists. Corporation Counsel
Stevens conducted the case for the government.

" Suppose," suggested Justice Robb, " some upholders of Billy
Sunday should go out on the streets with banners on which were
painted some of Billy's catch phrases, and should stand with
their backs to the fence, and a curious crowd gathered, some of
whom created disorder and threw stones at the carriers of the
banners. Who should be arrested, those who created the disorder, or the banner carriers? "

Mr. Stevens gave it as his opinion that both parties should be
arrested.

" Did I make myself clear that the banner carriers were perfectly peaceful? " Justice Robb asked.

" When it is commonly known there is a forty-foot sidewalk there? " Justice Van Orsdel reinforced him.

" Well, then," observed Attorney O'Brien, when he answered Mr. Stevens in his argument, " the honorable Justices obstruct traffic, according to learned counsel's definition, when court adjourns, and they walk down the street together."

On March 4, Judge Van Orsdel handed down the opinion, which was concurred in by the other two judges of the court, that in the case of those pickets who appealed, no information had been filed justifying their arrest and sentence. Since the offense of every other picket who was arrested was identical with that of these twelve who appealed their case, they were all illegally arrested, illegally convicted and illegally imprisoned. The Appellate Court thus reversed the decision of the District Police Court. In addition, it ordered the cases dismissed. All of the costs involved in the cases, it was decided, should be paid by the Court of the District of Columbia, for which an appropriation would have to be made by Congressional enactment.

Later, the case of Mrs. Harvey Wiley came up. It will be remembered that Mrs. Wiley was one of the forty-three women who picketed the President on November in the last picket line demonstration. She was sentenced to serve fifteen days in the District Jail. Dr. Wiley, her husband, appealed her case. Early in April the Court decided that there was no information filed justifying her arrest. So that she also was illegally arrested, illegally convicted, and illegally imprisoned.

Yet in spite of the brutalities to which the Courts sentenced the pickets, unconsciously they furthered the Suffrage cause. The women turned the Court sessions into Suffrage meetings. In defending their case at one of the early trials, the pickets, each taking up the story where the other left it, told the entire history of the Suffrage movement. Crowds thronged the Court People attended these trials who had never been to a Suffrage meeting in their lives.

5. *The Strange Ladies*

THE EMPTY CUP

Evening at Occoquan.   Rain pelts the workhouse roof.
The prison matrons are sewing together for the Red Cross.
The women prisoners are going to bed in two long rows.
Some of the Suffrage pickets lie reading in the dim light.
Through the dark, above the rain, rings out a cry.

We listen at the windows.   (Oh, those cries from punishment
        cells!)
A voice calls one of us by name.
" Miss Burns!   Miss Burns!   Will you see that I have a drink
        of water? "
Lucy Burns arises; slips on the coarse blue prison gown.
Over it her swinging hair, red-gold, throws a regal mantle.

She begs the night-watch to give the girl water.
One of the matrons leaves her war-bandages; we see her hasten
        to the cell.
The light in it goes out.
The voice despairing cries:
" She has taken away the cup and she will not bring me water."
Rain pours on the roof.   The Suffragists lie awake.
The matrons work busily for the Red Cross.

KATHERINE ROLSTON FISHER,
The Suffragist, October 17, 1917.

WOMAN'S PARTY SONG

Composed in Prison by the Suffrage Pickets

SHOUT THE REVOLUTION OF WOMEN

Tune (Scotch):
" Charlie Is My Darling."

Shout the Revolution
    Of Women, of Women,
Shout the Revolution
    Of Liberty

Rise, glorious women of the earth,
    The voiceless and the free,
United strength assures the birth
    Of True Democracy.
Invincible our army,
    Forward, forward,
Strong in faith we're marching
    To Victory.

Shout the Revolution
    Of Women, of Women,
Shout the Revolution
    Of Liberty.
Men's revolutions born in blood
    But our's conceived in peace
We hold a banner for a sword,
    'Til all oppression cease,
Prison, death defying,
    Onward, onward,
Triumphant daughters marching
    To Victory.

The preceding two chapters have been concerned mainly with the treatment of the pickets at the hands of the law. We now approach a much graver matter—their treatment at the hands of the prison authorities. This chapter describes what is one of the most disgraceful episodes in the history of the United States. It is futile to argue that what happened in the District Jail and at Occoquan Workhouse, and later at the abandoned Workhouse, was unknown to the Administration. The Suffragists, indeed, published it to the entire country. That the treatment to which the pickets were subjected was the result of orders from above is almost demonstrable. It must be remembered that the officials who are responsible for what happened to the pickets—the three Commissioners who govern the District of Columbia, the police court judges, the Chief of Police, the warden of the jail, the superintendent of Occoquan Workhouse, are directly or indirectly answerable to the President.

When the first pickets came out of prison (arrested on June 27, 1917), their spirit was that of women who have willingly gone to jail for a cause—and was in consequence entirely without self-pity.

In a speech at a breakfast tendered them in the garden at Headquarters, Mabel Vernon sounded this note:

I do not want any one here to think we have been martyrs because of this jail experience we have had. There was no great hardship connected with it. It was a very simple thing to do— to be imprisoned for three days, really two nights and a day. Do not think we have gone through any great sacrifices.

But I do not feel patient about this experience. I do not want to go back to jail, and I do not want others to go, *because it should not be necessary.*

The jail in which the women were first imprisoned was the conventional big white-washed octagonal building with wings at both sides. This was as filthy then as any place could be. The bathroom, with its shower was a damp, dank, dark place. The jail was filled with vermin and rats. Julia Emory said that, in the night, prisoners could actually hear the light cell chairs being moved, so big and strong were the rats. The prisoners complained so constantly that finally the prison officials put poison about; but this did not decrease them. Then they brought a dog, but the dog was apparently afraid of the rats. The girls used to hear the matrons telling visitors that they had got rid of the rats by means of this dog. One night, Julia Emory beat three rats in succession off her bed. Alice Paul says that among her group of jailed pickets was one whose shrieks nightly filled the jail as the rats entered her cell.

On July 17, however, when the sixteen women charged with obstructing traffic went to Occoquan Workhouse, things got much worse. Occoquan is charmingly situated, and, judged superficially, seems a model institution. It consists of a group of white buildings placed in a picturesque combination of cultivated fields with distant hills. All about lie the pleasant indications of rural life—crops; cows grazing; agricultural implements; even flower gardens. The District

Jail cannot compare with it for charm of situation. It has not even a pretense of the meretricious effect of cleanliness which Occoquan shows. Nevertheless, no picket who went to Occoquan emerged without a sinister sense of the horror of the place. Lucy Burns, of whom it may almost be said that she knows no fear, confesses that at Occoquan she suffered with nameless and inexplicable terrors. This evidence is all the more strange because, I reiterate, Occoquan has an effect of cleanliness, of open air, of comfort; almost of charm. One reason for this sinister atmosphere was that no question the pickets put was ever answered directly. If they asked to see Superintendent Whittaker, he was always out—they could see him tomorrow. If they made a request, it would be granted to them in two days, or next week. The women's ward was a long, clean, sunny, airy room with two rows of beds—like a hospital ward. Here they put colored prisoners to sleep in the same room with the Suffragists. Moreover, they set the Suffragists to paint the lavatories used by the colored women. The matron who handled the bedclothes was compelled to wear rubber gloves, but the Suffragists were permitted no such luxury—even in painting the lavatories. Indeed, often they slept in beds in which the blankets had not been changed or cleaned since the last occupant. It seemed a part of their premeditated system in the treatment of the Suffragists that they made them all undress in the same bathroom, and, without any privacy, take shower baths one after another.

The punishment cells, of which later we shall hear in reference to the Night of Terror, were in another building. These were tiny brick rooms with tiny windows, very high up.

A young relative of one of the jail officials, in the uniform of an officer of the United States Army, used to come into this building at night, and look in through the undraped grating of these cells. Once he unlocked the door, and came into a room where two young pickets were sleeping. "Are you a physician?" one of them had the presence of mind to ask.

He answered that he was not. She lay down, and covered her head with the bedclothes. Presently he left.

There were open toilets in all these cells, and they could only be flushed from the outside. It was necessary always to call a man guard to do this. They came, or not, as they pleased.

In the *Suffragist* of July 28, 1917, occurs the first account of Occoquan, by Mrs. Gilson Gardner. Mrs. Gardner, it will be remembered, was one of that early group of sixteen pickets whom the President pardoned after three days.

She says:

The short journey on the train was pleasant and uneventful. From the station at Occoquan the women sent to the Workhouse were put into three conveyances; two were filled with white women and the third with colored women. In the office of the Workhouse we stood in a line and one at a time were registered and given a number. The matron called us by number and first name to the desk. Money and jewelry were accounted for and put in the safe. We were then sent to the dining-room. The meal of soup, rye bread, and water was not palatable. . . .

From the dining-room we were taken to the dormitory. At one end of the long room, a white woman and two colored women were waiting for us. Before these women we were obliged, one by one, to remove all our clothing, and after taking a shower bath, put on the Workhouse clothes. These clothes consisted of heavy unbleached muslin chemises and drawers, a petticoat made of ticking, and a heavy dark gray cotton mother hubbard dress. The last touch was a full, heavy, dark blue apron which tied around the waist. The stockings were thick and clumsy. There were not enough stockings, and those of us who did not have stockings during our sojourning there were probably rather fortunate. We were told to wear our own shoes for the time being, as they did not have enough in stock. The one small rough towel that was given to us we were told must be folded and tucked into our aprons. The prisoners were permitted to have only what they could carry.

The dormitory was clean and cool and we longed to go to bed, but we were told we must dress and go into the adjoining room where Superintendent Whittaker would see us. Mr. Whittaker brought with him a man whom we afterward learned was a newspaper man. The superintendent informed us that for about an hour we could do as we chose, and pointing to the piano said that we might play and sing. The piano was not unlocked while we were there, but that night no one had a desire to sing. Although Mr. Whittaker's words were few and not unpleasant, we realized that our presence did not cause him either embarrassment or regret.

We were told that one dormitory was given up to colored women; in the other one, the one in which we were to sleep, there would be both colored and white women. We had asked to be allowed to have our toilet things and were told we could not have them until the next morning, that is, we would be permitted to have our combs and toothbrushes then. But we were not permitted to have these until Thursday. One woman told us we must not lend our comb to other prisoners and must not mingle with the colored women. . . .

The days were spent in the sewing-room. We were permitted to talk in low tones, two or three being allowed to sit together. While we were there, the sewing was very light. We turned hems on sheets and pillow slips and sewed on the machine. There were both white and colored women working in the sewing-room. The work was monotonous and our clothing extremely heavy.

The great nervous strain came at meal time. All the women ate in one big room. The white women sat at one side. The meal lasted thirty and sometimes forty minutes. The food to us was not palatable, but we all tried to be sensible and eat enough to keep up our strength. The real problem, however, was not the food; it was the enforced silence. We were not allowed to speak in the dining-room, and after a conscientious effort to eat, the silent waiting was curiously unpleasant. . . .

The use of the pencil is forbidden at all times. Each inmate is permitted to write but two letters a month, one to her family and one business letter. All mail received and sent is opened and read by one of the officials. Next to our longing for our own toilet articles was our desire for a pencil and a scrap of paper. Another rule which makes life in the Workhouse more difficult than life in the jail is that the Workhouse prisoners are not permitted to receive any food sent in from outside.

We found that the other prisoners were all amazed at the excessive sentences we had received. Old offenders, they told us, received only thirty days.

In the *Suffragist* of August 11, Doris Stevens, who was a member of the same group says:

No woman there will ever forget the shock and the hot resentment that rushed over her when she was told to undress before the entire company, including two negress attendants and a harsh-voiced wardress, who kept telling us that it was "after hours," and they "had worked too long already today," as if it were our fault that we were there. We silenced our impulse to resist this indignity, which grew more poignant as each woman nakedly walked across the great vacant space to the doorless shower. . . .

"We knew something was goin' to happen," said one negro girl, "because Monday," (we were not sentenced until Tuesday) "the clo'es we had on were took off us and we were given these old patched ones. We was told they wanted to take stock, but we heard they were being washed for you-all Suffragists."

It will be remembered that this was that early group of pickets whom the President pardoned after the appeals of J. A. H. Hopkins, Dudley Field Malone, and Gilson Gardner. Before leaving they were taken to Superintendent Whittaker.

Asking for the attention of Miss Burns and the rest of them, he said:

" Now that you are going, I have something to say to you." And turning to Miss Burns, he continued, *" And I want to say it to you. The next lot of women who come here won't be treated with the same consideration that these women were."*

Mrs. Virginia Bovee, an officer of Occoquan Workhouse, was discharged in September. At that time Lucy Burns filed charges with Commissioner Brownlow of the District of Columbia concerning conditions in the Workhouse. Evidence is submitted on Whittaker's brutal treatment of other prisoners, but our concern must be with his treatment of the Suffragists.

Lucy Burns says in that complaint :

The hygienic conditions have been improved at Occoquan since a group of Suffragists were imprisoned there. But they are still bad. The water they drink is kept in an open pail, from which it is ladled into a drinking cup. The prisoners frequently dip the drinking cup directly into the pail.

The same piece of soap is used for every prisoner. As the

prisoners in Occoquan are sometimes afflicted with disease, this
practice is appallingly negligent.

Mrs. Bovee's affidavit reads in part:

The blankets now being used in the prison have been in use
since December without being washed or cleaned. Blankets are
washed once a year. Officers are warned not to touch any of the
bedding. The one officer who has to handle it is compelled by
the regulations to wear rubber gloves while she does so. The
sheets for the ordinary prisoners are not changed completely,
even when one has gone and another takes her bed. Instead,
the top sheet is put on the bottom, and one fresh sheet given
them. I was not there when these Suffragists arrived, so I do
not know how their bedding was arranged. I doubt whether the
authorities would have dared to give them one soiled sheet.
The prisoners with diseases are not always isolated, by any
means. In the colored dormitory there are now two women in
advanced stages of consumption. Women suffering from syphilis,
who have open sores, are put in the hospital. But those whose
sores are temporarily healed are put in the same dormitory with
the others. There have been several such in my dormitory.
When the prisoners come, they must undress and take a
shower bath. For this they take a piece of soap from a bucket
in the storeroom. When they have finished, they throw the
soap back in the bucket. The Suffragists are permitted three
showers a week, and have only these pieces of soap which are
common to all inmates. There is no soap at all in the washrooms.
The beans, hominy, rice, corn meal (which is exceedingly
coarse, like chicken feed), and cereal have all had worms in them.
Sometimes the worms float on top of the soup. Often they are
found in the corn bread. The first Suffragists sent the worms to
Whittaker on a spoon. On the farm is a fine herd of Holsteins.
The cream is made into butter, and sold to the tuberculosis
hospital in Washington. At the officers' table, we have very good
milk. The prisoners do not have any butter, or sugar, and no
milk except by order of the doctor.

As time went on and great numbers of pickets were arrested, more and more indignities were put on them. They
were, in every sense, political prisoners, and were entitled to
the privileges of political prisoners. In all countries distinction is made in the treatment of political prisoners. Of

course, the hope of the Administration was that these de-grading conditions would discourage the picketing, and, of course, the results were—as has happened in the fight for liberty during the whole history of mankind—that more and more women came forward and offered themselves.

In the *Suffragist* for October 13, 1917 ("From the Log of a Suffrage Picket"), Katherine Rolston Fisher writes the following:

Upon entering Occoquan Workhouse, we were separated from the preceding group of Suffragists. Efforts were made by the officers to impress us by their good will towards us. Entirely new clothing, comfortable rooms in the hospital, and the sub-stitution of milk and buttered toast for cold bread, cereal, and soup, ameliorated the trials of the table. The head matron was chatty and confidential. She told us of the wonderful work of the superintendent in creating these institutions out of the wilder-ness and of the kindness shown by the officers to inmates. She lamented that some of the other Suffragists did not appreciate what was done for them. . . .

"Why are we segregated from all the white prisoners?" I asked the superintendent of the Workhouse. Part of the time we were not segregated from the colored prisoners, a group of whom were moved into the hospital and shared with us the one bathroom and toilet. "That is for your good and for ours," was the bland reply. . . .

That was quite in the tone of his answer to another inquiry made when the superintendent told me that no prisoner under punishment—that is, in solitary confinement—was allowed to see counsel. "Is that the law of the District of Columbia?" I inquired. "It is the law here because it is the rule I make," he replied.

We learned what it is to live under a one-man law. The doctor's orders for our milk and toast and even our medicine were countermanded by the superintendent, so we were told. Our counsel after one visit was forbidden, upon a pretext, to come again.

On Tuesday, September 18, we were made to exchange our new gingham uniforms for old spotted gray gowns covered with patches upon patches; were taken to a shed to get pails of paint and brushes, and were set to painting the dormitory lavatories and toilets. By this time we were all hungry and more or less weak from lack of food. A large brush wet with white paint weighs at least two pounds. Much of the work required our standing on a table or stepladder and reaching above our heads. I think the wiser of us rested at every opportunity, but we did not refuse to work.

All this time we had been without counsel for eight days. . . .

The food, which had been a little better, about the middle of the month reached its zenith of rancidity and putridity. We tried to make a sport of the worm hunt, each table announcing its score of weevils and worms. When one prisoner reached the score of fifteen worms during one meal, it spoiled our zest for the game. . . .

We had protested from the beginning against doing any manual labor upon such bad and scanty food as we received. . . .

Mrs. Kendall, who was the most emphatic in her refusal, was promptly locked up on bread and water. The punishment makes a story to be told by itself. It clouded our days constantly while it lasted and while we knew not half of what she suffered. . . .

All this time—five days—Mrs. Kendall was locked up, her pallid face visible through the windows to those few Suffragists who had opportunity and ventured to go to her window for a moment at the risk of sharing her fate.

Ada Davenport Kendall's story runs as follows:

For stating that she was too weak from lack of food to scrub a floor and that the matron's reply that there was no other work was "hypocritical," Mrs. Kendall was confined in a separate room for four days for *profanity*. She was refused the clean clothing she should have on the day of her confinement, and was therefore forced to wear the same clothing for eleven days. She was refused a nightdress, or clean linen for the bed in the room. The linen on her bed was soiled from the last occupant and Mrs. Kendall lay on top of it all. The only toilet accommodation consisted of an open pail. Mrs. Kendall was allowed no water for toilet purposes during the four days, and was given three thin slices of bread and three cups of water a day. The water was contained in a small paper cup, and on several occasions it seeped through.

Friends of Mrs. Kendall's obtained permission to see her. She was then given clean clothing, and taken from the room in which she was in solitary confinement. When the door opened upon her visitors, she fainted.

Aroused by an inspection of samples of food smuggled out to him by Suffrage prisoners, Dr. Harvey Wiley, the food expert, requested the Board of Charities to permit him to make an investigation of the food. " A Diet of Worms won one revolution, and I expect it will win another," promulgated Dr. Wiley.

The most atrocious experience of the pickets at Occoquan was, however, on the night known to them generally as *The Night of Terror*. This happened to that group of Suffragists who were arrested on November 14, sentenced to Occoquan, and who immediately went on hunger-strike as a protest against not being treated as political prisoners and as the last protest they could make against their imprisonment. Whittaker was away when they arrived, and they were kept in the office which was in the front room of one of the small cottages. Out of these groups there always evolved a leader. If the group included the suave and determined Lucy Burns, she inevitably took command. If it included Mrs. Lawrence Lewis, equally velvet-voiced and immovable, she inevitably became spokesman. This group included both. The Suffragists were then still making their demand to be treated as political prisoners, and so, when the woman at the desk—a Mrs. Herndon—attempted to ask the usual questions, Mrs. Lewis, speaking for the rest, refused to answer them, saying that she would wait and talk to Mr. Whittaker.

" You will sit here all night then," said Mrs. Herndon.

The women waited for hours.

Mrs. Lewis always describes what follows as a sinister reversal of a French tale of horror she read in her girlhood. In that story, people began mysteriously to disappear from a group. One of them would be talking one instant—the next he was gone; the space where he stood was empty. In this case, slowly, silently, and in increasing numbers, men began to appear from outside, three and then four.

Mrs. Herndon again tried to get the Suffragists to register, but they made no reply.

"You had better answer up, or it will be the worse for you," said one man.

"I will handle you so you'll be sorry you made me," said another.

The Suffragists did not reply. Mrs. Nolan says that she could see that Mrs. Herndon was afraid of what was going to happen.

Suddenly the door burst open, and Whittaker came rushing in from a conference, it was later discovered, of the District of Columbia Commissioners at the White House—followed by men—more and more of them. The Suffragists had been sitting or lying on the floor. Mrs. Lewis stood up.

"We demand to be treated as political pris——" she began. But that was as far as she got.

"You shut up! I have men here glad to handle you!" Whittaker said. "Seize her!"

Two men seized Mrs. Lewis, dragged her out of the sight of the remaining Suffragists.

In the meantime, another man sprang at Mrs. Nolan, who, it will be remembered, was over seventy years old, very frail and lame. She says:

I am used to being careful of my bad foot, and I remember saying: "I will come with you; do not drag me. I have a lame foot." But I was dragged down the steps and away into the dark. I did not have my feet on the ground. I guess that saved me.

It was black outside, and all Mrs. Nolan remembers was the approach to a low, dark building from which, made brilliantly luminous by a window light, flew the American flag.

As Mrs. Nolan entered the hall, a man in the Occoquan uniform, brandishing a stick, called, "Damn you! Get in there!" Before she was shot through this hall, two men brought in Dorothy Day,—a very slight, delicate girl; her captors were twisting her arms above her head. Suddenly they lifted her, brought her body down twice over the back of an iron bench. One of the men called: " The damned Suffrager! My mother ain't no Suffrager! I will put you through hell! " Then Mrs. Nolan's captors pulled her down a corridor which opened out of this room, and pushed her through the door.

Back of Mrs. Nolan, dragged along in the same way, came Mrs. Cosu, who, with that extraordinary thoughtfulness and tenderness which the pickets all developed for each other, called to Mrs. Nolan: " Be careful of your foot! "

The bed broke Mrs. Nolan's fall, but Mrs. Cosu hit the wall. They had been there but a few minutes when Mrs. Lewis, all doubled over like a sack of flour, was thrown in. Her head struck the iron bed, and she fell to the floor senseless.

The other women thought she was dead. They wept over her.

Ultimately, they revived Mrs. Lewis, but Mrs. Cosu was desperately ill all night, with a heart attack and vomiting. They were afraid that she was dying, and they called at intervals for a doctor, but although there was a woman and a man guard in the corridor, they paid no attention. There were two mattresses and two blankets for the three, but that was not enough, and they shivered all night long.

In the meantime, I now quote from Paula Jakobi's account. We go back to that moment in the detention room when they seized Mrs. Lewis.

" And seize her! " rang in my ears, and Whittaker had me by the arm. " And her! " he said, indicating Dorothy Day. Miss Day resisted. Her arm was through the handle of my bag. Two men pulled her in one direction, while two men pulled me in the opposite direction. There was a horrible mix-up. Finally, the string of the bag broke. Two men dragged her from the room. I saw it was useless to resist. The man at the right of me left me, and tightly grasped in the clutches of the man at my left, I was led to a distant building.

When Julia Emory, who was rushed along just after Mrs. Jakobi, entered the building, the two guards were smashing

Dorothy Day's back over the back of a chair; she was crying to Paula Jakobi for help; and Mrs. Jakobi, struggling with the other two guards, was trying to get to her. They placed Julia Emory in a cell opposite Lucy Burns.

Of the scene in the reception room of the Workhouse, Mrs. John Winters Brannan, who saw all this from a coign of vantage which apparently surveyed the whole room, says:

> I firmly believe that, no matter how we behaved, Whittaker had determined to attack us as part of the government plan to suppress picketing. . . . Its (the attack's) perfectly unexpected ferocity stunned us. I saw two men seize Mrs. Lewis, lift her from her feet, and catapult her through the doorway. I saw three men take Miss Burns, twisting her arms behind her, and then two other men grasp her shoulders. There were six to ten guards in the room, and many others collected on the porch—forty to fifty in all. These all rushed in with Whittaker when he first entered.
>
> Instantly the room was in havoc. The guards brought from the male prison fell upon us. I saw Miss Lincoln, a slight young girl, thrown to the floor. Mrs. Nolan, a delicate old lady of seventy-three, was mastered by two men. The furniture was overturned, and the room was a scene of havoc.
>
> Whittaker in the center of the room directed the whole attack, inciting the guards to every brutality.
>
> The whole group of women were thrown, dragged, and hurled out of the office, down the steps, and across the road and field to the Administration Building, where another group of bullies was waiting for us. The assistant superintendent, Captain Reams, was one of these, armed with a stick which he flourished at us, as did another man. The women were thrown roughly down on benches.

In the meantime, Lucy Burns, fighting desperately all the way, had been deposited in a cell opposite.

As always, when she was arrested, she took charge of the situation. In her clear, beautiful voice, she began calling the roll one name after another, to see if all were there and alive. The guards called, "Shut up!" but she paid no more attention to them than if they had not spoken. "Where is Mrs. Lewis?" she demanded. Mrs. Cosu an-

swered: " They have just thrown her in here." The guard
yelled to them that if they spoke again, he would put them
in strait-jackets. Mrs. Nolan and Mrs. Cosu were so terrified that they kept still for a while.

But Lucy Burns went right on calling the roll. When she
refused—at the guard's orders—to stop this, they hand-
cuffed her wrists and fastened the handcuffs above her head
to the cell door. They threatened her with a buckle gag.
Little Julia Emory could do nothing to help, of course, but
she put her hands above her head in exactly the same position
and stood before her door until they released Lucy Burns.
Lucy Burns wore her handcuffs all night.

Mrs. Henry Butterworth, for some capricious reason, was
taken away from the rest, and placed in a part of the jail
where there were only men. They told her that she was
alone with the men, and that they could do what they pleased
with her. Her Night of Terror was doubly terrifying—with
this menace hanging over her.

For a description of the rest of that night, and of succeeding days, I quote the account of Paula Jakobi:

I didn't know at the time what happened to the other women.
I only knew that it was hell let loose with Whittaker as the
instigator of the horror. In the ante-chamber to the cells, some
of the guards were standing, swinging night sticks in a menacing
manner. We were thrust into cells; the ventilators were closed.
The cells were bitter cold. There was an open toilet in the
corner of the cell, which was flushed from the outside. We had
to call a guard who had previously attacked us to flush them.
The doors were barred, there were no windows. The doors were
uncurtained, so that through the night the guard could look into
the cell. There was no light in the room, only one in the corridor. Three of us were thrown into every cell. There was a
single bed in each room and a mattress on the floor. The floors
were filthy as were the blankets.

In the morning, we were roughly told to get up. No facilities
for washing were given us. Faint, ill, exhausted, we were ordered
before the superintendent. It was eight o'clock and we had had
no food since the preceding day at twelve. None had been
offered us, nor were any inquiries made about our physical con-

dition. Whittaker asked my name; then whether I would go to the Workhouse and obey prison regulations and be under the care of the ladies. I told him I would not. I would not wear prison clothes, and I demanded the rights of political prisoners. He interrupted me with, " Then you'll go to the male hospital "—he emphasized the " male "—" and be in solitary confinement. Do you change your mind? " I said " No! " and was taken to the hospital by a trusty.

Then followed a series of bullying, of privileges, and of curtailing them. The first day at three o'clock milk and bread were brought to the room. After I refused it, it was taken away. That evening some more milk and bread were brought. These were left in the room all night. The second day toast and milk were brought. These were left in the room all night. The third day the matron suggested an egg and coffee for breakfast. I told her I did not want anything to eat. This day at lunch time fried chicken and salad were brought in. Later Miss Burns passed a note which read, " I think this riotous feast which has just passed our doors is the last effort of the institution to dislodge all of us who can be dislodged. They think there is nothing in our souls above fried chicken." No matter what was offered, a glass of milk and piece of bread were left from meal to meal, and once bouillon and bread was left.

The fast did not make me ill at this time, only weak. The second day there was slight nausea and headache; the third day, fever and dizziness; the fever remained, causing very dry, peeling skin and swollen lips. By the third day, I was rather nervous —there were no other manifestations except increasing weakness and aphasia. I could remember no names, and it was quite impossible to read.

We were summoned so often and so suddenly from our rooms to see Whittaker, or to have the rooms changed—we were in the same room scarcely two consecutive nights—that one was never sure when she would be searched and when the few remaining treasures would be taken from us, so I hid stubbs of pencils in my pillow, ripping the ticking with a hairpin, and one pencil in the hem of the shade. The dimes and nickels for the trusty I placed in a row over the sill of the door, paper behind the steam radiator pipes. It was difficult to find places to secrete anything, for the only furniture in the room was a single iron bed and one chair. Notes to one another are passed by tapping furtively on the steampipe running through the walls; then, when the answer comes, passing the note along the pipe. Everything is conducive to concealment.

The second day our writing materials were asked for (I did not give up those I had hidden). Then we were summoned to Whittaker—each of the hunger strikers. (There were now seventeen of us.) He had a stenographer with him. He asked my name; then, "Are you comfortable?" His manner was quite changed; he was as civil as he could be. I answered him with the little formula, "I demand the right to be treated as a political prisoner. I am now treated as a common criminal."

He: If you have steak and vegetables, will you go to the Workhouse and obey rules?

I: I will not.

He: If you will promise not to picket any more and to leave Washington soon, I will let you go without paying any fine and I'll take you to Washington in my own automobile.

I: I will not promise this.

He: What is it you want?

I: The right to keep my own clothes, to have nourishing food permanently, which will not be taken away and given back at your will, the right to send and receive mail, and above all, the right to see counsel and have fresh air exercise.

He: If I grant you all these things, will you go to the Workhouse and work?

I: I will not.

He: Are the matrons and internes kind to you?

I: Yes.

He: What food is left in your room?

I: Chiefly bread and milk, once bouillon and toast.

He: Anything else?

I: No.

He: Have you any request?

I: That I receive the rights due me—those of a political prisoner.

Whittaker will use these interviews in expurgated form, I am sure. When I said anything which did not please him, he said to the stenographer, "You needn't put that down."

After the above interviews, he absolutely refused to let our counsel who came from Washington see us.

After my visit to Whittaker this day, I was summoned to the Workhouse. My clothes were listed—those I wore—before two matrons, just as those of criminals are listed; then I was obliged to undress before the two matrons and two trusties, walk to a shower, take a bath, and dress before them in prison clothes. The clothes were clean, but so coarse that they rubbed my skin quite raw. They have two sizes of shoes for the prisoners—large and small.

The only message which reached me from "outside" was a telegram from a friend asking that I allow my bail to be paid. I answered that I would not. This day six girls in our section were taken away "somewhere." The sense of some unknown horror suddenly descending is the worst of the whole situation. Whittaker's suave manner was interrupted for a moment this day when he came into the hospital ward and saw Julia Emory in the corridor—she was returning from the wash-room—and taking Julia by the neck he threw her into her cell. "Get in there," he snarled, or words to that effect. . . . I was coming out of an adjoining wash-room at the moment, and saw this.

This night I had a most vivid dream. The interne brought in a rabbit. He held it up and told us he would cook it for us. The women—our women—did not wait for him to cook it, but rushed toward him, pulled it from his hands, and tore the living animal into pieces and ate it. I awoke, sobbing.

Next evening, there was great commotion in our corridor. The doors, which did not lock, were held; there were rapid footsteps to and fro. Distressed sounds came from the room adjoining mine, and soon it was evident that Miss Burns was being forcibly fed. Half an hour earlier, her condition was found normal by the doctor, who strolled casually through our ward, looked in at the door, nodded, felt her pulse, and went on. Now Miss Burns was being forcibly fed. What could it mean? Then there were more hurried steps, and the men went to Mrs. Lewis's room. Fifteen minutes later, they were both hurried into an ambulance and taken away—no one told us where. We had visions accentuated that night, of being separated, hurried out of sight to oblivion, somewhere away from every one we knew.

A detachment of the United States Marines guarded the place. The prisoners were kept incommunicado. That meant, not only were they not allowed visitors, but they were not allowed counsel—and counsel is one of the inalienable rights of citizenship.

In the meantime at Headquarters, the Suffragists, under the leadership of Doris Stevens, now that Alice Paul and Lucy Burns were both in prison, could not even find out where the prisoners were. They had received a jail sentence but were not in the District Jail. Katherine Morey, in great anxiety in regard to her mother, who was one of the prisoners, came from Boston to see her. She could not even locate her. Finally, she hit on the device of meeting the morning train, on which released prisoners always came from Occoquan, and one of them informed her that her mother was at the Workhouse.

In the meantime, sixteen of the women had gone on a hunger-strike. They were committed to Occoquan on Wednesday, November 14. By the following Sunday, Superintendent Whittaker became alarmed. He declared he would not forcibly feed any of them unless they signed a paper saying that they themselves were responsible for any injury upon their health. Of course, they all refused to do this, whereupon Superintendent Whittaker said: " All right, you can starve." However, by Sunday night, he was a little shaken in this noble resolution. He went to Mrs. Lewis, and asked her what could be done. Mrs. Lewis answered that all they asked was to be treated as political offenders, which provided for exercise, receiving of mail and visitors, buying food and reading matter. He asked her to write this statement out in his name, as though he demanded it. On Monday he brought the statement to the Commissioners of the District of Columbia. Commissioner Gardner gave out a statement that such demands would never be granted.

In the meantime too, Matthew O'Brien, the counsel for the Woman's Party, succeeded in getting an order from the Court which admitted him to Occoquan. He saw Mrs. Lewis, Mrs. Brannan, and Miss Burns once; but afterwards in spite of his Court order, they refused him admission.

It had been part of the system in attempting to lower Miss Burns's morale to take her clothes away from her. When Mr. O'Brien visited Miss Burns she was lying on a cot in a dark cell, wrapped in blankets. He came back to Headquarters filled with admiration for her extraordinary spirit. He said that she was as much herself as if they were talking in the drawing-room of Cameron House. Mrs. Nolan, released at the end of her six day sentence, also

brought the news of what happened back to Headquarters.
These were the things that made the Suffragists determine
on habeas corpus proceedings. Mr. O'Brien applied to the
United States District Court at Richmond for this writ. It
was granted returnable on November 27. Mr. O'Brien, however, afraid that, in combination with the indignities to which
they were being submitted, the women would collapse from
starvation, made another journey to Judge Waddill, who
set the hearing forward to the 23rd.

The next step was serving the writ on Superintendent
Whittaker. This was done by a ruse. On the night of the
21st, Mr. O'Brien called at Superintendent Whittaker's
home. He was told that the Superintendent was not there.
Mr. O'Brien went not far away, and telephoned that he
would not return until the morning. Then he returned immediately to Superintendent Whittaker's home, found him
there, of course, and served the papers.

In the meantime, Superintendent Whittaker began to fear
that Mrs. Lawrence Lewis and Lucy Burns would die. Unknown to the other prisoners—and thereby causing them the
most intense anguish—he had them taken to the hospital of
the District Jail. They had been forcibly fed at Occoquan,
and the feeding was continued at the jail.

Mrs. Lewis writes:

I was seized and laid on my back, where five people held me,
a young colored woman leaping upon my knees, which seemed to
break under the weight. Dr. Gannon then forced the tube
through my lips and down my throat, I gasping and suffocating
with the agony of it. I didn't know where to breathe from, and
everything turned black when the fluid began pouring in. I was
moaning and making the most awful sounds quite against my
will, for I did not wish to disturb my friends in the next room.
Finally the tube was withdrawn. I lay motionless. After a
while I was dressed and carried in a chair to a waiting automobile, laid on the back seat, and driven into Washington to the
jail hospital. Previous to the feeding I had been forcibly examined by Dr. Gannon, I struggling and protesting that I wished
a woman physician.

Lucy Burns was fed through the nose. Her note, smuggled out of jail, is as follows:

Wednesday, 12 m. Yesterday afternoon at about four or five, Mrs. Lewis and I were asked to go to the operating room. Went there and found our clothes. Told we were to go to Washington. No reason, as usual. When we were dressed Dr. Gannon appeared, said he wished to examine us. Both refused. Were dragged through halls by force, our clothing partly removed by force, and we were examined, heart tested, blood pressure and pulse taken. Of course such data was of no value after such a struggle. Dr. Gannon told me that I must be fed. Was stretched on bed, two doctors, matron, four colored prisoners present, Whittaker in hall. I was held down by five people at legs, arms, and head. I refused to open mouth, Gannon pushed the tube up left nostril. I turned and twisted my head all I could, but he managed to push it up. It hurts nose and throat very much and makes nose bleed freely. Tube drawn out covered with blood. Operation leaves one very sick. Food dumped directly into stomach feels like a ball of lead. Left nostril, throat, and muscles of neck very sore all night. After this I was brought into the hospital in an ambulance. Mrs. Lewis and I placed in same room. Slept hardly at all.

This morning Dr. Ladd appeared with his tube. Mrs. Lewis and I said we would not be forcibly fed. Said he would call in men guards and force us to submit. Went away and we not fed at all this morning. We hear them outside now cracking eggs.

We resume Paula Jakobi's account:

We were summoned two days later to appear at Alexandria jail next day, Friday of that week—that would make nine days spent in the Workhouse.

A writ of habeas corpus had been issued for our unjust imprisonment at Occoquan when we had been sentenced to Washington jail. This day I fainted. It was now seven and a half days since I had started hunger-striking. Three young doctors came in to have a look at the hunger-strikers. They did not take our pulse; they just gazed and departed. Later in the day, I was told that I could not go to court next day if I did not eat, as they would not take the responsibility for my trip. They prepared to forcibly feed me. I concluded to eat voluntarily, since I had to break my fast, so that evening I. had a baked potato and a baked apple. Next morning I ate no breakfast, but was threatened with forcible feeding at noon if I did not eat, so I ate again.

The next day we were taken to Alexandria Court House. There we found out why Miss Burns and Mrs. Lewis had been taken away from Occoquan. It was to prevent their appearance at Court, although it was shown that Whittaker had been removed after he had received the writ of habeas corpus. Our counsel pleaded for their appearance in Court. The warden of the Washington jail, where they now were, was so solicitous for their health that he feared to move them. Mr. Dudley Field Malone asked him whether they were being forcibly fed. The warden replied that they were. " How many men does it take to hold Miss Burns? " Mr. Malone quietly questioned, " while she is being forcibly fed? " Zinkham answered, " Four." " Then, your Honor," asked Mr. Malone, " don't you think that if it takes four men to hold Miss Burns to give her forcible feeding, she is strong enough to appear in Court? "

Next day, both Mrs. Lewis and Miss Burns were at the trial.

It was found that our detention in the Workhouse was illegal and we were given our freedom on parole. I refused to accept it, and with twenty-two other prisoners was taken to Washington jail to finish my term of imprisonment.

The Suffragists were brought from Occoquan to the Court on November 23, according to schedule. Their condition was shocking. They all showed in their pallor and weakness the effect of the brutal régime to which they had been subjected. The older women could hardly walk, and were supported by their younger and stronger companions. When they reached their chairs, they lay back in them, utterly worn out. Mrs. John Winters Brannan collapsed, and had to be taken from the Courtroom.

As Paula Jakobi has stated, Judge Waddill decided that the thirty-one Suffragists had been illegally committed to Occoquan Workhouse, and were entitled to liberation on bail pending an appeal or the return to the District Jail.

Rose Winslow, it will be remembered, was tried at the same time as Alice Paul and received a sentence of seven months.

Here are some extracts from the prison notes of Rose Winslow smuggled out to friends:

The women are all so magnificent, so beautiful. Alice Paul is as thin as ever, pale and large-eyed. We have been in solitary for five weeks. There is nothing to tell but that the days go by somehow. I have felt quite feeble the last few days—faint, so that I could hardly get my hair combed, my arms ached so. But today I am well again. Alice Paul and I talk back and forth though we are at opposite ends of the building and a hall door also shuts us apart. But occasionally—thrills—we escape from behind our iron-barred doors and visit. Great laughter and rejoicing! . . .

I told about a syphilitic colored woman with one leg. The other one was cut off, having rotted so that it was alive with maggots when she came in. The remaining one is now getting as bad. They are so short of nurses that a little colored girl of twelve, who is here waiting to have her tonsils removed, waits on her. This child and two others share a ward with a syphilitic child of three or four years, whose mother refused to have it at home. It makes you absolutely ill to see it. I am going to break all three windows as a protest against their boarding Alice Paul with these!

Dr. Gannon is chief of a hospital. Yet Alice Paul and I found we had been taking baths in one of the tubs here, in which this syphilitic child, an incurable, who has his eyes bandaged all the time, is also bathed. He has been here a year. Into the room where he lives came yesterday two children to be operated on for tonsilitis. They also bathed in the same tub. The syphilitic woman has been in that room seven months. Cheerful mixing, isn't it? The place is alive with roaches, crawling all over the walls everywhere. I found one in my bed the other day. . . .

In regard to the forcible feeding, she said:

Yesterday was a bad day for me in feeding. I was vomiting continually during the process. The tube has developed an irritation somewhere that is painful. . . .

I fainted again last night. I just fell flop over in the bathroom where I was washing my hands, and was led to bed, when I recovered, by a nurse. I lost consciousness just as I got there again. I felt horribly faint until twelve o'clock, then fell asleep for awhile. . . .

The same doctor feeds us both. . . . Don't let them tell you we take this well. Miss Paul vomits much. I do, too, except when I'm not nervous, as I have been every time but one. The feeding always gives me a severe headache. My throat aches afterward, and I always weep and sob, to my great disgust, quite against my will. I try to be less feeble-minded.

The final barbarity, however, in the treatment of the pickets came out in the experience of Alice Paul. Of course, the Administration felt that in jailing Alice Paul, they had the "ringleader." That was true. What they did not realize, however, was that they had also jailed the inspired reformer, the martyr-type, who dies for a principle, but never bends or breaks. Miss Paul was arrested, it will be remembered, on October 20. The banner that she carried had, in the light of later events, a grim significance. It bore President Wilson's own words:

THE TIME HAS COME TO CONQUER OR SUBMIT. FOR US THERE CAN BE BUT ONE CHOICE. WE HAVE MADE IT.

Her sentence was seven months.

"I am being imprisoned," said Miss Paul as she was taken from the District Police Court to the patrol wagon that carried her to jail, "not because I obstructed traffic, but because I pointed out to President Wilson the fact that he is obstructing the progress of justice and democracy at home while Americans fight for it abroad."

When Alice Paul reached the jail, she found ten other Suffragists who had been brought there four days before from Occoquan. The air of this jail was stifling. There were about seventy-five women prisoners locked in three tiers of cells, and no window had been opened. The first appeal of the Suffragists to Alice Paul was for air.

Alice Paul, not committed to her cell yet, looked about her. High up she saw a little, round window with a rope hanging from it. She asked the matron why they did not open the window. "If we started opening windows, we should have to give the colored women more clothes," the matron told her.

With her usual promptness and decision Alice Paul crossed the corridor and pulled the window open. There was no place to fasten the rope so she stood there holding it. The matron called for the guards. Two of them, unusually big and husky in comparison with Alice Paul's ninety-five pounds, tried to take the rope away. It broke in her hands, the window closed, and the guards carried Miss Paul to her cell.

Alice Paul had brought, in the pocket of her coat, a volume of Browning. Before they closed the door, she threw it with what Florence Boeckel describes as a " desperate, sure aim," through the window.

Miss Paul's confrères say that it is amusingly symbolic of the perfection of her aim in all things that she hit one of the little panes of that faraway window. As the glass had not been repaired when the Suffragists left jail, they had the pure air they demanded. They said that the old-timers told them it was the first good air they had ever smelled in jail.

Alice Paul and Rose Winslow went on hunger-strike at once. This strike lasted three weeks and a day. The last two weeks they were forcibly fed. Both women became so weak that they were finally moved to the hospital.

Two or three alienists with Commissioner Gardner were brought in to examine Alice Paul. They usually referred to her in her presence as " this case." One of the alienists, visiting her for the first time, said to the nurse, " Will this patient talk?" Alice Paul burst into laughter.

" Talk!" she exclaimed. " That's our business to talk. Why shouldn't we talk?"

" Well, some of them don't talk, you know," the alienist said.

" Well, if you want me to talk——" Weak as she was, Miss Paul sat up in bed and gave him a history of the Suffrage movement beginning just before the period of Susan B. Anthony and coming down to that moment. It lasted an

294

hour. This alienist told the present writer that in his report to the authorities he said in effect:

"There is a spirit like Joan of Arc, and it is as useless to try to change it as to change Joan of Arc. She will die but she will never give up."

Alice Paul says that she realized after a while that the questions of the alienists were directed towards establishing in her one of the well-known insane phobes—the mania of persecution. The inquiries converged again and again toward one point: "Did she think the President personally responsible for what was occurring?" As it happened her sincere conclusion in this matter helped in establishing their conviction of her sanity. She always answered that she did not think the President was responsible in her case—that he was perhaps uninformed as to what was going on.

Notwithstanding the favorable report of the alienist, after a while they removed Alice Paul from the hospital to the psychopathic ward. The conditions under which she lived here are almost incredibly sinister. It is difficult to avoid the conclusion that it was hoped that they would affect Alice Paul's reason; would certainly discredit the movement she led by making the world believe that she was mentally unbalanced. The room in which she was confined was big and square, pleasant enough. It had two windows, one of which they boarded up. They took off the wooden door and replaced it with a grated door. All day long patients— mentally unbalanced—came to that door and peered in at her. All night long, shrieks rang in her ears. Just before dawn would come an interval of quiet, then invariably it was broken by the long, harrowing, ululating cries of a single patient who kept this up for hours.

One of the alienists told the nurse to keep Miss Paul under observation. This observation consisted of flashing a light in her face every hour all night long. This—naturally —brought her with a start out of her sleep. She averaged, she says, only a little sleep between flashes. Of course one cannot but think that if she had been trembling on the verge of insanity, this process would certainly have pushed her over the edge.

The women nurses were almost unfailingly kind and thoughtful. One carried her kindness to the point of saying once, "You know, I don't think you are insane." Alice Paul says, it was staggering to have people express their friendliness for you by assuring you that they thought you were in your right mind. The doctor who forcibly fed her protested against having to do it. She was kept in the psychopathic ward a week incommunicado. When it was discovered where she was, Dudley Field Malone got her removed back to the hospital. Of course the forcible feeding went on.

In the files at Headquarters, there are dozens of affidavits made by the women who went to jail for picketing. It is a great pity that they cannot all be brought to the attention of a newly enfranchised sex. More burningly than anything else, these affidavits would show that sex what work lies before them, as far as penal institutions are concerned. I quote but one of them—that of Ada Davenport Kendall—because it sums up so succinctly and specifically the things that the prison pickets saw.

I went into Occoquan Prison as a prisoner on September 13, 1917.

I went in with the idea of obeying the regulations and of being a reasonable prisoner.

While there I saw such injustice, neglect, and cruelty on the part of the officials that I was forced into rebellion.

During my thirty days' imprisonment I saw that commissioners and other officials made occasional visits but that the people in charge were usually warned and used much deception on the occasion of these visits. Specially prepared food replaced the wormy, fermenting, and meager fare of ordinary days. Girls too frail to work were hurried off the scrubbing and laundry gangs, and were found apparently resting. Sick women were hidden. Girls were hurried out of punishment cells as the visitors proceeded through the buildings, and were hidden in linen rooms or rooms of matrons already inspected.

While there I was treated with indignities. I was insulted by loud-mouthed officials at every turn, was stripped before other women, stripped of all toilet necessities, warm underwear, and ordinary decencies, was deprived of soap, tooth-brush, writing materials, and sufficient clothing and bed coverings. I was dressed first in clean garments, but the officials later punished me by putting me in unclean clothing and into a filthy bed in which a diseased negress had slept. In the hospital I was obliged to use the toilet which diseased negro women used, although there was a clean unused toilet in the building.

With the four other women who were sentenced with me I was fed food filled with worms and vile with saltpeter; food consisting of cast-off and rotting tomatoes, rotten horse meat and insect-ridden starches. There were no fats: no milk, butter, nor decent food of any kind. Upon this fare I was put at hard labor from seven A.M. until five P.M., with a short luncheon out. We were not allowed to use the paper cups we had brought, but were forced to drink from an open pail, from common cups.

After several days of driven labor this group was ordered to wash the floors and clean the toilets in the dormitory for the colored inmates. I protested for the whole group: said we would not do this dangerous work. For this I was put in solitary confinement which lasted for nearly seven days. Water was brought three times in the twenty-four hours, in a small paper cup. Three thin slices of bread were brought in twenty-four hours. Several times matrons with attendants came in and threatened me and threw me about. They searched me for notes or any writing, and threw me about and tore my clothes. I was allowed no water for toilet, and the only toilet convenience was an open bucket. No reading nor writing materials were allowed. Mail was cut off, as it was nearly all of the time while I was in prison. I was not allowed to see an attorney during this period. The bed had been slept in and was filthy, and there was no other furniture. After six days, influential friends were able to reach my case from outside the prison, and I was taken out of solitary confinement.

While in prison I heard men and women crying for help, and heard the sound of brutal lashes for long periods,—usually in the evening, after visitors were not expected.

I saw a woman have a hemorrhage from the lungs at nine in the morning—saw her lie neglected, heard the matrons refuse to call a doctor; and at eleven saw the woman carry a tobacco pail filled with water to scrub a floor; saw her bleeding while she was scrubbing, and when she cried a matron scolded her.

Saw a young dope fiend who was insane run out of a door, and heard a matron at the telephone order men to loose the bloodhounds upon this girl in the dark. Soon heard the dogs howling and running about.

Saw men with fetters on legs being driven to and from work.

Saw matrons choke and shake girls.

Was continually disgusted with lack of fair play in the institution.

Inmates were set to spy upon the others, and were rewarded or punished, as they played the game of the matrons.

Saw sick girls working in laundry. Saw diseased women sleeping, bathing, and eating with other inmates.

Saw armed men driving prisoners to work.

Saw milk and vegetables shipped to Washington, and rotting vegetables brought up from city market.

Saw unconscious women being brought from punishment cells.

Saw sick women refused medical help, and locked in the hospital without attendance to suffer. Saw them refused milk or proper food. Saw them refused rest, and once I saw the only medical attendant kick at a complaining inmate and slam the office door in her face.

Found that while the institution was supposed to build and improve inmates, they were ordinarily not allowed any recreation nor proper cleanliness. No classes were held, and no teaching of any sort was attempted. They were deprived of all parcels, and mail was usually withheld both coming and going. Visitors and attorneys were held up, and the prisoners usually absolutely shut away from help.

Found that no rules governing the rights of the prisoners had been codified by the Congressional Committee responsible for the institution, and was told by the superintendent that the prisoners had no rights and that the superintendent could treat the inmates as he liked.

Under that management, the matrons, while apparently ordinarily decent and often making a good first impression, were found to be brutal and unreasonable in their care of inmates.

The inmates were driven, abused, insulted. They were not allowed to speak in the dining-room or workrooms or dormitories. It was a place of chicanery, sinister horror, brutality, and dread.

No one could go there for a stay who would not be permanently injured. No one could come out without just resentment against any government which could maintain such an institution.

As has been told before Judge Waddill decided that the
pickets had been illegally transferred from the Jail to
Occoquan and they were sent back to the Jail. But between
Occoquan and Jail occurred one night, in which the pickets
were released in the custody of Dudley Field Malone, their
counsel. They went immediately to Cameron House and
broke their hunger-strike—spent the evening before the fire,
talking and sipping hot milk. The next day they were committed to jail again and immediately started a new hunger-
strike.

The government, however, undoubtedly appalled by the
protests that came from all over the country, and perhaps,
in addition, staggered at the prospect of forcibly feeding
so many women, released them all three days later.

A mass-meeting was held at the Belasco Theatre early in
December to welcome them. The auditorium was crowded
and there was an overflow meeting of four thousand outside
on the sidewalk. The police reserves, who had so often, in
previous months, come out to arrest pickets, now came out
to protect them from the thousands of people who gathered
in their honor. Elsie Hill addressed this overflow meeting,
which shivered in the bitter cold for over an hour, yet
stayed to hear her story.

Inside, eighty-one women in white, all of whom had served
in the Jail or the Workhouse, carrying lettered banners and
purple, white, and gold banners, marched down the two
center aisles of the theatre and onto the stage. There were
speeches by Mrs. Thomas Hepburn, Dudley Field Malone,
Mrs. William Kent, Mrs. O. H. P. Belmont, and Maud
Younger. Then came an interval in which money was raised.
Two touching details were sums of fifty cents and thirty
cents pledged from Occoquan "because the Suffragettes
helped us so much down there." And Mrs. John Rogers, Jr.,
on behalf of the pickets gave "tenderest thanks for this
help from our comrades in the Workhouse."

Eighty-six thousand, three hundred and eighty-six dollars
was raised in honor of the pickets.

On that occasion, prison pins which were tiny replicas in silver of the cell doors, were presented to each " prisoner of freedom."

As Alice Paul appeared to receive her pin, Dudley Field Malone called, " Alice Paul," and the audience leaped to its feet; the cheers and applause lasted until she disappeared at the back of the platform.

It is a poignant regret to the present author that she cannot go further into conditions at the District Jail and at Occoquan in regard to the other prisoners there. But that is another story and must be told by those whose work is penal investigation. The Suffragists uncovered conditions destructive to body and soul; incredibly inhumane! One of the heart-breaking handicaps of the swift, intensive warfare of the pickets was that, although they did much to ameliorate conditions for their fellow prisoners, they could not make them ideal. Piteous appeal after piteous appeal came to them from their " comrades in the Workhouse."

" If we go on a hunger-strike, will they make things better for us? " the other prisoners asked again and again.

" No," the Suffragists answered sadly. " You have no organization back of you."

However, in whatever ways were open to them the Suffragists offered counsel and assistance of all kinds.

I asked one of the pickets once how the other prisoners regarded them. She answered: " They called us ' the strange ladies.' "

TELLING THE COUNTRY

In the meantime, the country had not been kept misinformed or uninformed in regard to the treatment of the pickets. Of course, the press teemed with descriptions of their protests and its results. Again and again their activities pushed war news out of the preferred position on the front page of the newspapers. Again and again they snatched the headlines from important personages and events. But despite flaming headlines, these newspaper accounts were inevitably brief and incomplete; sometimes unfair. The Woman's Party determined that the great rank and file, who might be careless or cautious of newspaper narration, should hear the whole extraordinary story. Picketing began in January, 1917. By the end of September, long before Alice Paul's arrest and through October and November, therefore, speakers were sent all over the United States. Alice Paul divided the States into four parts, twelve States each: Maud Younger went to the South; Mrs. Lawrence Lewis and Mabel Vernon to the Middle West; Anne Martin to the far West; Abby Scott Baker and Doris Stevens to the East. Ahead of them went the swift band of organizers who always so ably and intensively prepared the way for Woman's Party activity.

Public opinion became more and more intrigued, began to blaze oftener and oftener into protest as successive parties of pickets were arrested. The climax, of course, was the climactic Administration mistake—the arrest of Alice Paul. And as it began to dawn on the country that she was kept incommunicado . . . that she was in the psychopathic ward . . . alienists . . . hunger-striking . . . forcible feeding. . . .

The speakers had extraordinary experiences, especially those who went into the strongholds of the Democrats in the South. Again and again when they told about the jail conditions, and how white women were forced into association with the colored prisoners, were even compelled to paint the toilets used by the colored prisoners, men would rise in the audience and say, " There are a score of men here who'll go right up to Washington and burn that jail down." It has been said that Warden Zinkham received by mail so many threats against his life that he went armed.

From Headquarters, telegrams were sent to speakers as the situation grew at Washington, informing them as to the arrests, the actions of the police, sentences, et caetera. Often these telegrams would come in the midst of a speech. The speaker always read them to the audience. Once after Doris Stevens had read such a telegram, " Do you protest against this? " she demanded of her audience. " We do! " they yelled, rising as one man to their feet.

Suddenly while everything was apparently going smoothly, audiences large, indignantly sympathetic, actively protestive, change came. Everywhere obstacles were put in the way of the speakers. That this was the result of concerted action on the part of the authorities was evident from the fact that within a few days four speakers in different parts of the country felt this blocking influence.

In Arkansas they recalled Mabel Vernon's permit for the Court House. In Connecticut, newspapers began to call Berta Crone pro-German, to attack her in a scurrilous manner.

Anne Martin's meeting throughout the West had gone on without interruption of any kind. When, however, she arrived in Los Angeles, she was met by a Federal officer and told that there could be no meeting in Los Angeles. Miss Martin's answer was to read to him a section on the right of free speech and assemblage, to inform him that he could not prevent the meeting, to assure him that he was welcome to attend it, and to invite him to arrest her if she made any seditious remarks. The attempt was then made to get her right to use the hotel ball-room, in which she was to hold the meeting, canceled. However, when Miss Martin told the management that she had made the same speech at the St. Francis Hotel in San Francisco, they agreed to let her have the hall. Federal officers sat on the platform and interrupted her speech, saying, " You've said enough about the President now." Anne Martin replied, " If I've said anything seditious it's your duty to arrest me. Otherwise I'm going on with my speech." The audience applauded. Within a few minutes, five hundred dollars was collected in that audience for the struggle in the Capitol. Later, one of the Secret Service men warned Miss Martin not to make the same speech in San Diego. " I told him," Miss Martin said, " to follow me and arrest me at any time he wished to, but in the meantime to stop speaking to me." She had no further trouble in California.

Maud Younger's experiences in the South and West were so incredible in these days of free speech that it deserves a detailed narration.

She had passed through nine southern Democratic States. Every speech had been received enthusiastically, with sympathy, and without question. Suddenly the cry of " Treason," " Pro-German," was raised. She was to speak at Dallas, Texas, on Monday, November 18. But the organizer found she could not engage a hall nor even a room at the hotel in which Miss Younger could speak. The Mayor would not allow her to hold a street meeting. Miss Younger whose speeches are always the maximum of accuracy, informedness, feeling—coupled with a kind of diplomatic suavity—offered to submit her speech for censorship. They refused her even that. Finally on Monday morning a hall was found and engaged. The people who rented it canceled that engagement on Monday afternoon. The reporters flocked to see Miss Younger, who astutely said to them, " Of course the President is not responsible for——

etc, etc."—ad libitum—not responsible, in brief, for all the things she would have said in her speech. Miss Condon, who was organizing in that vicinity, had a little office on the top floor and decided to hold a meeting there. Miss Younger spoke to a small audience drummed up as hastily as possible, notifying newspaper and police when the audience was about to arrive. There were detectives present. Miss Younger takes great joy in the fact that in attending this meeting, these detectives, following the accepted tactics of detectives, heavy-handedly—or heavy-footedly—got out of the elevator on the floor below; tiptoed solemnly up to the floor of the meeting, thus proclaiming loudly to the world that they were detectives.

In Memphis, Miss Younger had the assistance of Sue White, who, not then a member of the Woman's Party, became subsequently one of its most active, able, and devoted workers. Miss White who is very well known in her State, had just gained great public approbation by registering fifty thousand women for war work. She fought hard and constantly to preserve Miss Younger's speaking schedule in the nine Tennessee towns. But it was impossible in many cases. Everywhere they were fought by the Bar Association and the so-called Home Defense Leagues; and often by civic officials. The Bar Association et caetera appointed a committee to go to all hotels, or meeting-places, to ask them not to rent rooms for Miss Younger's meetings, and to mayors to request them not to grant permits for street meetings. The Mayor of Brownsville, for instance, telephoned to the Mayor of Jackson: "I believe in one God, one Country, and one President; for God's sake keep those pickets from coming to Brownsville." Fortunately everywhere, as has almost invariably happened in the Suffrage movement, Labor came to their rescue.

In the towns where it was impossible to get a hall, Miss Younger did not stay to fight it out. First of all, she felt the situation had developed into a free speech fight between the people of these towns and their local governments. It was for them to make the fight. Moreover, she wanted as far as possible to keep to her schedule.

Sue White went on ahead to Jackson, which was her own home town, and appealed to the Judge for the use of the Court House. The Mayor said he could not legally prevent the meeting. Miss White opened the Court House and lighted it. In the meantime, the Chief of Police met Miss Younger in the Court House before the meeting began. He told her if she said anything against the President, he would arrest her. He came to the meeting that night, but left as soon as he discovered how harmless it was—harmless, that is, so far as the President was concerned. The audience unanimously passed a resolution asking the Mayor of Nashville, which was the next stop, to permit Miss Younger to speak.

However, when she got to Nashville, the Home Defense League had brought pressure on the local authorities and it was impossible for her to get a hall. The organizer had hired the ball-room of the hotel, had deposited twenty-five dollars for it; but the manager broke his contract, refused to allow them to use it, and refunded the money. The prosecuting attorney, months later, boasted, " I was the one that kept Miss Younger from speaking in Nashville."

The next two towns were Lebanon and Gallatin. In Lebanon, although they could get no hall, they were allowed to speak in the public square. Sue White introduced Miss Younger. It was a bitter cold day; but the weather was not colder than the audience at first. Gradually, however, that audience warmed up. When Miss Younger finished, they called, " We are all with you! " When the Suffragists reached Gallatin, they secured the schoolhouse. There was no time for any publicity, but Rebecca Hourwich hired a wagon and went about the town calling, " Come to the schoolhouse! Hear the White House pickets! "

In Knoxville, they met with the same hostility from the Bar Association. Their permit to speak in the town hall was revoked, and even the street was denied to them. Joy

Young, thereupon, went to Labor. The local Labor leader, who was the editor of the Labor paper, saw at once that it was a free speech fight. He said that Labor would make the fight for the Suffragists. He also pointed out that though the Mayor was a Democrat, the Judge was a Republican. He went to the Judge and asked for the Court House. The Judge said that it was not within his power to grant the Court House; that three county officials, to whom, twelve years before, jurisdiction in this matter had been given, must decide the question. These county officials agreed to the proposition. Again the Bar Association interfered. All day long telephone pressure, pro and con, was brought to bear on these county officials. In the end it was decided to have a preliminary rehearsal of Miss Younger's speech.

At high noon, therefore, Maud Younger went to the Court House. The prosecuting attorney opened the proceedings by reading from a big book an unintelligible excerpt on sedition. Miss Younger then made her forceful, witty, and tactful speech. Of course they gave her the Court House. The prosecuting attorney said, " For an hour I argued against you with the Judge. Now, I don't see how he could possibly refuse." The Judge said, " You women have a very real grievance." Late as it was, Joy Young got out dodgers, inviting the town to the meeting and scattered them everywhere, and the afternoon papers carried the announcement.

That night at dinner, the editor of the Labor paper called. He told them that the Sheriff had suddenly put up the claim of jurisdiction over the county Court House taken from him twelve years ago, and that he would be there with a band of armed deputies. " But," said the Labor leader, " Labor will be there with eighty armed Union men to meet them." Of course the two Woman's Party speakers did not know what would happen. But the only thing they did know was that they would hold the meeting as usual. So Maud Younger and Joy Young proceeded alone to the Court House. They both expected to be shot. The Sheriff with his deputies, instead of surrounding the building, went inside, holding the place against Suffrage attack. The Labor men stationed themselves in front of the door. The steps were filled with audience. Joy Young introduced the speaker. Maud Younger took up her position, and they held their meeting outside. Miss Younger always says: " The Sheriff had the Court House, but I had the audience."

At Chattanooga, Joy Young had explained the situation; The Mayor was with them; the Bar Association, the Chief of Police, the Sheriff were against them; so the Mayor with the assistance of Labor and the newspapers took up their fight. No hall was to be had, *and someone in the Bar Association instructed the Chief of Police to enter any private house and break up any meeting the Suffragists might hold; and the Sheriff to do the same in the country outside the city limits.* But Labor was not to be outwitted. They were holding a scheduled meeting in their own hall that night. Labor canceled that meeting and offered Maud Younger the hall free. They said they would like to see any police break up a meeting in *their* hall. All day long there was a stormy session of the Commissioners as to whether or not she might speak. But in the end she did speak.

Later, when Maud Younger returned to Washington, she met Senator McKellar in the course of her lobbying activities. Of course, she was astute enough to know that orders for all this persecution had come from above. She referred quite frankly to his efforts to stop her in Tennessee. With equal frankness, Senator McKellar said: " I wasn't going to have you talking against the President in Tennessee."

III

MORE PRESSURE ON CONGRESS

THE various activities described in the last six chapters all took place in the year 1917. But during all this year—when the picketing, the arrests, the imprisonments, were going on—work with Congress was of course proceeding parallel with it. It now becomes necessary to go back to the very beginning of the year to follow that work.

It will be remembered that early in this year there occurred in Washington an event of national political importance. The Congressional Union for Woman Suffrage and the Woman's Party merged into one organization.

This union of the Congressional Union with the Woman's Party occurred on March 2. On March 3—the last day of his first Administration—President Wilson despatched the following letter to the Hon. W. R. Crabtree, a member of the Tennessee Legislature.

May I not express my earnest hope that the Senate of Tennessee will reconsider the vote by which it rejected the legislation extending the Suffrage to women? Our Party is so distinctly pledged to its passage that it seems to me the moral obligation is complete.

WOODROW WILSON.

On April 26 occurred a hearing before the Senate Committee; Anne Martin presided. The note she struck in her opening speech sounded all through the hearing—the somber, sinister note of the Great War; and the necessity of accepting the Suffrage Amendment as a war measure.

"We regard it as an act of the highest loyalty and patriotism," she said, "to urge the passage of the Amendment at this time, that we may, as fully-equipped, fully-enfranchised citizens, do

307

our part in carrying out and helping to solve the problems that lie before the government when our country is at war."

Madeline Doty, who had traveled in Germany and in England since the beginning of the war, gave her testimony in regard to the degree of war-work women were contributing in those two countries. Others spoke: Mary Beard, Ernestine Evans, Mrs. Richard Wainwright, Alice Carpenter, Hon. Jeannette Rankin, and Dudley Field Malone, at that time still Collector of the Port of New York.

Altogether, there was a different sound to these Suffrage arguments. Women had discovered for the first time in the history of the world that they were a national necessity in war, not only because they bore the soldiers who fought, not only because they nursed the wounded, but because their efforts in producing the very sinews of war were necessary to its continuance.

On May 14, the Committee appointed by the National Party (the Party formed by the former Progressive leaders): J. A. H. Hopkins, Dr. E. A. Rumley, John Spargo, Virgil Hinshaw, Mabel Vernon, called on the President for the purpose of discussing the passage of the Federal Suffrage Amendment as part of the war program.

Mabel Vernon described the interview afterwards:

The President said frankly that the lines were well laid for the carrying out of a program in this session of Congress in which Suffrage, he intimated, has not been included and expressed his belief that the introducing of the question at this time might complicate matters. He seems to feel, however, that the coming of war has put the enfranchisement of women on a new basis.

He showed his appreciation of the rapid gains Suffrage has made through the country when he said, " Suffrage is no longer creeping, but advancing by strides."

The President told the Committee as proof of his willingness, as he said, " to help Suffrage in every little way," that he had written a letter to Representative Pou, Chairman of the Rules Committee of the House, saying he would favor the creation of a Woman Suffrage Committee.

The next day, May 15, a hearing was held before the Judiciary Committee of the House. The Progressive Committee, who had visited the President the day before, spoke, and also a group of the Woman's Party leaders: Mrs. William H. Kent, Mrs. John Rogers, Mrs. Donald R. Hooker, Lucy Burns, Anne Martin, Abby Scott Baker. Again the note of the Great War sounded through all the speeches, and the impatience of women because everything in the way of war service was demanded of them, but nothing given in return.

Mrs. Rogers said:

You men sit here in Congress and plan to take our sons and husbands and every cent in our pockets. Yet you say to us: " Do not be selfish; do not ask anything of the government now, but do your part."

Mrs. Rogers quoted the words of Lord Northcliffe:

The old arguments against giving women Suffrage were that they were useless in war. But we have found that we could not carry on the war without them. They are running many of our industries, and their services may be justly compared to those of our soldiers.

" It has taken England nineteen hundred years to find this out," said Mrs. Rogers.

Also, stress was laid on the fact that, since the last hearing before the Judiciary Committee, six States had granted Presidential Suffrage to women.

In this connection, a letter written by Chairman Webb of the Judiciary Committee to J. A. H. Hopkins of New Jersey, is interesting.

Mr. Hopkins wrote Mr. Webb:

The suggestion in your letter, that your caucus resolution provides that the President might from time to time suggest special war emergency legislation, puts the responsibility for the inaction of your Committee upon the President. As the President has already stated that he will be glad to do everything he can to promote the cause of Woman Suffrage, it seems to me quite

evident that he has at least given your Committee the opportunity to exercise their own authority without even the fear that
they may be infringing upon your caucus rules.

In the answer which Chairman Webb sent to Mr. Hopkins,
he put the responsibility of the inaction in regard to the
Suffrage situation directly on the President.
He said:

The Democratic caucus passed a resolution that only war
emergency measures would be considered during this extra session, and that the President might designate from time to time
special legislation which he regarded as war legislation, and such
would be acted upon by the House. The President not having
designated Woman Suffrage and national prohibition so far as
war measures, the Judiciary Committee up to this time has not
felt warranted, under the caucus rule, in reporting either of these
measures. If the President should request either or both of them
as war measures, then I think the Committee would attempt to
take some action on them promptly. So you see after all it is
important to your cause to make the President see that Woman
Suffrage comes within the rules laid down.

In May, the Rules Committee of the House of Representatives granted a hearing to Suffrage bodies on the question
of the creation of a Suffrage Committee in the House. It
will be remembered that this is the first time since December,
1913, that the Rules Committee had granted this request,
although women have worked for the creation of a Suffrage
Committee in the House since the days of Susan B. Anthony.
Chairman Pou presided.

A few days before, he had received a letter from President
Wilson, in favor of the creation of a Suffrage Committee.
For a long time now, the President had not been saying
anything about the State by State method of winning Suffrage, but this was the first time that he had shown a specific
interest in the Federal Suffrage Amendment.

The meeting was open to the public, and the room was
crowded. The members of the National American Woman
Suffrage Association spoke; a group of Congressmen from

the Suffrage States, and the following members of the Woman's Party: Anne Martin, Maud Younger, Mrs. Richard Wainwright, Mabel Vernon.

Mrs. Richard Wainwright said:

One of the members of the Commission from England said: "We came to America that America may not make the mistakes that we have! One of the mistakes that England is now trying to rectify is not giving justice to her women. I should like the Congress of the United States to remember what Wyoming said when asked to join the nation: 'We do not come in without our women.'"

Miss Younger said in part:

We regard this, however (the formation of a Suffrage Committee in the House), Mr. Chairman and gentlemen of the Committee, as only one step toward our goal. We will not be satisfied with this alone. It will not in any way take the place of the passage of the Amendment. Nor are we interested in any mere record vote which might come from the Suffrage Committee. We are working only for the passage of the Amendment at the earliest possible date. . . .

We ask for this measure now in war time, because the sufferings of war fall heavily upon women. In case of an invading army the greatest barbarities, the greatest cruelties, fall upon the women. In this war, as never before, the burdens are borne by women. Secretary Redfield said yesterday that three armies are necessary to the prosecution of this war, the army in the field, the army on the farm, and the army in the factories. In these two armies at home the women are taking an increasingly large part and the efficiency of their work depends largely upon the conditions under which they do this work. In England the output of munitions was not satisfactory. The government appointed a commission to investigate. They found that the trouble lay in the conditions under which the women worked, with the overlong hours. They could not get the best results under such conditions. In America today there is an effort to break down the protective legislation that through the years has been built up around women and children. And so for efficiency in the war as well as for the protection of the women, we urge Suffrage upon you now.

We do not know when this struggle may end nor to what extent the women here may replace men. An English shipbuilder said recently that should the war last two years longer he would build ships entirely with women. We know that all over Europe today they are doing men's work, in field, in factory, and in office. When the war is over and the armies march home, whether in victory or defeat, they will find the women in their places. Not without a struggle will the women give up the work, but give it up they probably will. And then, without the means of livelihood, many of them without husbands, with the men of their families killed in war, without the chance to marry, to bear children, they will turn to America. We can then look forward to an immigration of women such as this country has never known. Before that time comes we want the power to protect the women who are here, and to prepare to meet the new conditions that we may not be swamped by them.

We are asking for Suffrage in war time because other nations at war are considering it now. Over a year ago, in the Hungarian Parliament, a deputy asked the prime minister, "When our soldiers return from fighting our battles, will they be given the vote?" We find men everywhere in Europe asking for Suffrage for themselves now in war time. In Germany today the most powerful political party is urging the vote for women as well as for men. Russia, England, and France are on the verge of enfranchising their women. But two days ago in the British Parliament the Under Secretary of State for the Colonies urged the immediate passage of the Suffrage measure that the government might not be hampered by domestic problems when, at the end of the war, international problems will cry for settlement and a unified nation will be needed. In the period of reconstruction also we feel that women have something to contribute, that we may be of help in solving the new problems which will arise from the war and which will tax all the resources of the people. We ask you now to release to other service the time, the energy, the money that is being poured into the Suffrage movement.

Lastly, we urge this now that we may prove to other nations our sincerity in wanting to establish democracy and our unselfish motives in going into the war.

I think of that night on the 2nd of April when, from the gallery of the House, we heard President Wilson read his war message. We were going to war not for any gain for ourselves but to make the world safe for democracy. We sat there and heard him read, and, gentlemen, you applauded, " we shall fight for those things which we have always carried nearest our hearts, for democracy, for the right of those who submit to authority to have a voice in their own government." And while you applauded, some of us there in the gallery thought of the 20,000,000 of women in our own country who "submit to authority without a voice in their own government," which is the President's definition of democracy. We thought, too, of the women of other nations on the verge of enfranchisement themselves, and we wondered how they would welcome the United States at the peace council, to establish democracy for them—the United States, which does not recognize its own women.

And we went out into the night. The Capitol looked very beautiful and shining white against the dark sky. It seemed a great beacon light to the nations of the world. Suddenly a dark shadow fell across our path—the shadow of a mounted soldier. A troop of cavalry had encircled the Capitol holding back the people. We walked down the marble terraces and started across the Avenue. There, again, the troop of cavalry winding down the hill blocked our progress. Suddenly it seemed so symbolic of what war meant, the armed force, centralized authority, blocking progress, encroaching upon the people. And it came to us that our greatest foe is not the enemy without but the danger to democracy within. We realized then that the greatest service we could render today would be to fight for democracy in this country.

We are going into this war. We will give our service, our time, our money. We may give our lives and what is harder still, the lives of those dear to us. We lay them all down upon the altar for the sake of an ideal. But in laying them down let us see that the ideal for which we sacrifice shall not perish also. Let us fight to preserve that ideal, to make this a real democracy. And, gentlemen, the first step toward that end lies with you here today. We ask you to take that step and help make this nation truly a beacon light to nations of the earth.

Although—following the hearing before the Senate Committee, on May 15—the Chairman, Senator Jones of New Mexico, was unanimously instructed to make a report on the Amendment, he failed to do so. When so requested by the Woman's Party, he refused. After three months the minority (Republican) leaders of the Committee, led by Senator Cummins of Iowa, and backed by Senator Jones of Washington and Senator Johnson of California, attempted to get the Suffrage Amendment on the Senate Calendar by discharging the Senate Suffrage Committee from its further consideration.

In his own defense, Senator Jones of New Mexico pleaded lack of time and desire to make a report that would be " a contribution to the cause." Another Democratic member, Senator Hollis of New Hampshire, brought forward the picketing of the Suffragists as a reason for withholding the report. He expressed the amazing reason for not acting, his fear that this " active group of Suffragists " would focus public attention and " get credit." The Chairman of the Committee who had neglected week after week to make the report which he had been authorized to make by the Committee, was finally galvanized into action by a visit to the imprisoned pickets at Occoquan. Immediately, September 15, he made his report to the Senate. On September 24, the creation of the House Suffrage Committee came up for heated debate in the House of Representatives, though its passage was a foregone conclusion. Of course, there was much discussion of the picketing which was still going on. Many of the speakers harped on the note that this late action in regard to the creation of a committee, which the Woman's Party had been working for ever since 1913, would be interpreted by the country as being the result of the picketing. This was a quaint argument on their part, because of course, it *was* the result of the picketing. Why else would it have come so swiftly?

During this discussion, Mr. Pou, the Chairman, made the following statement:

I want to say in conclusion, Mr. Speaker, that this is no proposition to pack the Committee for a particular purpose. The friends of this resolution have distinctly stated time and again that they do not expect action at this session of Congress (first session of the Sixty-fifth Congress). The appointment of a Committee only is asked; but after this Committee is appointed, in the next Congress they expect to go before the people of America, and if the returns justify, then in the Sixty-sixth Congress, they will ask for Congressional action.

This boiled down meant of course there was no intention of passing the Suffrage Amendment before the Sixty-sixth

Congress. However, the Administration was to reverse its policy on this point less than three months later.

The House Suffrage Committee was created by a vote of one hundred and eighty-one yeas and one hundred and seven nays.

PART FOUR

VICTORY

"The vast and beckoning future is ours."
The Suffragist.

I

THE NEW HEADQUARTERS AND THE
LATER YEARS

At the opening of the year 1918, the Woman's Party made
another change in the location of its headquarters. It will
be recalled that during the first part of its history, it had
premises in F Street. In the middle years, it was located
at Cameron House. It was now to go directly across the
Park to 14 Jackson Place. Like Cameron House, this new
mansion had had a vivid and picturesque history. It was
built by the Hon. Levi Woodbury while he was serving in
the cabinet of President Jackson and President Van Buren.
Later, it became the home of Schuyler Colfax, when he was
Vice President. During the Civil War, Postmaster William
Denison, a member of Lincoln's cabinet, lived there. And
perhaps it was at this period that the house achieved the
apex of its reputation for official hospitality. Later, it was
the scene of the tragic triangle of General Sickles, his beautiful young Spanish wife and the brilliant Barton Key. Still
later it fell into the hands of Mrs. Washington McLean, and
then of her grandson's family—the Bughers. Then it was
turned into the Home Club.

It is a charming house. The façade is a pleasing combination of cream-colored tiling trimmed with white. Immediately, of course, the Woman's Party adorned that delicate, lustrous expanse with the red, white, and blue of the
big national banner, which always flies over their Headquarters, and the purple, white, and gold of the equally big
Party tri-color. Later, in the little oval made by the porte-
cochère, they erected a bulletin board presented by Mrs.
O. H. P. Belmont. By this means the casual passerby was

319

320

kept informed, by bulletin and by photographs, of the activities of the Woman's Party.

Inside there are rooms and rooms, rooms big and small, rooms of all sizes and heights. A spacious ball-room on the second floor with a seating capacity of three hundred, was of course of great practical advantage to the Party. The other rooms on this floor were made into offices; the rooms on the floor above into bedrooms. Mrs. Lawrence Lewis and Mrs. William Kent raised the money for the maintenance of this huge establishment.

Alice Paul, always economically inclined where expenditure is not absolutely necessary, immediately asked for contributions of furnishings. All kinds of things were given of course, from pianos to kitchen pans. From Mrs. Pflaster of Virginia came a load of heirlooms, in various colonial patterns—furniture which makes the connoisseur positively gasp. Chairs of the Hepplewhite and Sheraton periods; tables made by Phyffe; tables in the most graceful style of Empire furniture; mahogany cabinets, delicately inlaid—they gave the place an extraordinary atmosphere. Huge, dim, old-gold-framed mirrors and a few fine old paintings reinforced the effect.

Alice Paul's office, which is on the second floor, was done in purple and gold; the woodwork of gold, the furniture upholstered in purple velvet.

Later, a large room, originally a stable at the rear of the first floor, was transformed into a tea-room. Vivian Pierce had charge of the decorations here; and she made it very attractive. The brick walls were painted yellow, the tables and chairs black. The windows and doors were all enclosed in flat frames of brilliant chintz, of which the background was black, but the dominating note blue. The many hanging lights were swathed in yellow silk. The tea-room rapidly became very popular in Washington; and, as rapidly, became one of the most interesting places in the city. Visitors of many distinguished kinds came there in preference to the larger restaurants or hotels. They knew the members of the Woman's Party who lived in the house, and they gradually came to know the habitués of the tea-room. At meals, separated parties were always coalescing into one big party. People wandered from table to table. There was an air of comradeship and sympathy. Afterwards, groups often went up the little flight of stairs which leads to the ball-room, and sitting before the fire in the huge fireplace, drank their after-dinner coffee together. These talks sometimes lasted until midnight.

As for the atmosphere of the place itself—it can be summed up by only one word, and that word is—youth. Not that everybody who came to Headquarters was—as years go—young. There were, for instance, Lavinia Dock who was sixty, Mary Nolan who was seventy, and the Rev. Olympia Brown who was an octogenarian. Of course, though, when one considers that the Rev. Olympia Brown took part in that rain-drenched and wind-driven picket deputation of a thousand women on March 4, and that Mary Nolan and Lavinia Dock both served their terms in prison, one must admit that they were as young in spirit as the youngest picket there. But young pickets were there—I mean, young in actual years; young and fresh and gay; able and daring. Alice Paul, herself, whimsically relates what an obstacle their very youth seemed to them during the early part of the movement. When first they began to wage their warfare on the Democratic Party, old Suffragists rebuked them; and rebuked them always on the score that they were too young to know any better. "How hard we tried to seem old," Alice Paul said. "On all occasions we pushed elderly ones into the foreground and when Mrs. Lawrence Lewis became a grandmother, how triumphant we were. Oh, we encouraged grandmotherhood in those days." But now— triumphantly successful—they were no longer afraid of their own youth. They knew it was their greatest asset. They made the place ring with its gaiety. They made it seethe with its activity. They made it rock with its resolution. "The young are at the gates!" said Lavinia Dock. And these were young who would not brook denial of their demands.

As you entered Headquarters, that breath of youth struck you in the face with its wild, fresh sweetness. It was as pungent as a wind blowing over spring flowers. It was as vivid as the flash of spring clouds hurrying over the new blue of the sky. In actuality, youthful activity rang from every corner of the house. In the white entrance hall, a young girl sat at the switchboard; and she was always a very busy person. To the left was the Press Headquarters, full of that mad turmoil which, seemingly, is inevitable to any Press activity. Upstairs, Alice Paul was always interviewing or being interviewed; reading letters or answering them; asking questions or giving information; snatching a hurried meal from a tray; dictating all manner of business; or giving the last orders before she darted east, west, north, or south. She was sure to be doing one of these things, or some of them, or—this really seems not an exaggeration—*all* of them.

All about and from the offices that ran beside the ball-room sounded the click of typewriters—some one counted twenty-four typewriters in the house once. Everywhere, you ran into busy, business-like stenographers with papers in their hands, proceeding from one office to another. If it were lunch time, or dinner time, pairs of young girls, with their arms around each other's waists, chattering busily, were making their way to the tea-room. At night, the big ball-room was filled with groups reading magazines at the big (and priceless) tables; or talking over the events of the day . . . Congress . . . the picketing. Late at night, the discussions still went on. Upstairs, they followed each other from bedroom to bedroom, still arguing, still comparing notes, still making suggestions in regard to a hundred things: organizing, lobbying, personal appeal to political leaders, et caetera, ad infinitum. The huge, four-poster bed—big enough for royalty—in Mrs. Lawrence Lewis's room was the scene—with ardent pickets sitting all over it—of many a discussion that threatened to prolong itself until dawn.

And all day long, and all evening long—any time—organizers with their harvests of facts and ideas were likely to appear from the remotest parts of the country. Young, enthusiastic, unconscious of bodily discomfort, if the beds were all full, they pulled a mattress onto the floor and slept there or curled up on a couch—anything so long as they could stay at the friendly, welcoming Headquarters. To middle age, it was all a revelation of the unsounded, unplumbed depths of endurance in convinced, emancipate, determined youth. There was no end to their strength apparently. Apparently there was no possibility of palling their spirit. Arriving at nine at night from Oregon, they would depart blithely the next morning at six for Alabama. To those women who had the privilege of taking part, either as active participants, or enthralled lookers-on, this will always stand out as one of their most thrilling life experiences. Katherine Rolston Fisher's fine descriptive phrase in regard to it all inevitably recurs: " It was," she says, " the renaissance of the Suffrage movement."

Speed was their animating force: " The Suffrage Amendment passed at once," their eternal motto.

In the nomenclature of the Great War, the pickets were the shock troops of the Suffrage forces. They took the first line trenches. The forces of the organization back of them secured and maintained these positions; held those trenches until the time came for the next advance. As for the organizers working all over the country, they were the air force and—still using the nomenclature of that great struggle—they were like the little, swift, quickly-turning chasse-planes which so effectually harassed the huge enemy machines.

The Woman's Party never grew so big nor its organization so cumbrous that its object was defeated by numbers and weight. It was distinguished always by quality rather than quantity, and its mechanical organization was sensitive and light. It lay over its members as delicately as a cobweb on the grass; and it responded as instantly as a cobweb to the touch of changing conditions. News from Washington went to the uttermost parts of the country as swiftly as electricity could bear it. The results in action were equally swift. That was because youth was everywhere, not only youth of body, but, perhaps more important, youth of spirit. Senators and Representatives frequently marveled at the power and strength of an organization which had come to fruition in so few years. Had they all visited Headquarters —as some of them did—I think that all would have understood.

II

LOBBYING

I HAVE left until now all consideration of a department which had been, almost from the very beginning, of great importance to the Woman's Party; the most important department of all; the crux of its work; a department which steadily augmented in importance—the lobbying.

From the moment in 1912 that the Suffragists started their work in Washington, relations had to be established with the House and the Senate. At first, tentative, a little wavering, irregular, the lobbying became finally astute, intensive, and constant. The lobby grew in numbers. After the Congressional Committee had become the Congressional Union, and had separated from the· National American Woman Suffrage Association, the latter body sent its own lobbyists to Washington. The anti-Suffragists sent lobbyists too. By 1914, the stream had grown to a flood The halls of Congress were never free from this invasion. The siege lasted without cessation as long as a Congress was in session. "This place looks like a millinery establishment," a Congressman said once.

In the early days, the reception of the lobbyists at the hands of Congressmen lacked by many degrees that graciousness of which, at the very end, they were almost certain. A story of this early period taken from the Woman's Party card index, is most illuminating.

Two Suffrage lobbyists were calling on Hoke Smith. "As you are Suffragists," Mr. Smith said, "you won't mind standing." He himself sat, lounging comfortably in his chair. He took out a big cigar, inserted it in his mouth, lighted it. The two women said what they had to say, standing, while Mr. Smith smoked contemptuously on.

325

Those two women were Emily Perry and Jeannette Rankin.

The lobbying for the Woman's Party was directed at first by Alice Paul and Lucy Burns. Mrs. Gilson Gardner was the pioneer lobbyist, and the first-year lobbyists were all women voters. They made reports to Alice Paul and Lucy Burns every day. First these were oral; later they were written. This was the nucleus of the Woman's Party card catalogue which has since become so famous. Finally, these written reports were put in tabulated form by Mrs. Grimes of Michigan.

As the work grew, unenfranchised women lobbied as often as enfranchised. The early lobbyists were: Mrs. Gilson Gardner, Mrs. William Kent, Mrs. George Odell, Lucy Burns, Abby Scott Baker, Mrs. Lowell Millett. But not only the experienced lobbied. As has before been set down —following that wise instinct which impelled Alice Paul to give her workers glimpses of all phases of the movement— as fast as the organizers came back to Washington, she sent them up to the galleries of Congress to listen; she made them lobby for a while. And, as has elsewhere been stated, this was found to be a mutual benefit. Organizers took the temper and atmosphere of Congress back to the States, and sometimes to the very constituents of the Congressmen with whom they had talked; they put Congressmen in touch with what was happening at home. Whenever a woman visting Washington called at Headquarters, Alice Paul immediately sent her to the Capitol to lobby the Congressmen and Senators of her own State.

In November, 1915, Anne Martin, as Chairman of the Legislative Department, became the head of the lobbying. Miss Martin is a born general. She brought to this situation an instinct for the strategy and tactics of politics. She supervised the work of those who were under her, sent them up to Congress with specific directions; received their reports; collated them; made suggestions for the next day's work; developed a closer relation with the constituents and kept local chairmen in touch with the States of their own Congressmen and Senators. In 1916, Anne Martin ran for Senator in Nevada. She had of necessity to relinquish active work in Washington for the Woman's Party.

In the spring of 1916, therefore, Maud Younger who was in a position to give her whole time to it, became Chairman of the Lobby Committee and chief lobbyist for the Amendment.

At all times this work was hard, and sometimes intensely disagreeable. Maud Younger in her *Revelations of a Woman Lobbyist*, gives some of the actual physical strain. She says:

The path of the lobbyist is a path of white marble. And white marble, though beautiful, is hard. The House office building runs around four sides of a block, so that when you have walked around one floor, you have walked four blocks on white marble. When you have walked around each of the five floors you have walked a mile on white marble. When you have gone this morning and afternoon through several sessions of Congress you have walked more weary miles on white marble than a lobbyist has time to count.

But the Woman's Party lobbyists were not balked by the mere matter of white marble. In a week they were threading that interminable intricate maze of Congressional alleys with the light, swift step of familiarity and of determination. All day long, they drove from the Visitors' Reception Room to Senatorial offices, and from Senatorial offices back to the Visitors' Reception Room. They flew up and down in the elevators. They found unknown and secret stairways by which they made short cuts. They journeyed back and forth in the little underground subway which tries to mitigate these long distances. At first Congressmen frankly took to hiding, and the lobbyist discovered that the Capitol was a nest of *abris*, but in the end, even Congressmen could not elude the vigilance of youth and determination. As for the mental and spiritual difficulties of the task—at first,

Senators and Congressmen were frankly uninterested, or, more concretely, irritated and enraged with the Suffrage lobbyists. It is not pleasant to have to talk to a man who does not want to hear you. The lobbyists had to learn to be quiet; deferential; to listen to long intervals of complaint and abuse; to seem not to notice rebuffs; to go back the next day as though the rebuff had not occurred. This is not easy to women of spirit. Perhaps it could not have been borne, if it had not been a labor of love. Many times these women had to bolster a smarting sense of humiliation by keeping the thought of victory in sight.

In her *Revelations of a Woman Lobbyist*, Maud Younger tells interestingly and with a very arch touch some of these experiences:

Mr. Huddleston, the thin, blonde type of Congressman, sat at his desk in his low-ceilinged, well-lighted office.

"What is it?" he greeted me when I entered. His manner was very brusque, but I refused to be repelled by it. I began to speak.

"There's always some one hippodroming around here with some kind of propaganda," he snapped, interrupting. "We're very busy, we've got important things to do, we can't be bothered with Woman Suffrage." He made a jerky motion, rattling the papers on his desk, and turning his head to look through the window. I thought of several things to say to Mr. Huddleston, but this was obviously the time to say none of them. So I murmured, "Thank you," and withdrew. . . .

Mr. Whaley's face is red; his head is prematurely gray outside and his thoughts prematurely gray inside. "We don't need women voting in South Carolina," he said with a large masculine manner. "We know how to take care of our women in our State. We don't allow divorce for any reason whatever."

He was continuing with expressed contempt for Suffrage and implied contempt for Suffragists, when the door opened and a negro, evidently a clergyman, entered.

"Get out of here!" said Mr. Whaley. "You stand in the hall till you're called." As the negro hastily retreated, Mr. Whaley turned to me and said with pride, "That's the way to treat 'em." . . .

A few minutes later, I opened Mr. Sisson's door and saw him, very large and rugged, standing with some letters in his hand and dictating to a stenographer.

"I can't discuss that subject," he interrupted at my first words, and then he discussed it at length. He had meant that I was not to discuss it. He spoke of women in the kitchen, in the nursery, in the parlor. He spoke of her tenderness, her charm, her need for shelter and kindness. Wearily shifting from one foot to the other, I listened. At last I opened my mouth to speak, but he silenced me with a brusque gesture.

"The reason I'm so lenient with you," he explained—for he had allowed me to stand and listen to him—"is because you're a woman. If you were a man——" He left the end of the sentence in dark doubt. What would he have done to a man standing dumbly in my place, holding tight to a muff? I shall never know. Discretion did not allow me to ask him.

Mr. Reed sat at his mahogany desk—a large, rather good-looking Senator, with gray hair. His record in our card-index read: "He is most reactionary, not to say antediluvian." So I was not surprised to hear him say slowly and solemnly:

"Women don't know anything about politics. Did you ever hear them talking together? Well, first they talk about fashions, and children, and housework; and then, perhaps about churches; and then perhaps—about theatres; and then perhaps——" At each "perhaps," he gazed down at his finger-tips where his ideas appeared to originate, looking up at me at each new point. "And then, perhaps—about literatoor!" he ended triumphantly. "Yes, and that is the way it ought to be," he added, satisfied.

"But don't you believe that voting might make women think?"

At this suggestion he recoiled, then recovered and grew jocose.

"Do you think I want my wife working against my interests? That's just what she'd be doing—voting against me. Women can't understand politics."

I began to tell him about California women voters, but he interrupted. "Women wouldn't change things if they did vote. They'd all vote just like their husbands."

Sometimes they said to Miss Younger, "If you were a voter——"

"But I am a voter," Miss Younger, who is from California, would reply.

Their attitude invariably changed.

Miss Younger comments: "They *said* they respected

femininity, but it was plain that they *did* respect a voter."
It was hard, hard work.

The lobbying was immensely more detailed and complicated than an outsider would ever suspect. All the time, of course, they were working for the passing of the Anthony Amendment. That was their great objective, but, as in all warfare, the campaign for the great objective was divided into many tiny campaigns. At the beginning of the Congressional Union work in Washington, for instance, they lobbied Senators and Representatives to march in the big parade of March 3, 1913. Later they lobbied them to go to mass-meetings, to attend conventions. In 1916, when they were having such difficulty with the Judiciary Committee, they lobbied Republicans and Democratic members of that Committee to get them to act. By a follow-up system, they sent other lobbyists in a few days to see if they had acted. When the Suffrage Envoys came back from the West, they lobbied Congressmen to receive them. In the Presidential election of 1916, they lobbied Congress first to get Suffrage planks in both Party platforms and when these planks proved unsatisfactory, they lobbied the Republican Suffragists in Congress to get Hughes to come out for the Federal Amendment and when Hughes came out for it, they lobbied the Democratic Congressmen to get the President to come out for it. When the Special War Session met, in April, 1917, fifty Woman's Party lobbyists lobbied Congress— covering it in a month. When the Irish Mission visited Congress, and two hundred and fifty voted for the freedom of Ireland, they lobbied these Congressmen to vote for the freedom of women. When the arrests of the pickets began, they lobbied their Congressmen to go to see their constituents in jail. The Woman's Party kept track of how Congressmen voted on different measures and wherever it was possible, they linked it up with Suffrage. To the Congressmen who voted against war, they sent lobbyists who could show what an influence for peace the women could be. To those who voted for war, they sent the women, who were war workers, to show how women could work for war.

Before the six years' campaign of the Woman's Party was over, the Republicans were sometimes sending Congressmen of one State to convert the unconverted ones of another, and, in the end, the young Democratic Senators had actually appointed a committee to get Suffrage votes from their older confreres. After Congress passed the Amendment, they lobbied the Congressmen to write the governors to call special sessions of the Legislature in the interests of ratification; then they lobbied them to write the Legislators; then they lobbied them to write political leaders.

Perhaps the hardest interval in their work was that which followed the campaign of 1916. Wilson had been elected again on the slogan, " He kept us out of war." The Republicans did not want to hear anything about the women voters of the West. The Woman's Party lobbyists, who were often more informed on the Republican situation in parts of the West than were the Republicans 'themselves, had to educate them. They had to show them how remiss the Republicans themselves had been during that campaign, how Hughes for instance came out for Suffrage in the East, where women did not vote, and never mentioned it in the West, where they did. It was not easy work. Sometimes Congressmen would take up papers or letters and examine them, while the lobbyist was talking. Nevertheless, she would continue. And then, inevitably the degree of her information, her clear and forceful exposition of the situation, would arouse interest. Often in the end, the erstwhile indifferent Congressman would shake hands and bow her out.

As to the mechanics of lobbying work, perhaps nothing is more interesting than the cards themselves of the famous card-index.

No. 1—Contains the member's name and his biography as contained in the Congressional Directory.

No. 2—A key card has these headings:

Ancestry, Nativity, Education, Religion, Offices Held, General Information.

No. 3—A sub-card under the foregoing, as are those yet to be given, contains these headings: Birth, Date, Place, Number of Children, Additional Information.

Nos. 4, 5, and 6—Are respectively for Father, Mother, Brothers. They have headings to elicit full information on these subjects, as Nativity, Education, Occupation.

No. 7—Education: Preparatory School and College.

No. 8—Religion: Name of Church, Date of Entrance, Position Held in Church, Church Work.

No. 9—Military Service: Dates, Offices, Battles, Additional Information.

No. 10—Occupation: Past, Present.

No. 11—Labor Record.

Nos. 12 and 13—Are set aside for Literary Work and Lecture Work.

No. 14—Newspapers: Meaning what newspapers the member reads and those that have the most influence over him.

Nos. 15 and 16—Are respectively for Recreation and Hobbies.

Nos. 17 and 18—Are devoted to Health and Habits.

No. 19—Political Life Prior to Congress: Offices Held. Whether Supported Prohibition Amendment, Offices Run For.

No. 20—Political life in Congress: Terms, Date, Party, Bills Introduced, Bills Supported, Committees.

No. 21—Suffrage Record: Outside of Congress, In Congress.

No. 22—Votes cast in Election of Member.

In an interview in the *New York Times* of March 2, 1919, Miss Younger describes the working of this system.

If a Congressman said to a lobbyist, for instance, " I do not think my district is much interested in Woman Suffrage, I get very few letters in favor of it from my constituents," then, immediately, by means of the information gained through the card-index, a flood of pro-Suffrage letters would descend upon him. Always, as far as possible, these letters would come from people he knew or who were influential.

If a Congressman had a financial backer, they tried to get at him. If he were from a strong labor district, they appealed to Labor to bring its influence to bear upon him.

When the lobbyist started for Congress, she was given a lobbying slip which had a list of entries printed on it. For instance, one heading was " Exact statements and remarks."

Miss Younger told me of one Congressman who said to her: "Put me down on the mourners' bench. I am thinking about it." Immediately Headquarters became very busy with this Congressman.

Another said, "Women in my State do not want it." Miss Younger, commenting on that, said that it was always an encouraging case. We see immediately that he gets shoals of letters and telegrams from his State. One Congressman on whom such a campaign was waged said finally: "If you will only stop, I will vote for the Amendment. It keeps my office force busy all day answering letters about Suffrage alone."

The hardest Congressmen to deal with were those who said, "I will not vote for it if every voter in my State asks me." To such a one, we would send a woman from his own district. In one case, the Congressman was so rude to her that she came back to Headquarters, subscribed a hundred dollars to our funds, departed, and became a staunch Suffragist. We kept a list of men of this type and we sent to them any woman who was wavering on Suffrage. It never failed to make her a strong Suffragist.

Any bit of information on these cards might be used. If a man played golf, that might be a happy moment for a member of the Woman's Party to talk Suffrage with him. If he had the kind of mother who was an influence in his life, they tried to convert the mother. If it was the wife who was the ruling influence, they tried to convert the wife. They were careful even in regard to brothers. The habits of Congressmen as disclosed by this index were of great importance. Some of them got to their office early, and that was often the best time to speak with them. If a Congressman drank, it was necessary to note that. Then when the lobbyists found him muddled and inarticulate, they knew to what to impute it.

Of course information of a blackmailing order was occasionally offered from outside sources to the Woman's Party, but, of course, this was always ignored.

From 1916 on, the years in which Maud Younger was in charge of the lobby committee, twenty-two Senators changed their position in favor of Suffrage.

I have said that it was difficult for a Congressman to elude these swift and determined scouts of the Woman's Party. But harder still was it to elude a something, an unknown quality—an x—which had come into the fourth generation

of women to demand enfranchisement. That quality was
political-mindedness. Congressmen had undoubtedly before
run the gamut of feminine persuasiveness; grace; charm;
tact. But here was an army of young Amazons who looked
them straight in the eye, who were absolutely informed, who
knew their rights, who were not to be frightened by bluster,
put off by rudeness, or thwarted either by delay or political
trickery. They never lost their tempers and they never gave
up. They never took " No " for an answer. They were
young and they believed they could do the impossible. And
believing it, they accomplished it. Before the six years and
a half of campaign of the Woman's Party was over, Congressman after Congressman, Senator after Senator paid
tribute—often a grudged one—to the *verve* and *élan* of that
campaign.

But though they talked man fashion, eye to eye, the lobbyists, when returned to Headquarters, were full of excellent
information and suggestions and all that mysterious by-
product which comes from feminine intuition.

III

ORGANIZING

ALTHOUGH it is impossible to do justice to any department of the National Woman's Party, it seems particularly difficult in the case of the organizers. The reason for this is not far to seek. These young women were turned loose, sometimes quite inexperienced; sometimes only one to a State, with the injunction to come back with their shield or on it. They always came back with their shield—that is to say an organization of some sort in the State they had just left. As has been before stated, the National Woman's Party has organized in every State in the Union at some time during its history—that is between the years 1912 and 1919. As has also been stated, the organizers divided into three groups—those who worked in the first two years; those who worked in the middle two; those who worked in the last two.

It has been shown with what careful instruction Alice Paul sent these young adventurers into the wide wide world of unorganized States; but perhaps justice has not been done to the trust she placed in them and the consequent extraordinary results. She kept in close telegraphic communication with them all the time—and yet always, she left them free to make big decisions and sudden changes in policy. " She made us feel that we could do it in the first place," one of them said to me, " and somehow we did. That sense we had of her—brooding and hovering back there in Washington— always gave us courage; always gave us the physical strength to do the things we did and the mental strength to make the decisions we made."

As one looks through the lists of these three groups of organizers, one is astounded at the various kinds of work they did; their versatility. Mabel Vernon for instance. Her activities form an integral part of the Woman's Party history. Mabel Vernon traveling ahead of Sara Bard Field in her spectacular automobile trip across the country, was more responsible than anybody, except Mrs. Field herself, for the success of that trip. Mabel Vernon challenged the President in the course of his speech at the laying of the corner-stone of the new Headquarters of the American Federation of Labor in Washington. Mabel Vernon was one of the women who dropped the banner in the Senate when the President came to speak before them. Mabel Vernon picketed and went to jail. Mabel Vernon *seems* to have organized or spoken in every State in the Union.

Elsie Hill, Doris Stevens—you find them everywhere, luminous spirits with a new modern adjunct of political-mindedness. Abby Scott Baker was always on the wing.

One's mind stops at the names of Vivian Pierce, Lucy Branham, Mary Gertrude Fendall, Hazel Hunkins. How many and what varying and difficult things they did! Vivian Pierce in addition to speaking and organizing and picketing activities, edited the *Suffragist*, and designed the charming tea-room at Headquarters. As for Lucy Branham—she must have seemed a stormy petrel to all opposing forces—she had so much the capacity of being everywhere at once.

When one comes to the last group, a sense—almost of awe—is leavened by a decided sense of amusement. Julia Emory, Betty Gram, Anita Pollitzer, Mary Dubrow, Catherine Flanagan are all *little* girls. But in Suffrage work, they were active, insistent, and persistent in inverse ratio to their size. In ratification, that legislature was doomed on which any two of them descended.

What they accomplished! Once Alice Paul turned Anita Pollitzer loose on the entire State of Wyoming and Anita Pollitzer brought Wyoming into camp. It is impossible to do justice to all of them, to any of them. But as an example of how they worked, I am quoting from letters written by Anita Pollitzer describing various experiences in her work of organization. I use Miss Pollitzer's letters, not because they are exceptional but because they are typical. Space will not permit me to do equal justice to any of the others. But perhaps some day all those marvelous narratives will be collected. Miss Pollitzer writes me as follows:

Wyoming

" Campaign against the party in power "—late October, 1918 —snow on the ground and no friends in the State—traveled miles to get help of most influential woman, found her lying on the floor of a church with brass tacks and a hammer— She said she was " chairman of the committee on laying carpets in the church," and that was all she could undertake.

Cheyenne wonderfully beautiful—plains—most exceptional place for campaign purposes—forty minutes between street cars —snow miles high and every woman demanding a separate visit. Influenza epidemic so bad that it was considered immoral for six women to meet in a parlor—only way was to campaign by dodgers and street signs— Got permission from owner of building to put a forty foot purple, white, and gold sign, suspended it from the most prominent building— Town literally gathered in groups to see it— I got up next morning at seven and sign was down— I had " antagonized "—so I went to call on the Mayor and we toured the town, and rehung the sign on an even more important street, and I had double publicity, the Mayor taking full responsibility for the sign even inquiring if it would " run in the rain."

Such fearful snow, could get no billboard men to put up my big paper signs outside of the cities, and I wanted them on cross-country roads. I met a woman delivering newspapers, explained our campaign and my difficulties, and she offered us her eighteen-year-old daughter and a box of stickers, and we tramped the automobile roads and papered the tree trunks— Posters.

This is my first National Woman's Party trip. Wyoming a real adventure— South where I have always lived (Charleston, South Carolina) so utterly unlike— When I went out to mail my thousands of circular letters each night at two A.M. funny Filipino bell boys and other kinds would escort me and carry the thousands of circular letters to mail box. Local post-office *really* asked me to be " more considerate."

338

South Carolina

Getting Senator Pollock's vote seemed largely a question of getting the farmers of South Carolina. If Pollock (the Progressive) was to beat Senator Smith (the Reactionary) he must please the farm element.

So I journeyed out to Mayesville—arrived on hog-killing day —at the house of Dabs—impressive person, leading farmer of South Carolina. We ate all day, and sat around a glorious fire, and in the afternoon Mr. Dabs wrote a letter that he gave me to take to town to mail that helped more than we'll ever know. In the letter Dabs spoke for the farmers, urged Pollock to declare for the Suffrage Amendment, and ended, " We farmers are doing little talking but a lot of thinking."

I always believed if Pollock voted, he would vote " Yes." But Mrs. William P. Vaughan of Greenville, our State Chairman, and I tramped the State up and down, saying, " There'll be no vote—unless Pollock declares."

Finally one night Senator Pollock's secretary appeared at my hotel in Columbia, and he said, " Don't say again that Pollock is defeating Suffrage by delay." I said, " Well, then, get him to declare." He said, " I'm going to Washington, going tomorrow. Good night. We will have a surprise for you within a week— within three days." And at once, after weeks and weeks of campaigning, Senator Pollock of South Carolina broke the Conservative record of his State, declared " Yes," and voted " Yes," on the freedom of American women.

When it was all over—his vote and our campaign to get him to declare—I came back to Washington, had lunch with him at the Capitol, and sat, while he told me of the numerous people in South Carolina who had asked him to vote " Yes!" " You'll never know the sentiment that exists in South Carolina," was all he said. But I felt we knew.

Florida

Getting the South Florida Press Association at its annual meeting to endorse the Federal Suffrage Amendment was marvelous fun—I learned that Senator Trammell had gotten solid support from two counties, and owed this support to a man named Goolsby—editor. So I hired a car and made for Goolsby. He is a very powerful newspaper man. We sat around a log fire, with the wife, a parrot, and a cat, and finally he said he was going in two days to a meeting of the South Florida Press Association, and that he was President. I said, " I'm going too." He said, " Well, there's hope while there's life—they're against you, but you can try." I felt that we could do it, talked it all over with him, and said that I would be down to put the resolution in regardless of the results—but that I knew it could pass.

Two days seemed like years. At daybreak—five—I climbed in a Ford and arrived at the Press Conference at ten. Goolsby was the only one I knew. He introduced me to the Resolutions Committee. I sat through speeches and speeches. At noon came a luncheon. The Chairman of the Resolutions Committee took me to that. Then an auto ride all through the orange groves—we got out and picked them, talking Suffrage all the while. Only the Resolutions Committee and I were in the car. The Chairman of the Committee finally said out of a clear sky to the elderly gentleman at my left—a strong anti—" I believe we ought to pass a resolution or something, don't you, thanking Miss Pollitzer for coming? "—all in joke. I said: " No, but you ought to pass a resolution urging your own Florida Senators to stand behind President Wilson. They're not." He said, " They should." I said, " Well, let's pass it." So in the car, speeding along, thanks to the marvelously smooth roads and my luncheon friend—we wrote the resolution. The old editor said, " What? Suffrage! " My young one said, " Yes; Suffrage; standing back of President Wilson." When we got back, my old editor said: " Say, let's make that strong—we've got to go on record unmistakably for Wilson." He worked—Goolsby worked—of course the young one worked. I sat and ate oranges. It was all done—in less than fifteen minutes. The Resolutions Committee reported out a glorious resolution, calling on Senators Trammell and Fletcher to support the Susan B. Anthony Amendment, and it passed unanimously. The Resolution read: " Be it resolved that we stand with President Wilson in his advocacy of Woman Suffrage, and we urge our Representatives in Congress to vote for the enfranchisement of women!!! "

The most exciting adventure of my life was " holding up the Florida legislature " till midnight so Governor Catts could send a resolution in asking Trammell and Fletcher (Senators) to vote for Suffrage. I saw Senator Trammell in Washington, and he said he had not decided how he would vote on the Amendment. That his vote would represent " the people "—I asked him if in our government a State legislature didn't represent " the will of the people." He said, " Yes, but I don't intend to instruct my legislature." I said: " No, but maybe your legislature will instruct you." I came home and told Miss Paul, who said, "Will you go down to Florida tonight?" and Bertha Arnold and I went. Helen Hunt, a capable young Jacksonville lawyer, joined us, and the campaign began.

It was absolutely essential to get Governor Catts to send in the Resolution, as messages from the Governor only took a majority—others a two-third vote, but we didn't want this too soon. When we had our votes all there in the Senate, the leader, anti, moved that no new business not already in by noon, could come up at all—the legislature barring everything, to save themselves from Suffrage. This was fearful, as the House was most difficult, and we had planned to attack the Senate first. At four o'clock the last afternoon of the special session, called simply to discuss prohibition, we flew to the Governor's office. Helen Hunt, a senator, a member of the House, and I got Governor Catts to say he'd send a message at once. 4.30 came—5.30 came—no message. In terror, I flew down. The Governor's office was locked—I got one of the House to move a night session —we lobbied for that, it carried. The Night Session began at eight—Governor Catts still nowhere to be found. Finally, after phoning his home every five minutes it seemed—I called at ten and they said, "Governor Catts is in bed."—I said we had to have him. The person who answered the phone said nothing could be done. His secretary had the office keys; he was ill at home; his stenographer had the desk keys; she was at a movie. These obstacles to be overcome, and Governor Catts to be rushed to the Capitol. I flew back to our night session at the Capitol. I sent in a little slip-written message to Mr. Stokes, saying: "Trust us—you said you'd help—keep this session going— filibuster—do anything—don't let them adjourn." I stood in the door and saw him nod "All right," and flew.

Bertha Arnold in a taxi secured the outer key from the secretary—after arousing secretary and encountering a storm.

Helen Hunt in another taxi called for Governor Catts, waited till he got up from bed and dressed, and brought him and his daughter, Ruth, to the Capitol. I meanwhile stopped at a Western Union Office and got a messenger boy. He said, "What am I to take?" I said, "Me!" He knew the way, and together we ran through the streets of Tallahassee at midnight, covered every movie, and had the stenographer paged—brought her and her escort to the Capitol—produced the desk keys—got the resolution. Never was any sound more marvelous than Governor Catts' thud when he walked up those Capitol steps at midnight—instantly he rushed it up—the door of the House opened

—there stood my man Stokes, talking and hoarse. He had kept them there. The secretary announced, "Message from the Governor," and our resolution was read!

The vote was closer than close—didn't pass, but they had to stay till the next day at two—we stayed too, and in the morning —of the last day—we got a majority petition from the Florida legislature which showed Trammell and Fletcher that Florida wanted their Suffrage votes.

When I heard that Senator Trammell was arriving in Lakeland, I wired Miss Paul I would stay— Such a hectic and great day. I saw him with four antis in the hotel lobby. He looked dumbfounded, shook hands, discussed the climate, and acted as though I were touristing because Florida was beautiful—but he knew.

Then I went out of his life—but sent others in—all day I got out little delegations to him—the State Senator from that district—his minister—president of the Bank—leading Labor man —his editor. Mr. Trammell's one day in Lakeland was a Woman's Party event. I asked Mr. Smailes—a strong Labor man—boyhood friend of Trammell's, to see him. That night they all came to me at the hotel and each reported his achievement with Park Trammell.

Smailes said: "I looked at him and said, 'Park—it's funny you can't see it and those you were brought up with all can,' and Park looked at me, and he said, 'Well, there's one thing worrying me a little. I don't want women to get more than their share of electors.' I just looked at him, and I said: 'Park, you know Mrs. Smailes don't want more than her share, but she ain't got her share yet; that's what she's asking for.'"

I said, "Mr. Smailes, what do you think that Senator Trammell will do?" He said, "I don't know. I've known him since we were babies, but he's a Senator now."

Helen Hunt met Trammell in Jacksonville when he arrived— on his "one day" to Lakeland. He said, "Where is *she?*" (meaning me). "Is she still in the State?" (Miss Younger thinks this funny because it shows how scared they are of the Woman's Party—even one of us.)

Virginia

I think our hotel experiences are so funny.

We had a terrible time getting any one to consider taking action on Suffrage ratification at the Special Session. Virginia legislature called just for good roads—I went to Roanoke to see floor-leader Willis (strongest Suffragist in the House) and he announced he was scheduled himself to introduce a bill saying that nothing but good roads would come up. After a morning's work with Willis, he decided he would bring up Suffrage provided Senator Trinkle agreed. He promised to see Trinkle the next morning, so I decided I'd better see Trinkle that night. Fortunately a train was leaving in ten minutes. I arrived at Wytheville at nine P.M. It was black. Senator Trinkle was on the platform. I picked him out because he was the biggest man obviously and I asked where Senator Trinkle lived and he said, " I am Senator Trinkle." When my interview was at an end and it was fixed, he said that the last train out had left, and that I should go to the hotel, and say to the owner that he said to give me the best room. To my great consternation, the hotel proprietor escorted me into a room the size of a young stable, which contained six beds, explaining, " This is our best room. I'll call it a single room for tonight." Never can I describe the creaks of the empty five beds all night long. It doesn't sound funny, but it was—I and six beds, some of them double, and a box of Uneeda crackers and Hershey's milk chocolate.

The way we got the University of Virginia mass-meeting was amusing. I taught art at the University of Virginia Summer School. We had just staged a big pageant at the University. Director Maphis was grateful and said he'd do anything I wanted. That afternoon, Senator Martin arrived in Charlottesville, his home, and so I went to see Mr. Maphis to tell him I wanted Cabell Hall, the real University of Virginia Hall, and he said, " Yes." I phoned Miss Paul and she sent Lucy Branham—we advertised with huge sheets on the front of each of the eight street cars, in Charlottesville and hand-made slides at movies and posters that my Art classes all were given to do as a " problem."

The Hall was full and the wonderful old Jeffersonian University held its first Federal Suffrage Mass Meeting and passed resolutions urging Senator Martin to vote for the Amendment. Lucy Branham and I drove to his home the next morning, presented him with the resolutions, and described the meeting of his own constituents to him.

Here perhaps is the place to describe the work of the Political Department, of which Abby Scott Baker was Chairman. The Political Department supplemented the work of the Legislative and Organization Departments. Whenever the work of the National Woman's Party demanded instant pressure on Congress and on State Legislatures, Alice Paul despatched Mrs. Baker at once to the power who could exert that pressure. She was a kind of perpetual flying envoy for the Woman's Party.

IV

THE PRESIDENT CAPITULATES AND THE HOUSE SURRENDERS

IT will be remembered that after the eight months in which the Woman's Party picketed the President, the House of Representatives created a Suffrage Committee in September, 1917. It will also be remembered that during the discussion on the floor, in regard to that Committee, Mr. Pou, Chairman, made the statement that there was no intention of passing the Amendment before the Sixty-sixth Congress. That Congress adjourned on October 6, 1917. Also, it will be remembered that that day, Alice Paul marched over to the White House gates carrying a banner inscribed with the words of the President:

THE TIME HAS COME WHEN WE MUST CONQUER OR SUBMIT. FOR US THERE CAN BE BUT ONE CHOICE. WE HAVE MADE IT.

It will be remembered too that Alice Paul was arrested and sentenced to seven months in jail.

Following the publicity which came from the Woman's Party speakers all over the country and from the newspapers, protests of all descriptions began to pour into the White House and to the Democratic leaders: letters, resolutions, petitions.

Again it will be remembered that a week before Congress reconvened on December 3, 1917, all the imprisoned women were suddenly released.

In the new Session—a direct reversal of Mr. Pou's announcement of two months earlier that the House would not pass the Amendment before 1920—a day was set for the vote on the Suffrage Amendment, a week after Congress assembled.

Again, it should be pointed out that all these things happened after those eight months of picketing.

That important day which the House set was January 10, 1918. In September, the Suffragists lacked seventy-three votes of the passage of the Amendment. Naturally all December was spent in working up that vote. The National Woman's Party secured statements from Republican leaders like Mondell and Kahn, stating the strong Republican support of the measure and blaming the Democrats if it were defeated. The National Woman's Party worked up the Republican majority from three-quarters of the House to five-sixths. The Democrats began to be frightened at the press statements of the Republicans. They began to work to increase their showing, as they feared the country would blame them if the Amendment were defeated.

But more important than any of these things was the capitulation of the President which won, as the Woman's Party contended it would, the necessary votes in the house. On January 9, 1919, one year from the day the Inez Milholland Memorial Deputation visited him, President Wilson made his declaration for the Federal Amendment, and on January 10, the Amendment was passed in the House by a vote of two hundred and seventy-four to one hundred and thirty-six.

This important epoch in the history of the Suffrage Movement, Maud Younger describes in her *Revelations of a Woman Lobbyist.*

The atmosphere had changed when I returned to Washington. Republican Congressmen had suddenly realized what an asset to the Republican Party would be their support of Suffrage. Democrats, seeing the blame that would attach to them for its defeat, were becoming alarmed.

"The country is fixing to blame the Democrats," said Mr. Hull, of Tennessee, very thoughtfully, but not quite thoughtfully enough. As a member of the National Executive Committee of the Democratic Party he was thoughtful. As a Congressman with a vote in the House he was not quite thoughtful enough.

We lacked sixty votes in the House, and had only three weeks to get them. We worked day and night. Our friends in Congress, brightly hopeful, told us we had votes to spare, but we knew the truth. We lacked forty votes, then twenty, then ten, but we kept this to ourselves. Unless something happened we could not win.

Then, on January 9, the day before the vote, it happened. Late on that afternoon the President invited a deputation of Democratic Congressmen to wait on him. Knowing of the appointment, we went through the halls of Congress, on wings, all day. When the Congressmen went into the White House, a small group stood outside in the snow waiting for the first word of that interview. After what seemed an interminable time, the doors opened. Out came cheery Mr. Raker with the news: "The President has declared for the Susan B. Anthony Amendment, and will stay home from his game of golf tomorrow morning to see any Congressman who wishes to consult him about it." Thus, just a year from the day he had told us we must concert public opinion, President Wilson declared for Suffrage.

There was a feeling of victory in the air as we went through the corridors that night. Yet our secret poll showed that we still lacked votes. We could do nothing more. We could only wait and see how much force the President would put behind his declaration.

Scrub women were still at work with brushes and buckets of soapsuds when I reached the Capitol that fateful morning. From the front row of the gallery we looked down on the floor of the House, with its seven rows of empty seats rising in semicircular rows like an amphitheatre. A few people scurried here and there, the galleries were rapidly filling. We watched the Congressmen come in, sit down, walk about, or stand in groups talking and looking up at the galleries.

At the stroke of eleven all eyes turned toward the door of the Speaker's lobby. Chattering ceased. The door opened, and a Roman mace appeared and advanced, supported by the Deputy Sergeant-at-Arms, who held it in his two hands before him. Very solemn, very mindful of his step, he ascended the three steps to the Speaker's stand, followed by the Speaker, Champ Clark, dignified and magnificent in a tan frock coat, with a white flower in the buttonhole. Having ascended, the Sergeant-at-Arms laid the mace against the wall where all the Congressmen could look at it, and came down again with a little skip on the last step, while the Speaker impressively faced the House.

Prayer and routine business finished, the speeches began. Most of them were prosy and dull, delivered not for those who heard them, but for constituents hundreds of miles away. In the galleries we listened wearily. We had brought luncheon with us, which we ate as unobstrusively as possible. We would lose our seats if we left them, for through the ground-glass doors we dimly saw waiting multitudes trying to come in. All day the largest crowds the doorkeepers had ever known pressed against the doors. Inside the speeches droned on.

" What a dull ending for such a dramatic struggle," said a newspaper man, leaning over from the press gallery. I could have wished it had been duller, for we never for an instant forgot we still lacked votes. We did not know how far the President's message had carried since our last possible poll.

Suddenly a wave of applause and cheers swept over the floor. Every head turned toward the Speaker's door, and there, on the threshold, we saw Mr. Mann, pale and trembling. For six months he had lain in a hospital—his only visitors his wife and secretary. It had been said that he would never come back to the House. Yet he had come to vote for our Amendment.

Now, through the skylight, we could see that the afternoon had gone, and evening had come. At last the time for speech-making ended and the vote was taken. Forty years to a day from the first introduction of the Susan B. Anthony Amendment in Congress, one year exactly from the time the first picket-line went to stand before the White House, the Federal Suffrage Amendment passed the House of Representatives. It passed with just one vote to spare. Six votes came to us through the President. He had saved the day!

Outside the doors of the gallery a woman began to sing, *Praise God from whom all blessings flow*. Others took it up, more and more voices joined, and through the halls of the Capitol there swelled our song of gratitude. Louder and louder it rose and soared to the high arches, and was carried out into the night to die away at last in the far distances. And still in our hearts we sang, *Praise God from whom all blessings flow*.

But our minds were not at rest, nor our thoughts quiet. Our victory was worth nothing unless we could consolidate it quickly. To do this we had to win the Senate. And the Senate is farther from the people than the House, and much, much harder to move.

V

FIGHTING FOR VOTES IN THE SENATE

THE House of Representatives passed the Susan B. Anthony Amendment on January 10, 1918, by a vote of two hundred and seventy-four to one hundred and thirty-six. The work of the Woman's Party was now concentrated on the Senate. They needed only eleven votes there, and many Suffragists were optimistic—they thought victory a matter of but a few weeks. The Woman's Party knew better. However, in the siege of the Senate, they continued their policy—to work downwards through the President, and upward through constituents and political leaders from the people.

In summing up the situation in the Senate, Alice Paul said:

If the Republicans had the vision to see that it was a wise Party policy to secure the credit for the passage of the Amendment in the House, and the Democrats believed it an unwise Party policy to be responsible for its defeat—the same argument must hold for the vote in the Senate, for while more than two-thirds of the Republicans had already promised their votes, only half the Democrats are at present pledged in the Senate.

The effect of the passing of the Susan B. Anthony Amendment in the House was, however, not only profound, but immediate. In February, the Republican National Committee met in St. Louis for the selection of a Chairman. Abby Scott Baker appeared before the committee, urging a favorable stand on the Susan B. Anthony amendment. Two women representing the anti-Suffragists were also to speak. However, when the anti-Suffragist speakers presented themselves before the Committee, they found that it had already voted a resolution commending the stand of the Republican members

348

of the House of Representatives in favor of the Suffrage Amendment. This was the first favorable expression of the National Republican Party on the question of Federal Suffrage.

Minnie Bronson said of the anti-Suffragist members:

> I looked round for the thirty members who last night were opposed to Suffrage. I wonder what changed them over night.

Lucy Price, also an anti-Suffragist, asserted:

> Your action without even hearing us was worse than a betrayal of us who are opposed to Suffrage. It was an admission that Party pledges are meant to be broken.

The Executive Committee of the Democratic National Committee, which met that same day in Washington, held a telegraphic referendum of their entire national committee on the question of the Amendment. It is interesting to note that this was done at the instance of the Democratic woman who had charge of the Democratic campaign among women in 1916, when the Woman's Party made Suffrage the great issue. This telegraphic referendum showed more than a two to one desire for the national committee to take action that would put it on record as " urging the support " of the Amendment. The Executive Committee, therefore, adopted the resolution, endorsing the Federal Suffrage measure, and by a vote of five to two, calling upon the Senate to act at once favorably upon it.

For months thereafter, the Woman's Party concentrated on obtaining the necessary eleven votes in the Senate. It was a period of comparative calm. There was no militant action of any kind. The pickets had all been released in December, and, although the appeal cases were coming up in the courts at intervals, picketing seemed an abandoned weapon.

In her *Revelations of a Woman Lobbyist*, Maud Younger describes very delightfully how the first nine votes were obtained:

"We should get Senator Phelan now," said Miss Paul. "He opposed Federal Suffrage because the President did. Now that the President has come out for it, Senator Phelan should do so. Send for him."

I sent in my card and he came at once, very neat in a cut-away coat, his eyes smiling above his trimmed sandy beard. "Of course I'll vote for the Amendment," he said, as though he had never thought of anything else. He was plainly glad to have an excuse for changing his position.

"That leaves ten to get," said Miss Paul. "Let's go and see Senator McCumber." The Senator from North Dakota is sandy and Scotch and cautious, and, like many other Senators, thinks it would be weak and vacillating to change his opinion.

"I voted against it in 1914. I cannot vote for it in 1918," he said. "I cannot change my principles."

"But you can change your mind?"

"No, I could not do that."

"Then you might change your vote," said I, urging progress. He, too, saw progress, but was wary of it. Looking cautiously around the room and back of us, he said slowly, "If the legislature of my State should ask me to vote for it, I would feel obliged to do so."

That same night Beulah Amidon telegraphed to North Dakota, —her own State—to the Chairman of the Republican Party and the Non-Partisan League that controls the Legislature; to her father, Judge Amidon, and to others. The Legislature immediately passed a resolution calling on Senator McCumber to vote for our Amendment. Miss Amidon went to see him at once, with the news.

"But I haven't seen how the resolution is worded yet," said Senator McCumber cannily.

When the resolution arrived some one else went to see him.

"I want to look it over carefully," he said. When he had looked it over carefully, he admitted, "I will vote for the Amendment. But to show loyalty both to constituents and principle," he added hastily, "I will speak against it, and vote for it."

"That leaves nine to get," said Miss Paul, counting Senator McCumber off on her little finger and turning to a list of other legislatures in session. The difficulty was that the legislatures in session did not fit the Senators whose votes we must get. Mildred Glines, our Rhode Island chairman, was at our Headquarters, and Senator Gerry of Rhode Island was at the Capitol, and not for our Amendment. So Mildred Glines set out at once for Rhode Island, where she had a resolution presented and passed, and returned with it to Senator Gerry.

Then I went to see his colleague, Senator Colt. A scholarly-looking man, he sat at his desk deep in some volume of ancient lore. Arguing with himself while I sat listening, he stated the case for Suffrage and Senator Gerry. " But on the other hand," he said—and then stated the other side.

" Yes," he concluded deliberately, but with a twinkle in his eye, " Peter will vote for it."

" That leaves eight to get," said Miss Paul, very thoughtfully. " Have you seen Senator King lately? "

Though Senator King is not unpleasant to talk with, if one does not broach subjects controversial, persons who appealed to his reason had succeeded only in ruffling his manners. He smiled blandly and, leaning back in his chair, began what he believed to be a perfect case. " I've always been opposed to national Suffrage. I said so in my campaign, and the people elected me."

We must appeal to his constituents. But how? His Legislature was not in session. Alice Henkle went post-haste to Utah, and at once newspapers began to publish editorials; all sorts of organizations, civic, patriotic, religious, educational, social, began to pass resolutions. Letters poured in upon Senator King. But always Miss Henkle wrote us, " They tell me everywhere that it's no use; that Senator King is so ' hard-shelled ' that I might as well stop."

" Go to the Capitol and see," said Miss Alice Paul.

I had just entered the revolving door when Senator Sheppard, hurrying past, stopped to say, " Do you know King is coming around! I think we may get his vote."

So Miss Paul wired Alice Henkle that night: " Redouble efforts. They are having good effect." Four weeks later, three Senators told me that Senator King had said in the cloak room, " I'm as much opposed to Federal Suffrage as ever, but I think I'll vote for it. My constituents want me to."

" That leaves six to get," said Miss Paul, " counting Senator Culberson too." For while we had been busy in Washington, Doris Stevens and Clara Wolfe had been busy in Texas on the trail of Senator Culberson.

The national committees of both political parties had taken a stand for Federal Suffrage in February. Also, Colonel Roosevelt and other Republican leaders were writing to Senators whose names we furnished, urging their support.

" Now," said Senator Curtis, smiling, " I think we'll get

Harding and Sutherland. They both want to vote for it, but their States are against it. I'll go see them again. Keep the backfires burning in their States."

Senator Curtis has the dark hair and skin of Indian ancestry, and perhaps his Indian blood has given him his quick sense of a situation and his knowledge of men. Without quite knowing how it happened—it may have been his interest in listening or his wisdom in advising—he had become the guiding friend, the storm-center of our work on the Republican side of the Senate.

" Colonel Roosevelt has written to Senator Sutherland too," I thought hopefully, while I sat waiting for him in the marble room. He came out, and said almost at once, " I've just had a letter from Colonel Roosevelt asking me to vote for your Amendment! "

" Have you? " said I.

" Yes. But I wish he had told me how I can do it, when the overwhelming sentiment of my State is against it." I spoke of something else, but that night I reported this remark to Doris Stevens and Abby Scott Baker. Both of them immediately wrote to Colonel Roosevelt. Later, I again saw Senator Sutherland. He had evidently forgotten our former conversation.

" I've had a letter from Colonel Roosevelt about your Amendment," he said. " It's the second time he has written to me about it. He wants me to come to Oyster Bay so he can give me reasons for voting for it."

" I should think it would be awfully interesting to go," I encouraged gently. And soon we checked off Senator Sutherland's name on our lists, and said, " Five more to get."

" Do you think we can get Borah? " I asked Senator Curtis. " He's one of the fathers of the Amendment. He introduced it in 1910."

" He says he did that by request."

" It doesn't say so in the Record. Doesn't a man always say so when it is so? "

" That is usual," said Senator Curtis, stroking his mustache and not meeting my eyes, and I knew he said only half of what he thought.

" I think I'll go and see him at once."

Senator Borah is a most approachable person, but when you have approached, you cannot be sure you have reached. You see him sitting at his desk, a large unferocious, bulldog type of man, simple in manner. You talk with him, and you think he is with you through and through. . . . But you never quite know. . . . Sometimes you wonder if *he* knows.

In April, Senator Gallinger told Miss Paul that the Republicans counted four more votes for Suffrage—Kellogg, Harding, Page, and Borah. "We understand Borah will vote for the Amendment if it will not pass otherwise. But he will not vote for it if it will pass without him. But if his vote will carry it, he will vote for it."

Thus far we had come on our journey toward the eleven, when Senator Andreus Aristides Jones of New Mexico, Chairman of the Woman Suffrage Committee, rose in the Senate and announced that on May 10 he would move to take up the Suffrage resolution. There was great rejoicing. We thought that now the Administration would get the needed votes.

Indeed, with only two votes more to get, everything looked promising.

In May, members of the Woman's Committee of the Council of National Defense were received by the President and Mrs. Wilson.

Florence Bayard Hilles, State Chairman in Delaware for the National Woman's Party, who had campaigned for the Liberty Loan throughout her State, and was then working in the Bethlehem Steel Plant, as a munition maker, said to the President:

Mr. President, it would be a great inspiration to all of us in our war work if you would help towards our immediate enfranchisement.

Behind Mrs. Hilles came Mrs. Arthur Kellam, who is Chairman of the Woman's Party in New Mexico, who said:

Mr. President, we, women of the West, are growing very restless indeed waiting for the long-delayed passage of the Federal Suffrage Amendment. Won't you help to secure this recognition of citizens? The women of New Mexico and many other States have no redress save through the Federal Amendment. They are eagerly waiting for action on this measure in the Senate. Will you help us?

The President, with marked cordiality, answered:
" I will. I will do all I can."

In the meantime, the President was receiving picturesque groups of many descriptions: Pershing's Veterans went to the White House; the Blue Devils of France. Finally a group of women munition workers from the Bethlehem Plant, led by Florence Bayard Hilles, came to Washington to see the President in regard to Suffrage They were: Catherine Boyle; Ada Walling; Mary Gonzon; Lula Patterson; Marie McKenzie; Isabel C. Aniba; Lilian Jerrold; Mary Campbell; Mildred Peck; Ida Lennox. The experience of the war workers was amusing. They wrote at once asking for an interview with the President. Mr. Tumulty responded saying that the President bade him to tell them that " nothing you or your associates could say could possibly increase his very deep interest in this matter."

Mrs. Aniba despatched an answer, again asking for an interview. She said among other things:

The work I do is making detonators, handling TNT, the highest of all explosives. We want to be recognized by our country as much her citizens as soldiers are.

Every day this little group went to the White House and sat, waiting. They made a picturesque detail in the exceedingly picturesque war flood surging through the White House, wearing bands printed with the words, *munition workers* on their arm and their identification badges. They knitted all the time. At first, one of the secretaries explained to them, " You are very foolish. You may have to wait for weeks. Even Lord Reading had to come back four times before he saw the President! "

Later, an under-secretary said: " You are becoming a nuisance. Other people have more consideration than to keep coming back; but you persist and persist."

" Even Lord Reading had to come back four times before he saw the President," quoted one of the munition girls.

They waited two weeks, but in the end they had to go back to work. They wrote a letter to the Senate, however, which was read there.

May 10 approached. I resume Miss Younger's narrative:

When the proper time arrived next day, Senator Andreus Aristides Jones arose in his place. The galleries were packed. Our forces were all present except the three missing votes. There was Senator Smith of Michigan, who had come from California; Senator Smith of Arizona, who had left a sick relative to be present for the vote; and there were others who had come from far and wide. Senator Jones in the hush of a great moment, rose and announced that he would not call up the Amendment that day.

Our opponents looked at him and, grinning, taunted: "Haven't you got the votes?" "We want to vote today." "We're ready now."

Finally the women filed out of the galleries and went home, and the Senate resumed its usual business.

Later, however, Senator Jones announced that on June 27 he would take up the Suffrage Resolution.

Miss Younger says:

Senator Jones does not act on mad impulse. No one could imagine that placid, unhurried man buckling on his armor and brandishing his sword to lead his forces a second time up a blind alley only to lead them back again. Senator Jones was a strong Administration man and would not act without approval.

Moreover, he was a sincere Suffragist. In fact, he was a Father of the Amendment. So we kept at work, aiding and abetting all its Fathers. For the disabilities of fathers are manifest when you compare them with mothers. A father is so casual, especially when his child is an Amendment to the Constitution.

"Nagging!" said Senator Lenroot viciously, when I asked him to speak to Senator Borah. "If you women would only stop nagging!" And making a savage face at me, he hurried down the hall.

I stood still. It was but the second time we had spoken to him since he had come to the Senate. I wondered if he thought we liked "nagging"; if we liked going to the Capitol day after day, tramping on marble floors, waiting in ante-rooms—sometimes rebuffed, sometimes snarled at. I wondered if he thought we could do it for anything but a great cause—for the thousands of women toiling in the factories, for the thousands struggling under burdens at home. And then I bit my lips to keep back the

356

tears, and putting aside such uncomfortable things as feelings, and putting forward such solacing things as a lace jabot and a smile, I sent for another Senator.

Senator Martin, of silvery white hair and determined manner would not sit down and talk Suffrage, nor would he stand up and talk Suffrage. The only way to discuss Suffrage with Senator Martin was to run beside him down the hall.

" The good women of Virginia do not want Suffrage," he said, breaking almost into a trot, with eyes on his goal, which was an elevator.

" But if you were convinced that the good women of Virginia do want it? " you replied, breaking almost into a run, with your eyes on him.

" It's only the professional agitators I hear from," he answered.

It is interesting to talk Suffrage with Senator Martin, and very good exercise. But it was still more interesting to watch a deputation of good Virginia women talking to him.

" Every one knows where I stand, and yet the ladies waylay me all about the halls," he complained. Yet when we had spoken before the Platform Committee of the Democratic Convention in St. Louis, he told me: " I said to those men, ' There isn't an equal number of you that could make as good speeches as those women made.' " So he was not to be considered as hopeless, though the path to his salvation was a strenuous one.

In June, Carrie Chapman Catt, President of the International Woman Suffrage Alliance, transmitted to the President a memorial from the French Union for Woman Suffrage asking him in one of his messages to proclaim the principle of Woman Suffrage to be one of the fundamental rights of the future.

The President replied in the following letter:

I have read your message with the deepest interest, and I welcome the opportunity to say that I agree, without reservation, that the full and sincere democratic reconstruction of the world, for which we are striving, and which we are determined to bring about at any cost, will not have been completely or adequately attained until women are admitted to the Suffrage. And that only by this action can the nations of the world realize for the benefit of future generations the full ideal force of opinion. or the full humane forces of action.

The services of women during this supreme crisis of the world's history have been of the most signal usefulness and distinction. The war could not have been fought without them or its sacrifices endured. It is high time that some part of our debt of gratitude to them should be acknowledged and paid, and the only acknowledgment they ask is their admission to the Suffrage. Can we justly refuse it?

As for America, it is my earnest hope that the Senate of the United States will give unmistakable answer to this question by passing the Suffrage Amendment to our Federal Constitution before the end of this session.

Cordially and sincerely yours,
WOODROW WILSON.

Miss Younger says:

The twenty-seventh of June approached. Again we were in the marble room talking with Senators. Absentees were on trains hurrying to Washington. The antis were in the reception-room knitting votes into their wool. The Capitol thrilled with excitement. Even the Senators seemed to feel it. This time Sutherland would vote " yea," and several opponents were absent. If none of them paired with a Suffrage Senator we could just manage the necessary majority. And the White House was taking a hand. Senator James of Kentucky, in a Baltimore hospital, had promised Mr. Tumulty that he would not pair—that is, that he would not ask a Suffrage Senator to refrain from voting to counterbalance his own enforced absence. Victory seemed in our hands.

The day arrived. The galleries were filled. The Senators came in all dressed up for the occasion—here a gay waistcoat or a bright tie, there a flower in a button-hole, yonder an elegant frock coat over gray trousers.

Senator Jones arose to take up the Amendment. At once opposition developed. Our opponents were willing to have a vote, provided all absentees could be paired. Now, if all absentees were counted, we would not have enough votes. Senator James' promise not to vote had given us our majority. But, stunned, we heard Senator Underwood read a telegram from Senator James pleading that some Suffragist pair with him. Senator Underwood said he had just confirmed the telegram. It was not until too late that we learned the truth. The telegram had been sent six weeks earlier for another occasion.

And now Senator Reed had the floor. " Oh, who will pair

with Ollie James?" he cried. "That n-o-oble Ollie James! You all know that great, fine, noble specimen of manhood, Ollie James! A pair! A pair!" he cried with tears in his voice and arms outstretched. He went on and on.

We leaned over the balcony and watched Senator Curtis pleading with Borah, urging him to vote for us and save our Amendment. We watched breathlessly. We saw Borah listen, smile, and then, without a word, rise and walk slowly out of the room. We flew down to Senator Curtis.

"No, Borah won't do it. They say King is going to. Reed won't give up the floor unless we withdraw or furnish a pair. He and his friends will hold the floor for weeks, if necessary. And the military bill must pass before July first. The army needs money. You can see for yourself what's happening. It's a filibuster."

Reed was still talking. They say he knows about a great many subjects, and I think he talked about all he knew that day. But nobody will ever know what they were, for no one listened; and he never allowed the speech to be printed in the *Record*.

Finally Senator Jones arose and withdrew the motion to take up Suffrage. Senator Reed, satisfied, sat down. His filibuster had succeeded. He had threatened to hold up the military bill to defeat us, so we had withdrawn. The Senate took up the military bill, and we went home.

"Suffrage is dead for this session," said Senator McKellar. "The Senators don't like being nagged any more. They are all very tired of it."

But the Woman's Party did not think it was dead. They worked at their usual strenuous pace all summer long. They did feel, however, that if the President had exerted himself, he could have obtained the two necessary votes for the Amendment to pass. They were, moreover, highly indignant over the filibuster of a Democratic Senator—Reed. Their patience was beginning to wear thin.

In the meantime, the primary Senatorial elections were coming up, and the President was taking an active part in them. He was working against Senator Vardaman of Mississippi and Senator Hardwick of Georgia, both Democrats of course and Vardaman a Suffragist. In other States, he helped to elect anti-Suffragists in the places of Suffragists. It is true that the President threw a sop to the Suffragists in that he asked Senator Shields of Tennessee to come out for Suffrage. The Shields incident is interesting.

Senator Shields was making it his sole issue in the primary campaign that he would carry out all the President's war policies. Opposing Senator Shields was Governor Rye, a Democrat of course, and a Suffragist.

Maud Younger called at the White House on Secretary Tumulty one day to ask him if the President could not do something further for Suffrage. Mr. Tumulty's answer was to read a letter from President Wilson to Senator Shields, asking him to vote for the Suffrage Amendment. Maud Younger, with characteristic political astuteness, saw at once the possibilities in the publication of that letter. She asked Mr. Tumulty for a copy and Mr. Tumulty, with a sudden sense of indiscretion, refused. However, Miss Younger went back instantly with the story to Headquarters, and presently Sue White and Lucy Branham became very busy—oh, very busy indeed—in the Tennessee campaign.

On July 26, Senator Shields notified the Suffragists in Tennessee that he would see them at three that afternoon. He told the fifty women who gathered to meet him that "he would hold the matter in consideration." The same day a Columbia paper carried the story that President Wilson had requested Senator Shields by letter to vote for Suffrage. This brought the whole month-old correspondence before the public.

The letters ran as follows:

THE WHITE HOUSE, WASHINGTON.
June 20, 1918.

MY DEAR SENATOR:
I feel so deeply the possibilities latent in the vote which is presently to be taken by the Senate on the Suffrage Amendment that I am going to take a liberty which in ordinary circumstances I should not feel justified in taking, and ask you very frankly if it will not be possible for you to vote for the Amendment. I

feel that much of the morale of this country and of the world will repose in our sincere adherence to democratic principles, will depend upon the action which the Senate takes in this now critically important matter. If it were merely a domestic question, or if the times were normal, I would not feel that I could make a direct request of this sort, but the times are so far from normal, the fortunes of nations are so linked together, the reactions upon the thought of the world are so sharp and involve such momentous issues that I know that you will indulge my unusual course of action and permit me to beg very earnestly that you will lend your aid in clearing away the difficulties which will undoubtedly beset us if the Amendment is not adopted. With much respect,

Sincerely yours,
WOODROW WILSON.

UNITED STATES SENATE, WASHINGTON, D. C.
June 25, 1918.

MY DEAR MR. PRESIDENT:

Your valued letter concerning the joint resolution proposing an Amendment on the Federal Constitution favoring Equal Suffrage, now pending in the United States Senate, has challenged my most thoughtful consideration, as do all your views upon public matters. The resolution involves fundamental questions affecting the sovereignty and powers of the Federal and State governments, most important and vital to the people of the State which I have the honor in part to represent in the United States Senate, and those of States with which they are closely allied in all social, economical, and governmental interests, upon which I have most profound convictions, unfavorable to it, known, and I believe approved, by the great majority of the people of Tennessee—arrived at after full consideration of conditions existing when I voted against a similar one some years ago and those now confronting our country. The reasons for my conclusions are those controlling the majority of my colleagues from the Southern States, well known to you and which would not be interesting to here re-state.

If I could bring myself to believe that the adoption of the Resolution would contribute to the successful prosecution of the war we are waging with Germany, I would unhesitatingly vote for it, because my whole heart and soul is involved in bringing it to a victorious issue and I am willing to sacrifice everything save the honor and freedom of our country in aiding you to accomplish that end. But I have been unable to do so. We cannot reasonably expect the proposed Amendment to be ratified within less than two years and the discussion of it would, unquestionably, divert the minds and energies of the people from the one great absorbing subject before us—the winning of the war— by involving those of many States in a most bitter controversy contrary to our earnest desire for that unity of thought and action of the American people now so imperatively required.

These are my sincere convictions, but, out of my very high respect for your views, I will continue to give your suggestion my most thoughtful and earnest consideration.

With the highest respect, I am,

Sincerely yours,
JOHN K. SHIELDS.

WASHINGTON, D. C.
June 26, 1918.

Thank you very sincerely for your frank letter of yesterday about the Suffrage Amendment. I realize the weight of argument that has controlled your attitude in the matter, and I would not have written as I did if I had not thought that the passage of the Amendment at this time was an essential psychological element in the conduct of the war for democracy. I am led by a single sentence in your letter, therefore, to write to say that I do earnestly believe that our acting upon this Amendment will have an important and immediate influence upon the whole atmosphere and morale of the nations engaged in the war, and every day I am coming to see how supremely important that side of the whole thing is. We can win if we have the will to win.

Cordially and sincerely yours,
WOODROW WILSON.

Many believe that had President Wilson—in regard to Suffrage—gone over Shields' head to his constituents as— in regard to other war policies—he had gone over the heads of Vardaman and Hardwick to their constituents, Senator Shields would have declared in favor of Suffrage.

On August 2, a letter written by the President to Senator Baird of New Jersey was made public:

The President writes:

The whole subject of Woman Suffrage has been very much in my mind of late and has come to seem to be a part of the international situation, as well as of capital importance to the United States. I believe our present position as champions of democracy throughout the world would be greatly strengthened if the Senate would follow the example of the House of Representatives in passing the pending Amendment. I, therefore, take the liberty of writing to call the matter to your serious attention in this light and to express the hope that you will deem it wise to throw your influence on the side of this great and now critical reform.

(Signed) WOODROW WILSON.

In spite of these letters, which of course were mere requests, Alice Paul well knew, as did the Senators themselves, that President Wilson was doing a little for Suffrage, but not all he could. He was not of course doing for the Suffrage Amendment a tithe of what he did for other measures in whose success he was interested. Nothing continued to happen with monotonous, unfailing regularity.

The Woman's Party could wait no longer.

VI

BURNING THE PRESIDENT'S WORDS

AT half-past four on Tuesday afternoon, August 6, a line of nearly one hundred women emerged from Headquarters, crossed the other side of the street to the Park; turned into Pennsylvania Avenue. At the head of the long line floated the red, white, and blue of the American flag carried by Hazel Hunkins. Behind it came, banner after banner and banner after banner, the purple, white, and gold of the National Woman's Party tri-color. The line proceeded along Pennsylvania Avenue until it came to the statue of Lafayette just opposite the east gate of the White House. All along the way, the crowds cheered and applauded the women; soldiers and sailors saluted the red, white, and blue as it passed.

At the Lafayette monument, two banner bearers emerged from the group; and stationed themselves on the platform at the base of the statue.

One of them, Mary Gertrude Fendall, bore Inez Milholland's banner, inscribed with her memorable last words:

HOW LONG MUST WOMEN WAIT FOR LIBERTY?

The other, borne by Clara Wold and Blanche McPherson, carried what was really the message of the meeting:

WE PROTEST AGAINST THE CONTINUED DISFRANCHISEMENT OF AMERICAN WOMEN, FOR WHICH THE PRESIDENT OF THE UNITED STATES IS RESPONSIBLE.

WE CONDEMN THE PRESIDENT AND HIS PARTY FOR ALLOWING THE OBSTRUCTION OF SUFFRAGE IN THE SENATE.

WE DEPLORE THE WEAKNESS OF PRESIDENT WILSON IN PER-
MITTING THE SENATE TO LINE ITSELF WITH THE PRUSSIAN
REICHSTAG BY DENYING DEMOCRACY TO THE PEOPLE

WE DEMAND THAT THE PRESIDENT AND HIS PARTY SECURE
THE PASSAGE OF THE SUFFRAGE AMENDMENT THROUGH THE
SENATE IN THE PRESENT SESSION.

The other banner bearers marched to both sides of the
statue where they made solid banks of vivid color. Mrs.
Lawrence Lewis stepped forward. " We are here," she said,
" because when our country is at war for liberty and democracy. . . ."

At the word " democracy," the police, who had been drawing nearer and nearer, placed her under arrest. Other
women standing about her were arrested, although they had
not even spoken.

For a moment there was a complete silence.

Then Hazel Hunkins, who had led the line carrying the
American flag, leaped upon the base of the statue and said:

Here, at the statue of Lafayette, who fought for the liberty of
this country, and under the American flag, I am asking for the
enfranchisement of American women.

She was immediately arrested. Another woman took her
place, and she was arrested; another; and another; and on
and on, until forty-seven women had been taken into custody.

Alice Paul, who had not participated in the parade, was
standing in the middle of the street, watching and listening.
She had no banner. She had not spoken. She had not
moved. But a policeman, pointing at her, said: " That is
the leader; get her! " And she was arrested.

Many women asked on what charge they were arrested.
" Do not answer them! Do not tell them anything! " said
a policeman. Others answered with very labored charges,
which were not substantiated later by Police Headquarters.
Patrol wagon after patrol wagon appeared, was filled with

BURNING THE PRESIDENT'S WORDS AT THE LAFAYETTE
MONUMENT, WASHINGTON.

A SUMMER PICKET LINE.

women, and dashed off, followed by the purple, white, and gold flutter of the banners.

When Hazel Hunkins was arrested, she forbade the policemen to take the American flag which she carried from her. At the Municipal Building, she refused to relinquish it. After the preliminaries of their arrest were over and the women released on bail, they marched back in an unbroken line behind Hazel's flag.

The arrested women were the following:

Hazel Adams, Eva E. Sturtevant, Pauline Clarke, Blanche A. McPherson, Katherine R. Fisher, Rose Lieberson, Alice Kimball, Matilda Terrace, Lucy Burns, Edith Ainge, May Sullivan, Mary Gertrude Fendall, Julia Emory, Anna Kuhn, Gladys Greiner, Martha W. Moore, Cora Crawford, Dr. Sarah Hunt Lockrey, Mrs. Lawrence Lewis, Ellen Winsor, Mary Winsor, Mrs. Edmund C. Evans, Christine M. Doyle, Kate Cleaver Heffelfinger, Lavinia Dock, Harriet Keehn, Alice Paul, Mary E. Dubrow, Lillian M. Ascough, Edna M. Purtelle, Ruby E. Koeing, Elsie Hill, Helena Hill Weed, Eleanor Hill Weed, Mrs. Gilson Gardner, Sophie G. Meredith, Louise M. Black, Agnes Chase, Kate J. Boeckh, Hazel Hunkins, Cora Wold, Clara P. Wold, Margaret Oakes, Mollie Marie Green, Gertrude Lynde Crocker, Effie Boutwell Main, Annie Arniel, Emily Burke Main.

The forty-seven were ordered to appear in court the next morning at half-past nine. The United States attorney told them, when he arrived at 10:30, that the case was postponed for a week. The police clerk told Clara Wold that she was arrested " for climbing the statue."

Clara Wold describes her subsequent experiences when, dismissed by the court, she walked to Headquarters past the Lafayette monument, " there sat a colored man on the very same ledge—basket, bundles, and papers strewn about him as he comfortably devoured a sandwich."

Lafayette Park was not under the District of Columbia, but directly under the President's military aide—Colonel Ridley, who was also Superintendent of Public Buildings and grounds in Washington.

On August 13, the women appeared in the Federal Police Court, as ordered, for trial. The charge had been decided on; " For holding a meeting in public gounds." But again the Court announced postponement until August 15.

After vigorous protests by the Suffragists against further delay, the cases of the eighteen, who were charged in addition with " climbing a statue," were tried separately.

The women had no lawyers. Each spoke on her own behalf. They defended themselves on the ground of the constitutional right of free assemblage and appeal to the Government for the redress of grievances. They all pleaded, Not Guilty. Many of them added that they did not recognize the jurisdiction of the Court. Hazel Hunkins explained: " Women cannot be law-breakers until they are law-makers."

One of the witnesses was the Chief Clerk of Public Grounds, an elderly man. Elsie Hill suddenly asked him when he had taken office. He replied, " In 1878." " Do you realize," Miss Hill said, " that in that year a Federal Suffrage Amendment was introduced, and that since then women have been helping to pay your salary and that of other government officials under protest? " The Chief Clerk was so astounded that he merely shook his head.

The trial of the remainder of the women on the charge of " holding a meeting on public grounds " took place on August 15.

At the very beginning of proceedings Alice Paul said:

As a disfranchised class we feel that we are not subject to the jurisdiction of this court and therefore refuse to take any part in its proceedings. We also feel that we have done nothing to justify our being brought before it.

They then sat down and refused to answer any question put to them.

The judge was utterly nonplussed by this situation. He said that he would call a recess of fifteen minutes to consider the question of contempt. Among the spectators who packed the room was a lawyer—a visitor in Washington. He extracted a great deal of enjoyment out of this occasion, because, he said, "if the women are not afraid of jail, there is nothing the judge can do." He awaited the judge's decision with an entertained anticipation. Apparently the judge came to the same decision, for at the end of fifteen minutes, the Court reconvened and the trial went on as though nothing had happened.

The women refused to rise when charged. They refused to plead Guilty or Not Guilty. They sat and read, or knitted, or, as the proceedings bored them, fell asleep. The Park Police were, of course, the only witnesses. At last all the women whom they could identify were found Guilty. They were sentenced to pay fines of five or ten dollars or to serve in prison ten or fifteen days. They all refused to pay the fine. Mary Winsor said: "It is quite enough to pay taxes when you are not represented, let alone pay a fine if you object to this arrangement." The prisoners were then bundled in the Black Maria and taken off to prison.

Before the pickets were released from prison at the end of the previous year, Superintendent Zinkham said to them:

Now don't come back, for, if you do, I will have a far worse place than the jail fixed up for you. I will have the old workhouse fixed up for you, and you will have cells without sunlight, with windows high up from the ground. You won't be as comfortable as you are here.

Everything happened as Superintendent Zinkham prophesied, and a great deal more that was worse. The old Workhouse which he had promised them had been condemned in Roosevelt's Administration, and had not been used for years. The lower tier of cells was below the level of the ground. The doors of the cells were partly of solid steel and only partly of grating, so that little light penetrated. The wash basin was small and inadequate. The toilet was open, the cots were of iron and without springs, and with a thin straw mattress on them. Outside, they left behind a day so hot as to be almost insupportable, but in the Workhouse, it was so cold that their teeth chattered. It was damp all the time. When the present writer visited this old Workhouse in October, 1919, beads of water hung on everything. The walls were like the outside of an ice water pitcher in summer. Several of the pickets developed rheumatism. But the unendurable thing about it was the stench which came in great gusts; component of all that its past history had left behind and of the closeness of the unaired atmosphere. Apparently something was wrong with the water, or perhaps it was that the pipes had not been used for years. Most of the women believe they suffered with lead poisoning. They ached all over; endured a violent nausea; chills.

However, all the twenty-six, with the exception of two elderly women, went on hunger-strikes. Lucy Burns presented a demand on behalf of the entire company to Superintendent Zinkham. She said: " We must have twenty-three more blankets and twenty-three hot-water bottles. This place is cold and unfit for human habitation."

" I know it is cold and damp," he replied,, " but you can all get out of here by paying your fines."

The Woman's Party showed their usual ingenuity in bringing these conditions before the public. As fast as women were arrested, their State Senators and Representatives were besieged by letters and telegrams from home urging them to go to see these imprisoned constituents. The Press of their district made editorial question or comment. As long as this imprisoning of the pickets continued, there was a file of Representatives and Senators visiting the victims. Senator Jones of Washington was the first outside visitor to see them.

In the meantime, another meeting of protest, held at the Lafayette Monument on August 12, with the same speakers and many of the same banner bearers, was broken up by the police.

A curious feature of this case was that at Police Head-

370

quarters the police decided to confiscate, along with the banners, the Suffragist regalia—a sash of purple, white, and gold without any lettering whatever. The women refused to relinquish these sashes, and there was in every case a struggle, in which wrists were twisted, fingers sprained; bruises and cuts of all kinds administered. All the thirty-eight women were, however, released unconditionally.

On August 14, the women held two meetings of protest at the Lafayette Monument—one at half-past four in the afternoon, and one at eight o'clock in the evening.

This double protest came about in this way.

At the afternoon demonstration, the women were immediately arrested. They were held at Police Headquarters for two hours. The authorities feeling then that the hour was too late for further demonstrations, released them. They did not require bail, or a promise to appear in Court.

The women went at once to Headquarters, snatched a hasty dinner; slipped quietly out of the building, and marched to the Lafayette Monument. Everybody agrees that this evening demonstration was very beautiful. It was held in the soft dusk of the Washington August. The crescent moon, which seemed tangled in the trees of the park, gave enough light to bring out the Suffrage tri-color and the Stars and Stripes. As the women gathered closer and closer around the statue, the effect was of color, smudged with shadow; of shadow illuminate with color.

Elsie Hill, carrying the American flag in one hand, and the purple, white, and gold banner in the other spoke first; spoke wonderfully—as Elsie Hill always spoke. She said in part:

We know that our protest is in harmony with the belief of President Wilson, for he has stood before the world for the right of the governed to a voice in their own government. We resent the fact that the soldiers of our country, the men drafted to fight Prussia abroad, are used instead to help still the demand of American women for political freedom. We resent the suppression of our demands but our voices will carry across the country and down through time. The world will know that the women of America demand the passage of the Federal Suffrage Amendment and that the President insists that the Senate act.

There were only two policemen on duty. For two policemen to try to arrest nine lively and athletic pickets was a little like a scene in *Alice in Wonderland.* They would pull one woman down from the statue, start to get another, whereupon the first would be back again with her flying banner.

Finally, the police reserves arrived, but every woman had managed to make a speech.

While the Suffragists were still in the old Workhouse, Alice Paul, following her usual system of complete publicity, had announced another protest meeting at the Lafayette Monument.

Later Alice Paul received a letter from Colonel Ridley:

I have been advised that you desire to hold a demonstration in Lafayette Square on Thursday, August 22. By direction of the Chief of Engineers, U. S. Army, you are hereby granted permission to hold this demonstration. You are advised good order must prevail.

Miss Paul replied:

We received yesterday your permit for a Suffrage demonstration in Lafayette Park this afternoon, and are very glad that our meetings are no longer to be interfered with. Because of the illness of so many of our members, due to their treatment in prison this last week, and with the necessity of caring for them at Headquarters, we are planning to hold our next meeting a little later. We have not determined on the exact date but we will inform you of the time as soon as it is decided upon.

As a result of the first series of protest meetings, the Administration had yielded to the point of no longer interfering with the meetings at the Lafayette Monument. But as time went by and neither the Senate nor the President did anything about Suffrage, the National Woman's Party announced that a protest meeting would be held at the Lafayette Monument on September 16 at four o'clock. Immediately the President announced that he would receive a delegation of Southern and Western Democratic women that day at two.

The same day, September 16, as Maud Younger was coming back from the Capitol to Headquarters, Senator Overman of the Rules Committee came and sat by her in the car. In the course of his conversation, he remarked casually: "I don't think your bill is coming up this session."

That afternoon, Abby Scott Baker went to see Senator Jones of New Mexico, Chairman of the Suffrage Committee, to ask him to call a meeting of the Committee to bring Suffrage to the vote. Senator Jones refused. He said he would not bring up the Suffrage Amendment at this session in Congress.

When—still later—that delegation of Southern and Western Democratic women called on the President, he said to them:

I am, as I think you know, heartily in sympathy with you. I have endeavored to assist you in every way in my power, and I shall continue to do so. I shall do all that I can to assist the passage of the Amendment by an early vote.

This was the final touch.

The National Woman's Party hastily changed the type of its demonstration. Instead of holding a mere meeting of protest, they decided to burn the words which the President had said that very afternoon to the Southern and Western Democratic women. At four o'clock instead of two, forty women marched from Headquarters to the Lafayette Monument. They carried the famous banners:

HOW LONG MUST WOMEN WAIT FOR LIBERTY?

MR. PRESIDENT, WHAT WILL YOU DO FOR WOMAN SUFFRAGE?

At the Lafayette statue, Bertha Arnold delivered an appeal to Lafayette, written by Mrs. Richard Wainwright and beginning with the famous words of Pershing in France:

Lafayette, we are here!

We, the women of the United States, denied the liberty which you helped to gain, and for which we have asked in vain for sixty years, turn to you to plead for us.

Speak, Lafayette! Dead these hundred years but still living in the hearts of the American people. Speak again to plead for us, condemned like the bronze woman at your feet, to a silent appeal. She offers you a sword. Will you not use the sword of the spirit, mightier far than the sword she holds out to you?

Will you not ask the great leader of our democracy to look upon the failure of our beloved country to be in truth the place where every one is free and equal and entitled to a share in the government? Let that outstretched hand of yours pointing to the White House recall to him his words and promises, his trumpet call for all of us to see that the world is made safe for democracy.

As our army now in France spoke to you there, saying, " Here we are to help your country fight for liberty," will you not speak here and now for us, a little band with no army, no power but justice and right, no strength but in our Constitution and the Declaration of Independence, and win a great victory again in this country by giving us the opportunity we ask to be heard through the Susan B. Anthony Amendment?

Lafayette, we are here!

The police, having no orders to arrest the women, smiled and nodded. And while the crowd that had very quickly gathered applauded, Lucy Branham stepped forward. Beside her was Julia Emory, holding a flaming torch.

" We want action," Miss Branham stated simply, " not words." She took the torch from Julia Emory, held the words of the President's message of that afternoon in the flames. As it burned, she said:

The torch which I hold symbolizes the burning indignation of women who for a hundred years have been given words without action. In the spring our hopes were raised by words much like these from President Wilson, yet they were permitted to be followed by a filibuster against our Amendment on the part of the Democratic Senate leaders.

President Wilson still refuses any real support to the movement for the political freedom of women. . . .

We, therefore, take these empty words, spoken by President Wilson this afternoon, and consign them to the flames.

Photo Copr. Harris and Ewing, Washington, D. C.

LUCY BRANHAM BURNING THE PRESIDENT'S WORDS AT THE
LAFAYETTE MONUMENT.

Photo Copr. Harris and Ewing, Washington, D. C.

THE RUSSIAN ENVOY BANNER, AUGUST, 1917.

This is a symbol of the indignation of American women at the treatment given by the President to their plea for democracy.

We have protested to this Administration by banners; we have protested by speeches; we now protest by this symbolic act.

As in the ancient fights for liberty the crusaders for freedom symbolized their protest against those responsible for injustice by consigning their hollow phrases to the flames, so we, on behalf of thousands of Suffragists, in this same way today, protest against the action of the President and his Party in delaying the liberation of American women.

For five years, women have appealed to this President and his Party for political freedom. The President has given words, and words, and words. Today, women receive more words. We announce to the President and the whole world today, by this act of ours, our determination that words shall no longer be the only reply given to American women—our determination that this same democracy, for whose establishment abroad we are making the utmost sacrifice, shall also prevail at home.

Applause greeted these spirited words. As Jessie Hardy Mackaye started to speak, a man in the crowd handed her a twenty-dollar bill for the Woman's Party. Others began passing money to her. The Suffragists were busy running through the crowd collecting it. The crowd continued to applaud and cheer.

Mrs. Mackaye said:

Against the two-fold attitude on the part of the Senate toward democracy, I protest with all the power of my being. The same Congress and the same Administration that are appropriating billions of dollars and enlisting the services of millions of men to establish democracy in Europe, is at the same time refusing to do so common a piece of justice as to vote to submit the Woman Suffrage Amendment to the States.

This was the first time the President's words were burned.

The President's car drove up to the door during the progress of this demonstration, and President Wilson stepped in. But instead of going out at the usual gate, the driver turned the car about, so that he could make his exit elsewhere.

VII

THE PRESIDENT APPEALS TO THE SENATE TO PASS THE SUFFRAGE AMENDMENT

THE very next day occurred a remarkable example of direct action: that direct action coming within twenty-four hours. Senator Jones, who the day before had refused to bring up Suffrage in this session, arose in the Senate and announced that on September 26, he would move to take up the Suffrage Amendment, and keep it before the Senate until a vote was reached.

With this promise of definite action, the Woman's Party immediately ceased their demonstrations.

On September 26, Senator Jones brought the Amendment up. Maud Younger says, in her *Revelations of a Woman Lobbyist:*

Discussion began. Discussion went on. For five whole days it lasted, with waves of hope and waves of dismay, and always an undercurrent of uncertainty. Thursday, Friday, Saturday, the speeches went on. On Monday word went forth that the President would address the Senate on behalf of our Amendment.

I hurried to Senator Curtis, who was in his office signing letters. He said: " The other side claim that they have their men pledged: that the President comes too late. What do you expect? "

" I don't know what I should expect. I hope."

I went over to the Senate. There was very great excitement; a sense of something wonderful impending. On the floor there was the ceremonious atmosphere that attends the President's coming.

" Look," said a newspaper man in the gallery beside me, " he's brought all his heavy artillery with him." There on the floor of the Senate were the members of the Cabinet. Lesser dignitaries were scattered about the room. Congressmen stood, two-deep, lining the walls. The Sergeant-at-Arms announced in clear tones: " The President of the United States."

The President came in, shook hands with the presiding officer, turned and read his speech. There is always an evenness about his public utterances, in manner, in voice, in reading; yet I thought he read this message with more feeling than his War message, or his Fourteen Points.

The President said:

Gentlemen of the Senate: The unusual circumstances of a world war in which we stand and are judged in the view not only of our own people and our own consciences but also in the view of all nations and peoples will, I hope, justify in your thought, as it does in mine, the message I have come to bring you.

I regard the concurrence of the Senate in the constitutional Amendment proposing the extension of the Suffrage to women as vitally essential to the successful prosecution of the great war of humanity in which we are engaged. I have come to urge upon you the considerations which have led me to that conclusion. It is not only my privilege, it is also my duty to apprise you of every circumstance and element involved in this momentous struggle which seems to me to affect its very processes and its outcome. It is my duty to win the war and to ask you to remove every obstacle that stands in the way of winning it.

I had assumed that the Senate would concur in the Amendment because no disputable principle is involved but only a question of the method by which the Suffrage is to be extended to women. There is and can be no Party issue involved in it. Both of our great national Parties are pledged, explicitly pledged, to equality of Suffrage for the women of the country.

Neither Party, therefore, it seems to me, can justify hesitation as to the method of obtaining it, can rightfully hesitate to substitute Federal initiative for State initiative, if the early adoption of this measure is necessary to the successful prosecution of the war and if the method of State action proposed in Party platforms of 1916 is impracticable within any reasonable length of time, if practicable at all.

And its adoption is, in my judgment, clearly necessary to the successful prosecution of the war and the successful realization of the object for which the war is being fought.

That judgment I take the liberty of urging upon you with solemn earnestness for reasons which I shall state very frankly and which I shall hope will seem as conclusive to you as they seem to me.

This is a peoples' war and the peoples' thinking constitutes its atmosphere and morale, not the predilections of the drawing-room or the political considerations of the caucus.

If we be indeed Democrats and wish to lead the world to democracy, we can ask other peoples to accept in proof of our sincerity and our ability to lead them whither they wish to be led nothing less persuasive and convincing than our actions. Our professions will not suffice. Verification must be forthcoming when verification is asked for. And in this case verification is asked for—asked for in this particular matter. You ask by whom?

Not through diplomatic channels; not by foreign ministers. Not by the intimations of parliaments. It is asked for by the anxious, expectant, suffering peoples with whom we are dealing and who are willing to put their destinies in some measure in our hands, if they are sure that we wish the same things they do.

I do not speak by conjecture. It is not alone the voices of statesmen and of newspapers that reach me, and the voices of foolish and intemperate agitators do not reach me at all. Through many, many channels I have been made aware what the plain, struggling, workaday folk are thinking upon whom the chief terror and suffering of this tragic war falls.

They are looking to the great, powerful, famous Democracy of the West to lead them to the new day for which they have so long waited; and they think in their logical simplicity, that democracy means that women shall play their part in affairs alongside men and upon an equal footing with them. If we reject measures like this, in ignorance or defiance of what a new age has brought forth, of what they have seen but we have not, they will cease to believe in us; they will cease to follow or to trust us.

They have seen their own governments accept this interpreta· tion of democracy—seen old governments accept this interpreta-tion of democracy—seen old governments like that of Great Britain, which did not profess to be democratic, promise readily and as of course this justice to women, though they had before refused it, the strange revelations of this war having made many things new and plain, to governments as well as to people.

Are we alone to refuse to learn the lesson? Are we alone to ask and take the utmost that our women can give—service and sacrifice of every kind—and still say we do not see what title that gives them to stand by our sides in the guidance of the affairs of their nation and ours?'

We have made partners of the women in this war; shall we admit them only to a partnership of suffering and sacrifice and toil and not a partnership of privilege and right? This war could not have been fought either by the other nations engaged or by America, if it had not been for the services of the women—services rendered in every sphere—not merely in the fields of effort in which we have been accustomed to see them work, but wherever men have worked, and upon the very skirts and edges of the battle itself.

We shall not only be distrusted but shall deserve to be distrusted if we do not enfranchise them with the fullest possible enfranchisement, as it is now certain that the other great free nations will enfranchise them.

We cannot isolate our thought and action in such a matter from the thought of the rest of the world. We must either conform or deliberately reject what they propose and resign the leadership of liberal minds to others.

The women of America are too noble and too intelligent and too devoted to be slackers whether you give or withhold this thing that is mere justice; but I know the magic it will work in their thoughts and spirits if you give it to them.

I propose it as I would propose to admit soldiers to the Suffrage, the men fighting in the field for our liberties and the liberties of the world, were they excluded. The task of the woman lies at the very heart of the war, and I know how much stronger that heart will beat if you do this just thing and show our women that you trust them as much as you in fact and of necessity depend upon them.

Have I said that the passage of this Amendment is a vitally necessary war measure, and do you need further proof? Do you stand in need of the trust of other peoples and of the trust of our own women? Is that trust an asset or is it not?

I tell you plainly, as the commander-in-chief of our armies and of the gallant men in our fleets, as the present spokesman of this people in our dealings with the men and women throughout the world who are now our partners, as the responsible head of a great government which stands and is questioned day by day as to its purposes, its principles, its hopes, whether they be serviceable to men everywhere or only to itself, and who must himself answer these questions or be shamed, as the guide and director of forces caught in the grip of war and by the same token in need of every material and spiritual resource this great nation possesses—I tell you plainly that this measure which I urge upon you is vital to the winning of the war and to the energies alike of preparation and of battle.

And not to the winning of the war only. It is vital to the

right solution of the great problems which we must settle, and settle immediately, when the war is over. We shall need then in our vision of affairs, as we have never needed them before, the sympathy and insight and clear moral instinct of the women of the world. The problems of that time will strike to the roots of many things that we have not hitherto questioned, and I for one believe that our safety in those questioning days, as well as our comprehension of matters that touch society to the quick, will depend upon the direct and authoritative participation of women in our counsels. We shall need their moral sense to preserve what is right and fine and worthy in our system of life as well as to discover just what it is that ought to be purified and reformed. Without their counselings we shall only be half wise.

That is my case. That is my appeal. Many may deny its validity, if they choose, but no one can brush aside or answer the arguments upon which it is based. The executive tasks of this war rest upon me. I ask that you lighten them and place in my hands instruments, spiritual instruments, which I do not now possess, which I sorely need, and which I have daily to apologize for not being able to employ.

In this speech, the President had said: " The voices of foolish and intemperate agitators do not reach me at all."

It was generally felt that the President, there, indicated the Woman's Party. Commenting on that phrase the next day, the Republican Senators remarked, " Why it was that which brought him there!"

During the course of the debate between Poindexter and Pitman, Poindexter asked, " Wasn't it the pickets that got the President?"

The next afternoon when the vote was called for, and the last Senator had answered to his name, the presiding officer announced the result:

"The joint resolution does not pass."

The Suffrage Amendment still lacked two votes.

Miss Younger says in her *Revelations of a Lobbyist:*

Stunned, as though unable to grasp it, hundreds of women sat there. Then slowly the defeat reached their consciousness, and they began slowly to put on their hats, to gather up their wraps, and to file out of the galleries, some with a dull sense of injustice, some with burning resentment. In the corridors they began to form in groups. Every one wanted to discuss it. But Alice Paul took my arm.

"Come," she said, "we must find out about the short-term candidates and go into the election campaign at once."

Immediately after the vote was taken and defeated, Senator Jones of New Mexico changed his vote and moved that the measure be reconsidered; thereby placing it again on the Senate Calendar, ready to be called up any time and voted on.

By going to the Senate in this manner, the President had made his own record clean to the country at large. But he had not made it clean to the National Woman's Party, because, although he had done something, he had not done enough. He appeared to be doing more than he was, but there was a great deal more that he could have done. He did not, for instance, start his appeal to the Senate early enough. That appeal came only a fortnight before the vote was taken. Possibly he had underestimated the opposition; probably he had overestimated the strength of his own influence. But the country at large of course did not understand that. For the time being, therefore, the Woman's Party concentrated their drive on another point in the enemy line.

VIII

PICKETING THE SENATE

As the Senate was still sitting and could at any time reverse its action in regard to the Suffrage Amendment, the Woman's Party decided to protest against its defeat of the Amendment and to demand a reversal.

They began to picket the Senate and in especial the thirty-four Senators whose adverse vote had again delayed the passage of the Amendment.

On the morning of October 7, four banner-bearers ascended the steps of the Capitol. They were: Elizabeth Kalb; Vivian Pierce; Bertha Moller; Mrs. Horton Pope. The lettered banner, flanked as usual with the Suffrage tri-color, read:

WE DEMAND AN AMENDMENT TO THE UNITED CONSTITUTION
ENFRANCHISING WOMEN.

They had hardly mounted the steps when the Capitol police placed them under arrest. They took the prisoners to the guard room in the Capitol, kept them there for fifteen minutes, and then released them. It was, of course, not exactly an arrest; and no one seemed exactly responsible for the order. The banners were, however, confiscated.

That afternoon, the same women, except that Bertha Arnold was substituted for Mrs. Pope, mounted the steps bearing a large banner which read:

WE PROTEST AGAINST THE 34 WILFUL SENATORS WHO HAVE
DELAYED THE POLITICAL FREEDOM OF AMERICAN WOMEN.
THEY HAVE OBSTRUCTED THE WAR PROGRAM OF THE PRESI-
DENT. THEY HAVE LINED UP THE SENATE WITH PRUSSIA BY
DENYING SELF-GOVERNMENT TO THE PEOPLE.

All the afternoon, the banner-bearers were detained in the courtroom at intervals. When they were released, they went back to the Capitol; were arrested; detained in the court-room again; released again.

On the morning of October 10, four more pickets, Edith Ainge, Bertha Moller, Maud Jamison, Clara Wold, started for the Capitol. Crowds of men and women gathered in the park to see what was going to happen, and rows of police stood on the Capitol steps awaiting the pickets. As soon as the big protest banner was unfurled, the police seized it. Maud Jamison and Clara Wold tried to mount the steps with the tri-color, but several policemen rushed upon them, and conducted them up the steps and into the Capitol build-ing. As the police said over and over again that there were no arrests, the women insisted on carrying their banners.

Protesting against the curious and inconsistent action on the part of the police, the women were conducted into the presence of the captain. He iterated and reiterated that this action was all in accordance with the rules of Colonel Higgins, the Democratic Sergeant-at-Arms who is under the Rules Committee which carries out the Democratic pro-gram. The Suffragists demanded by what authority they were held and the captain informed them that it did not make any difference about the law, that Colonel Higgins had taken the law into his own hands. The four Suffragists waited for a few minutes. Their purple, white, and gold banners had been confiscated, but the protest banner was still there. Suddenly, without any interference from any-body, they took up their protest banner, walked out of the guard room, went over to the Senate Office Building and stood with it, at the top of the steps, the rest of the day. Later Vivian Pierce, Mrs. Stewart Polk, Mary Gertrude Fendall and Gladys Greiner joined this group of pickets.

In the meantime, other Suffragists were trying vainly to take the Suffrage colors to the Capitol steps. They walked from the Office Building on to the Plaza by twos. The instant they appeared, policemen, rushing down the steps, rushing from the curb, rushing from the crowd which had gathered, seized them. They tried to wrench the banners away; and this was, of course, an unequal contest, in which sometimes the women were pulled completely off the ground and always their wrists painfully twisted. But the women clung to the banners, walked as calmly as the situation permitted into the Capitol, and down to the guard room. Here the banners were always confiscated, but they, themselves, were released. If anybody in the crowd showed any disposition to resent the attitude of the police, he was placed under arrest too; but he also was released.

On October 11 the Suffragists picketed only the Senate Office Building, as Congress was not in session. At the beginning of the day, Mrs. George Atwater and Betty Cram held the banners. Mrs. Atwater's two little girls, Edith and Barbara, assisted their mother by holding the tricolors.

Others who picketed that day were: Grace Needham, Mrs. George Odell, Elizabeth Kalb, Virginia Arnold, Mary Gertrude Fendall, Gladys Greiner, Maud Jamison, Vivian Pierce, Bertha Moller, Clara Wold.

On October 13, plans for another demonstration were announced in the Washington papers. *Edith Ainge, bearing the American flag, was to lead a procession of Suffragists on to the Senate floor.* There the words of the anti-Suffrage Senators in praise of democracy were to be burned. For an hour before the line formed, the Capitol police were lined up, ready for the pickets. Above, Senators hung over the balcony where they could witness the demonstration. Below, motor after motor drove up to the curb and stopped, waiting to see what was going to happen. At length, the Suffragists arrived. They formed in line outside the Senate Office Building, and started towards the Capitol. They were beset by a battalion of police, and taken to the guard room. Women standing in the crowd, who were not in the procession, but who wore the Suffrage colors were taken along also.

Alice Paul, who wore no regalia of any kind, was caught in the net.

These women were: Alice Paul; Vivian Pierce; Bertha Moller; Bertha Arnold; Elizabeth McShane; Edith Ainge; Edith Hilles; Julia Emory; Clara Wold; Elizabeth Kalb; Virginia Arnold; Grace Frost; Matilda Young; Mrs. K. G. Winston.

The Woman's Party now decided to open a " banner " campaign on each of the Senators who had helped to defeat the Suffrage Amendment. They began with Senator Wadsworth. They unrolled on the steps of the Senate Office Building a banner which read:

SENATOR WADSWORTH'S REGIMENT IS FIGHTING FOR DEMOCRACY ABROAD.

SENATOR WADSWORTH LEFT HIS REGIMENT AND IS FIGHTING AGAINST DEMOCRACY IN THE SENATE.

SENATOR WADSWORTH COULD SERVE HIS COUNTRY BETTER BY FIGHTING WITH HIS REGIMENT ABROAD THAN BY FIGHTING WOMEN.

Later appeared another banner, proclaiming the case of Senator Shields:

SENATOR SHIELDS TOLD THE PEOPLE OF TENNESSEE HE WOULD SUPPORT THE PRESIDENT'S POLICIES. THE ONLY TIME THE PRESIDENT WENT TO THE SENATE TO ASK ITS SUPPORT, SENATOR SHIELDS VOTED AGAINST HIM. DOES TENNESSEE BACK THE PRESIDENT'S WAR PROGRAM OR SENATOR SHIELDS?

These banners were taken up by the newspapers of the Senators' States and focussed unfavorable attention upon them.

By this time, the Capitol police had found that their system of arresting and detaining what threatened to prove an inexhaustible army of Suffragists was futile. So now they reverted to their policy of 1917. They stood aside and let the crowd worry the Suffragists. Mainly, however, these were small boys, who seized the banners and dragged them through the streets.

On October 23 appeared:

GERMANY HAS ESTABLISHED "EQUAL, UNIVERSAL, SECRET, DIRECT FRANCHISE." THE SENATE HAS DENIED EQUAL UNIVERSAL SUFFRAGE TO AMERICA. WHICH IS MORE OF A DEMOCRACY, GERMANY OR AMERICA?

The small boys, generally office boys, were allowed to tear up this banner too.

On October 24, Julia Emory and Virginia Arnold succeeded in getting to the top of the Capitol steps, unseen by the police who were grouped on the sidewalk. Their banner said:

WE CONDEMN THE DEMOCRATIC PARTY. THE DEMOCRATIC PARTY DEFEATED SUFFRAGE. THE DEMOCRATIC PARTY HAS PLACED AMERICA BEHIND GERMANY AS A DEMOCRACY, IF GERMANY HAS, AS SHE SAYS, ESTABLISHED EQUAL, UNIVERSAL, SECRET, DIRECT FRANCHISE.

The instant they caught sight of this banner, the policemen took the two girls to the guard room, where they held them, until half-past seven that evening.

On October 25, as the Senate was not in session, the pickets returned to the Office Building, where hitherto they had been unmolested. There were four of them, and they carried the Great Demand banner. They were arrested, and held until six o'clock. They went back to the Capitol at eight in the evening, and were again arrested, and held until eleven o'clock. Friends or newspaper men, calling at the Capitol, could get no information about them. On various pretexts, the telephone answered nothing. These women were Matilda Young; Elizabeth Kalb; Julia Emory; Virginia Arnold.

On October 26, eight pickets bore the Wadsworth and Shields banners with the tri-color. As usual, the poles of their banners were broken; their banners themselves snatched from them; they were seized and held.

That afternoon, there was an aeroplane demonstration in Washington. Seven pickets went out with banners: Julia Emory, Maud Jamison, Bertha Arnold, Katherine Fisher, Minna Lederman, Elizabeth Kalb, Mrs. Frances Davies. They were handled with great roughness. Maud Jamison was knocked senseless by a policeman. Several men in uniform protested to the police.

On October 28, twenty-one women, each bearing the purple, white, and gold banners, started for the Capitol. They marched a banner's length apart across the Capitol grounds.

They had gone halfway up the steps, when policemen in plain clothes appeared from all sides and grappled with them. Many women were injured. Annie Arniel was thrown to the ground so violently that she fainted. An ambulance was summoned to take her to the hospital. The other women were locked in a basement room until six o'clock, when they were released. They were escorted through the Capitol grounds by a member of the vigilant force of guards. He bore the American flag which had been carried at the head of their line. As they reached the limit of the Capitol grounds, he returned that to them, but all the lettered banners and tri-colors were retained.

The twenty-one women were: Edith Ainge; Harriet U. Andrews; Bertha Arnold; Virginia Arnold; Annie Arniel; Olive Beale; Lucy Burns; Eleanor Calnan; L. G. C. Daniels; Frances Davis; Julia Emory; Mary Gertrude Fendall; Mrs. Gilson Gardner; Sara Grogan; Maud Jamison; Elizabeth Kalb; Augusta M. Kelley; Lola Maverick Lloyd; Matilda Young; H. R. Walmsley; Alice Paul.

On October 29, two pickets went to the Capitol with a banner inscribed:

RESISTANCE TO TYRANNY IS OBEDIENCE TO GOD.

They were seized and held until the afternoon.

By some divagation in the police policy, they were seized, while they were walking to the car after their release, and held for another hour.

On October 30, five pickets, carrying the Senator Baird banner and three tri-colors, picketed the north front of the Capitol for an hour. Then they marched to the south front, determined to take up their stand on the Senate steps. Half-way in their progress, they were seized, locked up, and held until six o'clock.

Indignant at these arrests without charge, the National Woman's Party decided to protest the next day—Thursday.

On October 31, therefore, after the usual morning arrest, their lawyer applied to Judge Siddons of the District Supreme Court for a writ of habeas corpus. The Judge declared that the sergeant-at-arms had no right to hold any one without a charge, that he must either make a charge, or release the Suffragists. The sergeant-at-arms released them at once. Nevertheless, when the pickets returned in the afternoon, they were seized in the usual violent fashion and conducted to the guard room. However, although their banners were not returned to them, they were detained but a few minutes. On Friday, they were released as soon as their banners were seized. Fresh banners appeared from time to time all day long. Again consulted, Judge Siddons said that the police had no right to keep the banners. On Saturday, however, the police did not have to seize the banners; there appeared a variation in the picket line. A group of women walked up and down in front of the Senate Office Building. They bore no lettered banners; they bore no tri-colors; but they wore on their arms black mourning bands

—in commemoration of the death of justice in the United States Senate.

On November 21, the Senate declared a recess without considering the Federal Suffrage Amendment. That day, twelve pickets protested against the recess, marching from the Senate Office Building to the Capitol. They were: Alice Paul, Mrs. Lawrence Lewis, Elizabeth Kalb, Clara Wold, Bertha Arnold, Sara Grogan, Julia Emory, Anita Pollitzer, Matilda Young, Mrs. Nicholas Kelly, Olive Beale, Maud Jamison.

They carried a banner which read:

AMERICAN WOMEN PROTEST AGAINST THE SENATE'S RECESSING WITHOUT PASSING THE SUFFRAGE AMENDMENT.

AMERICA ENTERS THE PEACE CONFERENCE WITH UNCLEAN HANDS FOR DEMOCRACY IS DENIED TO HER PEOPLE.

THE NATIONS OF THE WORLD CANNOT TRUST HER MEDIATION IF SHE PREACHES DEMOCRACY FOR ALL EUROPE WHILE AMERICANS ARE ARRESTED FOR ASKING FOR IT AT THE CAPITOL.

On this occasion, the women were treated outrageously. The police, two to a picket, pounced upon them as they approached the Capitol. One was heard to call, " Help! Help! They're coming!" Clara Wold was knocked down twice on the Senate steps; was shaken like a rat. They dragged and pushed Alice Paul about as though personally enraged with her. When they were taken into the basement room of the Capitol a crowd of indignant men and women followed. Policeman No. 21 threatened to arrest a man in the crowd because he said: " Sure! I believe in Woman Suffrage."

IX

THE THIRD APPEAL TO THE WOMEN VOTERS

ALL during this period, the National Woman's Party was, of course, taking its part in the autumn campaign—the campaign of 1918. It was in the Senatorial elections only that the Woman's Party was interested. The expedient quality of Alice Paul's policy manifested itself notably here. It has been shown again and again how swift she was to adapt the tactics of the Woman's Party to the needs of the moment. The Woman's Party, it must always be remembered, was organized for but one object—to enfranchise the women of the United States by federal amendment. Other Suffrage organizations could and did divide their interests; could and did deflect their forces for those interests. On this point, Alice Paul never swerved. But as has been again and again demonstrated, she was as fluid as water, as swift as light, to adapt that single adamantine policy to the situation of the moment. At this juncture she extended her policy.

The circumstances were these:

In the Senate, Suffrage needed two more votes.

In the West, as usual, the Woman's Party asked the women voters to defeat the Democrats as the Party in power and therefore the Party responsible. In two States in the East—New Jersey and New Hampshire—where the Republican candidates were anti-Suffragists and the Democratic candidates were Suffragists, the Woman's Party supported the Democratic candidates.

That campaign, short as it was, was intensive. In the West Elsie Hill took care of Nevada; Catherine Flanagan of Montana; Anita Pollitzer of Wyoming; Clara Wold of Oregon; Louise Garnett of Kansas; Iris Calderhead of Colorado. In the East, Doris Stevens, Betty Gram,

Bertha Arnold, Ruth Small, Rebecca Hourwich, Vivian Pierce, Bertha Moller, Lucy Branham, Caroline Katzenstein, Florence Bayard Hilles, Agnes Morey, Gladys Greiner, Maud Younger, Mary Beard, Abby Scott Baker, Mary Dubrow, Grace Needham, Lucy Burns, Mrs. Lawrence Lewis, Katherine Morey took care of New Jersey and New Hampshire.

The two vacancies in the Senate from New Jersey and New Hampshire had been caused by death. The Senators who would take those seats in November would fill out the remainder of the Congress then in Session. In New Jersey the Republican candidate—Senator Baird—had voted against the Suffrage Amendment in the Senate on October 1. The Democratic candidate—Charles O'Connor Hennessy— had fought all his public life in New Jersey for National Woman Suffrage.

In New Hampshire the Republican candidate—George H. Moses—was an anti-Suffragist. The Democratic candidate—John B. Jameson—was for the Federal Amendment.

The National Woman's Party thought of course the President would assist them in their campaign for Hennessy and Jameson, as they were both Democrats as well as Suffragists and, in particular, because he had just told the Senate that the passing of the Federal Amendment was necessary to the successful prosecution of the war. But he gave them no help until the Woman's Party forced him to do so, and then it was too late. But when the news came back from the Suffrage States of the West that the Woman's Party speakers were telling of his inaction, he sent—in the last week in October—the following letter to Hennessy of New Jersey:

May I not say how deeply interested I am in the contest you are conducting? I cannot but feel that in ignoring my earnest appeal with regard to the Suffrage Amendment, made in public interest, and because of my intimate knowledge of the issues involved both on the other side of the water and here, Senator

Baird has certainly not represented the true feeling and spirit of the people of New Jersey.

I am sure that they must have felt that such an appeal could not and should not be ignored. It would be a very great make-weight, thrown into the international scale, if his course of action while in the Senate could be reversed by the people of our great State.

Also, before the end of the campaign, the President came out in a statement endorsing Jameson. But he did not work so hard to elect these two Democrats, who were also Suf-fragists, as he did to defeat Vardaman and Hardwick, both of whom were Democrats and one a Suffragist. Hennessy and Jameson were both defeated. In the West, the election resulted in the defeat of Senator Shafroth of Colorado, thereby handing the Senate over to the Republicans. The defeat of Shafroth is universally ascribed to the Woman's Party. The Woman's Party believed that this election had brought them one vote, Pollock of South Carolina.

The Borah incident of the campaign of 1918 is a black page in the record of any gentleman who has Presidential aspirations. Catherine Flanagan and Margaret Whitte-more were campaigning in western Idaho, asking the Idaho people to bring pressure on Borah to vote for Suffrage.

Shortly after casting his vote against the Federal Amend-ment, Borah came to Headquarters to see Alice Paul. He said that that vote represented his personal belief, but that in the future he would have to be bound by the Idaho Party (Republican) platform which had endorsed the Amendment. He said he would not give a public statement as that would look like trying to get votes, but he wrote out a statement that the Woman's Party could understand as indicating his position. That statement is as follows:

We have talked over the Suffrage situation with Senator Borah and our understanding from the interview is that he will carry out his platform and vote for the Suffrage Amendment if re-elected.

The Woman's Party telegraphed this statement to Idaho and asked his constituents to get him to confirm it. He was

very evasive in replying to their questions and Alice Paul
finally sent him the following letter:

October 29, 1918.

SENATOR WM. E. BORAH,
    Senate Office Building,
        Washington, D. C.
DEAR SENATOR BORAH:
    In view of the statement that you have just telegraphed to one
of our members, Mrs. Marcella Pride, in Boise, and in view of
the statements which you have made to various newspaper cor-
respondents in Washington since Mrs. Baker's and my interview
with you, giving them the impression that there was no basis for
our understanding that you would vote for the Suffrage Amendment after November 5th, we feel that we have no course left
but to throw all the strength which we possess in Idaho against
you. I have, therefore, telegraphed to this effect today to Miss
Whittemore, who is in charge of our Idaho work.
    I am sure I need not tell you how much we regret that you
have not felt able to say frankly what you would do after election,
and that you are not willing to stand by the statement which you
authorized us to give out as expressing the understanding to be
derived by us from our interview with you.
               Sincerely yours,
                      ALICE PAUL,
                      National Chairman.

    Thereupon the Woman's Party campaigned against him
until election. Borah was re-elected. Here—anticipating by
three months—it must be mentioned that when on February
10, the Amendment came to a vote, Borah voted, " No."

X

THE PRESIDENT INCLUDES SUFFRAGE IN HIS CAMPAIGN FOR CONGRESS

For the third time the Woman's Party had waged in the West one of its marvelous campaigns against the Democratic Party. The repercussion of that campaign had reached the President. When Congress convened in December, he included the Federal Amendment in his message of Decembr 2 to Congress as a part of the Administration program. He said:

> And what shall we say of the women—of their instant intelligence, quickening every task that they touched; their capacity for organization and co-operation, which gave their action discipline and enhanced the effectiveness of everything they attempted; their aptitude at tasks to which they had never before set their hands; their utter self-sacrifice alike in what they did and what they gave? Their contribution to the great result is beyond appraisal. They have added a new luster to the annals of American womanhood.
>
> The least tribute we can pay them is to make them the equals of men in political rights as they have proved themselves their equals in every field of practical work they have entered, whether for themselves or for their country. These great days of completed achievement would be sadly marred were we to omit that act of justice. Besides the immense practical services they have rendered, the women of the country have been the moving spirits in the systematic economies by which our people have voluntarily assisted to supply the suffering peoples of the world and the armies upon every front with food and everything else that we had that might serve the common cause. The details of such a story can never be fully written, but we carry them at our hearts and thank God that we can say that we are the kinsmen of such.

This was the first time that any President ever mentioned Suffrage as a part of his administrative program. It was a step forward. The women waited ten days to see whether he would follow this message with action.

The President sailed for France.

When the Woman's Party discovered from the Administration leaders that he had left no orders to have Suffrage carried out, they decided to hold another protest meeting.

"In carrying on a campaign for Democracy abroad and utterly ignoring it at home," Alice Paul said, "he has exposed his whole broadside to our attack."

As always, whenever possible, the Woman's Party announced their protest meeting through the newspapers. Lucy Branham went to Police Headquarters. She explained her errand, asking for a permit.

"Here's your permit!" Colonel Ridley said.

Lucy Branham made further explanation, "We are going to burn the President's words," she warned him.

"Here's your permit!" Colonel Ridley said.

XI

BURNING THE PRESIDENT'S WORDS AGAIN

On December 16, a woman carrying an American flag, emerged from Headquarters. Behind her came a long line of women bearing purple, white, and gold banners. Behind them came fifty women bearing lighted torches. Behind them came women—more women and more women and more women. Always a banner's length apart they marched and on they came . . . and on . . . and on . . . and on. . . . People who saw the demonstrations say that it seemed as though the colorful, slow-moving line would never come to an end. Witnesses say also that it was the most beautiful of all the Woman's Party demonstrations. They marched to the Lafayette Monument. Their leader, Mrs. Harvey Wiley, stopped in front of a burning cauldron which had been placed at the foot of the pedestal. The torch bearers formed a semi-circle about that cauldron. The women with the purple, white, and gold banners—who were the speakers —grouped themselves around the torch bearers.

Among these women were the State Chairman or a Woman's Party representative from almost all the forty-eight States; some of whom had come great distances to be present on this occasion. There were three hundred in all.

In the meantime, a huge crowd, which augmented steadily in numbers and in excitement as the long line of Suffragists came on and on and on, formed a great, black, attentive mass, which hedged in the banner bearers, as the banner bearers hedged in the torch bearers. In that crowd were the National Democratic Chairman and many prominent Democratic politicians.

Dusk changed into darkness, and the flames from cauldron and torches mounted higher and higher.

After the Suffragists had assembled, there came a moment of quiet. Then Vida Milholland stepped forward and without accompaniment of any kind, sang with her characteristic spirit the *Woman's Marseillaise*. Immediately afterwards, Mrs. John Rogers opened the meeting, and introduced, one after another, nineteen speakers, each of whom, first reading them, dropped some words of President Wilson's on democracy into the flaming cauldron.

Mrs. John Rogers declared:

We hold this meeting to protest against the denial of liberty to American women. All over the world today we see surging and sweeping irresistibly on, the great tide of democracy, and women would be derelict to their duty if they did not see to it that it brings freedom to the women of this land.

England has enfranchised her women, Canada has enfranchised her women, Russia has enfranchised her women, the liberated nations of Central Europe are enfranchising their women. America must live up to her pretensions of democracy!

Our ceremony today is planned to call attention to the fact that the President has gone abroad to establish democracy in foreign lands when he has failed to establish democracy at home. We burn his words on liberty today, not in malice or anger, but in a spirit of reverence for truth.

This meeting is a message to President Wilson. We expect an answer. If it is more words, we will burn them again. The only answer the National Woman's Party will accept is the instant passage of the Amendment in the Senate.

Mrs. M. Toscan Bennett was the first speaker. She said:

It is because we are moved by a passion for democracy that we are here to protest against the President's forsaking the cause of freedom in America and appearing as a champion of freedom in the old world. We burn with shame and indignation that President Wilson should appear before the representatives of nations who have enfranchised their women, as chief spokesman for the right of self-government while American women are denied that right. We are held up to ridicule to the whole world.

We consign to the flames the words of the President which have inspired women of other nations to strive for their freedom while

398

their author refuses to do what lies in his power to do to liberate
the women of his own country. Meekly to submit to this dishonor to the nation would be treason to mankind.

Mr. President, the paper currency of liberty which you hand
to women is worthless fuel until it is. backed by the gold of
action.

The Reverend Olympia Brown of Wisconsin, eighty-four
years old, burned the latest words of President Wilson, his
two speeches made on the first day of his visit to France. She
said:

America has fought for France and the common cause of liberty. I have fought for liberty for seventy years and I protest
against the President leaving our country with this old fight here
unwon.

Mrs. John Winters Brannan burned the address made by
President Wilson at the Metropolitan Opera House in opening the Fourth Liberty Loan Campaign, in which he justified
women's protest when he said:

We have been told it is unpatriotic to criticise public action.
If it is, there is a deep disgrace resting upon the origin of this
nation. We have forgotten the history of our country if we have
forgotten how to object, how to resist, how to agitate when it is
necessary to readjust matters.

Mary Ingham burned President Wilson's speech of the
Fourth of July, 1914, in which he said:

There is nothing in liberty unless it is translated into definite
action in our own lives today.

Miss Ingham said:

In the name of the women of Pennsylvania who are demanding
action of the President, I consign these words to the flames.

Agnes Morey burned President Wilson's book, *The New
Freedom*. She said:

On today, the anniversary of the Boston Tea Party, in the name of the liberty-loving women of Massachusetts, I consign these words to the flames in protest against the exclusion of women from the Democratic program of this Administration.

Henrietta Briggs Wall burned President Wilson's address given at Independence Hall, July 4, 1919, when he said:

Liberty does not consist in mere general declarations of the rights of man. It consists in the translation of these declarations into action.

Susan Frost, of South Carolina, burned President Wilson's last message to Congress in which he again spoke words without results.

Mrs. Townsend Scott burned his message to the Socialists in France which declared:

The enemies of liberty from this time forth must be shut out.

Mrs. Eugene Shippen burned this message to Congress:

This is a war for self-government among all the peoples of the world as against the arbitrary choices of self-constituted masters.

Sara Grogan burned another message to Congress dealing with liberty for other nations.

Clara Wold burned the message to Congress demanding self-government for Filipinos.

Jessie Adler burned the speech to the Chamber of Commerce of Columbus:

I believe that democracy is the only thing that vitalizes the whole people.

Mrs. Percy Reed burned this message to Congress:

Liberty is a fierce and intractable thing to which no bounds can be set and no bounds ought to be set.

Sue White burned the President's reply to President Poincare of France.

Mary Sutherland burned the words:

I believe the might of America is the sincere love of its people for the freedom of mankind.

Edith Phelps burned the Flag Day address.

Doris Stevens burned a statement to Democratic women before election:

I have done everything I could do and shall continue to do everything in my power for the Federal Suffrage Amendment.

Dr. Caroline Spencer burned the words which President Wilson said when he laid a wreath on the tomb of Lafayette, " in memory of the great Lafayette—from a fellow servant of liberty."

Margaret Oakes burned the Suffrage message to the Senate:

We shall deserve to be distrusted if we do not enfranchise our women.

Florence Bayard Hilles ended the meeting with a declaration that women would continue their struggle for freedom, and would burn the words of President Wilson even as he spoke them until he and his Party made these words good by granting political freedom to the women of America.

After the meeting was over, the long line marched back to Headquarters. A big, applauding crowd walked along with them.

XII

THE WATCHFIRES OF FREEDOM

ALICE PAUL spent all day Christmas of 1918 in bed resting. At least, she was resting physically. Mentally . . .

On that day she evolved a new plan of bringing the attention of the President, the attention of the country, the attention of the world, to the fact that the Susan B. Anthony Amendment must be passed. It was impossible—because of the action of the police in putting out the fires and arresting those who tended them—to carry out, in all its detail, her original plan which was extraordinarily striking and picturesque. Perhaps at no time in the history of the world has there ever been projected a demonstration so full of a beautiful symbolism.

The original plan was to keep a fire burning on the pavement in front of the White House till the Susan B. Anthony Amendment was passed. Wood for this bonfire was to be sent from all the States. Whenever the President made a speech in Europe for democracy, that speech was to be burned in the watchfire. While this was going on a bell, which was set above the door of Headquarters, would toll.

On the afternoon of New Year's Day, 1919, therefore, a wagon drove up to the White House pavement and deposited an urn filled with firewood—on a spot in line with the White House door. Presently the bell at Headquarters began to toll, and a group of women marched from Headquarters to the urn. Edith Ainge lighted the fire, and Mrs. Lawrence Lewis dropped into the flames the most recent words, in regard to democracy, that President Wilson had addressed to the people of Europe.

The first was from the Manchester speech:

401

We will enter into no combinations of power which are not combinations of all of us.

The second was from his toast in Buckingham Palace:

We have used great words, all of us. We have used the words "right" and "justice," and now we are to prove whether or not we understand these words.

The third was from his speech at Brest:

Public opinion strongly sustains all proposals for co-operation of self-governing peoples.

The fourth was from the speech to the English wounded:

I want to tell you how much I honor you men who have been wounded fighting for freedom.

As Mrs. Lewis burned these "scraps of paper," Mary Dubrow and Annie Arniel, standing behind the urn, unfurled a lettered banner:

PRESIDENT WILSON IS DECEIVING THE WORLD WHEN HE APPEARS AS THE PROPHET OF DEMOCRACY.

PRESIDENT WILSON HAS OPPOSED THOSE WHO DEMAND DEMOCRACY FOR THIS COUNTRY.

HE IS RESPONSIBLE FOR THE DISFRANCHISEMENT OF MILLIONS OF AMERICANS.

WE IN AMERICA KNOW THIS.

THE WORLD WILL FIND HIM OUT.

This was the first of the many Watchfires of Freedom kindled by the Woman's Party.

After these words were burned, Mrs. Lewis addressed the crowd that had gathered. When Helena Hill Weed, who had followed her, was speaking, a group of soldiers and sailors rushed forward, overturned the urn, and began to stamp out the blazing pieces of wood. There were two sentinels on each side of the urn, Gertrude Crocker, Harriet U. Andrews, Mrs. A. P. Winston, Julia Emory. They bore the tri-color, but they also bore torches. They quickly lighted the torches from the embers, and held them aloft. The rioting continued, but Mrs. Weed went calmly on with her speech.

Suddenly there was an exclamation from the crowd. Everybody turned. Flames were issuing from the huge, bronze urn in Lafayette Square directly opposite the bonfire.

Hazel Hunkins—clinging to the high-pedestaled urn—was holding aloft the Suffrage tri-color. The flames played over the slender Tanagra-like figure of the girl and glowed through the purple, white, and gold. People said it was— that instant's picture—like a glimpse from the *Götterdämmerung*. Policemen immediately rushed over there, followed by a large crowd. They arrested Alice Paul, Julia Emory, Hazel Hunkins, Edith Ainge.

In the meantime, the fire in front of the White House had been rebuilt and rekindled. It burned all night long and all the next day. Alice Paul, who had been released with her three companions after being detained at the police station for a while, remained on guard until morning. Annie Arniel and Julia Emory stayed with her. It rained all night. But until late, crowds gathered, quiet and very interested, to listen to the speeches. This was Wednesday. All day Thursday succeeding groups of women took up their watch on the fire.

Friday afternoon, the same banner was carried out. As soon as it was unfurled, a crowd of soldiers, sailors, and small boys, a chief petty officer in the navy being most violent, attacked the Suffragists, Mary Dubrow and Matilda Young. They tore the banner, broke the urn and attacked the purple, white, and gold flags. The fires, were, however, at once rekindled. It was still raining, and the rain was mixed with snow, which became a steady sleet. But the fires continued. Finally a force of policemen put them out with chemicals. That night they were relighted. Mary Logue and Miss Ross guarded it until two in the morning; Mrs. Lawrence Lewis and Julia Emory from two until seven.

Saturday afternoon, the bell at Headquarters tolled again. Immediately the flames leaped up on the White House pavement. Alice Paul, Mrs. Lawrence Lewis, and Phœbe Munnecke burned the first speech on Liberty made by President Wilson on reaching Italy. They were arrested, and the police put out the watchfire with chemicals. Instantly the fire started in the urn. Mary Dubrow and Julia Emory were arrested. All five women were released on bail.

On Sunday, January 5, Julia Emory, Mary Dubrow, Annie Arniel, and Phœbe Munnecke started a fire in front of the White House. They burned the second speech on Liberty made by the President in Italy. All the time the bell pealed its solemn tocsin. The four sentinels were arrested. This time they refused to give bail and were sent to the house of detention. The fire had now burned all day and all night on Wednesday, Thursday, Friday, and Saturday.

All these sentinels were charged, when they were arrested, with breaking a Federal Park regulation. But when they came to court, they were charged with building a bonfire on a public highway between sunset and sunrise. Three of them went to prison for five days, and three for ten days. They all went on hunger-strike.

January 7, evidently the official mind changed. The fire which consumed the President's speech on democracy delivered in Turin was allowed to burn for three hours. Nevertheless the crowd kept kicking it about, so that there was a line of flames across the pavement and trailing into the gutter. By hook or by crook—three of the Suffragists— Harriet Andrews, Mrs. A. P. Winston, Mrs. Edmund C. Evans—managed to keep it going.

At the end of three hours, new orders seemed to materialize out of the air; for then the police took a hand and put the fire out. With the extinction of the last ember, however, a second fire burst into flames at the base of the Lafayette Monument across the street. The police rushed to it, and put it out. Immediately another fire started at the opposite corner of the Park. And then fires became general . . . here . . . there . . . everywhere. . . .

The police arrested the three women who had kept the fire going. On the following day they were sentenced to five days in jail.

On the afternoon of that day, Mrs. M. Toscan Bennet and Matilda Young burned the speech that the President had just made at the statue of Columbus in Genoa. They were arrested at once, and they too were given five days in jail.

By this time, there were eleven women in jail, all on a hunger-strike.

On the afternoon of January 13, just as the thousands of government clerks began to pour down Pennsylvania Avenue past the White House, twenty-five Suffragists, each one bearing a banner of purple, white, and gold, came round the corner of Lafayette Square. They proceeded to the White House pavement, where they built a watchfire. The crowds, of course, stopped to watch the proceedings. Policemen finally broke through them and arrested three of the women. The other twenty-two closed in their line a little, and went on with their fire-building. The police returned, but they did not arrest the others. But they tried to break up the fire with huge shovels and a fire extinguisher. They tried to trample it out. But it was useless. Wherever a bit of the watchfire fell, it broke into flames. Finally, they arrested seventeen more women. Four remained, holding the purple, white, and gold banners.

Suddenly a great tongue of flame leaped upwards from the urn in Lafayette Square. The crowd rushed towards it.

Then for a moment it seemed to go mad. A group of young men rushed over to the Headquarters; climbed up the pillars; tore down the flag, the uprights, and the pole. The bell ultimately crashed to the ground.

The police arrested the remaining four sentinels. By eight o'clock that afternoon, released on bail, all the women were back in Headquarters. Half an hour later, they went out with their banners again. The streets seemed deserted even by policemen. But, as they crossed the street, the park police began to materialize from the shrubs and trees of the square. However, they built their watchfire on the White House pavement, and stood there on guard for an hour and a half. Crowds gathered, of course. Occasionally, a man would rush over to one of the girls, and tear her banner from her. The girl would hold it as long as it was a physical possibility, the crowd meanwhile calling remonstrance or encouragement according to their sympathies. By ten o'clock the women were all arrested again. ·They spent the night in the house of detention. They were: Dr. Caroline Spencer; Adelina Piunti; Helen Chisaski; Mrs. C. Weaver; Eva Weaver; Ruth Scott; Elsie Ver Vane; Julia Emory; Lucia Calmes; Mrs. Alexander Shields; Elizabeth Kalb; Mildred Morris; Lucy Burns; Edith Ainge; Mrs. Gilson Gardner; Gertrude Crocker; Ellen Winsor; Kate Heffelfinger; Katherine Boyle; Naomi Barrett; Palys L. Chevrier; Maud Jamison; Elizabeth Huff.

Suffragists filled the court when these women came up for trial. Four of them were tried at once. They were sentenced to a ten-dollar fine or five days' imprisonment. Their entrance into court had been greeted with applause from the audience. When the next four women appeared, they too were applauded. The Judge said, " The bailiffs will escort the prisoners out and bring them in again, and if there is any applause this time . . ."

The prisoners returned, and the applause was a roar. Three women among those who applauded were taken out

ONE OF THE WATCHFIRES OF FREEDOM.
Taken Just Before the Arrest of the Picket Line.

A POLICEMAN SCATTERS THE WATCHFIRE.

of the mass. " The police will escort the women out of the courtroom," said the Court. When they reached the door, " And see that they do not return," added the Court. As the door closed, " And lock the doors," shouted the Court. Thereafter, the prisoners were brought in one at a time, and were sent to jail immediately. Twenty-two women were thus sentenced. There remained one for whom there was no prosecuting witness—Naomi Barrett.

The next day, Naomi Barrett was tried alone. As she came forward, applause greeted her—applause long and continued. The Judge ordered silence. The applause continued. He ordered the applauders to be brought forward. One, Mrs. Pflaster, sank to the floor in a faint. She was picked up and put on a chair, but as she fell from the chair, the Judge ordered her removed at once. A physician was sent for. Her fellow Suffragists demanded that they be permitted to see her. Finally one of them was allowed to go to her. The Court had scarcely reached the next case when word came that Mrs. Pflaster was in a serious condition. The Suffragists came rushing in and demanded that the Judge come off the Bench and see what had happened; the Court obeyed. In due time the doctor arrived, a stretcher came, and the patient was taken to the Emergency Hospital.

The Judge resumed his seat, and sentenced Bertha Moller, Gertrude Murphy, Rhoda Kellogg, and Margaret Whittemore—the applauders—to twenty-four hours in jail for contempt of court. Mrs. Barrett was sentenced to five days in jail. They joined the twenty-two women who were already there and hunger-striking.

On January 27, six women kindled a Watchfire on the White House pavement. They were arrested on the charge of starting a fire after sundown. They were as usual, tried the next day; sentenced to five days in jail. They went on a hunger-strike of course. They were: Bertha Moller; Gertrude Murphy; Rhoda Kellogg; Mary Carol Dowell; Martha Moore; Katherine Magee.

In the meantime an interesting event took place in France. President Wilson received a delegation representing the working women of France, Saturday, January 25, at the Murat Mansion in Paris. The delegation urged upon the President that the Peace Conference include Woman Suffrage among the points to be settled by the Conference. President Wilson replied as follows:

Mlle. Thomson and ladies: You have not only done me a great honor, but you have touched me very much by this unexpected tribute; and may I add that you have frightened me, because realizing the great confidence you place in me, I am led to the question of my own ability to justify that confidence?

You have not placed your confidence wrongly in my hopes and purposes, but perhaps not all of those hopes and purposes can be realized in the great matter that you have so much at heart—the right of women to take their full share in the political life of the nations to which they belong. That is necessarily a domestic question for the several nations. A conference of peace settling the relations of nations with each other would be regarded as going very much outside its province if it undertook to dictate to the several states what their internal policy should be.

At the same time these considerations apply also to the conditions of labor; and it does not seem to be unlikely that the conference will take some action by way of expressing its sentiments, at any rate, with regard to the international aspects at least of labor, and I should hope that some occasion might be offered for the case not only of the women of France, but of their sisters all over the world, to be presented to the consideration of the conference.

The conference is turning out to be a rather unwieldy body, a very large body representing a great many nations, large and small, old and new; and the method of organizing its work successfully, I am afraid will have to be worked out stage by stage. Therefore I have no confident prediction to make as to the way in which it can take up the question of this sort.

But what I have most at heart today is to avail myself of this opportunity to express my admiration for the women of all the nations that have been engaged in the war. By the fortunes of this war the chief burden has fallen upon the women of

Photo Copr. Harris and Ewing, Washington, D. C.

SUFFRAGIST REBUILDING THE FIRE SCATTERED BY THE POLICE.

Photo Copr. Harris and Ewing, Washington, D. C.

THE LAST SUFFRAGIST ARRESTED—THE FIRE
BURNS ON.

France, and they have borne it with a spirit and a devotion which has commanded the admiration of the world.

I do not think that the people of France fully realize, perhaps, the intensity of the sympathy that other nations have felt for them. They think of us in America, for example, as a long way off. And we are in space but we are not in thought. You must remember that the United States is made up of the nations of Europe: that French sympathies run straight across the seas, not merely by historic association but by blood connection, and that these nerves of sympathy are quick to transmit the impulses of one nation to the other.

We have followed your sufferings with a feeling that we were witnessing one of the most heroic, and may I add, at the same time satisfactory things in the world, satisfactory because it showed the strength of the human spirit, the indomitable power of women and men alike to sustain any burden if the cause was great enough.

In an ordinary war there might have been some shrinking, some sinking of effort; but this was not an ordinary war. This was a war not only to redeem France from an enemy, but to redeem the world from an enemy. And France, therefore, and the women of France strained their hearts to sustain the world. I hope that the strain has not been in vain. I know that it has not been in vain.

This war has been popular and unlike other wars in that it seemed sometimes as if the chief strain was behind the lines and not at the lines. It took so many men to conduct the war that the older men and the women at home had to carry the nation. Not only so, but the industries of the nation were almost as much a part of the fighting as the things that took place at the fronts.

So it is for that reason that I have said to those with whom I am at present associated that this must be a people's peace, because this was a people's war. The people won this war, not the governments, and the people must reap the benefits of the war. At every turn we must see to it that it is not an adjustment between governments merely, but an agreement for the peace and security of men and women everywhere.

The little obscure sufferings and the daily unknown privations, the unspoken sufferings of the heart, are the tragical things of this war. They have been borne at home, and the center of the home is the woman. My heart goes out to you, therefore, ladies, in a very unusual degree, and I welcome this opportunity to bring you this message, not from myself merely, but from the great people whom I represent.

Mary Nolan—over seventy years old—immediately made Suffrage capital of this speech by the President. Mrs. Nolan's record in the period of the Watchfires is positively heroic.

On January 19, with Bertha Arnold, Mrs. Nolan was arrested for the first time in connection with the Watchfires of Freedom demonstrations. On January 24, while under suspended sentence, the two women again fed the flames in front of the White House. They were immediately arrested; the next day, tried. Mrs. Nolan said:

I am guilty if there is any guilt in a demand for freedom. I protest against the action of the President who is depriving American women of freedom. · I have been sent to represent my State Florida, and I am willing to do or suffer anything to bring victory to the long courageous struggle. I have fought this fight many years. I have seen children born to grow to womanhood to fight at my side. I have seen their children grow up to fight with us.

So great a storm of applause greeted these remarks that the Judge had thirteen of the applauders brought immediately to the dock and tried for contempt of Court. Thirteen women were sentenced to forty-eight hours in jail with no alternative of fines. These thirteen women were: Lucy Burns; Edith Ainge; Mary Gertrude Fendall; Phœbe Munnecke; Lucy Branham; Annie Arniel; Matilda Young; Ruth Crocker; Elsie Unterman; Kate Boeckh; Emily Huff; Lucile Shields; Elizabeth Walmsley.

Bertha Arnold received a sentence of five days, but Mrs. Nolan was released.

On Monday, January 27, Mrs. Nolan went out on the picket-line again, this time with Sarah Colvin. As she burned in the Watchfire the text of the President's words to the French workingwomen, she said:

President Wilson told the women of France that they had not placed their confidences wrongly in his hopes and purposes. I tell the women of France that the women of America have placed their confidence in President Wilson's hopes and purposes for six years, and the Party of which he is a leader has continually, and is even now obstructing their enfranchisement.

President Wilson has the power to do for the women of this nation what he asserts he would like to do for the women of other nations.

There are thirty-one days left for the passage of the Suffrage Amendment in this Congress, of which his Party is in control. Let him return to this country and act to secure democracy for his own people. Then the words that he spoke for the women of Europe will have weight and will bear fruit. Sooner or later the women of the world will know what we know—that confidence cannot be placed in President Wilson's hopes and purposes for the freedom of women.

The police seemed loath to arrest Mrs. Nolan, but they finally did so. The Court as reluctantly sentenced her to twenty-four hours in jail. Mrs. Colvin received the customary five days. Three more applauding Suffragists were committed at this last trial, for forty-eight hours: Cora Crawford, Margaret Rossett, Elsie Unterman.

On January 31, Mrs. Nolan was again arrested at a Watchfire demonstration with Mary Ingham and Annie Arniel. She was discharged by the Court. Mary Ingham and Annie Arniel, it may be mentioned, were held in jail for two days before they were brought to trial. There were no witnesses against them, and so they were freed.

On February 4, Mrs. Nolan was arrested again with Elsie T. Russian and Bertha Wallerstein for burning the President's speech to French Deputies. There was the usual applause when the three women appeared in Court, and, as usual, the Judge ordered silence; as usual, the applause continued. Three applauders were thrown out.

Mrs. Russian made the following statement to the Court:

By burning the hypocritical words of President Wilson, we have expressed the unmistakable impatience of American women. In place of words, these women demand action. I am glad to have taken part in the expression of that demand.

414

The watchfires had been going since New Year's Day, growing in numbers until they culminated in the biggest demonstration of all, two days before the day set for the vote. On February 9, they burned the President in effigy.

At half-past four that Sunday, the bell at Headquarters began to toll. A procession of a hundred women, headed by Mrs. H. O. Havemeyer bearing the American flag, marched to the White House pavement. Behind Mrs. Havemeyer came Ella Riegel, bearing the purple, white, and gold banner. Behind the color bearers came Mrs. John Rogers and Mary Ingham, carrying a lettered banner which said:

ONLY FIFTEEN LEGISLATIVE DAYS ARE LEFT FOR
THIS CONGRESS.

FOR MORE THAN A YEAR THE PRESIDENT'S PARTY HAS
BLOCKED SUFFRAGE IN THE SENATE.

IT IS BLOCKING IT TODAY.

THE PRESIDENT IS RESPONSIBLE FOR THE BETRAYAL
OF AMERICAN WOMANHOOD.

Behind this came Sarah T. Colvin and Mrs. Walter Adams, carrying a second lettered banner:

WHY DOES NOT THE PRESIDENT ENSURE THE PASSAGE OF
SUFFRAGE IN THE SENATE TOMORROW?

WHY DOES HE NOT WIN FROM HIS PARTY THE ONE
VOTE NEEDED?

HAS HE AGREED TO PERMIT SUFFRAGE AGAIN TO BE
PUSHED ASIDE?

PRESIDENT WILSON IS DECEIVING THE WORLD. HE PREACHES
DEMOCRACY ABROAD AND THWARTS DEMOCRACY HERE.

Behind these banners came Nell Mercer and Elizabeth McShane bearing an earthen urn filled with fire. Behind them came Sue White and Gabrielle Harris, who were to perform the leading act of the demonstration.

After these came twenty-six wood bearers, and long eddying waves of the purple, white, and gold. The urn bearers deposited the urn in its place on the pavement opposite the White House door. The wood bearers and the banner bearers formed a guard about it. Sue White then advanced and dropped into the flames a paper figure—a cartoon—of the President. Mrs. Havemeyer then attempted to make a speech. Before she was arrested, she managed to say the following three sentences:

Every Anglo-Saxon government in the world has enfranchised its women. In Russia, in Hungary, in Austria, in Germany itself, the women are completely enfranchised, and thirty-four are now sitting in the new Reichstag. We women of America are assembled here today to voice our deep indignation that while such efforts are being made to establish democracy for Europe, American women are still deprived of a voice in their government here at home.

Speaker after speaker attempted to follow her, but they were all arrested. The police patrols were soon filled up, and nearby cars were commandeered. There was an enormous crowd present. The police—nearly a hundred of them—tried to force them back, and succeeded in getting them part way across Pennsylvania Avenue. When they turned back, more wood had been brought from Headquarters, and another fire started. Other women who came from Headquarters with further reinforcements of wood were stopped and arrested. The police then declared the open space between the encircling crowd and the banner-bearing women a military zone. No person was allowed to enter it. For an hour, therefore, the women stood there. For the most part, they were motionless, but at intervals they marched slowly round their small segment of sidewalk. The crowd stayed until the banner bearers started homeward. They followed them to the very entrance of Suffrage Headquarters.

All this time the bell was tolling.

Those arrested were: Mrs. T. W. Forbes, Mary Nolan, Sue White, Mrs. L. V. G. Gwynne Branham, Lillian Ascough, Jennie Bronenberg, Rose Fishstein, Nell Mercer, Amy Juengling, Reba Comborrov, Mildred Morris, Clara Wold, Louise Bryant, Bertha Wallerstein, Martha Shoemaker, Rebecca Garrison, Pauline Adams, Marie Ernst Kennedy, Willie Grace Johnson, Phœbe Munnecke, Mrs. H. O. Havemeyer, Edith Ainge, Lucy Daniels, Mary Ingham, Elizabeth McShane, Sarah T. Colvin, Ella Riegel, Mrs. William Upton Watson, Anne Herkner, Palys Chevrier, Anna Ginsberg, Estella Eylward, Annie Arniel, Cora Weeks, Lucy Burns, Helena Hill Weed, Mrs. John Rogers, Gladys Greiner, Rose G. Fishstein.

On February 10, the Anthony Amendment came up once more for the vote in the Senate of the United States. Perhaps at this juncture recapitulation in regard to the Senate situation will be illuminating.

It will be remembered that when the Amendment passed the House on January 10, 1918, the Suffragists were eleven votes short in the Senate, and how—Maud Younger told the story most vivaciously—nine of these votes were obtained. For a long time, the Suffragists continued to lack the remaining two votes. The first thing that promised to ameliorate this deadlock was the nomination in the South Carolina primaries of Pollock for the short term of the Sixty-fifth Congress, convening December 2, 1918. Senator Pollock confused the situation extraordinarily for the Suffragists. The South Carolina branch of the Woman's Party interviewed him immediately after his election and it was their understanding that he told them that he would vote " yes " on the Amendment. When he came to Washington, however, he refused to state how he would vote. The Suffragists were in a difficult situation. Many of them believed that he intended to vote for the Amendment but he would not say that he did. They believed they had one of the two necessary votes but they could never be sure of it.

All the time, therefore, they were trying to get the votes of Moses of New Hampshire, Gay of Louisiana, Hale of Maine, Trammell of Florida, and Borah of Idaho, as they seemed the most likely of the opposed or non-committal men.

Indeed, two kinds of campaigns were going on—one in the States among the constituents of these possible men and the campaign of the Watchfires in Washington. As soon as the Watchfires began, the President again began to work. He called various Senators asking them to support the Amendment. The Democratic leaders became alarmed at the effect on the country of this constant turmoil in front of the White House. In fact they did the thing they had always steadfastly refused to do—called a caucus to mobilize the Democrats back of the Suffrage Amendment. At this caucus, various Administration leaders appealed to the Party members in the Senate to give their support to the measure. Pollock then made his first public declaration that he would vote for the Suffrage Amendment.

The Amendment now needed but one vote.

The chairman of the Suffrage Committee then announced that another effort would be made to pass the measure and it would be brought up for a vote on February 10, although until the Watchfires started, they had repeatedly declared that it would be impossible to bring it up twice in the same session.

As Congress was coming to an end, it was decided to take the vote anyway, although, as things stood, even with Pollock, the Suffragists lacked one vote. Pollock did vote for Suffrage but the other vote was not forthcoming. The Amendment was therefore defeated on February 10.

From February 10 to June 4, the Woman's Party was working to get that one vote.

While the Senate was debating Suffrage, thirty-nine of the women who had burned the President in effigy the day before were being tried. Twenty-five sentences of five days and one of two days were pronounced. Then the Judge demanded, "How many more women are there out there?" When he found that several were still waiting, he dismissed them without trial.

They were not charged with burning the effigy of the President, but with unlawfully setting fire to certain combustibles in that part of the District of Columbia known as the White House grounds.

The prison conditions which these Suffragists endured were as unpleasant as before. At first they went to the District of Columbia jail. Since previous incarcerations and the resulting complaints and investigations, soap and water had been used to some extent in this jail. So much, indeed, had soap and water been used that the prisoners could now clearly distinguish the vermin of more than one species creeping up and down the walls. The rats ran about in hordes. While conditions were somewhat improved, they were still bad.

Harriet Andrews, writing of her impressions of the jail in the *Suffragist* of January 25, says:

The jail was real. And it was not funny. I had a book of poetry to read, but I was sorry I hadn't taken a volume from the works of the late Henri Fabre. It would have been interesting to study the habits of cockroaches. I lay on my straw pallet and watched them clustered in the upper right hand corner of my cell waiting for my light to be put out before they began their nightly invasion. And when my light went out, the bulb that still burned in the corridor enabled me to watch them crawling down in a long, uninterrupted line. . . . There were also other things that crawled.

The last group were sent to the old Workhouse in which Suffragists had been imprisoned the August before.

Of that Helena Hill Weed says in the *Suffragist* of February 22:

No fire had been built in the old Workhouse this winter until a few hours before we were imprisoned there. The dampness and cold of the first floor was quite unbearable. They permitted the women to sleep in the upper tier of cells, where the ventilation is better than on the ground floor where we were forced to sleep last summer. But these cells are too dark to stay in during the day, and the only other place is the cold, damp stone floor on the ground. The only fresh air in the prison enters the building through windows fifteen feet above the level of the floor where the women have to spend their waking hours. The warm air from the furnaces, which enters the building on the first floor immediately rises to the roof. The damp, icy winter air and all the noxious gases and foul odors sink to the floor, where the women have to sit. They are serving their imprisonment under practically cellar conditions. The authorities are not forcing us to drink the water in the pipes of the Workhouse this time, but are supplying fresh water.

Harriet Andrews said that in coming out, " the sense of air and light and space burst upon me like a shout."

In the meantime, the Woman's Party, carrying out its extraordinary thorough and forthright policy of publicity, had not failed to tell the country at large about all this. They sent throughout the United States a carfull of speakers; all women who had served sentences in prison. They were: Abby Scott Baker, Lucy Burns, Bertha Arnold, Mary Ingham, Mabel Vernon, Mrs. Robert Walker, Gladys Greiner, Mrs. A. R. Colvin, Ella Riegel, Mrs. H. O. Havemeyer, Mrs. W. D. Ascough, Mary Winsor, Elizabeth McShane, Vida Milholland, Sue White, Lucy Ewing, Lucy Branham, Edith Ainge, Pauline Adams, Mrs. John Rogers, Cora Week, and Mary Nolan.

This car was called the *Prison Special* and the newspapers soon called the women the *Prison Specialists*. On the platform the speakers all wore duplicates of their prison costumes. Perhaps in all its history, the Woman's Party has never gathered—not a more brilliant company of speakers —but speakers with so marvelous a story to tell. They spoke to packed houses. At their very first meeting in Charleston, South Carolina, traffic was actually stopped by the overflow meeting.

XIII

THE APPEAL TO THE PRESIDENT ON HIS RETURN

THE President of the United States returned to America from Europe on February 24, 1919, landing in Boston. Boston arranged an enormous welcome-home demonstration. The Woman's Party determined to take part in that welcome to remind him of the Suffrage work to be done, and they announced this to the world at large. Alice Paul went to Boston to arrange this demonstration. The Boston police announced in their turn that they would establish a dead line in front of the reviewing stand beyond which the Suffragists would not be allowed to penetrate. However, the Suffragists, following the Red Cross women, marched through the line of Marines who held the crowd back, and took up their position before the reviewing stand where the President was to appear. At the head of the line in the place of honor, waving the American flag, was Katherine Morey. On one side of the Stars and Stripes was the historic banner:

MR. PRESIDENT, HOW LONG MUST WOMEN WAIT FOR LIBERTY?

On the other side of the Stars and Stripes was a second historic banner:

MR. PRESIDENT, WHAT WILL YOU DO FOR WOMAN SUFFRAGE?

The special lettered banner for the occasion read:

MR. PRESIDENT, YOU SAID IN THE SENATE ON SEPTEMBER 30, " WE SHALL NOT ONLY BE DISTRUSTED BUT WE SHALL DESERVE TO BE DISTRUSTED IF WE DO NOT ENFRANCHISE WOMEN."

420

YOU ALONE CAN REMOVE THIS DISTRUST NOW BY SECURING
THE ONE VOTE NEEDED TO PASS THE SUFFRAGE AMENDMENT
BEFORE MARCH 4.

This banner was carried by Lois Shaw and Ruth Small.

The police politely requested the pickets to depart and the pickets politely refused to go; whereupon the police politely arrested them. The arrested women were: Jessica Henderson, Ruth Small, Lou Daniels, Mrs. Frank Page, Josephine Collins, Berry Pottier, Wilma Henderson, Mrs. Irving Gross, Mrs. George Roewer, Francis Fowler, Camilla Whitcomb, Mrs. H. L. Turner, Eleanor Calnan, Betty Connelly, Betty Gram, Lois Warren Shaw, Rose Lewis, Mrs. E. T. Russian.

They were charged with "loitering more than seven minutes."

In the afternoon while the President was making a speech in Mechanics Hall, a Watchfire demonstration occurred on Boston Common. A vast crowd gathered about it. From three o'clock in the afternoon until six, the women made speeches.

The speakers were: Louise Sykes, Mrs. C. C. Jack, Mrs. Mortimer Warren, Mrs. Robert Trent Whitehouse, Agnes H. Morey, Elsie Hill.

Louise Sykes burned the President's words—and they were the words that he was speaking that very afternoon. Mrs. Mortimer Warren and Mrs. C. C. Jack were arrested at six o'clock and released immediately. Elsie Hill was detained on the charge of speaking without a permit.

That day the President's carriage drove by the Boston Headquarters. When Wilson saw the purple, white, and gold colors, his expression changed. Quickly he looked the other way. It was observed that he held across his knees a newspaper whose flaring headlines announced that day's picketing.

The Suffragists were tried on February 25, by what was very like a Star Chamber proceeding, in the Judge's lobby on the second floor of the court house. The Press was not excluded from the hearing, but the public was. As usual, the Suffragists did not assist the Court by giving names or answering questions. As a result, in the words of the *Suffragist*, " There is quite a family of Jane Does in Boston." Sixteen of them—everybody, except Wilma Henderson, who was discovered to be a minor, and several others who could not be identified—were sentenced to eight days in jail.

Some person—I quote from the *Suffragist*—entirely unknown and untraceable and unidentified, whom the policemen gave the name " E. H. Howe " paid the fines of these women. Katherine Morey, Ruth Small, and Betty Connelly were released on February 26; Josephine Collins on February 27; the others came out two at a time.

As usual, the complaints of the Suffragists called the attention of the people of the commmunity to the filthy condition of their jail, which these experts pronounced one of the worst in the country. It was characterized by the " bucket system." In each cell stood two buckets for toilet purposes. One contained the water in which they bathed. The other was emptied once a day or once in two days, according to the frequency with which the prisoner was permitted to go into the jail-yard for the purpose.

The Boston papers gave this demonstration enormous publicity. Boston institutions received in the press a muckraking which they had not experienced in years.

When President Wilson arrived in the Capitol at Washington—after this welcome in Boston—one of the first pieces of legislation which he took up was the Federal Suffrage Amendment. He went to the Capitol and conferred with Senator Jones of New Mexico (Democrat) Chairman of the Woman's Suffrage Committee, about the Suffrage Resolution. After the vote of February 10,

Senator Jones of New Mexico refused to introduce the Suffrage Resolution again, but Senator Jones of Washington, the ranking Republican, introduced the identical bill. The President expressed his regret over the failure of the measure on February 10, but he did not exert his influence towards getting it passed.

The Sixty-fifth Congress was about to adjourn in a few days. On February 28, in order to overcome the Parliamentary difficulty of the reconsideration of a measure which had been once reconsidered, Senator Jones of New Mexico introduced a Suffrage Amendment which was a variation of the Anthony Amendment and so of course to Suffragists not so satisfactory. It was referred to the Woman Suffrage Committee. Soon after this, Senator Gay of Louisiana, who had voted against the Amendment on February 10, announced that he would now vote for it. The President had obtained this vote, but like all his action on Suffrage, it came too late. There were only three days left and Senator Jones of New Mexico made several attempts to obtain the necessary unanimous consent for the consideration of his Resolution, but he was unsuccessful. On Saturday, March 1, Senator Wadsworth (Republican) objected. On Monday, March 3, Senator Weeks (Republican) objected. On Tuesday, March 4, Senator Sherman (Republican) objected. The session came to an end in the Senate without action on the Suffrage Amendment. The Republicans did not want the Democrats to get the credit of passing it, and so prevented it from coming to a vote.

XIV

THE APPEAL TO THE PRESIDENT ON
HIS DEPARTURE

WHEN Congress adjourned at noon March 3, President
Wilson left immediately for Europe, stopping in New York
to speak at the Metropolitan Opera House. Alice Paul
arranged at once a demonstration in New York as a
protest against the President leaving the Suffrage question
still unsettled. Her plan was to have every word on democracy, uttered by the President inside the Opera House, immediately burned outside the Opera House.

On the evening of March 4 a long line of Suffragists
started from the New York Headquarters at 13 East Forty-
first Street. Margaretta Schuyler carried the American
flag. Lucy Maverick followed her carrying the purple,
white, and gold tri-color. Florence De Shan carried:

MR. PRESIDENT, HOW LONG MUST WOMEN WAIT FOR LIBERTY?

Beatrice Castleton bore:

MR. PRESIDENT, HOW LONG MUST WOMEN WAIT FOR LIBERTY?

The lettered banner for the occasion said:

MR. PRESIDENT, AMERICAN WOMEN PROTEST AGAINST THE
DEFEAT OF SUFFRAGE FOR WHICH YOU AND YOUR PARTY ARE
RESPONSIBLE. WE DEMAND THAT YOU CALL AN EXTRA SESSION
OF CONGRESS IMMEDIATELY TO PASS THE SUFFRAGE AMEND-
MENT. AN AUTOCRAT AT HOME IS A POOR CHAMPION FOR
DEMOCRACY ABROAD.

424

At the corner of Fortieth Street and Broadway, this line met a barrier of more than a hundred policemen. As the Suffragists tried to pass through them, the police—assisted by soldiers and sailors from the crowd—rushed upon them; bore down the banners; broke them.

In her book, *Jailed for Freedom*, Doris Stevens tells how in perfect silence, but in the most business-like way, the New York police clubbed the pickets. They arrested six of the women; Alice Paul, Elsie Hill, Doris Stevens, Beatrice Castleton, Lucy Maverick, Marie Bodenheim. These were taken to the police station charged with disorderly conduct. After half an hour, they were suddenly released.

They went back to Headquarters, re-formed into a second line and started for the Opera House. At Fortieth Street, the police again rushed them, tearing and breaking their flags. The women were knocked down. Some were trampled underfoot, and picked up later, limp and bleeding from scrapes and bruises. Elsie Hill succeeded in retaining her torch. She began her meeting of protest. A messenger emerged from the Opera House with some of the words which the President had just uttered, and she burned them. The police rushed upon her, but they were too late. In the meantime, Alice Paul had succeeded in bringing the line of Suffragists up to the wall of police. There the crowds dashed on them again.

With the wonderful spirit which always characterized her, Elsie Hill called out to one of the soldiers:

Did you fellows turn back when you saw the Germans come? What would you have thought of any one who did? Do you expect us to turn back now? We never turn back either—and we won't until democracy is won!

Finally the police pushed the crowds back so far that there was no audience. The pickets returned to Headquarters. There they found that all the evening long, lawless citizens had been breaking in, carrying out great bundles of banners and burning them in the street.

Doris Stevens tells in *Jailed for Freedom* how, when she attempted to enter Headquarters, she was knocked down by a hoodlum armed with one of their banner-poles.

That night and the following day, sailors, privates and officers—military and naval—called at Suffrage Headquarters to apologize for the conduct of other men in uniform. They begged the women to believe that their action was not representative of the attitude of service men in general.

The Sixty-sixth Congress convened in special session on May 19, 1919, with the Republicans in control.

The Suffragists knew before this Congress convened, that it would pass the Anthony Amendment.

This was how it happened.

XV

THE PRESIDENT OBTAINS THE LAST VOTE AND CONGRESS SURRENDERS

THE Suffrage situation was a little confused. Senator Baird, opposed to Suffrage, of the old Congress, was succeeded by Edge, favorable to it. Pollock, favorable, was succeeded by Dial, opposed. Vardaman of Mississippi, favorable, was succeeded by Harrison. Drew of New Hampshire, opposed, was succeeded by Keyes. Hardwick of Georgia, opposed, was succeeded by Harris. These three last new Senators—Harrison (Democrat), Harris (Democrat), and Keyes (Republican)—mantained a steady silence as to how they would vote. It was necessary to get one of them.

Senator Harris was a close supporter of President Wilson. Alice Paul knew that Matthew Hale, former Chairman of the Progressive National Committee, a Suffragist but not a Democrat, was influential with the Administration. She therefore suggested to Anita Pollitzer that she see Mr. Hale at once and lay the situation before him. This was early in May and Congress was convening May 19. Mr. Hale was enthusiastic in his desire to help. The situation was complicated by the fact that the President was in Europe. Mr. Hale and Miss Pollitzer went over the Senate poll and from among the most favorable non-committal senators chose Harris of Georgia. He too was in Europe. Suddenly the field of the campaign crossed three thousand miles of Atlantic Ocean to France. The Woman's Party concentrated their forces on getting President Wilson to influence Harris into declaring for Suffrage. Mr. Hale worked steadily with a group of people close to the President who rapidly increased in numbers. Ultimately this pressure bore fruit in a conference between Robert Woolley, Democratic Publicity Man-

427

ager in the 1916 campaign, Homer S. Cummings, Chairman
of the National Democratic Committee, William J. Cochran,
Director of Publicity of the Democratic Committee, Joseph
Tumulty, the President's Secretary, Senator Walsh. The
result of this conference was that Tumulty sent a cable
to the President, suggesting that he confer with Senator
Harris. Senator Harris was in Italy, but at the President's
request he went to France. Immediately came the news on
the cable that Senator Harris would support the Suffrage
Amendment.

Having secured Harris' vote, President Wilson cabled a
message to the new Congress on the night of May 20 which
contained the following reference to the Susan B. Anthony
Amendment:

> Will you permit me, turning from these matters, to speak once
> more and very earnestly of the proposed Amendment to the Con-
> stitution which would extend the Suffrage to women and which
> passed the House of Representatives at the last session of the
> Congress? It seems to me that every consideration of justice and
> of public advantage calls for the immediate adoption of that
> Amendment and its submission forthwith to the legislatures of the
> several States.
>
> Throughout all the world this long delayed extension of the
> Suffrage is looked for; in the United States, longer, I believe,
> than anywhere else, the necessity for it, and the immense advan-
> tages of it to the national life, has been urged and debated by
> women and men who saw the need for it and urged the policy of
> it when it required steadfast courage to be so much beforehand
> with the common conviction; and I, for one, covet for our country
> the distinction of being among the first to act in a great reform.

As soon as Suffrage was assured by this sixty-fourth vote,
Senator Keyes and Senator Hale in a convulsive effort to
leap on the fast disappearing band-wagon announced that
they would vote for the Amendment, thus giving the Suffragists two extra votes.

As this was a new Congress it was necessary for the House
to pass the Suffrage Amendment again. On May 21, 1919,
therefore, the new House passed it by three hundred and

four votes to eighty-nine—forty-two more than the required two-thirds. It will be remembered that, when the previous House passed it on January 10, 1918, the vote was two hundred and seventy-four to one hundred and thirty-six—only one vote more than the required two-thirds.

The Amendment then went to the Senate.

In her *Revelations of a Woman Lobbyist*, Maud Younger says:

Four months later, on June fourth, for the fifth time in a little more than a year, we sat in the Senate gallery to hear a vote on the Suffrage Amendment. The new Congress, coming in on March fourth, had brought us two more votes—we now had our eleven. There was no excitement. The coming of the women, the waiting of the women, the expectancy of the women, was an old story. A whole year had passed in the winning of two votes. Every one knew what the end would be now. It was all very dull.

We walked slowly homeward, talking a little, silent a great deal. This was the day toward which women had been struggling for more than half a century! We were in the dawn of woman's political power in America.

Several days before the Senate passed the Amendment, Alice Paul left Washington to arrange for an immediate ratification by the legislatures in session.

XVI

RATIFICATION

"WOMEN ARE FREE AT LAST IN ALL THE LAND"

Chant Royal

Waken, O Woman, to the trumpet sound
    Greeting our day of long sought liberty;
Gone are the ages that have held us bound
    Beneath a master, now we stand as he,
Free for world-service unto all mankind,
Free of the dragging chains that used to bind,
    The sordid labor, the unnoticed woe,
    The helpless shame, the unresisted blow,
Submission to our owner's least command—
    No longer pets or slaves are we, for lo!
Women are free at last in all the land.

Long was the stony road our feet have found
    From that dark past to the new world we see,
Each step with heavy hindrance hemmed around,
    Each door to freedom closed with bolt and key;
Our feet with old tradition all entwined,
Untrained, uneducated, uncombined,
    We had to fight old faiths of long ago,
    And in our households find our dearest foe,
Against the world's whole weight we had to stand
    Till came the day it could no more say no—
Women are free at last in all the land.

Around us prejudice, emotion-drowned,
    Rose like a flood and would not let us free;
Women themselves, soft-bred and silken gowned,
    Historic shame have won by their mad plea
To keep their own subjection; with them lined
All evil forces of the world we find,
    No crime so brazen and no vice so low
    But fought us, with inertia blind and slow,
And ignorance beneath its darkling brand,
    With these we strove and still must strive, although
Women are free at last in all the land.

430

The serving squaw, the peasant, toil-embrowned,
    The household drudge, no honor and no fee—
For these we now see women world-renowned,
    In art and science, work of all degree.
She whom world progress had left far behind
Now has the secret of full life divined,—
    Her largest service gladly to bestow;
    Great is the gain since ages far below,
In honored labor, of head and hand;
    Now may her power and genius clearly show
Women are free at last in all the land.

Long years of effort to her praise redound,
    To such high courage all may bend the knee,
Beside her brother, with full freedom crowned,
    Mother and wife and citizen is she,
Queen of her soul and body, heart and mind,
Strong for the noble service God designed;
    See now the marching millions, row on row,
    With steady eyes and faces all aglow,
They come! they come! a glad triumphant band,—
    Roses and laurels in their pathway strow—
Women are free at last in all the land!

ENVOI

Sisters! we now must change the world we know
To one great garden where the child may grow.
    New freedom means new duty, broad and grand.
To make a better world and hold it so
    Women are free at last in all the land.
            CHARLOTTE PERKINS GILMAN,
            The Suffragist, September, 1920.

THE Suffrage Amendment had now passed both the House of Representatives and the Senate. One step was necessary before it became a part of the Constitution of the United States—ratification by the legislatures of three-quarters of the States in the Union—by thirty-six States out of forty-eight. No time limit was set by Congress on ratification, but naturally Suffragists wanted it to come as soon as possible.

Some people believed it would take twenty years. They did not reckon with Alice Paul however.

As soon as Congress passed the Suffrage Amendment, the whole situation—as far as Suffrage was concerned—changed. Now the President, the leaders in the Administration, the leaders in the great political Parties became potential allies.

In four States—Wisconsin, Illinois, Pennsylvania, Massachusetts—the Legislatures were in regular session. In three States—Texas, Ohio, Michigan—called on matters not pertaining to Suffrage, the Legislatures were in special session. The first undertaking of the Woman's Party was to get the convening Legislatures to ratify and the remaining States to call special sessions.

A race as to who should be the first to ratify, set in between Wisconsin, Michigan, and Illinois. All three ratified on June 10. But Illinois had to re-ratify later on June 17 because of an error in printing the Amendment on its first ratification on June 10. As between the other two, Wisconsin won.

The story of Wisconsin's part in the race is interesting and humorous. D. G. James, the father of Ada James, former Chairman of the Wisconsin Branch of the Woman's Party, was spending the day in Madison when the Legislature ratified. His daughter was, of course, exceedingly desirous that Wisconsin should achieve the honor of the first ratification, and he was equally desirous of aiding her. He assisted her in every way to avoid official delays and in getting the action of the Legislature properly certified. He commandeered his daughter's traveling bag, made a few swift purchases of the necessities of traveling, and caught the first train to Washington. He procured a signed statement that Wisconsin's ratification was the first to be received from the Department of State, on June 13. He brought his trophy in triumph to Headquarters and told his story to the newspaper men while the statement was being photographed.

That statement runs as follows:

DEPARTMENT OF STATE

WASHINGTON.

June 13, 1919.

By direction of the Acting Secretary of State, I hereby acknowledge the receipt of a certified copy of the Joint Resolution of the Legislature of the State of Wisconsin, ratifying the proposed Amendment to the Constitution of the United States extending the right of Suffrage to women, which was delivered by Special Messenger, D. G. James, on June 13, 1919, and is the first ratification of the Amendment which has been received.

J. A. TOWNER,
Chief of Bureau.

Michigan, almost neck and neck in the race with Wisconsin, ratified on June 10. Kansas, Ohio, and New York ratified on June 16. Kansas was the first State to call its Legislature in special session to ratify the Suffrage Amendment, the first also in which the legislators paid their own expenses to attend the special session. Illinois, held up by that mistake in printing, ratified on June 17.

Pennsylvania, the first non-Suffrage State, ratified on June 24, but not without a struggle. The session of the Legislature was drawing to a close and it was difficult to get the measure introduced. The National Woman's Party made a strenuous campaign. Mrs. Lawrence Lewis, Chairman of the Pennsylvania Ratification Committee, enlisted the aid of Governor Sproul and in a conference with Senator Penrose, who had been one of the strongest opponents to the Suffrage Amendment in the United States Senate, persuaded him to give his support to ratification. Mary Ingham, the State Chairman, brought all the Woman's Party forces in the State to bear upon the situation. The scene in the Senate when the vote was taken was highly colorful. The floor was a waving mass of purple, white, and gold. The tri-color badges of the National Woman's Party appeared everywhere on the floor and among the audience. There was such demand for the Woman's Party colors that at the last moment the stock had to be replenished. After the final victory in the

House, a parade of purple, white, and gold blazed its way through Harrisburg.

Massachusetts followed close on Pennsylvania, ratifying on June 25. Agnes Morey, the State Chairman of the National Woman's Party, assisted by members of the State branch, and by Betty Gram, national organizer, made the intensive drive on the Legislature, which resulted in their bringing the Bay State into camp. Here, Senator Lodge, another hitherto unchangeable opponent to the Suffrage Amendment in the United States Senate, did not oppose the measure when it came up before the Massachusetts Legislature, although he did not give the support which Penrose of Pennsylvania gave.

Texas, the first Democratic " one-party " State to do so, ratified by special session on June 28. Iowa, after an appeal for a special session from Senator Cummins to Governor Harding—this was done at the instance of the Woman's Party—ratified on July 2; Missouri ratified by special session on July 3.

In the meantime the Legislature of Alabama, which only convenes once in four years, met and although Suffragists had not wanted this session and had very little hope of success, they conducted a campaign for ratification. As it was the first Democratic State in which there was difficulty, an appeal was made to the President. He despatched the following telegrams:

WHITE HOUSE,
July 12, 1919.

Hon. Thomas E. Kilby, Governor,
        Montgomery, Alabama.
I hope you will pardon me if I express my very earnest hope that the Suffrage Amendment to the Constitution of the United States may be ratified by the great State of Alabama.

It would constitute a very happy augury for the future and add greatly to the strength of the movement which, in my judgment, is based upon the highest considerations, both of justice and experience.

WOODROW WILSON.

WHITE HOUSE,
July 14, 1919.

Hon. H. P. Merritt,
 Speaker of House of Representatives,
  Montgomery, Alabama.
 I hope that you will not think that I am taking an unwarranted liberty in saying that I earnestly hope, as do all friends
of the great liberal movement which it represents, that the legislature of Alabama will ratify the Suffrage Amendment to the
Constitution of the United States. It would give added hope and
courage to the friends of justice and enlightened policy everywhere and would constitute the best possible augury for future
liberal policy of every sort.
                                        WOODROW WILSON.

 Alabama was the first State in which ratification was
defeated.
 By this time, the Legislature in Georgia was convening.
Suffragists had no more hope of ratification here than in
Alabama. Nevertheless the campaign was made. They ap-
pealed to the national Democratic leaders for help and the
President despatched the following telegram:

WHITE HOUSE,
July 14, 1919.

Governor Hugh M. Dorsey,
 State Capitol,
  Atlanta, Georgia.
 I am profoundly interested in the passage of the Suffrage
Amendment to the Constitution, and will very much value your
advice as to the present status of the matter in the Georgia legislature. I would like very much to be of help, for I believe
it to be absolutely essential to the political future of the country
that the Amendment be passed. It is absolutely essential to the
future of the Democratic Party that it take a leading part in this
great reform.
                                        WOODROW WILSON.

 Georgia defeated ratification July 24, although the national Democratic leaders had aided in the entire campaign.
 Arkansas ratified on July 20; Montana, July 20; Nebraska on August 2, all by special session.

436

Then came a lull in the ratification race. By August, only two States west of the Mississippi, had ratified and to the great surprise—and the intense disappointment—of Suffragists, the West continued to maintain this lethargy.

In the meantime, there came a special session for good roads in Virginia, another Democratic State. Since the session was meeting, the Suffragists had no alternative but to make the fight. In Virginia, they relied again on the Democratic national leaders to overcome the opposition of the local Democratic leaders. As in the case of Alabama and Georgia, although the national leaders did much, they did not do enough. The President, however, despatched the following letter:

August 22, 1919.

President of the Senate,
  Richmond, Virginia.

May I not take the liberty of expressing my profound interest in the action which the Legislature of my native State is to take in the matter of the Suffrage Amendment to the United States Constitution. It seems to me of profound importance to our country that this Amendment should be adopted and I venture to urge the adoption on the Legislature. With utmost respect and with the greatest earnestness,

WOODROW WILSON.

Virginia did not ratify.

During all this period campaigns for special sessions continued. Typical of these is the following account by Julia Emory, national organizer, in the July *Suffragist*:

"Good-by, good luck, and don't come back until Maryland ratifies!" This from the group of National Headquarters when I waved farewell and started over the hills and far away toward a special session in Maryland. Over the hills to Baltimore, and then early the next morning, very, very early, the big bay boat splashed down the Chesapeake to Cambridge where Governor Harrington was spending the week-end.

"It's good of you to come," the Governor greeted me. "Not good of me, but necessary, Governor, to let you know how much women need a special session in Maryland, now. Not just the 15,000 Maryland women of our organization who have asked me to come to you, but all the women in the United States." "Ah!" said he. "You ladies are too impatient. We will have a regular session in January, why can't you wait till then?" "Because," I answered, "there is no need of prolonging the struggle. We have the necessary thirty-six States in view. We want the special session so that we can vote for the next Governor of Maryland at the election this November, and for members of our legislature at the same election." "But the question of expense," he suggested. "That is easily eliminated," I said. "Take Kansas, for example, where the legislators waived all pay and mileage in order to push forward ratification. Surely our Maryland men will do the same. And, anyhow, two days at the outside would see the thing through. Think of the taxes women have paid for so many years. Think of the war for Democracy, think of the part women gave in human sacrifice, service and money, and then tell me if anybody would say that a special session called for the purpose of giving them a voice in their government would take too much out of the State treasury." "That's true," said the Governor, "but special sessions are unpopular, and suppose the resolution should fail——" "Oh!" I said with a beaming smile of relief, "if what you want is a convincing poll, I'll give you that," thinking of the poll which, though still not yet completed, already showed a majority pledged in both Houses. "Next Tuesday," said he. "Now," said I. It was then Friday. But the Governor said Tuesday, and told me that in the meantime he was going to "feel around" for sentiment. And so did I.

First I went to a State Senator. "Why the special session?" he wanted to know. And when he found the thirty-six States were in view, he sat up. "The thing is upon us," he said. We went over the situation from the political point of view from beginning to end. He was a Democrat. "And," said he in a low voice, "if I had to bet on the fall elections, I'd—well, all I have to say is, if the Democrats want to get any credit, it'll have to be by special session."

"Will you say that to the Governor?" I asked.

"I will, tonight," he said, "and as for the question of expense, I for one, will waive my pay." Just then the train whistled. "You can't make it," said the Senator. "We are some distance from the station." "I must," I said. "I have to see another man."

The Senator laughed and called to a man in an automobile and away I whisked and the conductor helped me to hop on the train as it moved off.

The man at the other end was in Chicago. And the next train was due in six hours. Then on to a little town where I sat on a pile of baggage and waited until the Republican delegate arrived. "I hope," he said, "that the Republicans will take the initiative and ask for a special session. Yes, you bet, I'll waive my pay."

Then a Democrat, who said he would fight a special session to a finish. "Knowing what it will mean to your Party if you do?" I asked. We went into it from the political viewpoint. Then he saw the end in sight. We carefully went over the thirty-six States. He rubbed his head and looked at the opposite wall (or it may have been the State of Maryland he was gazing at so intently). "You know," he said finally, "I am an anti-Suffragist at heart, but at the same time I am no fool. The thing is here, and the point is, what is the best thing to do about it. I will not urge a special session, but I will not fight it."

Then on Tuesday, Mrs. Donald Hooker, our Maryland Chairman, went over the poll with the Governor. Man by man, they considered the delegates and senators. Yes, this one was sure, that one was practically sure but wasn't pledged and so we wouldn't count him yet, another was hopeful, another was hopeless, and the then uncompleted poll stood fifty-nine to thirty-eight in the House and thirteen to eleven in the Senate. We looked expectantly at the Governor. "I need more time to consider," was what he said.

"In the meantime," said Mrs. Hooker to me as we went out, "we will complete the poll as fast as possible. A big majority will surely convince him that it must go through."

So off to Southern Maryland and the counties around Washington. One legislator I found in Washington in a big, cool office, dressed in a Palm Beach suit and on the point of departing for a vacation. I looked at him and thought of canoes and bathing suits which had been shoved aside for me till after the special session. "I hope you will have a good time," I told him. "Mine will come after you have voted 'yes.'" He smiled happily and his reply made me smile happily too.

One man was in his wheat field. 'Way into the country we went by automobile where no trains ran and no electric cars penetrated. We reached the town and inquired at the hardware store for our legislator: "Mr. F——? Oh, he don't live here, he just has his mail sent here, he lives 'bout fo'teen mile round yonder." "Fo'teen mile round yonder," we finally found his home. "Well, you see it's this way," explained his wife. "He might've been home, but Mr. So-and-So is thrashing wheat and my husband went over to help him get it in before the storm." We noticed clouds in the sky. We went on to the So-and-Sos' farm. At the farmhouse, we all alighted. My companions immediately made for the chicken yard where they made friends with Mrs. So-and-So and helped her to feed the chickens. Afterward, they told us of the strong Suffrage speech the farmer's wife had made to them, who being the mother of eight children— six girls and two boys—had come to the conclusion that nobody needed Suffrage more than the farmer's wife. Two of the little girls took me out to the field, up a dusty white road we walked, climbed rail fences and—oh! how good! picked a few blackberries—and came at last to the thrashing field. "No," said my man, "I can't see that Suffrage is right, and I can't therefore vote for it." "Did you think the war was right?" I asked. "Oh! of course." "And why did we go to war?" I asked. "To get democracy," he answered. "Exactly," I said. "And President Wilson said that democracy was 'the right of all those who submit to authority to have a voice in their own government.'" "Now look here, Missie," said my friend, "I believe women are superior beings to men, and if they were to vote, they'd have to be equals. Now look at this hay stack. You could no more pitch hay than——" "Will you lend me your fork?" I asked. I stuck in the form, gave it the peculiar little twist, then the little flop, squared my shoulder and up it went on the wagon. Three times. "Well, I'll be jiggered," laughed the legislator, "labor is scarce and now I'll know where to look for help when I need it!" "Yes," said I. "And we have come to you for help. We need your vote."

On to the next, we climbed into the machine and sped away.

And so it runs. Sometimes, we strike an obstinate anti who will not even listen to what we have to say, even though I have traveled weary miles in trains and on foot to find him. Sometimes we have to put up at a funny little village hotel because an inconsiderate legislator has gone out of town for a day. Sometimes they are cordial, and offer all sorts of help. Sometimes the road lies through beautiful country, occasionally in hot, stuffy little towns. At fastest, it is slow work. Why do legislators live so far apart and in such inaccessible places? And generally so very far from anything to eat! Some evenings as it begins to grow dark, I am keenly aware that I have had nothing to eat since breakfast. But that is part of the game, and after all what does it matter when I can write to Headquarters before

I fall into bed, " We can add the following names of legislators to the list of pledged, and all of them have offered to waive their pay." So far only one has refused to waive pay.

So, with a big majority in both houses pledged to vote for the measure, there remains nothing but the calling of the special session. This, it is up to Governor Harrington to do at once.

And this, according to the following answer to Attorney-General Palmer's letter, he still refuses to do. Yet the Governor must surely yet see the light, as he knows that there IS no question of defeat if a special session is called to ratify.

The poll which has been so carefully and accurately drawn up demonstrates that fact most convincingly, and we are going to keep right on working until Governor Harrington sees it that way!

Maryland defeated ratification later.

Owing to the fact that most of the governors who must call special sessions were Republicans, the National Woman's Party made a drive on the national Republican leaders to get them to act upon these governors. On August 14, Abby Scott Baker went to the Governors' Conference at Salt Lake City where, assisted by Louise Garnett, State Chairman of the Woman's Party in Utah, she succeeded in getting governors whose Legislatures had already ratified to organize an informal committee to work upon those whose Legislatures had not ratified. Some of these governors of these backward States—or rather some of the backward governors of these States—made tentative promises in regard to special sessions, but these promises were so vague that Mrs. Baker started, at the close of the Governors' Conference, to California. We shall hear about her work there later.

Minnesota ratified on September 8; New Hampshire on September 10, both in special session. Utah—but there is a story about Utah.

Utah was backward. Alice Paul interested Isaac Russell, a newspaper man, and a native of Utah, in the situation. He prevailed upon Senator Smoot, Republican, to write a letter to Alice Paul saying that he was disappointed that Governor Banberger, Democrat, was not calling a special session.

Alice Paul gave this letter to the Press, and of course, the Republican papers of Utah carried it. Alice Paul waited a while and then she sent Anita Pollitzer to see the Democratic Congressmen from Utah, and to put it clearly to them that the responsibility for the delay was on their Party. As a result of Miss Pollitzer's representations, Congressman Welling, a Democrat and a friend of Governor Banberger, wrote a strong telegram to him in which he urged him to set the date of a special session at once. Early the next morning, Congressman Welling telephoned Headquarters that the telegram had brought results and read a message from Governor Banberger announcing the date on which he would call that special session. Utah ratified on September 30.

In the meantime, we must go back to Abby Scott Baker, whom we left on her way to California. She found that an enormous amount of work had been done by Genevieve Allen, the State Chairman for California, and by the members of her organization, assisted by Vivian Pierce, a national organizer. Governor Stevens, however, seemed immovable on the subject of a special session. But with additional assistance from Mrs. William Kent, one of its national officers, the Woman's Party inaugurated a vigorous newspaper campaign. Governor Stevens found himself inundated by an avalanche of telegrams, letters, petitions, resolutions; and finally of entreaties of the men who surrounded him. Governor Stevens is a Republican, and the Democratic women began to organize for ratification. Senator Phelan, Democrat, gave them his assistance. National leaders of both Parties brought pressure to bear. It was impossible to resist this current. Governor Stevens issued a call for a special session for November 1, and on that date California ratified.

The Woman's Party refers to Maine as the first close call. This story is very interesting. Maine called a special session, but Maine was, so to speak, on the fence in regard to Suffrage, as, when the National Woman's Party approached the State on the subject of ratification, a referendum on Presidential Suffrage was pending. So important was the situation there that Alice Paul joined Mrs. Lawrence Lewis and Mrs. Robert Treat Whitehouse, the State Chairman, who were working hard. In Maine, too, the antis were troublesome. They managed to introduce a resolution in the Legislature proposing postponement on the subject of ratification until after the referendum. The President and Secretary of the State Federation of Labor sent an official appeal to the Legislature to vote for this resolution. Immediately the Woman's Party in Washington obtained a letter from Secretary Morrison of the American Federation of Labor to the Maine Federation, stating that the A. F. of L. stood strongly for ratification. Mrs. Whitehouse gave this letter to the newspapers; gave copies to every member of the Legislature. She conferred with the President of the State Federation, persuaded him to repudiate his former letter and to issue an appeal for the support of ratification. National leaders of both the Democratic and Republican Parties sent telegrams to legislators. Maine ratified on November 5—by a narrow margin of four votes.

After a long siege by the Woman's Party on the Governor, North Dakota ratified in special session on December 1.

In the case of South Dakota, Governor Norbeck agreed to call a special session of the Legislature if the majority of the members would serve without mileage. Late in November, Alice Paul received a telegram from Governor Norbeck saying that the session would not be called as he was sixteen answers short of a majority who were willing to serve without expense to the State. Alice Paul immediately sent Anita Pollitzer to the Capitol to see Senator Sterling of South Dakota. Miss Pollitzer showed him Governor Norbeck's telegram to Miss Paul and told him that the Suffragists would be greatly disappointed if the Republican Legislature of South Dakota refused to meet, and a Republican Governor refuse to call a special session. He agreed that was a political mistake and in Miss Pollitzer's presence, sent telegrams to his law partner, the chief politician of the State, telling him to do everything possible to have a special session called; to the Chairman of the Republican State Committee, asking him to telegraph each member of the Legislature, urging him to answer the Governor's appeal and to agree to come to the special session as the Governor had stipulated, at his own expense. Examining this situation superficially—or even closely—one would think that Miss Pollitzer had done everything that was possible. But there is no reckoning with Alice Paul. When Miss Pollitzer returned to Headquarters, Miss Paul said simply, " We can do more."

That afternoon Miss Pollitzer visited Mr. McCarl, the Secretary of the Republican Congressional Committee in Washington, who sent telegrams to all the Republican leaders in the State, urging that they make clear to the Republican Governor and to the members of the Legislature the importance to the Republican Party of a good record on ratification. Three days later, a telegram came to Washington announcing that a majority, willing to serve at their own expense, had been secured. South Dakota ratified on December 4.

Colorado, the last State to ratify in 1919, did so on December 12—but only after a long campaign, the result of local conditions.

January of 1920, in which five States came into the fold, was a highly successful month for the ratification record. Rhode Island and Kentucky ratified in regular session on January 6. Oregon, whose Governor broke his promises many times, finally ratified in regular session on January 12. The State Chairman, Mrs. W. J. Hawkins, campaigned vigorously here, assisted by her State organization and Vivian Pierce, national organizer. Much equally vigorous work in Washington supplemented her.

Indiana ratified January 16 in special session.

Wyoming was the last of the five January States. For months, Governor Carey had refused to call a special session. He had been peculiarly obstinate at the Governors' Con-

ference at Salt Lake City on August 14, where he had stated
that he would not call a special session even if it were needed
as the very last State. Wyoming, it should be remembered,
was the pioneer Suffrage State. Representatives of the
Woman's Party went at once to Wyoming. Mrs. Richard
Wainwright, who was staying in the West, made it her special
work to bring pressure on the Governor. Alice Paul sent
Anita Pollitzer to the Capitol to talk with the Congressman
and Senators from Wyoming. They said that circumstances
had arisen which made it impossible for them to try to force
the Governor. On the trolley car Miss Pollitzer met Frank
Barrow, Secretary to Congressman Mondell, and asked him
for help. He agreed to give it. Mr. Barrow had edited the
Cheyenne Tribune, the leading Republican paper of the State,
when Anita Pollitzer campaigned in Wyoming the year before. He began urging that a special session be called and
charged the Governor with hurting the Republican record on
Suffrage. Immediately a statement appeared in the Press
from the Governor, saying that he would call a special session, but not at the expense of the State; that the men must
come without pay or mileage. Wyoming is a huge State,
and this was in January, a month of terrific snow storms.
Unless extra political pressure was applied, the legislators
might not come from far-away ranches at their own expense. In the meantime, whenever politicians from Wyoming
arrived in Washington, members of the Woman's Party saw
them at once. Party members learned that a close political
advisor of Governor Carey was going to spend one night in
Washington. They called on him at his hotel and told him
that the responsibility of all this delay lay squarely on the
Republicans and on Governor Carey. He was highly indignant at the attitude of the Woman's Party and their Press
campaign. Nevertheless, he said that the Governor was
going to call a special session at once.

It was necessary to bring extra political pressure to bear,
so long as Governor Carey's request for a special session put
it up to the members of the Legislature, themselves, whether

they would attend that session. Anita Pollitzer went to the Capitol and got the political line-up from the political leaders. They divided the State into districts for her and told her who were the political bell-wethers of each district. With this information, Miss Pollitzer went to Dr. Simeon Fess, Chairman of the National Republican Congressional Committee. Dr. Fess sent strong telegrams to every one of the Republican State leaders asking them to round up the legislators of their district, to see that they agreed to go to the special session at their own expense; asked them for a reply; told them he would wire again if a reply was not received.

On January 27, both Houses of the Wyoming Legislature ratified unanimously.

The Governor of Nevada, a Democrat, had refused to call a special session for many months because he was afraid that other measures besides Suffrage would be brought up; but after a long pressure brought upon him by the national Democratic leaders, he was induced to call the session. Nevada ratified February 7.

The next State in the ratification line was New Jersey, and New Jersey gave the Woman's Party a terrific fight. Mrs. J. A. H. Hopkins, State Chairman, realized that with both the Republican and Democratic bosses opposed to Suffrage, New Jersey would never ratify unless the Woman's Party made it a matter of the greatest political importance to the majority Party—the Republican Party. She engineered the fight, assisted by Betty Gram and Catherine Flanagan.

In Washington, Alice Paul sent Anita Pollitzer to Frank Barrow, Secretary to Congressman Mondell, who had assisted the Woman's Party so signally in the Wyoming campaign, and asked him to go to New Jersey. "But I could speak with no authority," he said, "and Mr. Mondell will need me here." Anita Pollitzer told him that the Woman's Party would attend to all those matters. She then went again to Dr. Fess, Chairman of the National Republican Congressional Committee, and told him that they were likely to lose New Jersey unless somebody was immediately sent from the Congressional Committee to assist. At once, Dr. Fess wrote a letter to Mr. Barrow authorizing him to go to New Jersey in behalf of the National Republican Congressional Committee. Miss Pollitzer next went to Senator Poindexter, Chairman of the National Republican Senatorial Committee, and told him that the Woman's Party wanted Mr. Barrow to go to New Jersey; that Dr. Fess had asked him to urge ratification on behalf of the Republican Congressional Committee and that the Woman's Party wished him in addition to urge on behalf of the Republican Senatorial Committee. Senator Poindexter, thereupon, wrote a letter to Mr. Barrow authorizing him to go to New Jersey in behalf of the ratification of the Suffrage Amendment.

Last of all, Miss Pollitzer went to Congressman Mondell and broke the news to him that the Woman's Party would like to commandeer his Secretary to go to New Jersey for as long a time as necessary, to work among Republicans for the ratification of Suffrage. Following an entirely natural impulse, Mr. Mondell said, " I am vitally interested in Suffrage, but I must say I need my own secretary in Washington!" Miss Pollitzer of course represented to him how much it meant to the National Woman's Party to have Mr. Barrow go—that it would take at the most only a week out of his work; and that it might mean several years out of the lives of the women, if the Republicans allowed New Jersey to fail in ratification. She added that the responsibility was on him and got up to leave. Mr. Mondell said, " Tell Mr. Barrow to be in his office in ten minutes, as I shall want to see him there." Fifteen minutes later, Miss Pollitzer called on Mr. Barrow, who told her that Mr. Mondell had asked him to go to New Jersey. In a letter to Miss Paul, Mr. Barrow listed the obstacles which he found in the way in the big New Jersey battle:

1. The last Republican State platform on which members of the legislature were elected, declared for a referendum.
2. The Republican State Chairman was an open and avowed anti-Suffragist.

3. The biggest Republican boss in N. J. was actively hostile to the Suffrage movement.

4. The biggest Democratic boss of N. J. was actively hostile to the Suffrage movement.

5. The tremendous political influence exerted through the liquor interests was actively and openly working against them.

New Jersey ratified on February 10.

In regard to the New Jersey campaign, Betty Gram has a vivacious article in the *Suffragist* on March, 1920.

She says:

Miracles happen sometimes—but the ratification of the Suffrage Amendment on February 10th by the New Jersey Legislature was not the result of a miracle.

Every organizer of the Woman's Party who had worked in the State whispered in my ear, " Don't try New Jersey—it will never ratify." It was therefore with reluctance that at the bidding of Miss Paul and Mrs. J. A. H. Hopkins, New Jersey State Chairman, I invaded the territory of the enemy and went to Trenton, where on September 30th both the Republican and Democratic State platform committees were sitting.

Despite all our efforts the Republicans that day in open convention under the leadership of Republican State Chairman Edward Caspar Stokes, declared in favor of a referendum, though each individual who had given a pledge to his constituents to support the Suffrage Amendment was left free to do so.

In significant contrast to this, the Democrats, holding convention just across the street, declared for immediate ratification. This was done upon the persistent demand of the Democratic candidate for governor, Edward I. Edwards, at the probable cost of the support of the most influential Democratic boss in the State, James R. Nugent, who in open convention fought the issue bitterly and pledged his twelve Essex County Assembly candidates against immediate ratification. They ran on that issue.

We watched the election returns on November 4th with acute anxiety. It was a critical point, for we had much to gain and everything to lose. The decision brought joy in one respect. Edwards, a Suffrage governor, was victorious, but alas! the result showed that the Republicans, who had adopted the referendum plank in their platform, had carried the Legislature. They had a majority in the Senate of fifteen to six and in the Assembly of thirty-three to twenty-seven—and among the twenty-seven Democratic members were the twelve Nugent men from Essex.

We had only a fighting chance at best—but we set about the task resolutely. As usual, the first duty was to obtain an authentic report of the position of each newly elected man. We had secured pre-primary pledges from the fifteen Edwards Democrats, as well as a few from some staunch Suffragists on the Republican side, but only a very few, for not only was their State Chairman opposed, but the Republican boss of South Jersey—former Senator Davis Baird, whom we knew would fight us to the end—through his tremendous influence.

In a few days our poll was completed. The Senate showed a bare but safe majority of one, for there we needed eleven votes. In the House our poll was much less encouraging. We needed thirty-one votes out of sixty—and we could count only twenty-five positive yeas. Where and how to get the six more supporters out of a Republican opposition was the bewildering—almost stupefying question. Political pressure—both national and local——was the one way out. The time had passed for meetings at which to arouse sentiment of constituents—only pressure of the most intimate nature would move a vote to our side.

We first set about to choose our leaders in the respective houses. We wanted wide-awake, active militants—parliamentarians who would not demand the assurance of the usual excess number of votes before moving; men who would take up the fight eagerly, revel in the chance of victory, and with odds against them enter enthusiastically into a neck to neck race.

At a dinner given by the National Woman's Party at Newark on December 10th we accomplished our purpose—Senator Wm. B. MacKay, Republican, made an impassioned speech, publicly accepting the responsibility of leading our forces in the upper House. At this same dinner the newly chosen speaker-elect of the Assembly, W. Irving Glover, Republican, pledged his unequivocal support and straightforwardly stated that he would do all in his power to bring New Jersey into the line of ratified States. The happiest moment of the evening arrived when Republican majority leader of the House, Harry Hershfield, made known his position on the Suffrage issue and expressed his desire that New Jersey ratify. Great applause greeted his words that the backbone of opposition had been broken and that he anticipated victory and would exert every influence to that end. The day after the dinner, Mr. Hershfield permitted to be given out from our Headquarters a statement declaring that he would lead the fight in the House.

The next day I went to Washington. The interest of the two United States Senators from New Jersey as well as the Congressmen had to be recruited. Soon letters and telegrams were pouring into the State from Washington. The resolution passed unanimously by the Republican National Committee in Washington on December 10th did much to strengthen our position and before long the importance of the issue from a national standpoint began to dawn on the vision of some New Jersey Republicans.

The situation took on a more hopeful aspect—a few finishing touches only were needed—but just whose magic touch to summon was the problem.

We were at a standstill. Two votes were still needed to reach the required thirty-one. Then something happened.

Inauguration day came and with it the tactical error of the opposition which acted as a boomerang and assured the House majority leader his position as head of his party. It gave into our hands the strategic parliamentary advantage—which we had coveted and desired for so long. An unexpected resolution calling for a referendum on all constitutional amendments, including pending ones, wedged in among routine measures, was surreptitiously introduced on Inauguration Day by Assemblyman Coles of Camden and by a viva voce vote passed before more than fifteen members knew what had happened. Twelve Nugent men from Essex and three Baird men from Camden were responsible for the railroading through of this resolution. This act of course was a planned and deliberately malicious thrust at Suffrage.

The House adjourned and the anti-Suffragists believe they had scored a point. The reckoning came later. Editorials appeared in papers all over the State denouncing such methods. On the following Monday the House reconsidered the Coles' resolution with a vote of forty-four to thirteen—and we proceeded with our fight. The ratification resolution was introduced immediately after and sent to the Federal Relations Committee, which was favorable to our measure—four to one. The referendum resolution had gone to the same committee.

Then the problem came of getting our resolution reported out first. We did not have a sufficient number of votes to hazard the chance of having the referendum resolution considered before ours, though some of our supporters preferred this procedure. A conference of leaders was called, to which I summoned Miss Paul, for the political leaders had had little comparative experience in handling constitutional amendments, while she had sponsored ratification in two dozen States.

A hearing before the committee was held on February 2nd. Our State Chairmàn, Mrs. Hopkins, and United States Senator Selden Spencer of Missouri, who came from Washington, made splendid appeals for Suffrage. That evening our resolution passed the Senate eighteen to two as a result of the Republicans having caucused in its support, after an appeal had been made to them to do so by Senator Spencer. There was no dissenting Democratic vote in the upper House. That same evening the House rejected the minority report of the Committee and accepted the favorable majority report on our measure. It was voted to a second reading and made the first order of business for Monday evening, February 9th.

That same week influenza seized various members of the Legislature and four of our most ardent supporters were ill. Their absence meant defeat. Every day we anxiously inquired after their welfare. For a time it seemed we would never have our thirty-one yeas together.

The day before the vote the National Republican Senatorial and Congressional committees sent a representative, Mr. Frank Barrow, from Washington to our aid. He worked with the doubtful Republican members.

At last the long looked-for moment arrived. At eight o'clock on Monday evening the Legislature which was either to reject or accept the ratification resolution convened.

The fight began with opposing men as aggressors and soon one resolution after another was being rushed to the speaker's desk as a subterfuge of delay. Roll calls were asked on each and every occasion, and as we strained our ears for the yeas and nays we received each time a shock at the transference of a vote. A roll call to postpone lacked only one of the necessary thirty-one votes.

Debate lasted until one o'clock Tuesday morning—five hours of continuous fiery combat—and then a motion to move the previous question fell like a pall on the troubled assembly. With trembling, tired hands we turned to our last spotless roll call and began to mark the records of men on the sands of time. Clear and decisive came the yeas—inaudible and slow came the nays, and after them all the called, " Joint resolution number one adopted—thirty-four to twenty-four."

Silence followed for long seconds and then the wild, almost hysteric cheers of women reverberated through the halls. Never had there been such a demonstration of joy in the New Jersey

Capitol and out of the galleries poured countless smiling women—
bearing banners of victory, to take their places among the liberated peoples.

Idaho, which ratified on February 11; Arizona on February 12; New Mexico on February 19; Oklahoma on
February 27 did so only after a struggle, but their cases
were special only in detail.

In the meantime, there had been two January defeats,
Mississippi and South Carolina; two February defeats, Virginia for the second time, and Maryland.

West Virginia, which came into the fold on March 10,
presents to ratification another dramatic story. I quote an
article by Mary Dubrow, in the April *Suffragist*.

They are all true—the old adages about pride and falls,
boasters who forget to rap on wood, chickens and hatchings—
West Virginia proved it.

Last August the card catalogue files carefully compiled by
Maud Younger, Legislative Chairman of the Woman's Party,
showed an overwhelming majority for ratification in the West
Virginia legislature. To check up on this poll, a member of
the Legislature took another and discovered the same overwhelming majority. Our National Headquarters kept in touch
with the situation until the special session was called.

The West Virginia delegation in Congress, the Democratic
governor of the State, and the Republican National Committee-
man, all alike expressed certainty of ratification.

As I left for West Virginia I confided to every one I met how
happy I was to go to a State which would probably ratify
unanimously, and every leading citizen I interviewed for the
first four days confirmed my expectation.

Then the legislators began to assemble at the Kanawha Hotel,
the political center of Charleston. I had their written pledges
and I approached them more to exchange pleasant anticipations
of victory than for any other purpose, and my fall began—a
gradual inch-by-inch fall. The first man I met said: " Well, I
haven't been here very long and I don't know just how I will
vote. You see our great State voted Suffrage down by a majority of——" And the second man said the same thing, and
the third repeated the remark.

Then the splendid men who were leading our fight and who
were standing staunch came to me with appalling reports of the

wavering of this one and that one. It was an opposition stampede—nothing less.

I hurriedly told the Washington Headquarters the situation and the National Republican Senatorial Committee was prevailed upon to send a representative, Mr. Frank Barrow, to West Virginia to urge the Republicans in the Legislature to remember their Party and vote for ratification.

Our chairman in West Virginia, Mrs. William Gay Brown, a staunch Democrat, conferred with the Democrats and made them appreciate their responsibility. Miss Anita Pollitzer, legislative secretary of the Woman's Party working in Washington, convinced Senator Sutherland that his State could not afford to defeat the Amendment.

We re-polled the House of Delegates and one hour before the vote was taken in that body on March 4 we knew we had forty votes and the opposition had forty-one, and that there were six members who would tell neither friend, enemy, nor Party leader how they stood—the silent six they were called.

In the Senate we were certain of fourteen both ways. But the Republican leaders were sure they could get one more. Some of them were even sure they could get three! Senator Harmer, who led the fight in the Senate and who is one of the best parliamentarians in the State, nevertheless was not for allowing ratification to come to a vote.

The vote was taken—and the clerk announced it—" fourteen to fourteen." Senator Harmer saved the situation by changing his vote and making reconsideration possible. The Senate adjourned. It was the turn of the House. When the debate began speeches were tossed from man to man like balls in a game, and never for four hours was there a moment of silence in the House. At six o'clock the vote was taken. Forty-six men, in the face of the action of the Senate, stood sound—not as Republicans, not as Democrats, but as Suffragists, every one of the silent six voting for us.

With the announcement of the tie in the Senate, national leaders who had paid no attention to our repeated warnings of peril sprang into action. Representative Fess, Chairman of the Republican Congressional Committee, immediately wired the following telegram to Republicans:

" Can not overestimate importance from Party standpoint of Republican legislature West Virginia ratification and desire to maintain this position. Any attempt substitute referendum would be grave mistake. Can we count on your active and immediate aid? "

Senator Poindexter, Chairman of the Republican Senatorial Committee, told of the situation by leaders in Washington, sent the following message:

"Republican Senatorial Committee is deeply concerned over result of Suffrage vote in your Senate. We count on West Virginia's ratification. Republican Party has pioneered every fight for Suffrage and every State where Republicans had control of the Legislature has ratified. Party will be greatly embarrassed if West Virginia breaks that most gratifying record through failure to co-operate with us in this critical time."

Senator Capper and Senator Kendrick likewise sent messages urging the Republicans to reconsider this fatal step.

Senator Owen, Senator Walsh, and Attorney General Palmer, Secretary Daniels and Secretary Baker all used every effort to make it a Democratic victory.

As a climax to all this, the President himself, realizing that one Democratic vote could save the situation, sent every opposed Democratic member of the Senate a telegram urging him to cast the deciding vote. If we could not obtain one vote from this pressure, there was only one chance left to us.

Senator Bloch, who was wintering in California, had asked to be paired for Suffrage. The opposition refused to consider his request and no pressure could obtain from the opposed Senators this ordinary Senatorial courtesy. A long-distance call was put in for Senator Bloch in San Francisco. That night he started east.

Now came the test of all our resources and of the loyalty of our friends, and I do not believe that any stauncher loyalty has been displayed by any group of men in the whole ratification campaign than by the fourteen Suffrage senators of the West Virginia Legislature.

For five days these fourteen men had to wait in Charleston while the fifteenth vote crossed the continent. Every day they held conferences and buoyed one another up, while Betty Gram, who had been sent from Washington to help in the campaign, and I hovered round about trying, with radiant cheerfulness, to instill into every one the feeling: "Senator Block is on his way and all is well with the world." Telegraphic despatches constantly arrived saying Senator Block was in New Mexico or Omaha or some other remote place that gradually grew nearer.

Our enemies once more began their attack in the House. The opposition tried to reconsider and were beaten; tried a referendum and were beaten; tried to prevent consideration from being tabled and were beaten. Nevertheless, all of the delegates of the lower House had to be held in Charleston as well as the Senators. One man got as far as his comfortable seat in the train, but we heard that he had bought a ticket. I took a taxi-cab, Miss Gram and Mrs. Puffenbarger, Chairman of the Woman's Committee of West Virginia, took another. We arrived simultaneously and that bewildered delegate was rushed off the train and back to his less comfortable seat in the Capitol.

At one time it looked as if we could not get enough votes to recess from day to day until Senator Bloch arrived, and our friends prepared for continuous session. They carried pillows in their hands and playing-cards in their pockets, and we on the outside had our arrangements made for relaying them sandwiches and coffee. It was the opposition that weakened in the face of this ordeal.

Then came Monday, the day set for Mr. Bloch's arrival and suddenly a senator disappeared. We thought that he had been abducted. His thirteen Suffrage colleagues rushed about searching for him. Miss Gram and I walked the streets, even daring to peer into barber-shop windows.

At last the mystery was solved. He had gone home and was delayed by a blizzard.

The Senate did not convene until he reappeared at 2:50 and saved the situation.

And then Senator Bloch arrived—one man alone in two coaches bouncing behind an engine that broke the world record for speed. He had chosen the special train rather than the airplane that was put at his disposal by the Republicans, but, as he said himself, he was traveling in the air most of the way to Charleston. As he got off the train, pale but smiling, he was grasping his golf sticks desperately in one hand and a thermos bottle of coffee in the other. And at 2:40 A.M., when his private train pulled in, the town was out to meet him.

While the senator tried to catch his breath, he gave this statement to the press:

"The fourteen men who have so splendidly held together until my arrival deserve all the credit for the victory which we hope to gain tomorrow."

Even then our victory was won as by a miracle, for while we brought our vote from California, the anti-Suffragists were also bringing a senator more quietly from Peoria, Ill. Senator Montgomery, who had moved out of the State and resigned from the Senate, was persuaded to come back and attempt to regain his seat. But one of the opposition whom it had happened by chance Senator Montgomery had told personally of his resignation, refused to dishonor himself by voting to reseat even a member of his own Party under these conditions, and the day was saved again for the women of America.

The last Western State—Washington—ratified on March 22.

Thirty-five States had now accepted the Susan B. Anthony Amendment. One more and it would become part of the Constitution. However, that last State, every one knew, would be hard to get. The chances looked brightest in Delaware and the Woman's Party concentrated all its energies there.

Ratification was brought up twice in Delaware, the first time on April 1 and the second time on May 5. The fight was an intensive one, but it failed. This campaign had a quality of picturesqueness given to it by its *mise en scene*— the open square where the State House stands. Dover Green is surrounded by charming colonial houses with a beautiful colonial Capitol dominating them. Here, when the news came from Philadelphia of the signing of the Declaration of Independence, a crowd burned the picture of King' George— " Compelled by strong necessity, thus we destroy even the shadow of that King who refused to reign over a free people." The ancient whipping-post still stands in a yard adjoining the State House. A log cabin, which was put up fifty years ago, is still used as a lawyer's office. The *Suffragist* noted the fact that a yoke of oxen, drawing a plow in the ancient way, had been seen near Dover when the ratification campaign was going on. This accumulation of historic atmosphere added its subtle weight to the regret of the Suffragists when Delaware failed them.

Against highly organized opposition, the Suffragists began work in Delaware. Florence Bayard Hilles, State Chairman, conducted this important fight. She had the assistance of six national organizers: Mary Dubrow, Anita Pollitzer, Catherine Flanagan, Betty Gram, Vivian Pierce, Elsie Hill; of Mrs. Lawrence Lewis, National Ratification Chairman; of Mabel Vernon, National Secretary of the Woman's Party. Ultimately Alice Paul joined them. This able group produced a triumph of Suffrage ratification in the Senate on May 5. The vote was eleven to six. In the usual course of events, the ratification measure would have gone, after the Senate passed it, to the House. The votes necessary to pass it in the House were not forthcoming. The Legislature adjourned.

The Woman's Party used the interval until May 17 when the Legislature reconvened to wage a campaign against their opponents, by means of petitions, mass-meetings, and appeals to State leaders. President de Valera, Frank Walsh, and other champions of Irish freedom used their influence with the four Irish members of the Lower House. The American Federation of Labor also helped in this campaign. On June 2, when it became evident that the Republicans in this strongly Republican Legislature, would not ratify, President Wilson asked the Democrats to give their aid. The President's telegram ran:

May I not as a Democrat express my deep interest in the Suffrage Amendment, and my judgment that it will be of the greatest service to the Party if every Democrat in the Delaware Legislature should vote for it.

Delaware had been the first to ratify the Constitution of the United States but it failed to ratify this second great instrument of freedom.

For two months the Delaware members of the Republican Party had delayed the ratification of the Amendment. In spite of repeated appeals to them, the Republican national leaders refused to give the necessary support to assure victory in that State.

On May 18, Will H. Hays, Chairman of the Republican Party, spoke at the Hotel Willard, Washington, to women especially selected because of their wealth—in the hope that they would answer an appeal for funds for the support of the Republican Party. As each member of the audience took her seat, she found on her chair a slip which read in effect,

" For the use of the Republican National Committee, I herewith enclose a check for $1,000."

When Mr. Hays arose from his seat, Elsie Hill, well known as a national organizer of the Woman's Party, arose from hers. As he started to speak, she said, " Before you ask us to support the Republican Party, Mr. Hays, won't you tell us what the Republican Party is going to do about ratification in Delaware? "

The Chairman immediately intervened. " I am sure Mr. Hays, if he has time in the course of his remarks, will answer that." Instantly Sue White, one of the State chairmen, arose and demanded that the question be answered at once. Mr. Hays apparently did not hear. He moved to the front of the platform, opened his lips to speak. Immediately Benigna Green Kalb, a well-known member of the Woman's Party, arose and said, " Mr. Hays, women will not give money for the next elections until they know whether or not they are going to vote in them. In Delaware, Connecticut, and Vermont the Republican Party can answer that question."

Mr. Hays said, " I suppose I may as well take this matter up at once. My dear ladies, if any one of you know anything whatever about practical politics, you would know that we do not carry Legislatures around in our pockets. Why don't you go to Delaware and work for Suffrage? "

Instantly Anita Pollitzer was on her feet. " I have been working in Delaware, Mr. Hays, for six months. The legislators of Delaware seem to think that the Republican Party can do something about Suffrage in that State. Some of the leading Republicans of the Lower House telephoned to me last night and asked, ' What are the national Republican leaders going to do about this dead-lock here? ' "

Mr. Hays attempted explanation; apology; prophecy. " Every Republican hopes that Delaware will ratify. Some one of the remaining States will be intelligent enough to act between now and election time. I feel sure women will vote in the next elections."

Abby Scott Baker interposed, "Mr. Hays, why are you sure women will vote in the next elections? If the Republican Party cannot persuade the Republican Legislature of Delaware to ratify, can it persuade the Republican governors of Connecticut and Vermont to call special sessions, or are you depending upon the Democratic States to enfranchise the women to whom your Party is now appealing for funds?"

Woman after woman arose and brought up the matter of Delaware. Mr. Hays' speech was rapidly disappearing before the onslaught. He had spoken on nothing but Suffrage. Many of the audience liked the interruptions no better than Mr. Hays. They groaned and hissed. But the Suffragists kept on. Edith Ainge spoke. Elsie Hill arose for a second time and a third. Finally, definitely enraged, Mr. Hays accused her of being a Democratic woman who had come to interrupt his meeting. Miss Hill replied, "My father was for twenty years Republican Congressman from Connecticut and for several years ranking member of the Ways and Means Committee."

Mr. Hays talked for nearly five minutes after this last interruption. He slid off the subject of Delaware. He progressed as far away as Abraham Lincoln. Lucy Branham arose to bring his mind back to Delaware. Mr. Hays was saying, "The great Republican leaders of the past——" and his hands were uplifted to emphasize his statement. Glancing down between them, his gaze was attracted by Miss Branham's movement. "Not now, young lady, not now," he commanded, or suggested, or perhaps begged. Miss Branham bore up the aisle. Neither Mr. Hays' gesture nor sentence completed itself. "In conclusion," he said, "I desire to state that the few women who are about to be enfranchised could do no better——" Mr. Hays' conclusion merged with air.

In the meantime, the anti-Suffragists in Ohio had brought a suit attacking the validity of the Ohio ratification on the ground that the State of Ohio had the initiative and referendum on all acts by the State Legislature and therefore must have it on ratification, if it were demanded by petition. They therefore demanded a referendum on the ratification of Suffrage. The Woman's Party contested this suit, engaging the following counsel: Shippen Lewis, George Wharton Pepper, and William Draper Lewis. It went through the Courts of Ohio to the Supreme Court of the United States, which sustained the validity of the Ohio ratification.

The Republican Convention began on June 8 in Chicago. Delaware—whose Legislature and Governor were Republican—had just defeated ratification. There were only two other States from which it seemed possible at this time to obtain final ratification—Vermont and Connecticut. There were, to be sure, two other States which had not acted on the Amendment—Florida and Tennessee. But there were clauses in their constitutions which provided that an election must occur between the submission of an Amendment and its ratification. The fact that both Vermont and Connecticut were Republican put the responsibility of finishing up ratification on the Republicans. As repeated appeals to the National Republican leaders had failed to induce them to bring sufficient pressure on the Republican governors of Vermont and Connecticut, the Suffragists felt that it was necessary to make a stronger protest than hitherto they had exerted against this Republican inaction. They therefore decided to picket the Republican National Convention. The first day of the Convention, Mabel Vernon led a long white-clad line of women, carrying lettered banners and the purple, white, and gold tri-color, from the Woman's Party Headquarters to the Coliseum, directly opposite, where the Convention was held. They marched across the street and took up their brilliant tri-color stand at intervals against its dull walls.

Mary Ingham bore a banner which said:

THE REPUBLICAN PARTY HAS THE POWER TO ENFRANCHISE WOMEN. WHEN WILL IT DO SO?

Doris Stevens' banner read:

> WE HAVE HAD ENOUGH RESOLUTIONS.
> GIVE US THE 36TH STATE.

Mrs. H. O. Havemeyer's banner said:

> THEODORE ROOSEVELT ADVOCATED WOMAN SUFFRAGE.
> HAS THE REPUBLICAN PARTY FORGOTTEN THE
> PRINCIPLES OF THEODORE ROOSEVELT?

Mrs. M. Toscan Bennett's banner said:

> WE PROTEST AGAINST THE CONTINUED DISFRANCHISE-
> MENT OF WOMEN FOR WHICH THE REPUBLICAN
> PARTY IS NOW RESPONSIBLE.
> THE REPUBLICAN PARTY DEFEATED RATIFICATION OF
> SUFFRAGE IN DELAWARE.
> THE REPUBLICAN PARTY IS BLOCKING SUFFRAGE IN
> VERMONT.
> THE REPUBLICAN PARTY IS BLOCKING SUFFRAGE IN
> CONNECTICUT.
> WHEN WILL THE REPUBLICAN PARTY STOP BLOCKING
> SUFFRAGE?

This banner was also carried by Catherine Flanagan and Lou Daniels.

These banners were held during the first two days of the Convention. On the third day, each of thirty women carried a new banner:

> VOTE AGAINST THE REPUBLICAN PARTY AS LONG
> AS IT BLOCKS SUFFRAGE.

This quotation from Susan B. Anthony also appeared on the picket line:

> NO SELF-RESPECTING WOMAN SHOULD WISH OR WORK FOR THE
> SUCCESS OF A PARTY THAT IGNORES HER SEX.
> —Susan B. Anthony in 1872 and 1894.

THE OLDEST AND THE YOUNGEST PICKETS.

Rev. Olympia Brown and Miss Rowena Green at the Republican Convention, Chicago, 1920.

A favorite banner was:

REPUBLICANS WE ARE HERE.
WHERE IS THE 36TH STATE?

These banners were typical; many others appeared.

During the course of the Convention the Republicans inserted the following plank in their platform:

We welcome women into full participation in the affairs of government and the activities of the Republican Party. We earnestly hope that Republican legislatures in States which have not yet acted upon the Suffrage Amendment will ratify the Amendment to the end that all of the women of the nation of voting age may participate in the election of 1920, which is so important to the welfare of our country.

On the last day, therefore, a group of pickets hung, from the balcony in the Convention hall, facing the speakers platform, a banner which was the answer to this ratification plank. It read:

WHY DOES THE REPUBLICAN PARTY BLOCK SUFFRAGE?
WE DO NOT WANT PLANKS.
WE DEMAND THE 36TH STATE.

The effect of all this was that instant and urgent pressure to call special sessions was brought on the Republican governors of Vermont and Connecticut by Republican leaders.

In contrast to the treatment which the police of Washington, Boston, and New York had accorded the pickets, the police of Chicago were friendly and accommodating. Sometimes they even held the banners for them.

Immediately following the nomination of Senator Harding, members of the Woman's Party met him in Washington in an interview arranged by Genevieve Allen. Miss Paul introduced Mrs. Albion Lang, Helena Hill Weed, and Florence Bayard Hilles, each representing one of the three Republican States which had not acted favorably on ratification; Mrs. John Carey, Helen Hoy Greeley, Emma Wold and Genevieve Allen, representing women who could vote, and

Sue White, Mary Ingham, Mrs. John Gordon Battelle, Mrs. Donald R. Hooker, representing women who could not vote. The interview was utterly unsatisfactory—Senator Harding listened and evaded.

On June 15, Lousiana, which met in regular session, defeated ratification. Here, anticipating a little, it may be stated that on August 19, North Carolina defeated ratification, also in regular session.

In the meantime, the Woman's Party turned its attention to Tennessee. Up to this time, it had been considered impossible to ratify there, as there is a clause in the Tennessee State Constitution which says that the Tennessee Legislature cannot act on any Amendment to the Federal Constitution unless a new Legislature is elected between the time when the Federal Amendment shall have passed Congress and its ratification by Tennessee. The decision in the Ohio case which was handed down at this moment and which indicated that both Tennessee and Florida could ratify legally, changed the whole complexion of the Suffrage fight. The Ohio decision, it will be remembered, was that ratification was an act of a Legislature which was not subject to a referendum to the people. The Woman's Party pointed out—and they had consulted many eminent lawyers on this subject—that the clause in the Tennessee Constitution was equal to requiring a referendum before submitting a constitutional amendment to the Legislature. Since by the Ohio decision a referendum on such a matter was illegal, that clause in the Tennessee constitution could not stand in the way of ratification by the existing Legislature. Sue White, Tennessee State Chairman, instituted an immediate campaign on Governor Roberts, pointing this out to him and asking him to call a special session. The Woman's Party concentrated on getting the National Democratic leaders to bring pressure on Governor Roberts.

In the meantime, leading Democrats had gathered in San Francisco, preparing for their National Convention. Abby Scott Baker took charge of the campaign to get the Democratic leaders to bring pressure on the Governor of Tennessee. The Democratic National Committee passed a resolution calling on the Governor to convene his session. Homer S. Cummings, Chairman of the National Democratic Committee, called him on long-distance telephone and asked this of him. Many others appealed to him. On June 23, President Wilson telegraphed Governor Roberts as follows:

It would be a real service to the Party and to the Nation if it is possible for you to, under the peculiar provisions of your State Constitution, having in mind the recent decision of the Supreme Court in the Ohio case, to call a special session of the Legislature of Tennessee to consider the Suffrage Amendment. Allow me to urge this very earnestly.

The President also sent a letter to acting United States Attorney General William L. Frierson, asking his opinion on the constitutionality of ratification by a special session of the Tennessee Legislature.

Mr. Frierson's reply closed with this sentence:

I am therefore confident that if the Tennessee Legislature is called in session, it will have the clear power to ratify the Amendment notwithstanding any provision of the Tennessee Constitution.

The Democratic National Convention met in San Francisco on June 28. On the opening day of the Convention, Governor Roberts announced that he would call the session on August 9. Among the women who represented the Woman's Party at the Convention were Abby Scott Baker, Betty Gram, Mrs. Lawrence Lewis, Mrs. William Kent, Sara Bard Field, Ida Finney Mackrille, Izetta Jewel Brown. The Democratic Party inserted a plank in their platform endorsing the Federal Amendment and calling for ratification.

Tennessee then became the center of the Woman's Party campaign—a storm center. It was a foregone conclusion that a tremendous anti-Suffrage pressure would be brought on Tennessee, the last State necessary to ratification, as it had been brought on Delaware when Delaware seemed likely to be the last State. Alice Paul realized that great national political pressure must be brought upon the Tennessee legislators.

Governor Cox, the Democratic nominee, was, of course, a focus for most of this political pressure. The Woman's Party determined to make him realize, if possible, that Tennessee, as a Democratic State, was his responsibility. A huge deputation of Woman's Party leaders from all over the country called upon Governor Cox in his office in Columbus on July 16. Governor Cox said that he would co-operate with the Woman's Party in this matter and he asked to have a committee appointed to confer with him in regard to Tennessee. The Democratic National Committee met on July 20. The Woman's Party lobbied this Committee and got a resolution through urging immediate ratification by Tennessee. On July 23, Governor Cox conferred with the Committee—consisting of Sue White, Anita Pollitzer, and Mrs. James Rector—which he had asked Miss Paul to appoint.

The Republican National Committee met on July 21. Anita Pollitzer, Mrs. H. O. Havemeyer, Mrs. James Rector, and others saw the members of this Committee and secured from them a resolution urging that the Republicans do all they could to obtain the last State.

On July 22, the date of Harding's notification that he was nominated for the Presidency, two hundred members of the Woman's Party, coming from all over the United States, dressed in white and carrying purple, white and gold banners, marched through Marion to Senator Harding's lawn. The lettered banners, borne by two pioneer Suffragists, Mrs. L. Crozier French and Mrs. E. C. Green, read:

THE REPUBLICAN PLATFORM ENDORSES RATIFICATION OF SUFFRAGE.

THE FIRST TEST OF THE PLATFORM WILL COME WHEN THE TENNESSEE LEGISLATURE MEETS IN AUGUST.

WILL THE REPUBLICANS CARRY OUT THEIR PLATFORM BY GIVING A UNANIMOUS REPUBLICAN VOTE IN TENNESSEE FOR SUFFRAGE?

Mrs. John Gordon Battelle, Sue White, Mrs. H. O. Havemeyer, addressed Senator Harding and told him that he, as the Republican leader, had the power to line up the Republican members of the Tennessee Legislature and would be held responsible for them.

All this time the campaign in Tennessee had been going on.

That campaign, which was to become fiercer and more intensive until it moved like a whirlwind, was conducted in three ways.

First, Sue White, the State Chairman and other members of the State organization, assisted by Betty Gram, Catherine Flanagan and Anita Pollitzer, national organizers, conducted the campaign. After the Legislature convened Mrs. Florence Bayard Hilles, Delaware State Chairman, and Mary Winsor, of the Advisory Council, assisted in Nashville. Mabel Reber and Edith Davis carried on an extensive and intensive work of publicity.

Second, in Ohio, Abby Scott Baker, co-operating with Mrs. James Rector, kept in close touch with Cox and Harding, in order to get them to act upon the specific requests of the Woman's Party which began to come from Tennessee.

Third, Alice Paul remaining in Washington, planned every move, and kept in close communication with the political leaders who could influence Cox and Harding.

Sue White, immediately on her arrival at Nashville, opened Woman's Party Headquarters and took charge of the campaign on the legislators.

Anita Pollitzer went to the eastern part of the State and concentrated on the Republican leaders.

Betty Gram went to the western part of the State and worked in the Speaker's district.

Catherine Flanagan went into the districts of men soon to be elected, and secured pledges from some of the nominees that they would support ratification. In one case, Miss Flanagan secured the pledge of a Republican candidate whose Democratic opponent was a strong anti-Suffragist. A prominent Democrat in the district came out in support of the Republican nominee because he was for ratification.

If the three organizers had not made this intensive survey of these sections, they would not have realized that ratification votes were rapidly dropping away. Legislators gave the excuse that although they voted for Presidential Suffrage in a previous session, they would not vote for ratification in this session because they considered it unconstitutional. Alarmed at this defection, which was particularly noticeable among the Republican legislators, Anita Pollitzer secured opinions favorable to the constitutionality of ratification by Tennessee at this special session from the most eminent legal minds in the State, and sent them to each member of the Legislature.

Anita Pollitzer also sent a telegram to Abby Scott Baker, who, it will be remembered, was standing guard over the two Presidential candidates in Ohio, stating that the situation demanded Harding's immediate active support. Mrs. Baker telegraphed Alice Paul that she had seen Harding in regard to this matter and that he had telegraphed two Republican Congressmen to give their support to ratification, and his friend, ex-Governor Ben Hooper of Tennessee, to send him a poll of the Republicans. Immediately on receipt of a telegram from Alice Paul giving this information, Anita Pollitzer hurried to the " hill-billy " region of the State, where ex-Governor Hooper lived. Miss Pollitzer went over the entire situation with him in detail, giving him the only first-hand information that he had received. The result was that he spent the whole day telephoning the doubtful Republican legislators. He also telegraphed Harding that the situation was critical and urged him to give all possible aid to the Tennessee situation.

Miss Pollitzer then told ex-Governor Hooper that it was absolutely necessary to have a Republican caucus. Candler, the Chairman of the Joint Caucus Committee, was an anti-Suffragist. Congressman J. Will Taylor had, however, a strong influence with him. Miss Pollitzer started late that afternoon for Knoxville, where Congressman Taylor lived, and arriving early in the evening put her case to him. He said that he had voted for Suffrage in Congress and would do all he could to help. The next afternoon Miss Pollitzer saw Congressman Taylor to see what had been accomplished. He said that he had been unable to get Candler all day, was leaving the city in an hour. Miss Pollitzer called up the operator in Athens. She said, " This is a matter of life and death. Congressman Taylor must speak with Senator Candler. I have been in Athens myself and I know it is such a tiny place that you have only to look out of the door to know where Senator Candler is. You must find him for me." In a few minutes Senator Candler came to the telephone. Congressman Taylor asked him if he would call a caucus of the Republicans, and he agreed to do it. That night Miss Pollitzer took notices of this to all the papers. A telegram was sent to every Republican member urging him to come to the Legislature in time to attend this caucus. It was a necessary step to call this caucus, but it was equally necessary that all the important Republican leaders of the State be there. Catherine Flanagan and Anita Pollitzer brought so much pressure to bear on these leaders—and this included getting their reservations and actually seeing them on the train—that they were all there. The Republican leaders said in effect to the Republican members of the Legislature who were present, " We want the Republican members of the Legislature to give a majority of votes to ratification for the sake of their Party."

Before the Legislature convened, Betty Gram saw the Speaker of the House, Seth Walker, a very influential person and to the Suffragists, because of his position, probably the most important member of the Legislature. He told Miss Gram that he was looking into the question of the constitutionality of ratification at this session, and if he became convinced of its constitutionality, he might even lead the fight for ratification. A few days later, just before the Legislature convened, he told Miss White and Miss Gram that he had decided that it was constitutional for Tennessee to ratify and that they might count on his support. On the opening day of the Legislature, Betty Gram asked Speaker Walker to go over the poll with her. To her intense astonishment, he told her that he had changed his mind and could not vote for ratification in this session.

When the Woman's Party forces joined Miss White in Nashville at the convening of the Legislature, the town had filled with strangers. The anti-Suffrage forces had poured into the Capital. Lobbyists for railroads, manufacturing interests, and corporations of various kinds, came too.

One curious member of this army used to interrogate legislators as to their views. He said he was a reporter for a syndicate. Nobody had ever heard of the syndicate he represented. When Parley Christensen, candidate for President on the Farmer Labor ticket, came to Nashville to help with ratification among the labor members of the Legislature, he investigated the record of this gentleman, accused him, through the Press, of sinister purposes in lobbying. When this accusation appeared, the man hastily left town.

To off-set all this, the Suffragists of the State, as was usual in the State campaigns, poured into the Capital.

The atmosphere of Nashville grew rapidly more active . . . tense . . . hectic.

The Tennessee legislature convened on the ninth of August. It ratified on the eighteenth of August. The nine days between were characterized by work more intensive than ratification had yet known.

The Tennessee campaign was a miniature reproduction of the big national campaign which the Woman's Party had been waging ever since 1912. Here the Woman's Party was confronted with a double responsibility. It had to prove to the Democratic governor, Roberts—and it never relaxed for an instant in bringing it home to him—that he, as leader of the dominant Party in this Democratic Legislature, was responsible for ratification and could bring it about. In addition and at the same time, the Woman's Party had to make the Republican minority realize that they were responsible for votes favorable to ratification from their men.

In all this work in Tennessee, the Woman's Party was enormously assisted by the political sagacity of their chairman, Sue White, and the fact that all the politicians recognized that political sagacity. The experienced politicians said that they had never seen a more bitter fight in Tennessee. When the Legislature met, the Suffragists had a majority on paper. But they knew from previous experience they could not trust this paper majority to remain stable.

The ratification resolution was introduced in the House and the Senate on the same day, August 10. It was referred to a committee in both Houses and these committees held a joint hearing on August 11. This hearing, a notable and picturesque occasion, took place in the great Assembly Hall of the Capitol. Both floor and gallery were dotted with the colors of the opposing forces. The most famous State authorities on constitutional law appeared in behalf of the Suffragists.

The Woman's Party had, of course, immediately ascertained who were the members of both Houses who always supported Governor Roberts' measures. They found that many of these were not supporting ratification. They went with a list of these men to Governor Roberts, called his attention to this significant state of things. They also sent the news to Abby Scott Baker, who approached Cox daily on the subject. Cox responded by urging Governor Roberts to do all in his power to put ratification through.

Sue White gave out daily statements that were models of succinctness and comprehensiveness, which warned Governor Roberts that he would be held responsible and warned the Democratic Party that it would be held responsible, if ratification did not go through.

Realizing that they were strongest in the Senate, the Woman's Party wanted first to bring the matter to a vote there. They accomplished that on August 13, when ratification passed by twenty-five to four. Until this vote was cast, the Suffragists themselves did not realize what a degree of interest—due to their pressure on and from political leaders—they had developed in Tennessee. The vote proved a great stimulus to the men of the Lower House, who, up to this point, had been much more wavering in their attitude towards ratification.

The Capitol in these last few days presented a scene of activity on the part of the Woman's Party members such as no ratification campaign had ever known. They were at the House morning, noon, and night. They had to be there all the time because the fact that a member was numbered among their forces in the morning did not at all mean that he would be among them at night. The enemies of ratification made every possible attempt to steal Suffrage adherents. Realizing at last that they could not deflect men who were immovable on the ratification side, they began to introduce measures the passage of which would have been tantamount to defeat. For instance, a resolution was suddenly brought up one morning providing that the question of ratification should be referred to mass-meetings of the people to be held in every district on August 21. This would have meant a fatal postponement of ratification. Many of the legislators would have liked to hide behind a measure of this sort, but realizing this, the Woman's Party members told them that they would consider such a vote hostile to Suffrage and would hold them responsible. The Suffragists obtained sufficient support against the measure to get it tabled.

When it came to the last few days, the Woman's Party members seemed to work twenty-four hours out of the twenty-four, and some think they worked twenty-five. The situation was complicated, as always at the last hour, by rumors. Reports started and gained force every day that men were being bribed; so that legislators, about to declare for Suffrage, were often held up by the feeling that that act might lay them open to suspicion. This brought about a condition of such uncertainty that neither side, Suffragist nor anti-Suffragist, could prophesy the outcome. The instant a man wavered, the Woman's Party members, who, before the Legislature convened, had been working in the legislative districts, immediately got in touch with the political leaders who controlled the situation in those districts. Notwithstanding that nothing seemed stable at this period, the Woman's Party members met every few hours and compared polls. These polls served a second purpose. They gave political leaders definite data as to the position of every man in the Legislature. In all this confusion, the Woman's Party always knew where it stood.

On the morning of the vote the Suffrage workers rounded up all their legislative forces and saw that they arrived safely at the Capitol. More rumors were afloat that legislators would change their vote at the last moment. In every case, the Woman's Party saw these men again and made them realize that they were committed, not only to them, but to their political leaders.

Just before the vote was taken, Seth Walker ruled all the women off the floor of the House.

Two dramatic incidents marked the close of the campaign. The hero of one of these episodes was Banks Turner, of the other Harry Burn. To the very end the Woman's Party was uncertain of both their votes.

Banks Turner was one of Governor Roberts' closest friends. In considering the case of Banks Turner, it must always be held in mind that the Woman's Party steadfastly kept the Democrats to their pledges through Cox's constant pressure on Governor Roberts. It had at last penetrated Roberts' psychology that if he permitted ratification to fail in Tennessee, the Democrats would be held responsible by the women in the coming elections. The Woman's Party saw Governor Roberts before the vote and reminded him of this. The Woman's Party also saw Cox before the vote and reminded him of this; also reminded him to remind Roberts. When the vote was actually imminent, the Roberts forces began to get alarmed; for they realized they had played with the issue too long. As has been said Banks Turner was one of the Governor's closest friends. Banks Turner had never actually said he was against ratification, but he had never said he was for it. No Suffragist counted on him.

As for Harry Burn——

When Anita Pollitzer had been working among Republican leaders, she had gone to Harry Burn's Republican county chairman to ask him if they could count on Harry Burn's support for ratification. In her presence, he telephoned to Harry Burn and assured Miss Pollitzer that the Suffragists could depend on him. When Mr. Burn appeared in the Legislature, he was approached by Suffragists and anti-Suffragists in close and quick succession. After a while, he announced that he was uncertain. The fact that he was the youngest member of the Legislature—scarcely more than a lad indeed—and that he was immensely popular and beloved—seemed to add an especial acuteness to the situation. To Suffragists who approached him a few days before the vote, he said, " I cannot pledge myself, but I will do nothing to hurt you."

Of course that could be translated that he would not vote *yes*, but would not vote *no*—not vote at all in short.

With the poll virtually a tie, the Suffragists could take no chances. Miss Pollitzer telephoned at once to the county chairman who had assured her of Harry Burn's vote and told him the situation. The next day Betty Gram saw a letter, written to Harry Burn by one of the foremost political leaders of the State, which practically urged him—for his own political good—to vote no. Members of the Woman's Party saw Harry Burn and told him that they knew pressure was being brought upon him from State leaders against ratification. He would make no statement of support but he urged them to trust him and begged the Suffragists not to tell the political leaders of the State that they knew these political leaders had broken faith and were persuading him not to vote for ratification. He was obviously much wrought up over the situation.

The date of the vote came and on the Suffrage poll, Harry

Burn was still marked doubtful. When he appeared in the corridors of the House, however, he wore the red rose of the anti-Suffragists. One of the Woman's Party organizers said to him just before the vote was taken, "We really trusted you, Mr. Burn, when you said that you would never hurt us." He said, "I mean that—my vote *will* never hurt you."

Still he continued to wear the red rose of the anti-Suffragists. . .

It was known to many that Harry Burn had recently received a letter from his mother asking him to support ratification. It was known only to the Woman's Party how much political pressure to support it had been brought upon him.

The supreme moment arrived. Ninety-six members were present out of a total membership of ninety-nine. The first test of strength came in a motion to table the Resolution. Harry Burn's name was called early in the roll. True to the promise of that red rose, he voted yes. The roll-call went on, the members answering exactly according to expectation. What would Banks Turner do? If he voted with the Suffragists, the result would be a tie, forty-eight to forty-eight; the motion would not be tabled. His name was called; he did not answer. The vote was now inevitably forty-eight to forty-seven for the motion to table. All seemed lost. But before the final announcement of the vote, Turner arose and after a moment's hesitation said:

"I wish to be recorded as against the motion to table."

The Resolution was still before the House, but this test vote showed a tie—one short of a majority.

Then came the final vote.

Now the stillness was like death. Unless Turner stayed with the Suffragists and, in addition, another vote was gained, the Amendment was lost. When Harry Burn's name was called, he answered in a clear, loud voice, "Yes." The death-like stillness settled again over the audience in the

galleries as the roll-call approached the name of Banks
Turner. He had voted against tabling; that did not make it
certain that he would vote for the Resolution.

"Banks Turner!" called the clerk.

"Yes," he answered in a solemn, low voice.

The Resolution had carried—forty-nine to forty-seven.

Instantly Speaker Walker, white-faced, was on his feet.
"I change my vote from ' No ' to ' Yes,'" he said. Of course
he made this lightning change in order that he might move to
reconsider the Resolution. But he missed one point. The
vote now stood fifty to forty-six. His vote had given the
Resolution a *constitutional majority*, that is a majority, not
only of the membership present of the Lower House but of
the entire Lower House. Unwittingly, Speaker Walker
killed one legal attack already prepared by the anti-Suffragists in case the measure should pass.

An uproar of enthusiasm greeted the vote. State
leaders who had assisted the Suffrage campaign, yelled,
clapped, stamped. Women alternately laughed and wept;
cheered and applauded. One legislator producing a bell
from somewhere, rang it steadily. As for the Suffragists themselves, naturally they went wild with joy; particularly the Tennessee women, who were triumphant that
their State had proved to be the needed thirty-sixth to give
the franchise to women.

Of course, the anti-Suffragist red roses were in great
evidence all during the voting. But after the vote was
taken, they seemed to fade into the background. The
yellow jonquils of the Suffragists, the great purple, white,
and gold banners of the Woman's Party made tiny flares
and big slashes of light and color everywhere.

The bizarre and sensational moves of the opposition—the
withdrawal of the anti-Suffragist members of the Tennessee
Assembly to Alabama until the Suffrage members got tired
and went home, the return of the anti-Suffragist members,
their assembly in a Rump Legislature, their " reconsidered "

National Photo Co., Washington, D. C.

THE FLAG COMPLETE.

Alice Paul Unfurls the Ratification Banner with 36 Stars.

vote against the Amendment—all that seemed important at the time. Now it has faded to insignificance. The anti-Suffragists, on this and other grounds, instituted a suit against the validity of the Tennessee ratification. That suit and six attacks, also directed against the validity of ratification, are still pending.

In the meantime, however, Connecticut has ratified.

In brief, the facts in regard to Connecticut are these: Governor Marcus Holcomb, one of the foremost anti-Suffragists in the country, called a session of the Connecticut legislature to provide the legal machinery to enable the women of Connecticut to vote in the coming elections. The call was issued for September 14. The Suffragists instantly took advantage of this special session to institute a campaign for ratification.

In addressing the legislators Governor Holcomb said in effect: " Do not ratify this session. It will be illegal, as ratification was not mentioned in my call. I will call you again for that purpose a week from today."

Nevertheless Connecticut ratified on September 14.

Catherine Flanagan of the Woman's Party personally brought the ratification from the Secretary of State of Connecticut to the State Department in Washington.

A week later, to avoid any question as to the legality of the first ratification, which had been attacked on the ground that the subject was not included in the governor's message, Connecticut ratified again.

The women of the United States voted in the Presidential election of 1920.

XVII

THE LAST DAYS

TO A COMRADE

Oh, you of the unquenchable spirit—
How I adore you!
I could light forever the waning fires of my courage
At the incessant, upleaping flame of your being!

You,—creature of light and color and vivid emotions—
Of radiant action,—who ever could dream of you passive,
Submissive, your small ·self stilled into lazy contentment?
You, fired with the beauty of ardor,
Lovely with love for all that is clean and earnest and forceful,
Yourself daring anything
So long as it be for Womanhood, and the cause of justice and
        progress—
Daring to lead and daring to follow—
Giving us each of your unfailing inspiration.

You, over whom the jeers and the mockings and the ugly thoughts
        of those who understand not
Pass lightly, like a spent breath of foul air in a still cavern,
Unflicking the steadfast torch of you—
I could re-light forever the waning fires of my courage
At the incessant, upleaping flame of your being!

ELIZABETH KALB,
The Suffragist, January 25, 1919.

IN 1917 occurred the great leap forward in the activity
of the Woman's Party; in swift succession came the picketing; the burning of the President's words; the Watchfires of Freedom. And Headquarters from 1917 on—as
can be easily imagined—was a feverishly busy place.
From the instant the picketing started, it grew electric with
action. As for the work involved in making up the constant succession of picket lines——

478

It was not easy at an instant's notice to find women who had the time to picket. But always there were some women willing to picket *part* of the time and some willing to picket *all* of the time. Mary Gertrude Fendall was in charge of this work. That her office was no sinecure is evident from the fact that on one occasion alone—that memorable demonstration of March 4, 1917—she provided a line of nearly a thousand. Of course, too, as fast as the women went to jail, other women had to be found to fill their places. In those days Miss Fendall lived at the telephone and between telephone calls, she wrote letters which invited sympathizers to come from distant States to join the banner-bearing forces. Those women who could always be depended on for picketing were, in the main, Party sympathizers living in Washington; Party workers permanently established at Headquarters; organizers come back suddenly from their regular work. But volunteers came too—volunteers from the District of Columbia and from all parts of the United States. In the winter, as has been before stated, picketing was a cold business. The women found that they had to wear a surprising amount of clothes—sweaters and coats, great-coats, mufflers, arctics and big woolly gloves. Many of the pickets left these extra things at Heaquarters and the scramble to disengage rights and lefts of the gloves and arctics was one of the amusing details of the operation of the picket line. Banners took up space too; but they added their cheering color to the picture.

When the arrests began, the atmosphere grew more tense and even more busy. But just as—when trouble came—a golden flood poured into the Woman's Party treasury, so volunteer pickets came in a steadily lengthening line. Anne Martin had said to the Judge who sentenced her: "So long as you send women to jail for asking for freedom, just so long will there be women willing to go to jail for such a cause." This proved to be true. Volunteers for this gruelling experience continued to appear from all over the country. Mrs. Grey of Colorado, sending her twenty-two year old daughter, Nathalie, into the battle, said:

I have no son to fight for democracy abroad, and so I send my daughter to fight for democracy at home.

It interested many of the Woman's Party members to study the first reactions of the police to the strange situation the picketing brought about. Most of the policemen did not enjoy maltreating the girls. Some of them were stupid and a few of them were brutal, but many of them were kind. They always deferred to Lucy Burns with an air of profound respect—Miss Lucy, they called her. But a curious social element entered into the situation. Large numbers of the women were well-known Washingtonians. The police were accustomed to seeing them going about the city in the full aura of respected citizenship. It was very difficult often, to know—in arresting them—what social tone to adopt.

Mrs. Gilson Gardner tells an amusing story of her first arrest. In the midst of her picketing, an officer suddenly stepped up to her. He said politely: " It is a very beautiful day." She concurred. They chatted. He was in the meantime looking this way and that up the Avenue. Suddenly, still very politely, he said: " I think the patrol will be along presently." Not until then did it dawn on Mrs. Gardner that she was arrested.

Later, when the Watchfires were going, Mrs. Gardner was again arrested while she was putting wood on the flames. There was a log in her arms: " Just a minute, officer," she said, in her gentle, compelling voice, and the officer actually waited while she crossed the pavement and put the remaining log on the fire. Later, when Mrs. Gardner's name was called in the court, she decided that she preferred to stand, rather than sit in the chair designated for the accused. The policeman started to force her down. Again she said, in the gentle, compelling tone:

"Please do not touch me, officer!" and he kept his hands off her from that time forth.

Of course, the unthinking made the usual accusation that these women were doing all this for notoriety. That was a ridiculous statement, whose disproof was easy. The character and quality of the women themselves were its best denial. The women who composed the Woman's Party were of all kinds and descriptions; they emerged from all ranks and classes; they came from all over the United States. The Party did not belong exclusively to women of great wealth and social position, although there were many such in its list of membership; and some of these belonged to families whose fortunes were internationally famous. It did not belong exclusively to working women, although there were thousands of them in its ranks; and these represented almost every wage-earning task at which women toil. It did not belong exclusively to women of the arts or the professions; although scores of women, many nationally famous and some internationally famous, lent their gifts to the furtherance of the work. It did not belong exclusively to the women of the home, although scores of wives left homes, filled with the beauty which many generations of cultivation had accumulated—left these homes and left children; and although equal numbers left homes of a contrasting simplicity and humbleness—left these homes and left children to go to jail in the interests of the movement. It may be said, perhaps, that the rank and file were characterized by an influential solidity, that they were women, universally respected in their communities, necessary to it. It was an all-woman movement. Indeed, often women who on every other possible opinion were as far apart as the two poles, worked together for the furtherance of the Federal Amendment. On one occasion, for instance, on the picket line, two women who could not possibly have found a single intellectual congeniality except the enfranchisement of women stood side by side. One was nationally and inter-

nationally famous as a conservative of great fortune. The
other was nationally and internationally famous as a radi-
cal. In other words, one stood at the extreme right of
conservatism and the other at the extreme left of radical-
ism. It was as though, among an archipelago of differing intellectual interests and social convictions, the Party
members had found one little island on which they could
stand in an absolute unanimity; stand ready to fight—to
the death, if it were necessary—for that conviction.

Some of the stories which they tell at Headquarters to
illustrate the Pan-woman quality of the Party are touch-
ingly beautiful. There is the case, for instance, of a woman
government clerk, self-supporting, a widow, and the
mother of a little girl. Every day for weeks, she had
passed that line of pickets standing silently at the White
House gates. She heard the insults that were tossed to
the women. She saw the brutalities which were inflicted
on them. She witnessed arrests. Something rose within
fluttered . . . tore at her. . . . One day when Alice
Paul was picketing, this young woman, suit-case in
hand, appeared before her. She said " I am all ready to
picket if you need me. I have made all the necessary arrangements in case I am arrested. Where shall I go to
join your forces so that I may picket today? " She was
arrested that afternoon and sent to prison.

Two other government clerks, who appeared on the
picket line, were arrested and jailed. They appealed to
the government authorities for a month's leave of absence
on the score of their imprisonment. All these three
women, of course, ran the risk of losing their positions.
But in their case the instinct to serve their generation
was stronger than the instinct to conserve any material
safety. It is pleasant to record that they were not compelled to make this sacrifice. Others, however, suffered.
A school teacher in the Woman's Party, for instance, lost
her position because of her picketing.

If the foregoing is not denial enough of the charge, com-

mon when the picketing began, that these women were no-
toriety-seeking fanatics, perhaps nothing will bring conviction. It scarcely seems however that the most obstinate antagonist of the Woman's Party would like to believe that delicately reared women could enjoy, even for
the sake of notoriety—aside from the psychological effect
of spiders and cockroaches everywhere, worms in their
food, vermin in their beds, rats in their cells—the brutalities to which they were submitted. Yet many women who
had endured this once, came back to endure it again and
again.

One of the strong points of the Woman's Party was its
fairness. In reference to the President, for instance,
Maud Younger used to say that the attitude of the
Woman's Party to him was like that of a girl who wants a
college education. She teases her father for it without
cessation, but she goes on loving him just the same.
Another strong point of the Woman's Party was its sense
of humor on itself. They tell with great delight the amusing events of this period—of the grinning street gamin
who stood and read aloud one of the banners, *How long
must women wait for liberty?* and then yelled: " T'ree
months yous'll be waitin'—in Occoquan."—of a reporter
who, coming, into Headquarters in search of an interview,
found a child sliding down the bannisters. Before he
could speak, the child announced in a tone of proud triumph: " My mother's going to prison."

A story they particularly like is of that young couple
who, having had no bridal trip at the time of their marriage,
came to Washington for a belated honeymoon. They visited Headquarters together. The bride became so interested in the picketing that she went out with one of the
picket-lines and was arrested. She spent her belated
honeymoon in jail, and the groom spent his belated honeymoon indignantly lobbying the Congressmen of his own
district.

Later, when they were lighting the Watchfires of Free-

dom on the White House pavement, the activity at Headquarters was increased one hundred-fold.

The pickets themselves refer to that period as the most
" messy and mussy " in their history. Everything and
everybody smelled of kerosene. All the time, there was
one room in which logs were kept soaking in this pervasive
fluid. When they first started the Watchfires they carried
the urn and the oil-soaked logs openly, to the appointed spot
on the pavement in front of the White House. Later,
when the arrests began and the fires had to be built so
swiftly that they had to abandon the urn, they carried
these logs under coats or capes. The White House pavement was always littered with charred wood even when the
Watchfires were not going. Once the fires were started it
was almost impossible to put them out. Kerosene-soaked
wood is a very obstinate substance. Water had no effect
on it. Chemicals alone extinguished it. Amazed crowds
used to stand watching these magic flames. Often when
the policemen tried to stamp the fires out, they succeeded
only in scattering them.

It was an extraordinary effect, too, when the policemen
were busy putting out one fire, to see others start up, in
this corner of the Park, in *that* corner, in the great bronze
urn, near the center.

Building a fire in that bronze urn was as difficult a matter as it seems. A Woman's Party member, glancing out
from a stairway window at the top of the house at Headquarters, had noted how boldly the urn stood out from the
rest of the Park decoration. . . .

At three o'clock one morning, Julia Emory and Hazel
Hunkins, two of the youngest and tiniest pickets, bore over
to the Park from Headquarters several baskets of wood
which they concealed in the shadows under the trees. The
next problem was to get a ladder there without being
seen. They accomplished this in some way, dragging it
over the ground, slow foot after slow foot, and placed it
against the urn. At intervals the policeman on the beat,

EVERY GOOD SUFFRAGIST THE MORNING AFTER RATIFICATION.
Nina Allender in *The Suffragist*.

who was making the entire round—or square—of the Park, passed. While one girl mounted the rudder and filled the urn with oil-soaked paper, oil-soaked wood, and liberal libations of oil, the other remained on guard. When the guard gave the word that the policeman was near, the two girls threw themselves face downward on the frozen grass. It is a very large urn and by this stealthy process it took hours to fill it. It was two days before they started the fire. Anybody might have seen the logs protruding from the top of the urn during those two days, but nobody did.

The day on which the urn projected itself into the history of the Woman's Party, the Watchfires were burning for the first time on the White House pavements. The street and the Park were filled with people. A member of the Woman's Party, passing the urn, furtively threw into it a lighted asbestos coil. The urn instantly belched flames which threatened to lick the sky. The police arrested every Woman's Party member in sight. All the way down the street as the patrol carried them away, Hazel Hutchins and Julia Emory saw the flames flaring higher and higher.

" How did they do that? " one man was heard to say. " I've been here the whole afternoon and I didn't see them light it."

Twice afterwards fires were started in the urn. For that matter, fires were started there after the police had set a watch on it.

Hazel Hunkins, young, small, slender, took the urn under her special patronage. One of the pictures the Woman's Party likes to draw is the time Hazel was arrested there. She had climbed up onto the pedestal and was throwing logs into the pool of oil when two huge policemen descended upon her. The first seized one foot and the second seized the other; and they both pulled hard. Of course in these circumstances, it was impossible for her to move. But she is an athlete and she clung tight to the urn edge. Still the policemen pulled. Finally she said gently, "If you will let go of my feet, I will come down myself."

Later asbestos coils were introduced into the campaign. This—from the police point of view—was more annoying than the kerosene-soaked logs; for they were compact to carry, easy to handle, difficult to put out, and they lasted a long, long time.

Another picture the Woman's Party likes to draw is of Mildred Morris starting asbestos coils. With her nimbus of flaming hair, Miss Morris seemed a flame herself. She was here, there, everywhere. The police could no more catch up with her than they could with a squirrel. One night, with the assistance of two others, she—unbelievably—fastened some asbestos coils among the White House trees; but to her everlasting regret the guards found them before the illumination could begin.

The stories they tell about arrests at this time are endless. Little Julia Emory, who was arrested thirty-four times, is a repository of lore on this subject.

They were a great trial to the police—the arrests of these later months. While under detention, the pickets used to organize impromptu entertainments. This was during the period, when at their trials, the Suffragists would answer no questions and the court authorities were put to it to establish their identities. They related with great glee how in his efforts to prove Annie Arniel's identity, a policeman described one of their concerts in court.

And then, your Honor, that one there said, "We'll now have a comb solo from a distinguished combist, who has played before all the crowned heads of Europe, Annie Arniel," and then, your Honor, the defendant got up and played a tune on a comb.

When, for instance, Suffragists refused bail, the police did not like to hold them overnight because it was such an expense to the District of Columbia to feed them. Julia

Emory describes one evening when a roomful of them, arrested, and having refused to put up bail, were waiting the will of the powers. During this wait, which lasted several hours, they entertained themselves by singing.

Once a policeman came in:

" Will you pay your bail if we put it at twenty-five dollars? "

" No," answered the pickets promptly.

He went out, but later he returned.

" Will you pay your bail if we put it at five dollars? "

" No."

" Then march out."

But those light moments were only foam thrown up from serious and sometimes desperate times. When a crowd of ex-pickets gather together and indulge in reminiscences, extraordinary revelations occur. Looking at their faces and estimating their youth, one wonders at a world which permitted one per cent of these things to happen.

And as for their experiences with the mobs. . . . Not the least of the psychological factors in the situation was the slow growth of the crowds; the circle of little boys who gathered about them first, spitting at them, calling them names, making personal comments; then the gathering gangs of young hoodlums who encouraged the boys to further insults; then more and more crowds; more and more insults; the final struggle.

Often of course the pickets stood against the White House fence, an enormous mob packed in front of them, with the knowledge that police protection—according to the orders of the day—might be given them or might not. . . . Sometimes that crowd would edge nearer and nearer until there was but a foot of smothering, terror-fraught space between them and the pickets. Literally those women felt they had their backs to the wall. Occasionally they had to mount the stone coping! Always too they feared that any sudden movement within the packed, slowly approaching hostile crowd might foam into violence. Occasionally, when the police followed orders to protect the pickets, violent things happened to people in the crowd. Catherine Flanagan saw a plain-clothes man hit six sailors over the head in succession with a billy. They went down like nine pins. Yet when after hours of a seemingly impressive waiting the actual struggle came— something—some spiritual courage bigger than themselves —impelled them to hold on to their banner poles to the last gasp. They were big in circumference—those banner poles—but the girls clutched them so tightly that often it took three policemen to wrench them away. Catherine Flanagan had deep gashes on the inside of her palms where her own nails had penetrated her flesh and great wounds on the outside of her hands where the policemen had dug their nails into them. Virginia Arnold's hands and arms were torn as though in a struggle with some wild beast.

Yet, I repeat, Headquarters saw its lighter moments even in those most troubled times. And during those most troubled times, that gay spirit of youth managed to maintain itself. The onlookers marveled at it. But it was only because it was a spiritual quality—youth of the soul, in addition to youth of the body—that it could endure. During the course of the eight years of its history, the members of the Woman's Party had been subjected to disillusion after disillusion. The older ones among them bore this succession of shocks with that philosophy which a long experience in public affairs engenders. But the younger ones—believing at first, as youth always believes, in the eternal verities, and in their eternal prevalence— witnessed faith-shaking sights and underwent even more faith-shaking experiences.

In their contact with public men, they saw such a man as Borah for instance—perhaps the chief of the Knights of the Double Cross—give the Woman's Party what virtually amounted to his pledged word to support the Amendment and then coolly repudiate it. They saw Moses of New Hampshire play a quibbling trick on them which involved them in weeks of the hardest kind of work only calmly to ignore his own pledge at the end. They contended with such differing personalities as the cold, cultured mind, immutably set in the conventions of a past generation, of Henry Cabot Lodge; the unfairness, or fatuity, or brutality of such men as Penrose of Pennsylvania, Thomas of Colorado, Wadsworth of New York, Reed of Missouri, Brandegee of Connecticut, Hoke Smith of Georgia.

When the picketing began, they saw outside forces get their Headquarters from them; saw them influence scores of property owners sometimes after an advance rent had been paid, not to let houses to them; saw them try to influence the people who gave money, to withhold such financial support; saw them try to influence the newspapers to be less impartial in their descriptions of Woman's Party activities. As the picketing went on and the burning of the President's words and the Watchfires succeeded it— while they were exercising their inalienable right of peaceful protest—they knew the experience of being harried by mobs at the very door of the President of the United States; harried while the President passed in his carriage through their midst; later to be harried in collaboration by both mobs and police. Under arrest and in prison, they underwent experiences which no one of them would have believed possible of the greatest republic in the world. They were held incommunicado; they could see neither counsel nor Party members. They were offered food filled with worms. They were submitted to incredible brutalities.

And yet, I have said that spirit of youth prevailed. It prevailed because they were speaking for their generation. They developed a sense of devotion to their ideal of freedom which would have stopped short of no personal sacrifice, not death itself. They developed a sense of comradeship for each other which was half love, half admiration and all reverence. In summing up a fellow worker, they speak first of her "spirit," and her "spirit" is always *beautiful*, or *noble*, or *glorious*, or some such youth-loved word.

Once, when one party of pickets, about to leave Occoquan, was in the dining-room, a fresh group, just sentenced, were brought into luncheon and placed at another table. Conversation was not permitted. Not a word was spoken, but with one accord the released pickets raised their water-glasses high, then lowered them and drank to their comrades.

Yes, that was their strength—spirit of youth. Lavinia Dock said, "The young are at the gates." The young stormed those gates and finally forced them open. They entered. And leaving behind all sinister remembrance of the battle, they turned their faces towards the morning.

THE END

INDEX

Abbot, Minnie D.   232
Adams, Abigail   105
Adams, Hazel   366
Adams, Pauline   243, 245, 416, 419
Adams, Mrs. Walter   414
Addams, Jane   13, 40, 43
Adler, Jessie   399
Ainge, Edith   245, 366, 383, 384,
  385, 387, 402, 403, 406, 412, 416,
  419, 458
Allen, Genevieve   441, 462
Allender, Nina   15, 19, 20, 47, 215
American Federation of Labor   169
Amidon, Beulah   48, 126, 198, 209,
  239, 349
Andrews, Harriet U.   387, 403, 404,
  quoted 418
Anglin, Margaret   109
Aniba, Isabel C., quoted   354
Arizona ratifies   435
Arkansas ratifies   451
Armes, Mrs. George A.   64, quoted
  94
Arniel, Annie   227, 228, 245, 366,
  387, 402, 403, 404, 412, 413, 416,
  487
Arnold, Bertha   340, 372, 382, 385,
  387, 389, 391, 412, 419
Arnold, Virginia   72, 79, 126, 227,
  228, 237, 240, 384, 385, 386, 387,
  489
Ascough, Lillian M.   366, 416
Ascough, Mrs. W. D.   154, 419
Ashurst, Senator   55
Asquith, Herbert   10
Atwater, Mrs. George   384
Austin, Mary   116

Baird, Senator Davis   391, 427, 448
Baker, Abby Scott, quoted 155; 180,
  207, 245, 299, 309, 326, 336, 342,
  348, 352, 391, 419, 440, 441, 458,
  463, 464, 466, 467, 470
Baker, Secretary of War   163, 453
Banberger, Governor   440

Bar Association   303, 305
Barnes, Mrs. Charles W.   258
Barnett, John T.   91
Barrett, Naomi   406, 408
Barrow, Frank   444, 450, 452
Barry, John D.   262
Bartelme, Judge Mary A.   160
Bartlett, Dorothy   245
Battelle, Mrs. John Gordon 463, 466
Beach, Cornelia   245
Beale, Olive   387, 389
Beard, Mary   13, 44, 52, 147, 158,
  308, 391
Beckwith, Mrs. Carol   147
Beim, Mrs. A. N.   258
Belmont, Mrs. O. H. P.   52, 74,
  quoted 107; 108, 116, 131, 207,
  298, 319
Bennett, Mrs. M. Toscan, quoted
  397; 405, 460
Bergen, Mrs. William   258
Black, Judge W. W.   90
Black, Louise M.   367
Blair, Henry W.   222
Blatch, Harriot Stanton   13, 98,
  154, 156, 170, 177, 200
Bloch, Senator   453, 454
Blumberg, Hilda   250, 259
Bodenheim, Marie   425
Boeckel, Florence Brewer   47, 48,
  190
Boeckh, Kate J.   243, 365, 412
Boissevain, Inez Milholland   22,
  26, 98, 160, 177, memorial service,
  189-191
Borah, Senator   352, 358, 392
Bovee, Mrs. Virginia,   275, quoted
  276
Boyle, Catherine   354, 406
Brady, Senator   86
Brandeis, Miss   83
Branham, Lucy   126, 245, 336, 342,
  359, quoted 373; 391, 395, 412,
  419, 458
Branham, Mrs. L. V. G. Gwynne
  416

492

Brannan, Mrs. John Winters 131, 195, 207, 233, 257, 258, quoted 259; 282, 287, 290, 398

Brannenberg, Jennie 416
Brisbane, Arthur 161
Bristow, Senator 57
Bristow-Mondell Amendment 37, 79
British Mission 214
Bronson, Minnie, quoted 263, 348
Brooke, Minnie E. 67, 179
Brown, Izetta Jewel 464
Brown, Miss 11
Brown, Mrs. William Gay 452
Brown, Rev. Olympia 210, 321, quoted 398
Brownlow, Commissioner 275
Bruere, Mrs. Henry 147
Bryan, J. W. 95
Bryant, Louise 416
Burn, Harry 472, 473, 474
Burns, Lucy 9, 13, 16, 18, 43, 47, 52, quoted 63, 69; 70-71, 75, 79, 131, 151, 154, 184, 207, 215, 217, 227, quoted 230, 237, 240, 245, 258, 272, quoted 275-6; 282, 287, quoted 289; 309, 326, 366, 369, 387, 391, 406, 412, 416, 419, 480
Burritt, M. Tilden 258
Butterworth, Mrs. Henry 258, 283

Calderhead, Iris 126, 229, 390
California ratifies 441
Calmes, Lucia 406
Calnan, Eleanor 245, 387, 421
Campbell, Agnes 154
Campbell, Mary 354
Candler, Senator 467
Capper, Governor 150, 453
Caraway, Representative 139
Carey, Governor 443, 444
Carey, Mrs. John 462
Carlin, Representative 135, 139
Carpenter, Alice 158, 308
Casey, Josephine 79
Castleton, Beatrice 424, 425
Catt, Mrs. Carrie Chapman 165, 356
Catts, Governor 339-340
Chamberlain-Mondell Amendment 37
Chamberlain, Senator 36
Chandler, Representative 139
Chase, Agnes 366
Chevrier, Palys L. 406, 416

Cheyenne Tribune, quoted 90
Chi, Mrs. Chem. 103
Chicago Republican Convention 459, 462
Chisaski, Helen 406
Chisholm, Mrs. W. W. 245
Christensen, Parley 469
Churchill, Winston 10
Clark, Champ 346
Clark, Maude F. 71
Clarke, Pauline 47, 126, 227, 366
Club Women's Deputation 61
Cochran, William J. 428
Cohen, Cynthia 258
Coles, Assemblyman 449
College Equal Suffrage League 35
Collins, Josephine 421, 422
Colorado ratifies 443
Colt, Mrs. William L. 184, 259
Colt, Senator 351
Colvin, Sarah T. (Mrs. A. R.) 153, 412, 414, 416, 419
Comborrow, Reba 416
Condon, Miss 303
Congressional Committee 3, 32-3, 34, 36, 40, 46-7
Congressional Union 38, 48-9, 50, 56, quoted 90-95, 103-9, 125, 131, 133-4, 159, 160
Connecticut ratifies 477
Connelly, Betty 421, 422
Constable, Anna 154
Cosu, Alice 258, 281
Cox, Governor 465, 470
Crabtree, Hon. W. R. 307
Crans, Lillian 216
Crawford, Cora 366, 413
Crewe, Lord 10, 11
Crocker, Gertrude Lynde 130, 207, 255, 365, 403, 406
Crocker, Ruth 130, 240, 249, 412
Crone, Berta 227, 301
Culberson, Senator 351
Cummings, Homer S. 428, 464
Cummins, Senator 313, 434
Curtis, Senator 84, 182, 351, 358, 376
Cuthbert, Mrs. Lucius M. 80

Dabs, Mr. 338
Dale, Representative 139
Daniels, L. G. C. 387
Daniels, Lou C. 252, 258, 421, 460
Daniels, Lucy 416

Daniels, Secretary 453
Davis, Edith 466
Davis, Mrs. Frances 387
Day, Dorothy 258, 280
Dean, Ella Morton 237, 238
Debs, Eugene 156
Decker, Eva 258
Democratic Women's Deputation, 64
Dennett, Mary Ware 13, 39
De Shan, Florence 424
De Valera, President 456
Devoe, Emma Smith 40, 67
De Young, M. H. 108
Dial, Senator 427
Dixon, Edna 243
Dixon, Mary Bartlett 258
Dock, Lavinia, quoted 219; 227, 228, 243, 321, 366
Doolittle, Representative 91
Dorr, Rheta Childe 47, 61, 161
Dorsey, Hugh M. 435
Doty, Madeline 308
Dowell, Mary Carol 408
Doyle, Christine M. 366
Drew, Senator 427
Drumheller, Roscoe 94
Dubrow, Mary E. 126, 336, 366, 391, 402, 403, 404, quoted 451-55
Dyer, Mrs. E. Tiffany 147
Dyer, Representative 139

Eastman, Crystal 13, 52, 67, 161
Edge, Senator 427
Edwards, Edward I. 447
"E. H. Howe" 422
Emory, Julia 126, 245, 258, 271, 281, 283, 336, 366, 373, 385, 386, 387, 389, 403, 404, 406, quoted 436-40, 484, 487, 488
Evans, Mrs. 20
Evans, Mrs. Edmund C. 366, 404
Evans, Ernestine 308
Evans, Mrs. Evan 158
Evans, Mrs. Glendower, quoted 60
Ewing, Lucy 236, 243, 419
Eylward, Estella 416

Fendall, Mary Gertrude 126, 142, 225, 336, 363, 366, 383, 384, 387, 412, 479
Fess, Simeon 445, quoted 452
Field, Sara Bard, quoted 103; 107, 109-10, quoted 110-16; 116, 117, 120, 156, 160, 167, 168, 177, quoted 192; 195, 336, 464
Findeisen, Ella 258
Fisher, Katherine Rolston 249, quoted 269; 277, 323, 366, 387
Fishstein, Rose 416
Fishstein, Rose G. 416
Fitch, Ruth, quoted 187-8
Fitzgerald, Representative 130
Flanagan, Catherine 126, quoted 237-9; 240, 243, 256, 257, 336, 390, 392, 445, 455, 460, 466, 468, 477, 489
Flegel, Mr. 94
Forbes, T. W. 416
Fotheringham, Janet 232
Fotheringham, Margaret 243, quoted 244; 245
Fowler, Frances 421
French Commission 214
French, Mrs. L. Crozier 465
Frierson, William L., quoted 464
Frost, Grace 385
Frost, Susan 399
Fuller, Clara Kinsley 243, quoted 244

Gale, Zona, quoted 68; 190
Gallagher, Andrew, quoted 106
Gallinger, Senator 353
Gannon, Dr. 288
Gard, Representative 120, 139
Gardner, Commissioner 287
Gardner, Gilson 26, 209, quoted 210; 233, 234, quoted 241; 242, 275
Gardner, Mrs. Gilson 21, 52, 70, 71, 96, quoted 97; 131, 136, 207, 232, quoted 273; 274, 326, 366, 387, 406, 480
Garnett, Louise 390, 440
Garrison, Rebecca 416
Gasch, Marie Manning 258
Gates, Wellington H. 90
Gay, Senator 423
Gerberding, Elizabeth 158
Germany, war declared 212
Gerry, Senator 350
Gilbert, Mildred 184
Gilman, Charlotte Perkins, quoted 430-1
Ginsberg, Anna 416
Glines, Mildred 350
Glover, W. Irving 448
Goode, Edith 154

Goode, Jane 154
Gonzon, Mary 354
Goolsby, Mr. 338
Gram, Alice 48, 258
Gram, Betty 126, 258, 336, 384, 390, 421, 434, 445, quoted 447-51; 453, 454, 455, 464, 466, 468, 473
Gray, Natalie 240, 243, 480
Gray, Mrs. S. H. B. 227, 480
Greeley, Helen Hoy 462
Green, Mrs. E. C. 465
Green, Mrs. Frances 230
Green, Mollie Marie 366
Greiner, Gladys 227, 229, 249, 255, 366, 383, 384, 391, 416, 419
Grey, Sir Edward 11
Grimes, Mrs. 326
Grogan, Sara 23, 387, 389, 399
Gross, Mrs. Irving 421
Guggenheim, Leo U. 90
Guilford, Ella 258
Gwinter, Eleanor 249

Hale, Matthew 427
Hamilton, Elizabeth 258
Hara, Ernestine 250
Harding, Warren G. 353, 434, 462, 467
Hardwick, Senator 358, 427
Hardy, Jennie C. Law 119
Harmer, Senator 452
Harper, Ida Husted 44
Harrington, Governor 436
Harris, Gabrielle 415
Harris, Senator 427
Harrison, Senator 427
Hasbrouck, Olive 67
Havemeyer, Mrs. H. O. 177, 414,, quoted 415; 416, 419, 460, 465, 466
Hawkins, Mrs. W. J. 443
Hawley, ex-Governor 86
Hawley, Senator 94
Hayden, Congressman 85, 92
Hays, Will H. 456, quoted 457
Hearst, Phoebe A. 160
Heffelfinger, Kate Cleaver 252, 254, 256, 365, 406
Henderson, Jessica 421
Henderson, Wilma 421-2
Henesy, Minnie 252, 254, 256
Henkel, Alice 126, 351
Hennessy, Charles O'Connor 391-2
Henry, Mr., quoted 69; 70, quoted 96-7; 129

Hepburn, Mrs. Thomas 298
Herendeen, Anne, quoted 7
Herkner, Anne 416
Herndon, Mrs. 279
Hershfield, Harry 448
Higgins, Colonel 383
Hill, Alberta 64
Hill, Elsie 35, 52, 126, 131, 135, 178, 179, 212, 298, 336, 366, 367, quoted 370, 390, 421, 425, 455, 457, 458
Hilles, Florence Bayard 119, 154, 184, 207, 232, quoted 353; 354, 391, 400, 455, 462, 466
Hinchey, Margaret, quoted 59
Hinshaw, Virgil 308
Holcomb, Governor Marcus 477
Hollis, Senator 314
Hooker, Mrs. Donald R. 52, 131, 207, 309, 438, 463
Hooper, ex-Governor 467
Hopkins, J. A. H. 233, 234, 275, 308, quoted 309
Hopkins, Mrs. J. A. H. 207, 232, 234, 445, 447, 450
Hornesby, L. H. 258
Hourwich, Rebecca 126, 304 391
House Suffrage Committee 310 314, 315
Howe, Julia Ward 105
Howell, Representative 111
Howry, Elizabeth 190
Huddleston, Mr. 328
Huff, Elizabeth 406
Huff, Emily 412
Hughes, Charles Evans 28, 29, 164, 165
Hull, Mr. 345
Hunkins, Hazel 126, 180, 216, 227, 229, 232, 335, 363, 364, 366, 367, 484
Hunt, Helen 340
Hunter, Gertrude 74, quoted 82; 243
Hurlburt, Julia 154, 232
Hutton, May Arkwright 157
Hyattsville, Mayor of 39

Idaho ratifies 451
Igoe, Representative 139
Illinois ratifies 432
Indiana ratifies 443
Indianapolis News, quoted 114
Industrial Workers deputation 58

Ingham, Mary H., quoted 388, 401, 414, 416, 419, 433, 459, 463
Iowa ratifies 434

Jack, Mrs. C. C. 421
Jackson, Mrs. Mark 249
Jacobson, Pauline, quoted 252
Jakobi, Paula 258, 281, 283, quoted 286, 289
James, Ada 432
James, D. G. 432
James, Senator 357
Jameson, John B. 391-2
Jamison, Maud 227-8, 245, 252, 254, 256, 383, 384, 387, 389, 406
Jerrold, Lilian 354
Johns, Peggy Baird 250, 258
Johnson, Senator 313, 314
Johnson, Willie Grace 416
Joliffe, Frances 107, 109-10, 115, 116, 117, 120
Jones, Margaret Graham 48
Jones, Senator Andreus Aristides 313, 353, 355, 357, 376, 423
Jones, Senator Wesley L. 41, 313, 370, 423
Jost, Mayor 111
Judiciary Committee 36
Juengling, Amy 258, 416

Kahle, Louise Lewis 252
Kalb, Benigna Green 457
Kalb, Elizabeth 47, 382, 384, 385, 387, 389, 406, quoted 478
Kansas ratifies 433
Katzenstein, Caroline 154, 391
Keating, Senator 94
Keehn, Harriet 366
Kellam, Mrs. Arthur, quoted 353
Keller, Helen 161
Kelley, Augusta M. 387
Kelley, Florence, quoted 103-4, 115
Kellogg, Rhoda 408
Kellogg, Senator 353
Kelly, Mrs. Nicholas 389
Kelly, Representative 72
Kendall, Ada Davenport 278, 295-7
Kendall, Anna Norris 210
Kendall, Mrs. Frederick Willard 249
Kendrick, Senator 453
Kennedy, Marie Ernst 416
Kent, Representative 130

Kent, Mrs. William 19, 52, 96, 102, 131, 136, quoted 146, 177, 190, 200, 207, 226, 258, 260, 298, 309, 320, 326, 441, 464
Kentucky ratifies 443
Kessler, Margaret Wood 250
Keyes, Senator 427
Kilby, Thomas E. 434
Kimball, Alice 366
Kin, Dr. Yami, quoted 107
Kincaid, Mrs. B. R. 232
Kindberg, Maria 109
Kindstedt, Ingeborg 109
King, Dr. Cora Smith 35, 92
King, Senator 351
Koeing, Ruby E. 366
Kruger, Hattie 258
Kuhn, Anna 366
Kuli Khan, Mme. Ali 107

Ladd, Dr. 289
Lamont, Mrs. George W. 170
Lancaster, Elsie 79, 91
Lang, Mrs. Albion 462
Latimer, Edna S. 79
Latimer, Mrs. quoted 83-4
Laughlin, Gail, quoted 105; 156, 177
Lawrence, David 261
Lederman, Minna 387
Lennox, Ida 354
Lenroot, Senator 355
Lewis, Mrs. Lawrence 13, 52, 67, 131, 207, 227, 230, 258, 287, quoted 288; 300, 320, 321, 364, 366, 389, 391, 401, 404, 433, 442, 455, 464
Lewis, Rose 421
Lewis, Shippen 459
Lewis, William Draper 459
Lieberson, Rose 366
Lincoln, Kathryn 258
Lloyd, Lola Maverick 387
Lockrey, Dr. Sarah Hunt 366
Lockwood, Mrs. Henry L. 243
Lodge, Senator 434
Logan, Mrs. Ellis 61
Logue, Mary 404
Lloyd George 10
Lowenburg, Mrs. Harry 184
Lowry, Catherine 216
Ludlow, Dr. Clara E. 71

McCarl, Mr. 443
McCormick, Mrs. Medill 124

McCormick, Vance, quoted 183
McCoy, Representative 41, 42
McCue, Anne 79
McCumber, Senator 350
McDuffie, Mrs. S. B. 71
McKellar, Senator 358
McKenzie, Marie 354
McPherson, Blanche A. 363, 366
McShane, Elizabeth 258, 260, 385, 414, 416, 419
Mackay, Senator 448
Mackaye, Mrs. Benton 209
Mackaye, Jessie Hardy, quoted 375
Mackrille, Ida Finney 177, 464
Magee, Katherine 408
Main, Effie Boutwell 366
Main, Emily Burke 366
Maine ratifies 442
Maki, Mayi 104
Mallon, Winifred 15, 24, 154
Malone, Dudley Field 207, 246-49, 261, 267, 275, 290, 295, 298, 308
Malone, Maude 245
Mann, Representative 95, 347
Maphis, Director 342
Marion, Kitty 229, 230, 232
Marlborough, Duchess of 74
Maroney, Lieut 157
Marsden, Edith 47
Marsh, Eleanor Taylor 48
Martin, Anne 15, 24, 96, 110, 117, 131, 133, quoted 136-8; 152, 160, 190, 207, 232, quoted 267; 300, 301, 307, 309, 311, 326, 327, 479
Martin, Senator 342, 356
Martinette, Catherine 258
Massachusetts ratifies 434
Maverick, Lucy 424, 425
Mead, Mrs. Cyrus 154
Mellett, Mrs. Lowell 136
Men's League for Woman Suffrage 46
Mercer, Nell 414, 416
Meredith, Mrs. Sophie 256, 366
Merritt, H. P. 435
Michigan ratifies 432
Milholland, Inez, see Boissevain
Milholland, Vida 208, 229, 256, 397, 419
Miller, Alice Duer 132, 133
Millett, Mrs. Lowell 326
Minnesota ratifies 440
Missouri ratifies 434
Mitchell, Mayor 116

Moller, Bertha 382, 383, 384, 385, 391, 408
Mondell, Representative 36, 68, 70, 116, 118, 130, 444, 445
Monroe, Lila Day 151
Montana ratifies 435
Montessori, Mme. Marie, quoted 107
Montgomery, Senator 454
Moore, Martha W. 366, 408
Moran, Mrs. F. B., quoted 169
Morey, Agnes H. 154, 258, 391, quoted 398-9, 421, 434, 155, 215, 216, 217, 227-8, 238, 257, 286, 391, 420, 422
Morgan, Mary 189
Morgan, Representative 139
Morris, Mildred 406, 416, 487
Morrison, Secretary 442
Moses, George H. 391
Moss, Mr. Hunter 123, 139, 140
Moulton, Arthur L. 81
Moyle, James H. 94
Mullowney, Judge 233, 250, 255, 256, 259
Munds, Mrs. Frances 92
Munnecke, Phoebe 404, 412, 416
Murdock, Senator 84
Murphy, Gertrude 408

National American Woman Suffrage Association 3, 13, 43, 44, 67, 171
National Association Opposed to Woman Suffrage 262-3
National Council of Women Voters 35, 40
National Federation of Women's Clubs 60
Nebraska ratifies 435
Needham, Grace 384, 391
Neely, Representative, Kansas 84, 94
Neely, Representative, W. Va. 139
Nelson, Representative 134, 135, 139
Newell, Gertrude B. 155
New Freedom, quoted 204
New Hampshire ratifies 440, 447
New Jersey Women's Deputation 41-2
New Mexico ratifies 451
New York ratifies 433
New York Tribune, quoted 116, 124

498   INDEX

Nevada ratifies 445

Nolan, Mrs. Mary A. 258, 321, 280, quoted 412; 416, 419

Northcliffe, Lord, quoted 309

North Dakota ratifies 442

Noyes, Ruth 79

Nugent, James R. 447

Oakes, Margaret 366, 400

O'Brien, Matthew 245, 267, quoted 268; 287, 388

Occoquan Workhouse 271-86

Odell, Mrs. George 326, 384

Ohio ratifies 433

Oklahoma ratifies 451

Older, Mrs. Fremont, quoted 107

Oregon ratifies 443

Overman, Senator 372

Owen, Senator 453

Page, Mrs. Frank 421

Page, Senator 353

Palmer, Attorney General 453

Pankhurst, Mrs. 9

Panama Pacific Exposition 102

Papandre, Elizabeth 184

Patterson, Lulu 354

Paul, Alice, résumé of achievements, 4-5; youth and training, 7-8; work in England, 8-9; meeting with Lucy Burns, 9; Scottish campaign, 10-11; experiences in Glasgow, 11; starts work for Constitutional Amendment in Washington, 12-13; Convention of National American Association in Philadelphia, 13; Chairman Special Committee of National American Woman Suffrage Association, 13; description and tributes, 14-16; starts work in Washington, Dec., 1912, 19; methods of working, 20-29; and President Wilson, 33; leads Congressional Committee Deputation, 34; deputation of New Jersey women, 42; plans for 1914, 52; preparations for demonstration May 2, 1914, 67; Congressional Union deputation, 70; quoted, 75-79; outline for 1915, 101; Telegraph Editor of San Francisco Bulletin, 108; and Judiciary Committee,

Dec., 1915, 118-24; Congressional Union National Convention, 130; and William Elza Williams, 135; quoted 144, formation of Woman's Party, 152-53; Hughes campaign, 164-5; White House picketing, 202; National Woman's Party organized, 205; declaration of war with Germany, 213; assaulted while picketing, 239; arrested, 252; quoted 253-4; in prison, 256; interviewed in prison, 261; in psychopathic ward, 276; in Occoquan, 292; hunger striking, 293; lobbying, 326; Susan B. Anthony Amendment passes House of Representatives, 348; quoted 367; Lafayette Monument meetings, 369-372; arrested, 387, 389; and Senator Borah, 392-3; watchfires, 403; President Wilson's homecoming demonstration, 420; Metropolitan Opera House demonstration, 424-5; Utah ratification, 440; Maine ratification, 442; Delaware ratification, and Senator Harding, 462; Cox and Harding campaign, 466

Peck, Mildred 354

Pendleton Tribune, quoted 93

Pennsylvania ratifies 433

Penrose, Senator 433

Pepper, George Wharton 459

Perry, Emily 326

Pflaster, Mrs. 320, 408

Phelan, Senator 350, 441

Phelps, Edith 400

Philippine Bill 95

Picketing, details 478-82

Pierce, Vivian 47, 126; quoted 180; 227, 245, 251, 320, 336, 382, 383, 384-7, 385, 391, 441, 443, 455

Pinchot, Mrs. Amos 147

Pincus, Jane 77, quoted 85

Piunti, Adelina 406

Poindexter, Senator 446, quoted 453

Polk, Mrs. Stewart 383

Pollitzer, Anita 126, 336, quoted 336-41; 389, 390, 427, 441, 442, 443, 444, 445, 446, 452, 455, 457, 465, 466, 467, 468, 473

Pollock, Senator 338, 392, 416, 427
Pope, Mrs. Horton 382
Pottier, Berry 421
Pou, Mr. 70, 129, quoted 314
Price, Lucy 349
Pride, Mrs. Marcella 393
"Prison Special" 419
Puffenbarger, Mrs. 454
Pugh, Judge 243, 244
Pullman, Major 217, 241
Purtelle, Edna M. 366

Quay, Mrs. R. B. 258

Raker, Mr. 346
Rankin, Hon. Jeannette 308, 326
Read, Mrs. Percy 155
Reading, Lord 354
Reans, Captain 267
Reber, Mabel 466
Rector, Mrs. James 465, 466
Reed, Mrs. Percy 399
Reed, Senator 111, 329, 357
Reyneau, Mrs. Paul 232
Rhode Island ratifies 443
Ridley, Colonel 366, 371, 395
Riegel, Ella 155, 414, 416, 419
Robb, Justice, quoted 267
Roberts, Governor 463, 469, 460
Robertson, Mrs. C. T. 258
Robinson, Senator Helen Ring 43
Roewer, Mrs. George 421
Rogers, Mrs. John, Jr. 155, 157, 184, 233, 298, quoted 309, 397; 414, 416, 419
Roosevelt, Theodore 26, 158, 164, 223, 351
Root, Elihu 236
Ross, Margery 21, 126, 404
Rossett, Margaret 413
Rowe, Clara Louise 126
Rumley, Dr. E. A. 308
Russell, Isaac 440
Russell, Mrs. Charles Edward 136, quoted 138
Russian Commission 215
Russian, E. T. 413
Russian, Mrs.. H. D., quoted 413, 421
Rye, Governor 359

Salt Lake City Republican Herald, quoted 91
Samardin, Nina 249

San Francisco Bulletin, quoted 108
Sargent, Senator 37
Schuyler, Margaretta 424
Scott, Melinda, quoted 58
Scott, Mrs. George 258
Scott, Mrs. Townsend 155, 184, 227, 399
Scott, Ruth 406
Seattle Times, quoted 90
Seldomridge, Representative 94
Shafroth-Palmer Resolution 55-7
Shafroth, Senator 55, 392
Shaw, Anna Howard 13, 38, 43, 45
Shaw, Lois Warren 421
Sheinberg, Belle 258
Sheppard, Senator 351
Sherman, Senator 423
Sherwood, General 222
Shields, Lucile 230, 412
Shields, Mrs. Alex 406
Shields, Senator, 359, letters quoted 360-1; 385
Shippen, Mrs. Eugene 399
Shoemaker, Martha 416
Short, Mrs. J. H. 258
Siddons, Judge 388
Sisson, Mr. 328
Smailes, Mr. 341
Small, Ruth 391, 421, 422
Smith, Elizabeth 240, 259
Smith, Hoke 325
Smith, Senator Ellison D. 338
Smith, Senator John M. C. 355
Smith, Senator Marcus A. 85, 92, 94, 355
Smoot, Senator 440
Smyth, Chief Justice 267
South Dakota ratifies 443
Spargo, John 308
Spencer, Dr. Caroline 184, 251, 255, 400, 406
Spencer, Senator Seldon 450
Sproul, Governor 433
Stafford, Kate 258
Steele, Representative 130, 139
Sterling, Senator 442
Stevens, Counsel, quoted 267
Stevens, Doris 79, 80, 108, 126, 147, 200-1, 207, 256, quoted 275, 286, 300, 301, 336, 351, 352, 390, 401, 425, 426, 460
Stevens, Governor 441
Stimson, Secretary of War 30
Stokes, Edward Caspar 447

Stone, Lucy 105
Stowe, Harriet Beecher 105
Stubbs, Jessie Hardy 67, 79, quoted 80; 81
Sturgess, Georgiana 238
Sturtevant, Eva E. 366
Stuyvesant, Elizabeth 227, 230, 237, 238, 239, 240
Suffrage Amendment 3, 35-7, 44, 164, 416-7, 429, 433
"Suffrage Special" Western tour 155 .
Suffragist, established 47; quoted 46, 50, 53, 61, 69, 96-7, 116, 136, 167-8, 170, 172, 181, 222, 244 251
Sullivan, May 366
Sutherland, Mary 400
Sutherland, Senator 116, 118, 165, 352, 452
Sykes, Louise 421

Taggart, Representative 119, 121 139
Tarbell, Ida M., quoted 161
Taylor, J. Will 467
Tennessee ratifies 469; Anti-Suffrage suit 477
Terrace, Matilda 366
Texas ratifies 434
Thomas, Representative R. Y. 139
Thomas, Senator Charles S. 94
Thompson, Mayor, quoted 113
Thompson, Mrs. Sinclair 126
Todd, Helen 119, 155, 170, 177
Torrence, Olivia Dunbar 258
Trammell, Senator 338
Trax, Lola C. 79, quoted 81
Trinkle, Senator 342
Tumulty, Joseph 147, 150, 354, 359, 428
Turner, Banks 472-73
Turner, Mrs. H. L. 421

Ueland, Mrs. Andreas 119
Underwood, Senator 357
Unterman, Elsie 412, 413
Utah ratifies 441

Van Gasken, Dr. Frances G. 64
Van Orsdel, Justice 267-8
Van Winkle, Mina 170
Vardaman, Senator 358, 427
Vaughan, Mrs. William P. 338

Vernon, Mabel 8, 47, 67, quoted 87; 108, 113, 119, 126, 150, 160, 169, 184, 207, 217, 227-8, quoted 271; 300, 301, quoted 308; 311, 336, 419, 455, 459
Ver Vane, Elsie 406
Volstead, Representative 123, 139

Waddill, Judge Edmund 261, 288, 290, 298
Wadsworth, Senator 385, 423
Wainwright, Mrs. Richard 308, quoted 311; 372, 444
Walker, Amelia Himes 232
Walker, Mrs. R. 419
Walker, Representative 139
Walker, Seth 468, 469, 472, 475
Wall, Henrieta Briggs 399
Wallace, Alfred, quoted 160
Wallace, W. R. 91
Wallerstein, Bertha 413, 416
Walling, Ada 354
Walmsley, Elizabeth 412
Walmsley, H. R. 387
Walsh, Frank P., quoted 106, 112, 456
Walsh, Senator 115, 428, 453
Warren, Mary 105
Warren, Mrs. Mortimer 421
Washington Post, quoted 44, 184
Washington ratifies 455
Watson, Madeline 239, 243
Watson, Mrs. William Upton 416
Weaver, Eva 406
Weaver, Mrs. C. 406
Webb, Representative 119-20, 129, 132, 139, 309, quoted 310
Weed, Eleanor Hill 366
Weed, Helena Hill 15, 79, quoted 86-7, 159; 229, 230, 258, 366, 402, 416, quoted 418-19; 462
Weeks, Cora 258, 416, 419
Weeks, Senator 423
Welling, Congressman 441
West Virginia ratifies 451
Whaley, Representative 139, 328
Whitcomb, Camilla 258, 421
White, Mrs. John Jay 38, 108
White, Sue 47, 303, 304, 359, 399, 415, 416, 419, 457, 463, 465, 466, 469, 470
Whitehouse, Mrs. Robert Trent 421, 442
Whitman, Governor 115
Whittaker, Superintendent of Occoquan 229, 267, 272, 288

Whittemore, Margaret 79, 80, 126, 229, 392, 408
Whittemore, Mrs. Nelson 155
Wiley, Dr. Harvey 279
Wiley, Mrs. Harvey 61, 258, quoted 259; 260, 268, 396
Williams, Genevieve 258
Williams, Senator 120, 129, 130
Williams, William Ezra 135-6 quoted 136-8
Willis, Senator 342
Wilson, Woodrow, 3; election campaign, 29; inauguration, 30; attitude toward Woman Suffrage, 32-3; reply to New Jersey deputation, 42; reply to Industrial Women's deputation, 59-60; reply to Club Women's deputation, 61-3; reply to Democratic Women's deputation, 65-6; and the Filipinos, 96; votes for Woman Suffrage, 110; receives San Francisco petition, 117-8; delegation of New York women, 146-50; visits Kansas, 150-1; letters, 165-8; addresses National American Woman Suffrage Association, 172-74; letter to National Woman's Party Conference, 175-7; receives resolutions passed at Inez Milholland Memorial, 192-3; acknowledges resolutions of National Woman's Party, 212; declares for Federal Amendment, 263; becomes actively interested in Woman Suffrage, 310; receives Woman's Committee of the Council of National Defense, 353; reply to French Union for Woman Suffrage, 356; correspondence with Senators re Suffrage Amendment, 359-62; delegation of Southern and Western Democratic Women, 372; address to Senate re Woman Suffrage, 377-80; letter to Senator Hennessy, 391-2; message to Congress Dec. 2, 1918, 394; sails for France, 395; reply to delegation of French Working Women, 409-11; burned in effigy, 415; returns from Europe, 420; Boston demonstration, 420-2; leaves for Europe, 424; cabled message to Congress quoted,

428; ratification in Alabama and Georgia, 434-6; requests Delaware ratification, 456; requests Tennessee ratification, 464
Wilson and Marshall League 65
Winslow, Rose, quoted 59; 79, 177 180, 252, quoted 254-6 291
Winsor, Ellen 366, 406
Winsor, Mary 236, 245, 366, quoted 368, 419, 466
Winston, Mrs. A. P. 403, 404
Winston, Mrs. K. G. 385
Winthrop, Hannah 105
Wisconsin ratifies 432
Wold, Clara P. 47, 363, 366, 383, 384, 385, 389, 390, 399, 416, 462
Wold, Cora 366
Wolfe, Clara 351
Woman's Committee of the Council of National Defense 353
Woman's National Democratic League 168
Woman's Party 15, 29, 30, 175-7, 161-2, 205, 266, 319, 283, 390, 440, 465, 470-2, 481, 483
Woman Suffrage Committee 36, 37, 44
Women's Trade Union League 58
Woolley, Robert 427
Wyoming Leader, quoted 89
Wyoming ratifies 445
Wyoming State convention 21-2

Young, Joy 126, 230, 252, 305, 306
Young, Matilda 252, 259, 385, 387, 389, 403, 405
Younger, Maud 15, 22, 26, 29, quoted 106; 126, 133, 146, quoted 159; 177, 180, 188, 207, quoted 262; 298, 300, 302-4, 306, quoted 311-3; quoted 332; 359, 372, 391, 412, 483; Revelations of a Woman Lobbyist quoted, 134, 140-44, 194-95, 327-32, 345-7, 349-53, 355-58, 376-81, 429
Yuma Examiner quoted 93

Zinkham, Warden at Washington Jail 257, 266, 368

M